Get the eBooks FREE!

(PDF, ePub, Kindle, and liveBook all included)

We believe that once you buy a book from us, you should be able to read it in any format we have available. To get electronic versions of this book at no additional cost to you, purchase and then register this book at the Manning website.

Go to https://www.manning.com/freebook and follow the instructions to complete your pBook registration.

That's it!
Thanks from Manning!

Building Ethereum Dapps

Building Ethereum Dapps

DECENTRALIZED APPLICATIONS
ON THE ETHEREUM BLOCKCHAIN

ROBERTO INFANTE
FOREWORD BY THOMAS BERTANI

MANNING

SHELTER ISLAND

Manning Publications Co.
20 Baldwin Road
PO Box 761
Shelter Island, NY 11964

Acquisitions editor:	Michael Stephens
Development editor:	Candace West
Technical development editor:	Alain Couniot
Review editor:	Ivan Martinović
Production editor:	Anthony Calcara
Copy editor:	Carl Quesnel
Proofreader:	Melody Dolab
Technical proofreader:	Kumar Unnikrishnan
Typesetter:	Dennis Dalinnik
Cover designer:	Marija Tudor

ISBN: 9781617295157
Printed in the United States of America
1 2 3 4 5 6 7 8 9 10 – SP – 24 23 22 21 20 19

To my wonderful wife Estrella and beautiful daughters Bianca and Clio.

brief contents

contents

8 *Managing smart contracts with Web3.js* 225

foreword

Some believe blockchain is going to reinvent everything; others see it as a despicable hype-machine deserving no attention. I think the truth lies somewhere in between, and since blockchain technology is here to stay, I truly believe that reading this book may be one of the best investments you will ever make.

The blockchain space is growing rapidly—major conferences are starting to attract thousands of participants, and new companies are forming in the blockchain ecosystem at an ever-increasing rate. Despite this, adoption remains slow. I believe there are two reasons for this. The first is the disruptive impact of cryptocurrency speculation on unregulated financial markets. This can put off potential new developers, who may not be comfortable with it or may see such speculation as a distraction. Instead, I see it as a fantastic indicator of just how much potential this new form of programmable money has.

The second reason for the sluggish adoption of blockchain technology is, I believe, a fundamental misalignment of expectations. Imagine if in the late '90s we had decided to ignore the potential of the internet. What if we called it a scam just because today's Facebook or Netflix weren't quite there yet? The opportunity cost would have been enormous!

Having been in the blockchain space since 2012, I've witnessed firsthand both this phenomenal growth and the slow adoption. The community is larger by several orders of magnitude now, but its ideals remain similar to what I experienced when I first fell down the blockchain rabbit hole. Over 10 years have passed since the groundbreaking release of the Bitcoin whitepaper, but innovation is still being driven primarily by an ethos that says, "Don't trust—verify." This initial concept is alive and well and is growing stronger as it endures technical and social attacks.

The pioneering thinkers working behind the scenes on Bitcoin have helped decentralized blockchains become the innovative and powerful technology we have today. These thinkers saw early on how the concepts of "permissionless innovation" and "reinterpretation of trust" (whose roots reach back as far as the mid '80s with Ken Thompson and his ACM article "Reflections on Trusting Trust"[1]) were potential threats to preexisting systems, and they took that into account when designing the fundamentals of the new financial system they were dreaming of.

And now this new, decentralized, financial system they designed from scratch has become self-sustaining. Today, hundreds of developers are collectively securing the Bitcoin blockchain with their knowledge and expertise, and thousands more are contributing to the development of it and other blockchain platforms, such as Ethereum. Yet we still need more of these types of pioneering developers, these adversarial thinkers who are not afraid to go against the grain, who are blockchain-aware and have fresh ideas to contribute to this space. And here is where this book comes in.

Creating a decentralized application on a blockchain like Ethereum is a complex process, but Roberto Infante manages to present it in a simple manner that allows any good developer to successfully navigate the complexities, understand the implications, and ultimately realize their potential of writing blockchain applications.

This book shows the many tools, services, and protocols that have been created in this ecosystem, and demonstrates how everything works well together to support a decentralized application's needs. Blockchain is about interoperability, and Roberto understands this innately. He arms you with the tools of the experts while keeping you aware of the bigger picture.

Writing secure smart contracts is both difficult and a necessity when creating new, critical cogs for the existing blockchain. This book facilitates this while avoiding reinventing the wheel. It will help you to find new ways to connect these basic building blocks and create use cases that go above and beyond those already explored.

Crowdfunding and the spectacular returns from Initial Coin Offerings have been huge in the last year, and have doubtlessly contributed to the growth of the blockchain scene. But what use case will drive the next growth cycle? You, armed with this book, will have all the tools you'll need to answer that question.

The next financial revolution is already underway. And you do not want to miss it.

—THOMAS BERTANI, CEO of Oraclize

---

[1] See Ken Thompson, "Reflections on trusting trust," *Communications of the ACM*, August 1984, https://dl.acm.org/citation.cfm?id=358210.

preface

If you've followed the meteoric rise (in December 2017) and subsequent fall of Bitcoin, you've also heard about blockchain. Blockchain is the technology behind Bitcoin and other cryptocurrencies like Litecoin and Dash. It's a decentralized database, replicated across a large network, on which transactions are secured cryptographically. Most blockchains have a single purpose: to support a decentralized currency.

Ethereum was created in 2013 as a general-purpose blockchain. It allows developers to develop any decentralized application (Dapp), so it's considered a programmable blockchain.

Having followed Bitcoin and being a software developer, I was blown away by this idea and excited about the impact Ethereum could have on many industries and on society, so I started to experiment with it a couple of years ago.

I found my own learning experience very inefficient. There were no books initially, and only a few blogs, and the official documentation moved slower than the technology. Although more resources started to spring up, they were scattered all over the web, and their quality was inconsistent. So I proposed a project to Manning: a convenient book that aims to bring together in one place all you need to know to build a full Ethereum Dapp. This is the book I would have liked to read when I started my blockchain journey. I hope that by reading it you'll learn Ethereum much more quickly than I did!

acknowledgments

Although I've written this book in my spare time, I've tried to minimize, as much as possible, time stolen from my family by working on it late at night and early in the morning. In some cases, though, this hasn't been possible, so I thank my wife Estrella and my daughters Bianca and Clio for their patience and support. I look forward to spending more time with them now that the project is complete.

Before I became the author of this book, I'd already been a longtime reader of Manning books, so I was delighted when Manning gave me the chance to write for them. In particular, I'd like to thank Michael Stephens for getting this project started and placing it on the right track from the beginning, Marjan Bace for believing in it, Candace West for guiding me throughout the whole journey, and Bert Bates for making sure I was moving in the right direction. I'd also like to thank Ivan Martinović for coordinating the review process and Candace Gillhoolley, Ana Romac, Marko Rajkovic, and Christopher Kauffman for promoting the book. The reviewers who read the manuscript at varying stages of development and for whose comments and insight I am grateful include Alan Lenton, Arnaud Bailly, Duncan McRae, Garry Turkington, Godfred Asamoah, Gopala Krishna, James Nyika, Joel Kotarski, Jose San Leandro, Jürgen Hötzel, Massimo Dalla, Matthew Kiser, Michael Bright, Nasser Ugoji, Olivier Ducatteeuw, Rahul Rai, Tatiana Fesenko, Tomo Helman, Vinod Panicker, Vittal Damaraju, Win Lwin Oo, and Zhuo Hong Wei.

The content of the book has been considerably improved thanks to immensely useful feedback received from early readers, reviewers, technical editors, and key members of the Ethereum community. First of all, I'd like to thank Rehan Malik, a longtime friend of mine, for thoroughly reviewing the first draft of each chapter before I sent it to anyone else. The very detailed feedback that Alfredo Ielpo provided has contributed to clarifying and simplifying the first part of the book and making it more readable. Special thanks to Dr. David Buján, lecturer and researcher in the faculty of engineering at the University of Deusto, and Oscar Lage, head of cybersecurity and blockchain researcher at Tecnalia, who have helped me refine both terminology and explanations, especially for the more theoretical topics. A big thank you as well to my technical reviewers. The book wouldn't have been as complete and accurate as it is without the invaluable feedback of my technical development editor, Alain Couniot, to whom I am very grateful, and my technical proofer, Kumar Unnikrishnan, who identified a few bugs in my code and patiently tested the fixes before the book went to production. I would also like to thank Anthony Calcara for coordinating production very smoothly and particularly thank Carl Quesnel, my copy editor, and Melody Dolab, my proofreader, for polishing the text and perfecting the fine details.

Finally, the friendly Ethereum community has also lent me a big hand. First of all, I'd like to thank Nick Johnson, the creator of the Ethereum Name Service (ENS), for reviewing my coverage of ENS and of smart contract upgradeability. I also wish to thank Dr. Christian Reitwiessner, lead of Solidity and of the C++ client at Ethereum, for his feedback on chapters on Solidity and smart contracts. Many thanks to Thomas Bertani and his team at Oraclize, who have always been very kind and helpful since I met them in the early days of this adventure. I am also grateful to Tom Lindeman from ConsenSys Diligence for allowing me to reference content from their "Ethereum Smart Contract Best Practices" guide and for providing me with useful information on contract security. Finally, I'd like to thank Josh Quintal from Truffle for coordinating an internal review of my coverage of their tools.

about this book

This book is about Ethereum decentralized applications (Dapps). If you're new to blockchain, learning how to develop a Dapp isn't as straightforward as learning a new programming language or a new development framework. It requires you to learn a completely new technology, different from what you might have seen before. In short, it requires you to shift to a new paradigm, a new way of developing applications.

This objective of this book is to help you transition to this new paradigm as easily as possible. This doesn't mean I'll show you a magic shortcut to the new technology. On the contrary, I'll accompany you along a step-by-step path, based on hands-on explanations, through which you'll acquire all the concepts, tools, programming languages, and frameworks you need to develop an Ethereum application. I hope the sample applications you'll build while progressing through the chapters will make your journey as smooth as possible.

The goal is that after reading this book, you'll have gained a solid understanding of the main components of the Ethereum platform and its wider ecosystem, and you'll be able to design, implement, and deploy a complete Ethereum Dapp.

Who should read this book

Blockchain technology has just become mainstream, mostly on the back of the spectacular rise that cryptocurrencies experienced in December 2017. People from all walks of life are trying to figure out the potential and opportunities blockchain platforms such as Ethereum can offer to improve and revolutionize many industries. Different people are trying to learn at different levels, depending on their background and aspirations.

This book is aimed at software developers, architects, and anyone with intermediate programming skills who'd like to understand how Ethereum works by using it. Generally, I expect you to have interest in learning the technology, but I assume you have no prior deep knowledge of it. I believe any junior developer with knowledge of basic JavaScript, Java, or a C-like language should be able to follow along with no difficulty. If you also have some background in object-oriented programming and Node.js, your journey will be even easier. If you've read some general, high-level articles on blockchain or Ethereum, you're good to go!

Roadmap

The book is divided into four parts. Unless you have prior knowledge of blockchain platforms, I recommend you read it from front to back because I introduce concepts and tools progressively. Most chapters assume you've read the previous ones.

If you're familiar with blockchain and have basic knowledge of Ethereum, you might be able to skip part 1. On the other hand, if you're interested in learning the technology, but you're not planning to build a production application, you can skip part 4 on advanced topics, except perhaps chapter 15 on the current blockchain landscape:

- Part 1 is a general introduction to decentralized applications (chapter 1); blockchain technology and smart contracts (chapter 2); and the Ethereum platform, including the Ethereum Virtual Machine (EVM), the Go Ethereum client, and the Ethereum wallet (chapter 3). You'll get the foundation necessary to progress through the book, and you'll also implement your first Dapp—a simple cryptocurrency—which, in chapter 4, you'll also deploy on a public test network.
- Part 2 is focused on smart contracts, the technology that Ethereum introduced, which allow a blockchain to go beyond the traditional use of supporting cryptocurrencies to being a building block for any decentralized application. Chapter 5 gives an overview of Solidity, the most popular language for writing smart contracts on the Ethereum Virtual Machine. Chapter 6 presents the structure of a typical smart contract through a sample crowdsale application and explains its main elements: constructor, state variables, functions, and events. You'll also learn how to generalize the contract functionality through inheritance. Chapter 7 is focused on more advanced object-oriented features, such as abstract contracts and interfaces, which I introduce progressively for you to improve and extend the initial crowdsale application. This chapter also presents libraries, which provide yet another way of making code more maintainable. Chapter 8 explains how to deploy a smart contract to a public test network and interact with it through Web3, an Ethereum communication library; the Go Ethereum console; Node.js; and a web user interface. It also explains how to set up a private network and how to use a mock network client, such as Ganache.
- In part 3, which is the core of the book, you'll learn about real-world Ethereum. At this point, I assume you've developed a good foundation in Ethereum, so in

chapter 9 you'll start to familiarize yourself with the wider ecosystem. This includes, among other elements, the Ethereum Name Service (ENS), decentralized storage networks such as IPFS and Swarm, and oracle and other development frameworks. Then you'll start to use professional development tools. In chapter 10 you'll learn how to test smart contracts with the JavaScript Mocha framework, and in chapter 11 you'll improve the development cycle with the Truffle framework, which will allow you to easily compile, test, and deploy your contracts. Finally, in chapter 12, you'll put everything together by building an end-to-end voting Dapp from scratch. At this point, you can consider yourself graduated!

- Part 4 is aimed at readers who are not only interested in learning about the technology but are also planning to deploy a Dapp in production. Chapter 13 gives advice on operational aspects, such as event logging and contract upgradeability. Chapter 14 is entirely focused on security and gives you a heads-up on common vulnerabilities and typical forms of smart contract attack. I recommend all readers proceed through chapter 15 as well to get an overview of the current blockchain and distributed ledger landscape. If you want to continue the journey, it provides you with a short list of next destinations to consider.

Source code and downloads

The code snippets and listings throughout the book are mainly in Solidity and JavaScript. The source code is always represented in fixed-width font to make it stand out from the surrounding text. The code is annotated and has been formatted with careful indentation and page breaks so it fits the size of the book page well and shows clearly.

You can download all the listings and code snippets from Manning's book website at www.manning.com/books/building-ethereum-dapps.

Software and hardware requirements

The Ethereum tool set is available for Windows, Linux, and macOS; screenshots shown throughout the book are from Windows. Code is, in most cases, operating system-agnostic, but in a few cases I've escaped it for Windows (for example: curl-based RPC calls). You should be able to follow all the examples, regardless of what operating system you're using.

If you want to download the entire Ethereum MAINNET blockchain, you'll need around 1 TB of disk space. But you can get away with around 100 GB if you retrieve it in fast mode, as I explain in more detail in the early chapters. The TESTNET blockchain, which I use for most of the book, requires around 75 GB at the time of writing.

liveBook discussion forum

Purchase of *Building Ethereum Dapps* includes free access to a private web forum run by Manning Publications where you can make comments about the book, ask technical questions, and receive help from the author and from other users. To access the forum, go to https://livebook.manning.com/#!/book/building-ethereum-dapps/discussion. You can also learn more about Manning's forums and the rules of conduct at https://livebook.manning.com/#!/discussion.

Manning's commitment to our readers is to provide a venue where a meaningful dialogue between individual readers and between readers and the author can take place. It isn't a commitment to any specific amount of participation on the part of the author, whose contribution to the forum remains voluntary (and unpaid). We suggest you try asking the author some challenging questions lest his interest stray! The forum and the archives of previous discussions will be accessible from the publisher's website as long as the book is in print.

Tool set used in the book

These are the versions of all the tools I've used in this book. I recommend you install these exact versions, if you can, so you'll be able to follow my explanations more smoothly:

- Remix
  - URL: http://remix.ethereum.org
  - Solidity compiler version used (Settings tab): 0.4.24+commit.e67f0147.Emscripten.clang
- Ethereum wallet
  - URL: https://github.com/ethereum/mist/releases
  - Version: Ethereum-Wallet-win64-0-11-1.zip
- Geth
  - URL: https://ethereum.github.io/go-ethereum/downloads/
  - Version: Geth & Tools 1.8.13
- Solc
  - URL: https://github.com/ethereum/solidity/releases
  - Version 0.4.24 => solidity-windows.zip
- Solc in node (version 0.4.24):
  - `C:\>npm install solc@0.4.24`
- Web3 in node (version 0.20.4):
  - `C:\>npm install web3@0.20.4`
- Ganache 6.1.8
  - `C:\>npm install -g ganache-cli@6.1.8`
- Truffle 4.1.15
  - `C:\>npm install -g truffle@4.1.15`

about the author

 ROBERTO INFANTE has been writing software professionally for the last 20 years, mainly for retail and investment banks, brokers, hedge funds, and insurance underwriters. Throughout his career, he has worked on a variety of innovative projects, such as the first internet mortgage approval system in the UK, one of the first internet insurance underwriting systems in the London market, and a cutting-edge portfolio trading platform. He currently works on financial risk management applications and on blockchain-related projects.

about the cover illustration

The figure on the cover of *Building Ethereum Dapps: Decentralized Applications on the Ethereum Blockchain* is captioned "Habit of a Woman of Wotiac in Siberia in 1768." The illustration is taken from Thomas Jefferys' *A Collection of the Dresses of Different Nations, Ancient and Modern* (four volumes), London, published between 1757 and 1772. The title page states that these are hand-colored copperplate engravings, heightened with gum arabic.

Thomas Jefferys (1719–1771) was called "Geographer to King George III." He was an English cartographer who was the leading map supplier of his day. He engraved and printed maps for government and other official bodies and produced a wide range of commercial maps and atlases, especially of North America. His work as a map maker sparked an interest in local dress customs of the lands he surveyed and mapped, which are brilliantly displayed in this collection. Fascination with faraway lands and travel for pleasure were relatively new phenomena in the late 18th century, and collections such as this one were popular, introducing both the tourist as well as the armchair traveler to the inhabitants of other countries.

The diversity of the drawings in Jefferys' volumes speaks vividly of the uniqueness and individuality of the world's nations some 200 years ago. Dress codes have changed since then, and the diversity by region and country, so rich at the time, has faded away. It's now often hard to tell the inhabitants of one continent from another. Perhaps, trying to view it optimistically, we've traded a cultural and visual diversity for a more varied personal life—or a more varied and interesting intellectual and technical life.

At a time when it's difficult to tell one computer book from another, Manning celebrates the inventiveness and initiative of the computer business with book covers based on the rich diversity of regional life of two centuries ago, brought back to life by Jeffreys' pictures.

Part 1

Part 1 is a high-level introduction to Ethereum Dapps and related technologies. Chapter 1 introduces decentralized applications. Chapter 2 presents the blockchain and smart contracts. In chapter 3, you'll meet the Ethereum platform, including the Ethereum Virtual Machine (EVM), the Go Ethereum (geth) client, and the Ethereum wallet. In this part, you'll establish the foundation you need to progress through the book. You'll also implement your first Dapp—a simple cryptocurrency—and, in chapter 4, deploy it on a public test network.

A first look at decentralized applications

1

This chapter covers

- What a decentralized application is
- What a Dapp looks like and how it works
- Dapp terminology
- Suitable and less suitable Dapps

How many times have you found yourself in the following situation? You were browsing around to buy the latest gadget and were comparing prices online, when you came across SmallWebRetailer.com that was offering it 30% cheaper than Well-Known.com. You quickly put the item in the basket, fearing the price would rise at any moment, and entered your postal address and credit card details, but suddenly...you got cold feet. You started to wonder: Is the price too good to be true? What if this unknown SmallWebRetailer.com is a scam? Will they run off with my money? After a few minutes of hesitating on the Buy button, you opened a new browser tab and went straight to WellKnown.com. You submitted the order, aware you might have overpaid 30% for your gadget.

Why did you panic? Perhaps you didn't trust SmallWebRetailer.com. Perhaps you didn't want to waste your time contacting the credit card company and possibly waiting for a refund if the transaction turned sour.

What if you could've bought the gadget from the same small, unknown retailer through an "alternative e-commerce application" that guaranteed the seller couldn't access your money until you'd confirmed safe delivery of your order? What if that guarantee hadn't been provided by the seller or by a single third party, but by many independent parties participating in a platform designed to process transactions according to conditions encoded in software anyone could inspect? Hold on, probably I've said it too fast. I'll repeat it more slowly:

1 What if the money transfer was held until delivery, not by the retailer or a third party but by many participants in the platform?
2 What if the rules for escrowing and then releasing the money transfer were encoded in logic, not subjected to manual interaction?
3 What if, in case you were still unconvinced, you could inspect the code yourself?

I bet you'd click Buy, confident your funds would be safely stored on this platform until the delivery arrived. Such systems do exist, and they're called *decentralized applications*. Decentralized marketplaces, such as OpenBazaar (https://openbazaar.org/), work this way. The mechanism by which funds are routed to the seller only when you've confirmed safe delivery of the goods is called a *smart contract*.

Decentralized applications, also known as *decentralized apps* or *Dapps* (generally pronounced dee-apps), are part of a new wave of web applications meant to increase the transparency around commercial transactions, governmental processes, supply chains, and all those systems that currently require mutual trust between customer and supplier, user and provider. The objective of Dapps is to minimize or eliminate the need for any trust between the participants in a system interaction, with the aim of empowering users beyond what Web 2.0 has delivered. Some claim Dapps could be the backbone of Web 3.0.

Assuming you have programming experience—even better if it's in JavaScript—and some familiarity with web applications, this book will teach you how to build Dapps made of one or more smart contracts controlled by a user interface. By the end of this book, you'll be able to not only write smart contract code but design, implement, test, debug, deploy, and secure a full end-to-end decentralized application. Along the way, you'll also learn a new language, a new platform, and, most of all, a new way of thinking about, designing, and running applications.

In this first chapter, I'll give you a high-level overview of Dapps. I'll explain in detail what they are, what they look like, what technology stack they're built on, and when it makes sense to build them. Best of all, I'll help you start building your own! Let's start our journey.

1.1   What is a Dapp?

Before I talk about decentralized applications, I'll refresh a concept you're already familiar with, most likely without realizing it: that of a *centralized application*. Probably you've never heard this expression before because conventional web and enterprise applications are implicitly centralized with respect to their users. I can hear you asking, what does "centralized" mean exactly?

A *centralized application* or system is controlled by a single or *central* entity: an individual, company, institution, governmental agency, and so on. The entity hosts the system directly on its premises or through a service or cloud provider and has full control of all the components and layers of the system architecture. The user trusts the good faith of the central entity and decides whether to access its system depending on the entity's reputation. From the point of view of the user, the system is either *trusted* or not. This is how most web and enterprise applications are designed today.

Figure 1.1 illustrates a typical interaction between a user and a *centralized trusted* system. You shouldn't find anything surprising about it.

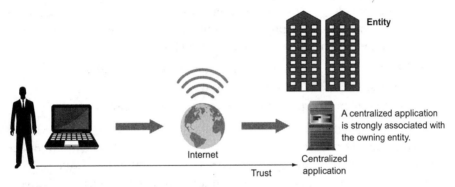

Figure 1.1 A centralized application is strongly associated with the single entity controlling it. Consequently, users decide whether to access it depending on their trust of the entity.

Let's move on to decentralized applications. If you consider for a moment the alternative e-commerce application I introduced earlier, you'll agree it has advantages with respect to SmallWebRetailer.com:

- *Favorable transaction conditions*—The transaction would be completed and the money would be fully transferred to the retailer only when the retailer had complied with all the conditions associated with the transaction, such as your confirmation of safe delivery. This would remove one of the biggest reservations you had about SmallWebRetailer.com: uncertainty whether you'd get the delivery and what would happen to your money if not.
- *Independent transaction execution and verification*—The transaction wouldn't be processed by the retailer or a single third party but by one of many participants in the platform supporting the e-commerce application, and then all the participants in the platform would independently verify it. The mechanism that all parties would use to agree on the verification of a transaction is called *consensus* (defined in the callout). The consensus mechanism would reassure you that the promised transaction conditions would be enforced and verified by many independent parties rather than an unknown retailer.

DEFINITION   Consensus is a *distributed and trustless* form of agreement on the verification of a transaction. *Distributed* means that an independent central authority doesn't perform the verification of a transaction; instead, all parties contribute to and agree on its verification. *Trustless* means that parties don't need to trust each other to agree on the verification outcome. Consensus is reached when a qualified majority of the participants have agreed on the outcome of the transaction.

- *Transparency*—You'd be able to check the code processing the transaction and verify that it was observing the specified conditions before transferring your money to the retailer. This would give you a further level of reassurance that the application was executing under the promised terms.

You can deliver all of these requirements by building the alternative e-commerce application as a network of processing nodes of equal importance and functionality, each owned by a different party. Each node would

- be able to process a transaction the same way other nodes do
- verify all transactions in the same way other nodes do
- contribute in an equal way to the outcome of a transaction

The consequence of this architecture would be that the processing would be decentralized to a network of independent nodes rather than being centralized to a specific set of servers that a specific entity owns. Such decentralization would relieve the user from having to trust a specific entity: the user would have to trust only the design of the network as a whole.

Applications built on this architecture are known as *decentralized applications*. I'll provide another example to make the concept clearer.

1.1.1 Dapps vs. conventional centralized applications

To explain more clearly the benefit of building a Dapp, as opposed to developing a conventional centralized application, I'll illustrate for you a typical use case: an electronic voting application.

CENTRALIZED VOTING APPLICATION

Traditional centralized voting applications are generally provided by a company to facilitate shareholder voting or by a local administration or government to facilitate the approval or selection of law proposals. The institution running the application owns it, directly or indirectly, at least during the voting session.

As you can see at the top of figure 1.2, a centralized voting application runs on one or more application servers connected to a central database. The system is exposed to the voters through one or more web servers hosting the voting website. The institution can have the web, application, and database servers hosted directly on the premises or in the cloud. Cloud hosting can happen through a cloud computing provider offering Infrastructure as a Service (IaaS) if the voting system has been implemented in-house by the institution, or through a cloud application provider offering Software as a Service (SaaS) if the voting system is only leased or rented from an external provider during the voting session. This architecture might not be ideal from the point of view of the voter, because of potential worries about trust and security.

TRUST IN CENTRALIZED VOTING

Given all the financial and accounting scandals that have happened at both corporate and governmental levels in the last few years, it's understandable if you don't fully *trust* the organizations you're a shareholder or citizen of. You might wonder whether the outcome of electronic voting might get manipulated in some way.

It's easy to imagine, for example, that a malicious developer or administrator of the voting application, colluding with some party interested in a certain outcome of the voting, could access key parts of the system and tamper with the way votes are collected, processed, and stored at various levels of the application architecture. Depending on how the application has been designed, it could be possible for some malicious database administrators to even modify votes retroactively.

SECURITY IN CENTRALIZED VOTING

When voting through a centralized application, you'd worry about not only the good faith of the company or institution organizing the election, but also whether the system was secured adequately against external manipulation. For example, external parties might be interested in having the voting go a certain way and might try to get their desired outcome by hacking into the system.

As I explained earlier, a centralized voting system includes only a certain number of servers located within the same network. Each server generally provides only one function, and it's therefore a single point of failure, not only from a processing point of view but also, and especially, from a security point of view. For example, if a hacker managed to alter code on the web server so that votes were intercepted and modified in that layer, the entire system would be compromised. The same outcome could be achieved by hacking only into the application server or, even better, into the database server. A breach of security in one part of the system is sufficient to compromise the security of the entire system.

DECENTRALIZED VOTING APPLICATION

A decentralized application is based on two key technical principles:

- Its application logic is present and executed simultaneously and independently on each server of a *peer-to-peer (P2P) network*. In theory, a different participant owns each server, also known as a *node*. A central node doesn't control or coordinate the servers; instead, they communicate directly with each other and are consequently also known as *peer nodes*. They continuously verify each other's output, so a user need only trust the P2P network, not an individual organization. The application data and state are stored on a local copy of a database on each server of the network, as shown at the bottom of figure 1.2.
- Its database technology, called *blockchain*, guarantees that data can't be modified retroactively.

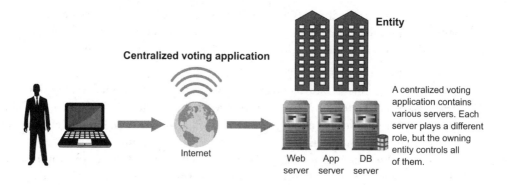

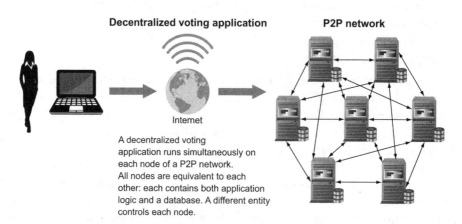

Figure 1.2 Comparison of a centralized voting application with a decentralized one. One institution owns all servers of a centralized application. A decentralized voting application runs simultaneously on multiple nodes of a network that different entities own.

TRUST AND SECURITY IN DAPPS THANKS TO P2P NETWORK REPLICATION

How can you address trust and security concerns by decentralizing the voting application according to the two principles I outlined? A decentralized voting application makes trust and security breaches pointless by replicating its execution over a network including many servers, each in theory owned by a different party. Think about it: if votes were processed and verified not by one single server but independently by many servers owned by different parties, and they were stored not in a single database but in many databases, each one local to the processing party, both trust and security concerns would be addressed:

- *Trust*—If one of the participants tried to maliciously alter a vote and propagate the modified vote to the network, the other participants would detect the vote as modified during their validation and would reject it. They wouldn't store it in their local copy of the database and wouldn't propagate the altered vote further throughout the network, so the malicious modification would become pointless.

- *Security*—Hackers would find trying to alter votes in a decentralized system much more difficult than trying to do so in a centralized one. Even if they managed to modify votes on one server, or they hosted themselves on one server of the decentralized voting application network to do so more easily, other participants would spot and reject the alteration, as seen earlier. Successful hacking would therefore require compromising not one server of the network but at least 51% of the nodes of the network simultaneously, assuming the state of the application is what is agreed among the majority of the network nodes. As you can understand, trying to manipulate a large part of a network including thousands of servers is an incredibly challenging task, especially if each one is managed independently. Also, each one might potentially be set up with a different way of preventing security breaches.

TRUST AND SECURITY IN DAPPS THANKS TO THE BLOCKCHAIN

A blockchain database is based on a data structure that, as its name suggests, is a chain of blocks. A block can be seen as a record containing a set of transactions, each one digitally signed, some metadata (such as block number and time stamp information), and a link to the previous block. Each transaction, each block as a whole, and the links between blocks are secured with cryptographic technology, which makes them *immutable*: retroactive alteration of single transactions is nearly impossible, especially as more blocks are added to the chain. A blockchain database therefore addresses trust and security concerns by providing further protection against manipulation attempts by malicious participants and external parties.

OUTSTANDING QUESTIONS ON LOW-LEVEL ASPECTS

At this stage, you might find the decentralized voting application concept promising from a logical or a high-level point of view, but you might still be confused about physical and lower level aspects of its architecture. You might have doubts in various areas:

- *System architecture*—Is the network hosting the decentralized voting application a special kind of network? Do servers communicate with each other using a special protocol or using standard internet technology?
- *Vote processing and validation*—How does vote submission get propagated across the network so that a vote gets processed on each server of the network? How does a vote get counted and then stored on the blockchain? How does a member of the network verify the authenticity of the consolidated vote records received from other members?

I'll try to answer these questions in the next two sections, which cover low-level details of the decentralized voting application. I'll also assume the voting Dapp has been developed for Ethereum, the blockchain and Dapp platform this book is focused on. Doing so will allow me to start introducing Ethereum and to refer to concrete infrastructural components while presenting two complementary low-level views of the system:

- *A structural Dapp view*—I'll describe the low-level architecture of the client and server sides of our voting Dapp.
- *A transactional Dapp view*—I'll walk you, step-by-step, through the entire lifecycle of a voting transaction.

1.1.2   *Structural view: Anatomy of a Dapp*

The *structural view* of the decentralized voting application includes a description of the components of both the client side, represented by the web UI through which a voter submits a vote, and the server side, represented by a network of servers running the application logic.

DAPP CLIENT SIDE: A WEB APPLICATION

The voting application web client, shown in figure 1.3, gets initially downloaded into the user browser from a conventional web server, generally as a web application containing HTML and JavaScript. The web user interface doesn't contain any server-side scripts and communicates directly with a specific server of the network through a client-side JavaScript library called Web3.js. It might also allow the user to communicate with a network node located on their premises. So far, this application differs in no major way from a conventional web application.

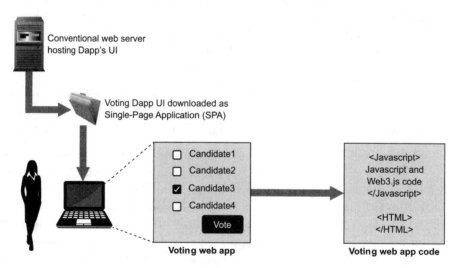

Figure 1.3   A decentralized voting application is exposed to the voter as a web application, which contains both HTML and JavaScript and is downloaded from a conventional web server. The web application, which doesn't contain any server-side scripts (otherwise, it would be partially centralized), is generally configured to communicate directly with a specific node of the network.

DAPP SERVER SIDE: A P2P NETWORK

The server side of a decentralized application is a P2P network of servers that run the same code and have identical copies of a blockchain database. As you know, a key characteristic of this network topology is that it uses no central coordination, but instead uses direct communication between each node and a number of other nodes, known as *peer nodes* or simply *peers*. No master node is needed. As shown in figure 1.4, a node doesn't need to be connected to all of the other nodes of the network. Being connected to a few nodes is sufficient to ensure transactions are rapidly propagated to the whole network.

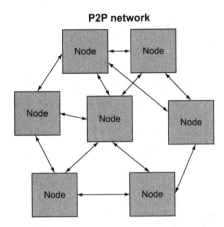

P2P network

Figure 1.4   A peer-to-peer (P2P) network is made of nodes that communicate directly with each other without the coordination of a master node.

THE ETHEREUM NETWORK

Various P2P networks supporting blockchain platforms exist. The most well-known one is the Bitcoin network.

In this book, I'll focus on the Ethereum network, whose *participant* nodes, as shown in figure 1.5, host a *blockchain database* and a piece of software called a node *client*, which allows a node to communicate with other nodes. Because all nodes are equivalent to each other, within the Ethereum network you have no clear-cut concept of client and server. Each node is a server to other nodes, but, at the same time, it's also a client of other nodes. That's why the software element of an Ethereum node is called a client.

Ethereum clients expose a common client interface and communicate with each other through a P2P protocol called *Wire*. That protocol enforces a standard way of sending data throughout the network, specifically a *transaction*, such as a submitted vote, and a *block*, such as a set of votes consolidated in the blockchain database.

Various implementations of an Ethereum client exist. As you can see in figure 1.5, they're written in various languages, from C++ to Go, but all implement the standard client interface and the Wire protocol, so they can interact seamlessly.

The advantage of an Ethereum node client over a Bitcoin node client is that it's able not only to propagate cryptocurrency transactions and blocks throughout the

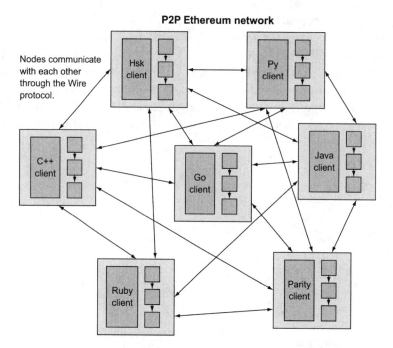

Figure 1.5   Each node of the Ethereum network hosts a blockchain database and a node client capable of executing application code stored in the blockchain. Nodes communicate through the Wire protocol and expose the same interface but can be implemented in different languages.

network, as a Bitcoin node does, but also to execute application code hosted on the blockchain database. From this point of view, platforms such as Ethereum are known as *programmable blockchains.* The code of decentralized applications is structured in *smart contracts*, which encapsulate logic and state in the same way classes do in most object-oriented languages. The voting decentralized application, for example, would be structured on various smart contracts that would be hosted on the Ethereum blockchain. I'll explain shortly what a smart contract is, how you deploy it, how you execute it, and where a smart contract is stored and runs. Bear with me.

THE ROLE OF NETWORK NODES

Although all network nodes communicate seamlessly through the common P2P Wire protocol, not all nodes perform the same function. Broadly, as shown in figure 1.6, the two main types of nodes, which are functionally different, are as follows:

- *Full node*—Most nodes have a standard setup that allows them to process transactions passively: they can read from the blockchain database, but they can't create new blockchain blocks. But they can append blocks received from peer nodes to the local blockchain. They do execute transactions, but only to verify the correctness of the blockchain blocks they receive from peer nodes. In the

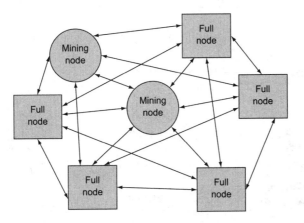

Figure 1.6 The Ethereum network includes two main types of nodes. Full nodes process transactions passively and can read, but can't write on, the blockchain. Mining nodes process transactions actively: they validate the correctness of transactions as full nodes do, but they also assemble transactions into new blocks that are appended onto the blockchain.

case of the voting application, full nodes propagate votes received from their peers to other peers. They also verify that the blocks received are correct and contain authentic votes by running the voting Dapp smart contracts. But full nodes don't store votes in new blockchain blocks.

- *Mining node*—Some of the nodes are configured to process transactions actively: they group and store transactions in new blockchain blocks. They're rewarded in Ether, the cryptocurrency supported in the Ethereum platform, for performing such computationally intensive and energy demanding work. They then propagate these new blocks to the rest of the P2P network. Such nodes are called mining nodes because the process of consolidating a new block to the blockchain and being rewarded for it in cryptocurrency tokens is known as *mining*. In the case of the voting Dapp, mining nodes group votes received from peer nodes into a new block, append the block to the blockchain, and propagate the block through their peers.

PUTTING EVERYTHING TOGETHER

You've examined the structural view of the voting Dapp. Figure 1.7 shows the entire system, including the client and server sides.

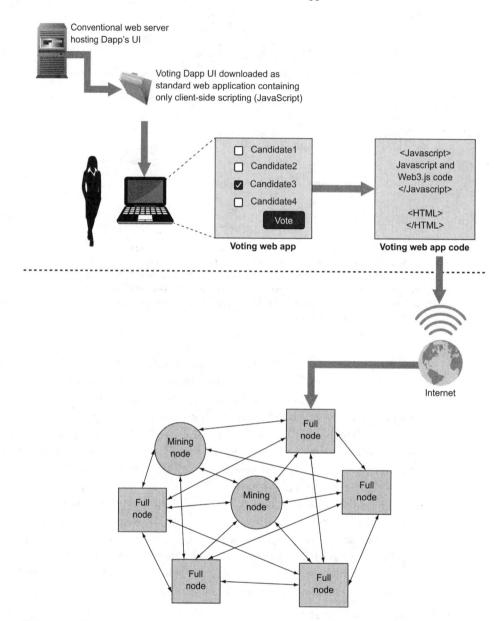

Figure 1.7   The entire static view of a decentralized voting application, including client and server sides

1.1.3 *Transactional view: Through the lifecycle of a transaction*

Adding a temporal dimension to the static view you saw in figure 1.7, figure 1.8 illustrates step-by-step the full lifecycle of a voting transaction:

1 The user selects one of the possible voting options from a drop-down list box on the web client and clicks Vote.

2 A JavaScript function handles the click event and grabs the voting selection. Then, through various web3.js library functions, it sets up the communication with a configured Ethereum node, connects with the voting smart contract, and calls the castVote() function on it. The invocation of castVote() generates a transaction message that's digitally signed against the account of the user to prove they're the genuine sender.

3 The contacted local Ethereum node handles the transaction message, verifies it, and relays it to its peer nodes.

4 Peer nodes do the same and keep propagating the transaction, until the transaction hits mining nodes. This will happen relatively quickly, depending on the ratio of full nodes to mining nodes. Mining nodes perform the same steps (steps 2 and 3) of a full node. In addition, a mining node picks a transaction, such as a voting transaction. A transaction is considered profitable if it's expected to generate an acceptable transaction fee, higher than the electricity costs the mining node faces while processing transactions. If so, the mining node executes the castVote() function and competes with other mining nodes to store the transaction on the blockchain. The winning mining node (which is the mining node successfully solving the so-called consensus algorithm, a cryptographic problem) consolidates the voting transaction among other transactions in a new block of the blockchain. It then relays the new block to all its peer nodes (regardless of whether they're full or mining nodes).

5 Each node that has received a new block verifies whether the individual transactions included in it are genuine and whether the block as a whole is valid. It then processes all the transactions present in it. While doing this, it implicitly verifies the validity of the contract state. For example, the vote submission logic might include an invariant verifying that the number of votes cast for a candidate, or the total number of votes cast for all candidates, isn't higher than the number of registered voters. If the node verifies the block successfully, it relays it to its peer nodes, which perform the same validation and propagation action until the whole network has acquired the new blockchain block. (The verification process will become clearer to you in the next chapter, when I'll present the cryptographic techniques it's based on.)

6 The local Ethereum node with respect to the user receives the new block and verifies it by executing all the transactions present on it, as all the other nodes have done. One of these is the voting transaction, which has been programmed

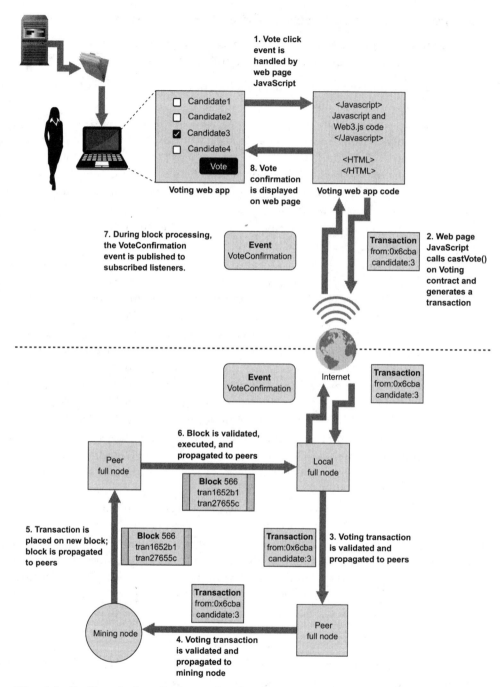

Figure 1.8   The lifecycle of a voting transaction. A voting transaction is created when a voter browser invokes the `castVote()` function on the Voting smart contract on a local node of the Ethereum network. This is then validated and propagated throughout the network until it's included on a new blockchain block by a mining node. The new block is propagated throughout the network, and then it finally gets back to the local node.

to raise a `VoteConfirmation` event on successful completion. The event is published to all the clients subscribed to it, including the Dapp web UI.

7 The JavaScript code present on the voting web client contains a callback function registered against the `VoteConfirmation` event, which then gets triggered.

8 Finally, the callback function shows a vote confirmation notification on the voter's screen.

1.1.4 Some Dapp terminology

Although decentralized applications are a relatively new idea, standard terminology around them started to appear relatively soon after the first Dapps were built. In this section, I'll provide a summary of the key terms that Vitalik Buterin, the creator of Ethereum, described in a famous blog post[1] he wrote to explain key Dapp concepts. You've already come across some of these terms in the previous sections, but now I'll define them more precisely.

SMART CONTRACT

A *smart contract* is an arrangement between two or more parties that involves an exchange of digital assets. One or more of these parties allocates digital assets to the contract at its initiation. Subsequently, the assets are redistributed among the parties according to a predefined protocol encoded in logic and a state that's initialized at the start of the contract.

AUTONOMOUS AGENT

An *autonomous agent* is a software entity that interacts autonomously with external software services and can reconfigure or even reprogram itself following verified changes in the external environment.

DECENTRALIZED ORGANIZATION

A traditional *centralized organization* contains assets and different classes of individuals, typically investors, employees, and customers. Investors control the organization by owning a part of it through the purchase of shares. Interactions between some classes of individuals are influenced by whether they control the organization. For instance, employees can get recruited by investors or by other employees authorized directly or indirectly by investors.

A *decentralized organization* (DO) isn't controlled by any one person or entity. Predefined protocols are what determine interactions between classes of individuals involved in the organization. But such protocols can be designed so that certain individuals have more power than others—for instance, depending on the number of shares owned—exactly as with centralized organizations.

DECENTRALIZED AUTONOMOUS ORGANIZATION

A *decentralized autonomous organization* (DAO) is both a DO and an autonomous agent. Like an autonomous agent, it's a software entity that interacts autonomously with

---

[1] Vitalik Buterin, "DAOs, DACs, DAs and More: An Incomplete Terminology Guide," http://mng.bz/vNrq.

external software services. Individuals involved with the DAO interact, as with DOs, through predefined protocols.

The main difference between a DAO and a DO is that interactions between DAOs and external parties are largely automated, and the interaction protocols are programmed in a *smart contract*, whereas interactions between the individuals who own the DO and external parties are subject only to a *manual protocol*. The key point is that from the point of view of external parties, DAOs are more trustworthy than DOs because automated interactions are predictable, whereas interactions based on a manual protocol rely entirely on the reputation of the individuals following it.

According to these definitions, opinions diverge as to whether blockchain platforms built with the main or only purpose of supporting a cryptocurrency can be classified as DAOs or DOs. Because the Bitcoin infrastructure doesn't allow for implementation of easily automated interaction protocols, some think it should be classified as a DO.

DECENTRALIZED AUTONOMOUS CORPORATION

A *decentralized autonomous corporation* (DAC) is a DAO that can be partially owned through a purchase of shares. As with classic (centralized) corporations, a DAC redistributes dividends periodically, depending on its financial success. A pure DAO, on the other hand, is generally a nonprofit organization, and participants benefit economically exclusively by contributing to its ecosystem and increasing its internal capital.

> **NOTE** The current widely accepted definition of *decentralized application* corresponds to that of DAO described previously, which is still in use among Ethereum purists. I'll use this definition for Dapp for the rest of this book. The reason why the initial terminology used the word *organization* rather than *application* was because the Ethereum founders wanted to put emphasis on the fact that a decentralized application can transact with other parties exactly like conventional organizations: by following rules and protocols and exchanging monetary value, obviously in the form of cryptocurrency rather than conventional currency.

The key aspects of each of these terms are summarized in table 1.1.

Table 1.1   Matrix summarizing key aspects of each term, with DAO standing for Dapp

	Is software	Has capital	Is autonomous	Is owned
Autonom agent	YES	NO	YES	NO
DO	NO	YES	NO	YES
DAO	**YES**	**YES**	**YES**	**NO**
DAC	YES	YES	YES	YES

Although you've learned some of the high-level terms, you can't truly understand the purpose of Dapps and how they work without familiarizing yourself with the concept of blockchain. Because Dapps are built on top of the blockchain and rely heavily on it, you should learn about it and its underlying technologies. I'll cover this in the next section.

Decentralized vs. distributed applications

Decentralized applications shouldn't be confused with *distributed* applications. The two concepts have similarities, but they're not the same thing.

An application is distributed if it runs over multiple servers within a network. The simplest example of a distributed application is a web application, which is typically distributed over a web server, an application server, and a database server, and possibly an email server and legacy mainframes. The centralized voting application seen earlier is an example of a distributed application. It's distributed because it's spread over several servers, but it's also centralized because all the servers are owned by the same institution.

A distributed application runs over multiple servers of a network. A decentralized application is replicated in its entirety over each node of a wide network.

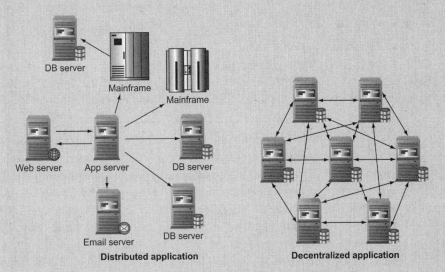

Distributed application　　　　**Decentralized application**

Comparison of the structures of distributed and decentralized applications

An application is decentralized if it's replicated in its entirety over each node of a network, with each node being theoretically owned by a different entity. The higher the number of entities owning nodes of the network, the more trustful the network in its entirety is. Obviously, networks that have only a few owners can't be considered trustful because they don't truly decentralize the processing.

A centralized application is generally distributed, but decentralized applications can also be distributed over multiple servers within each logical node.

1.2   Good and bad Dapps

In the last few years, many Dapps have been developed. Some have received various rounds of venture capital funding and have been deployed successfully into production. Others have failed to convince investors and users and never passed the proof-of-concept stage.

1.2.1   Good use cases

Given the novelty of the technology, it's hard to predict what's going to work and what's going to fail. Nevertheless, various use cases are being widely recognized as a good fit for the blockchain and in particular for Ethereum. Ideal Dapps are those that take advantage of the main benefits of these technologies, specifically record immutability, decentralization, security, and resilience. As a result, the main fields likely to be revolutionized by Dapps are provenance and ownership tracking, authenticity tracking, identity verification, regulatory auditing, charity expense auditing, prediction markets, customer loyalty management, crowdfunding, electronic voting, investing, gambling, lending, online games management, author royalty payment, Internet of Things, cloud computing, and even freedom of speech. Let's see what innovative solutions have already been found in some of these areas.

PROVENANCE AND AUTHENTICITY TRACKING

One of the biggest problems affecting supply chain management, particularly when involving long chains of processed goods crossing several countries, is tracking the authenticity of materials. Here are some Dapps that are innovating in this area with blockchain-based solutions:

- Dapps such as Provenance provide blockchain-based provenance tracking of materials to ensure no information is lost or manipulated within the supplier chain and goods of expected quality reach the end customer. One of the first applications built on Provenance has been focused on the food industry, to track the supply chain of ingredients from the point of collection, though the process of food manufacturing, to the final point of consumer sale. The aim of this system is to prove the food being sold has the claimed characteristics advertised to the consumers, such as location and sustainability of harvesting or breeding, whether the sources are organic or have been genetically modified, whether they're coming from fair trade, and so on.
- Unilever, the multinational consumer goods corporation, is developing a blockchain-based system in collaboration with a number of start-ups to track the tea supply chain starting from farmers in Malawi.
- Everledger is a Dapp that aims to replace the paper certification process for diamonds with a blockchain-based system. A full digital record of a diamond, including its certificate ID and many properties, such as cut, grade, clarity, color, and carat, is stored on the blockchain, and the certificate ID is then engraved with a laser on the stone. All the information related to a diamond

can then be retrieved at any point of the supply chain with the help of a scanner that reads the certificate ID from the stone. Almost 2 million diamonds have already been stored on Everledger.

- The pharmaceutical company Pfizer is partnering with the biotechnology company Genentech to develop MediLedger, a blockchain-based drug delivery tracking system. The aim is to verify the provenance and authenticity of Pfizer drug deliveries throughout the entire distribution chain to prevent thefts, fraud, and counterfeiting.

IDENTITY VERIFICATION

As with provenance tracking, verification of proof of identity tries to protect businesses and individuals from the consequences of fraud and identity theft. KYC-Chain is a novel platform built on the Ethereum blockchain that allows users to manage their digital identity securely. It also helps businesses and financial institutions to manage customer data in a reliable and easy manner. The system is designed so that users own the "keys" to their personal data and identity certificates. Consequently, identity owners, who can be individuals or companies, are the only ones who get to choose which part of their information is shared, with whom, and under what terms. Such information is digitally attested by notaries and institutions before being shared by owners and registered agents.

PROVING OWNERSHIP

Traditional blockchains associated with cryptocurrencies such as Bitcoin as ledgers implicitly prove the ownership of digital assets, such as the amount of Bitcoin stored at a certain address. Only the legitimate owners of the address are able to transfer funds because they're the only ones who know the private key.

TrustToken tries to go further. It's a Dapp conceived for proving the ownership of physical assets, such as real estate; financial assets, such as stocks and bonds; commodities, such as gold; and even intellectual property, such as music, books, and patents, through smart contracts. The idea is that you can transfer the ownership of these assets from one person to the other in the same way Bitcoins are transferred between addresses. The underlying assumption for TrustToken to be successful is that proof of ownership recorded through the system should be enforceable under law.

ECONOMY OF THINGS

The tech startup Slock.it (https://slock.it/) is building the infrastructure for the "economy of things," which lies at the intersection between the Internet of Things and blockchain technology. This infrastructure, which the company has named the Universal Sharing Network, has the potential to be used as a financial internet, where connected autonomous objects can not only sell and rent themselves but also pay for each other's services. The technology the company is developing, based on Ethereum smart contracts, aims to provide autonomous objects an identity and the ability to receive payments and enter into agreements without the need for intermediaries. Smart lockers, which enable the unlocking of physical objects when a fee is paid, are some of the applications already created on this platform. Because smart lockers make renting of sports equipment, hotel rooms, bicycles, and offices easy, this solution is thought to provide the foundation for the sharing economy.

DECENTRALIZED PREDICTION MARKETS

Prediction markets reward people for correctly predicting real-world events, such as the winner of a presidential election, the outcome of a referendum, the level of interest rates at a specific date, or the winner of a sports competition. Aside from speculative uses, they're also useful tools for economists, public administration planners, and corporate strategists, who can base their decisions on the event probabilities being currently traded, which are thought to reflect the "wisdom of the crowds."

Although centralized markets such as predictit.org (www.predictit.org) exist, several decentralized initiatives are starting to emerge. Augur is a decentralized market prediction platform built on Ethereum. The idea is that decentralization brings the following benefits:

- Being based on the Ethereum network, it has no central point of failure, so it's inherently highly available.
- Nobody controls the definition of markets: anyone can start a new market on a new prediction and can get rewarded for having created that market.
- The official outcome of each prediction isn't decided centrally; it's crowdsourced from market participants, so it's less likely to be subject to manipulation.
- Funds are stored on the blockchain, which eliminates counterparty risk, makes payment to prediction winners fast, and reduces the likelihood of errors.

INTERNATIONAL TRADE FINANCE

International trade between a supplier and a manufacturer located in different countries is a complex business. As you can see in figure 1.9, it's generally based on a complicated workflow involving many parties, such as banks that facilitate the payment, commercial intermediaries that facilitate the distribution, shipping and delivery companies that transport the goods, insurers that cover financial risks while the goods are in transit, and customs officials who check the legality of the goods and the payment of import duties.

Parties involved in a specific transaction often have never dealt with each other previously. But for the transaction to complete successfully, they must communicate with each other effectively, generally through established lengthy protocols designed to protect a party against the malicious behavior of another party. Parties cross-check each other, and this takes a huge amount of paperwork and time, which often causes long delays.

we.trade is a platform sponsored by a consortium of banking partners (including Société Générale, Deutsche Bank, Nordea, Santander, and HSBC) that aims at simplifying and streamlining such processes with the help of blockchain technology. The platform tracks each step of the transaction openly and transparently so that each party is able to submit and consume the relevant documentation with the confidence

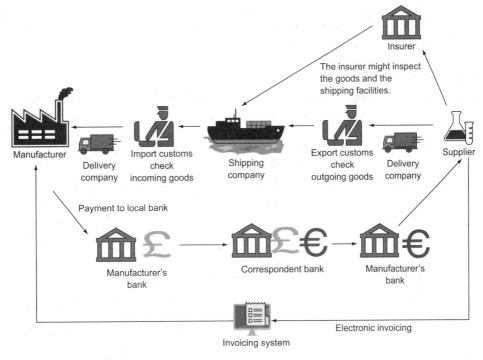

Figure 1.9 Typical international trade involving many parties: banks, commercial intermediaries, shipping companies, insurers, customs officials, and so on

that no one will tamper with it. Trades that used to take weeks can be now completed in a few days.

REGULATORY AUDITING

The blockchain is particularly suitable for ensuring that records stored on it haven't been altered or tampered with. Balanc3 is a Dapp built on Ethereum that ensures the integrity of accountancy records for regulatory purposes.

CROWDFUNDING

WeiFund aims at providing open source modular and extensible decentralized crowdfunding utilities based on the Ethereum blockchain. Users can set up and manage crowdfunding campaigns through these utilities. The possibility of encoding funding rules based on smart contract technology allows users to know precisely what will happen with their money if the campaign fails or is successful.

GAMBLING

Intuitively, a natural fit for a decentralized application is a gambling platform, because users get the benefit of being assured that bets are processed fairly and predictably. Edgeless is an example of such a platform, and it's currently being developed after a successful crowdfunding campaign.

Now that you've learned about some successful Dapp implementations, you might be wondering whether it's always worth basing your application on blockchain technology. We'll explore this in the next section.

1.2.2   Pointless Dapps

Deciding whether the blockchain is a suitable technology for an application you're planning to build might be difficult. What you should ask yourself is whether the functionality that a blockchain platform offers will meet your business requirements. More importantly, consider whether the benefits of using such a platform would be outweighed by all the technical limitations and additional complexities that come with this technology. A sobering blog post titled "Avoiding the Pointless Blockchain Project"[2] analyzes the requirements necessary to justify the use of a blockchain platform over more traditional technologies such as SQL or NoSQL databases. It concludes that a blockchain project only makes sense if you can answer yes to all of the following questions:

- Does your application require a shared database?
- Does the database need to support multiple writing parties?
- Do the writing parties have no trust in each other?
- Do the writing parties want to modify the state of the database directly, without requiring a central entity trusted by all participants?
- Do transactions that the writing parties create interact collaboratively with each other?

According to these criteria, for example, an internal enterprise application that wouldn't expose any data to external parties wouldn't be a suitable choice for a Dapp. Other poor Dapp candidates are applications for which confidentiality around the business rules is important. A smart contract is, by definition, completely open and transparent to all interacting parties. Therefore, preventing participants from accessing and understanding the logic of the rules would defeat the purpose.

Although decentralized microblogging applications such as EthTweet are considered sensible Dapps to those who value the fact that messages can't be censored and altered after they're sent, an instant messaging Dapp, such as a "decentralized WhatsApp," wouldn't be a particularly useful product for a fundamental reason. One of the technical downsides of the blockchain platform is that processing transactions (in this case instant messages) requires roughly 15 seconds to consolidate a new blockchain block. Therefore, messages would never be *instant* at all.

When building a Dapp, you also should keep in mind some operational aspects that, given the novelty of the technology, may cause some issues down the road. For instance, although a smart contract can automatically guarantee funds are routed and released subject to certain conditions, a commercial transaction might also be subject to real-world

---

[2] Gideon Greenspan, "Avoiding the Pointless Blockchain Project," http://mng.bz/4Oqg.

conditions that programming logic can't enforce. A classic example for a non-fully automatically enforceable smart contract is that of an electronic loan. If the borrower had to keep the borrowed money stuck on a blockchain account so a smart contract could automatically give it back to the lender if the borrower missed an interest payment, the borrowing wouldn't make any economic sense. In these cases, it isn't clear yet whether a court of law would be able to enforce the nonautomated elements of a smart contract or it would be necessary to complement the deal with a traditional legal arrangement.

1.3 A five-minute Dapp implementation

By now, you should have a good understanding of what a Dapp is, the purpose of Dapps over conventional apps, the main architectural components of a decentralized application, and whether it makes sense to embark on a project based on blockchain technologies. It's now time to take one little step further and get on with some programming. In the rest of the chapter, you'll start building the smart contract for a custom cryptocurrency. You'll then activate it and interact with it.

1.3.1 Building SimpleCoin, a basic cryptocurrency

Most Dapps are designed using functionality based on the exchange of cryptocurrency or tokens through rules encoded in one or more smart contracts. You'll start to get a feel for Dapps programming by building SimpleCoin, a basic cryptocurrency that will present useful preliminary concepts about smart contracts and the Ethereum platform. You'll progressively build on it in the following chapters, where you'll learn more about Dapp development. You'll also use or reference SimpleCoin from other Dapps that you'll build in later chapters.

Because you haven't installed an Ethereum platform client on your computer yet, you'll be writing code on the Remix Solidity (previously known as Browser Solidity) integrated development environment (IDE) for now. This online tool will allow you to implement smart contracts in a high-level language called Solidity, similar to JavaScript, and run them on a local JavaScript VM that emulates the Ethereum Virtual Machine that you'll meet in the next chapter. It's also possible through this tool to interact with real smart contracts deployed on the Ethereum network.

Open a web browser and go to: http://remix.ethereum.org/. You should see a screen like figure 1.10. On the website, the left side of the IDE is a file explorer (which you can hide by clicking the double arrow toggle at the top left); in the middle you have the code editor; and the right side contains various panels to run the code and interact with it.

In your first encounter with Solidity, you'll implement the simplest possible smart contract. If you think of a smart contract as the equivalent of a class in an object-oriented language, you'll write a single class with only one member field, one constructor, and one method. Then you'll run it and interact with it.

Hide the file explorer by clicking the double arrow toggle at the top left, and then enter the code in listing 1.1 in the Remix editor, in the left side of the screen.

File explorer toggle   **Code editor**   **Panels for running code**

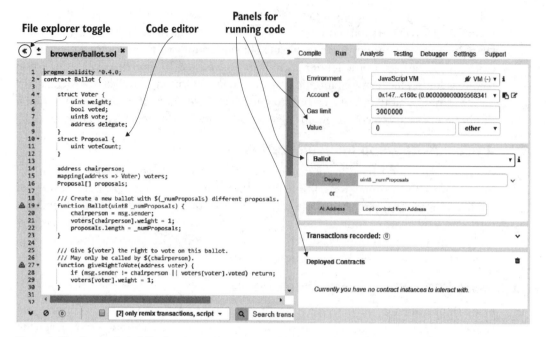

Figure 1.10   Screenshot of the Remix opening screen, with the code on the left and the code execution panels on the right. I've hidden the file explorer by clicking the double arrow toggle at the top left.

Listing 1.1   First implementation of SimpleCoin, a basic cryptocurrency

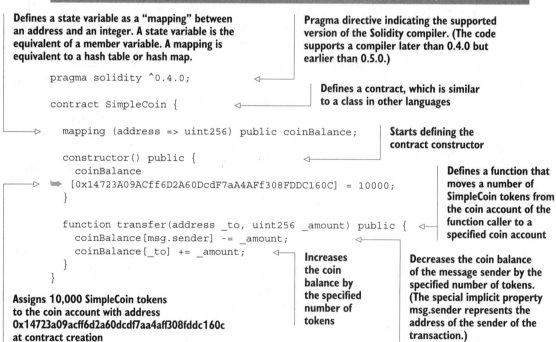

Defines a state variable as a "mapping" between an address and an integer. A state variable is the equivalent of a member variable. A mapping is equivalent to a hash table or hash map.

Pragma directive indicating the supported version of the Solidity compiler. (The code supports a compiler later than 0.4.0 but earlier than 0.5.0.)

```
pragma solidity ^0.4.0;

contract SimpleCoin {

  mapping (address => uint256) public coinBalance;

  constructor() public {
    coinBalance
    [0x14723A09ACff6D2A60DcdF7aA4AFf308FDDC160C] = 10000;
  }

  function transfer(address _to, uint256 _amount) public {
    coinBalance[msg.sender] -= _amount;
    coinBalance[_to] += _amount;
  }
}
```

Defines a contract, which is similar to a class in other languages

Starts defining the contract constructor

Defines a function that moves a number of SimpleCoin tokens from the coin account of the function caller to a specified coin account

Assigns 10,000 SimpleCoin tokens to the coin account with address 0x14723a09acff6d2a60dcdf7aa4aff308fddc160c at contract creation

Increases the coin balance by the specified number of tokens

Decreases the coin balance of the message sender by the specified number of tokens. (The special implicit property msg.sender represents the address of the sender of the transaction.)

Let's examine this code in detail. A *contract* in Solidity is a type similar to a class in any other language: it has *state variables* (such as `coinBalance`), a constructor, functions (such as `transfer`), and events.

The `coinBalance` state variable is defined as a `mapping`. A *mapping* is a hash map, equivalent to a hashMap in Java, Dictionary in C#, or dict in Python. In this example, the type of the key is an `address`, whereas the value is a `uint256`—an unsigned 256-bit integer. An *address* holds a 20-byte value and can identify a specific smart contract account or a specific user account. An account, as you'll see later in detail, is the sender or the receiver of a transaction. The `coinBalance` state variable therefore represents a collection of coin accounts, each holding a number of SimpleCoin tokens.

The `transfer` function is meant to move a number of SimpleCoin tokens from the coin account of the function caller to a specified coin account. In smart contract terminology, a function caller is the *transaction sender*. `msg` is a special implicitly defined variable that represents the incoming message. It has various properties, among which `msg.sender` represents the address of the sender of the transaction, who is the caller of `transfer`.

The body of the transfer function is simple to understand. It involves subtracting the specified amount from the cash account associated with the function caller and adding the amount specified in the `_amount` parameter to the account associated with the address specified in the `_to` parameter. To keep this initial code simple, this implementation isn't performing any boundary checks yet on the number of SimpleCoin tokens owned by the transaction sender, who, for example, shouldn't be allowed to send more tokens than they own. You'll perform such checks when we revisit Simple-Coin in later chapters.

At this point, you should understand that your `SimpleCoin` contract is, in practice, a class with a constructor (`SimpleCoin` function), some state (`coinBalance` variable), and a method (`transfer` function). Table 1.2 gives a quick summary of the Solidity keywords you've come across.

Table 1.2 A summary of Solidity keywords used in the first code sample

Keyword	Explanation
`contract`	Type similar to class in any other language
`mapping`	Data structure similar to a hash table or hash map
`address`	20-byte value representing an Ethereum user account or contract account
`uint256`	Unsigned 256-bit integer
`msg`	Special variable representing an incoming message object
`msg.sender`	Property of the msg object representing the address of the message sender

1.3.2   *Running the contract*

Move now to the right side of the screen to deploy the SimpleCoin contract. First, make sure the Auto Compile option in the Compile tab is checked, as shown in figure 1.11, so that Remix will recompile the code at every change. Also, make sure you've selected version 0.4.24 of the compiler (for example 0.4.24+commit.e67f0147), because this is the version I've been using when writing SimpleCoin.

Figure 1.11   The Auto Compile option in the Compile tab makes sure the code entered in the editor is recompiled at every change.

If you've typed your code correctly (I recommend you copy the code from the files provided on the book website!), and no compilation errors have occurred, you should see the following buttons in the Run tab: Deploy and At Address, as shown in figure 1.12. Ignore At Address for now and focus your attention on Deploy. By clicking this button, you'll deploy the SimpleCoin contract on an emulated blockchain within Remix.

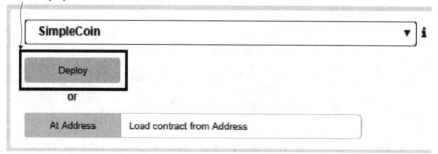

Figure 1.12   Once the code has been compiled correctly, the Run tab will show two buttons: Deploy and At Address. You can instantiate the contract by clicking Deploy.

The contract will be stored against an address on the emulated Ethereum blockchain, and a new Deployed Contracts panel will appear, as shown in figure 1.13. You can read the deployment address by clicking the Copy Address icon and pasting it in Notepad, for example.

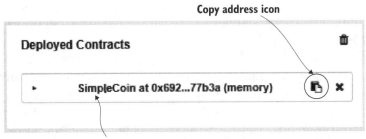

Figure 1.13   After deploying the contract, the Deployed Contracts panel appears, containing a drop-down with a SimpleCoin option; click it, and you'll see the contract operations.

1.3.3   Interacting with the contract

Now that the `SimpleCoin` contract has been deployed, you'll be able to perform simple operations against it: you'll check SimpleCoin token balances and move tokens across accounts.

Click the SimpleCoin drop-down list within the Deployed Contracts panel. Two new buttons will appear: CoinBalance and Transfer, as shown in figure 1.14.

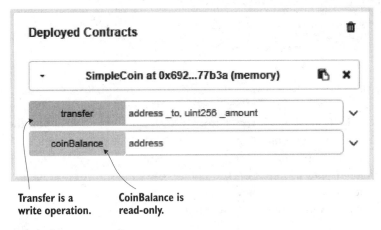

Figure 1.14   SimpleCoin operations buttons: CoinBalance and Transfer. CoinBalance is a getter of the coinBalance state variable and is a read-only operation. Transfer allows you to transfer the specified number of tokens to the indicated address.

The Remix IDE shows two types of buttons:

- *Blue buttons*—They perform read operations against the contract, such as checking the value of state variables or calling read-only functions.
- *Red buttons*—They perform write operations against the contract, such as instantiating the contract through the constructor (Create), or call functions that modify any state variables.

In this case, CoinBalance is blue because it allows you to read the coin balance associated with an address. Transfer is red because by clicking it you'll alter the state of the contract, specifically by changing values contained in the `coinBalance` mapping state variable.

Now check that the `coinBalance` associated with the address specified in the constructor has the full initial supply of SimpleCoin you set at construction. Wrap the address with double quotes: `"0x14723A09ACff6D2A60DcdF7aA4AFf308FDDC160C"`. Enter it in the text box and click CoinBalance. Some output will appear. At the bottom, you should see the expected number of SimpleCoin tokens you specified in the constructor: 10,000.

`0x14723A09ACff6D2A60DcdF7aA4AFf308FDDC160C` is the address of one of the five test accounts present on the Remix IDE. You can see them in the Transaction Origin drop-down list box on the top-right of the screen. Although they aren't fully visible on the screen, their full addresses are reported in table 1.3. (I've retrieved them one by one by clicking the Copy Address icon next to the Account drop-down.)

Table 1.3   Remix test accounts whose full address is hidden behind the HTML

`0xca35b7d915458ef540ade6068dfe2f44e8fa733c`
`0x14723a09acff6d2a60dcdf7aa4aff308fddc160c`
`0x4b0897b0513fdc7c541b6d9d7e929c4e5364d2db`
`0x583031d1113ad414f02576bd6afabfb302140225`
`0xdd870fa1b7c4700f2bd7f44238821c26f7392148`

You can double-check that the amount of SimpleCoin tokens associated with any address different from `0x14723A09ACff6D2A60DcdF7aA4AFf308FDDC160C` is zero. For instance, enter the following address, wrapped with double quotes as you did earlier, in the CoinBalance text box: `"0x583031D1113aD414F02576BD6afaBfb302140225"`. After clicking the button, you'll see a zero, as expected.

To recap, when you instantiated the contract, an amount of 10,000 SimpleCoin tokens got assigned as initial money supply to the address starting with `0x14723A09`. No other address owns any tokens yet, as summarized in table 1.4.

Table 1.4   Balance of each Remix test account after contract instantiation

Account address	Account balance
`0xca35b7d915458ef540ade6068dfe2f44e8fa733c`	0
`0x14723a09acff6d2a60dcdf7aa4aff308fddc160c`	10,000
`0x4b0897b0513fdc7c541b6d9d7e929c4e5364d2db`	0
`0x583031d1113ad414f02576bd6afabfb302140225`	0
`0xdd870fa1b7c4700f2bd7f44238821c26f7392148`	0

Now you'll call the transfer function to move some tokens from the account with the address starting with 0x14723a09 to a different test account. Because the transfer function moves tokens from the account of its caller, the function must be called from the contract creator's address starting with 0x14723a09. Pick this address from the Account drop-down at the top right of the Run tab, then enter in the text box of the transfer method the destination address—for example, the address starting with 0x4b0897b0—and a number of tokens to be transferred—for instance, 150 tokens. You should separate the values of these parameters with a comma:

```
"0x4B0897b0513fdC7C541B6d9D7E929C4e5364D2dB", 150
```

Now click Transfer. The function returns no result, as expected.

Check the number of tokens present in the contract creator's address by clicking CoinBalance after entering the contract creator's address ("0x14723A09ACff6-D2A60DcdF7aA4AFf308FDDC160C") in the related text box. The value is now 9,850, as expected.

If you perform the same check on the destination address ("0x4B0897b0513f-dC7C541B6d9D7E929C4e5364D2dB"), you'll get 150. All other addresses still have zero tokens, as summarized in table 1.5.

Table 1.5 Balance of each Remix test account after a transfer operation

Account address	Account balance
0xca35b7d915458ef540ade6068dfe2f44e8fa733c	0
0x14723a09acff6d2a60dcdf7aa4aff308fddc160c	9,850
0x4b0897b0513fdc7c541b6d9d7e929c4e5364d2db	150
0x583031d1113ad414f02576bd6afabfb302140225	0
0xdd870fa1b7c4700f2bd7f44238821c26f7392148	0

As an exercise, you can try to transfer coins from the address starting with 0x4b0897b05 to a different address and recheck if the amounts are correct. While doing so, please don't perform any crazy transactions yet, such as trying to move more coins than a certain address is holding. To keep the code simple for the moment, you haven't coded any boundary conditions to handle such situations. You'll learn about these in the next chapter.

Although the code you've written so far is simple, your main objective at this stage was only to start to familiarize yourself with smart contracts, the Solidity language, and Remix. By now, you should have achieved that objective, and you should understand how contract instantiation works and how to interact with a contract from different accounts.

SimpleCoin is still at the stage of an embryonic Dapp. So far, you've only executed its code on a JavaScript VM-based simulator and, because it's lacking a UI, you've seen its output through Remix. In the next chapter, you'll take a step further and install an Ethereum client. You'll then deploy SimpleCoin to a real Ethereum network and interact with it again.

> **WARNING**   If the compiler configured in the Compile tab is version 0.4.25, Remix will only allow you to enter addresses with a valid checksum in the code editor. I'll explain what a valid checksum is in chapter 5. But for now, it means 0x14723a09acff6d2a60dcdf7aa4aff308fddc160c (all in lowercase) and 0x14723A09ACff6D2A60DcdF7aA4AFf308FDDC160C aren't interpreted as being equivalent to each other. Unfortunately, addresses in the Account drop-down within the Run tab are all in lowercase and therefore aren't compliant. If you want to know the corresponding address with a valid checksum, you can use Etherscan, the online blockchain viewer (https://etherscan.io/). Enter the incorrectly formatted address (for example, 0x14723a09acff6d2a60dcdf7aa4aff308fddc160c) in the text box at the top of the screen, and you'll see the correctly formatted corresponding address (0x14723A09ACff6D2A60DcdF7aA4AFf308FDDC160C) in the Address header also at the top of the screen.

Summary

- A decentralized application is a novel type of application that isn't owned or controlled by any entity and runs on a trustless decentralized P2P network.
- The topology of a decentralized application is different from that of a conventional, centralized, one because both its business logic layer and its data layer (the blockchain) are fully replicated on each node of the network.
- Dapps rely on blockchain technology, which is based, in turn, on public key cryptography, cryptographic hash functions, and the concept of mining through a consensus protocol.
- Many appropriate use cases exist for decentralizing an application, especially in the fields of provenance and authenticity tracking, identity verification, regulatory auditing, prediction markets, and crowdfunding.
- Decentralized applications aren't always the best solution for a business problem. For example, it doesn't make sense to decentralize an internal enterprise application that isn't shared with any external participant.
- You can implement smart contracts, which are at the heart of Dapps, within the Ethereum platform in a language called Solidity, similar to JavaScript. It's possible to write simple smart contracts through the Remix Solidity IDE and simulate their activation and interaction with various mock Ethereum accounts.

Understanding the blockchain 2

I intended chapter 1 to give you a high-level overview of decentralized applications without overwhelming you with too many details. Consequently, I'm sure you're still wondering what technical stack you need to learn to build a full Dapp. Also, you might feel the architectural presentation on Dapps didn't go as far as you'd have liked, and you might still have doubts about how a blockchain exactly works. If you're asking yourself these questions, I'll address them in this chapter.

I'll start by revisiting the voting Dapp I introduced in the previous chapter, and I'll cover some aspects of an Ethereum node I skipped earlier for simplicity. I'll then cover the entire technology stack required to implement a full end-to-end decentralized application. Additionally, I'll introduce the cryptographic concepts and foundations you need to acquire to appreciate how a blockchain works. Before closing the chapter, I'll present technologies specific to the Ethereum blockchain and give you some information on Ethereum's history and governance.

2.1   *A deeper look at decentralized applications*

When I presented the structural and transactional views of a decentralized application in chapter 1, I decided to keep them at a relatively high level. I'm aware blockchain technology might be completely new to you, so I wanted to make sure you understood the high-level architecture and the purpose of decentralized applications without confusing you with too much jargon and too many technologies. Now that you've acquired a solid foundation, it's time to have a deeper look at Ethereum Dapps. Let's start by stepping into an Ethereum node.

2.1.1   *Inside an Ethereum node*

As shown in figure 2.1, each node of the Ethereum P2P network contains two main components:

- *An Ethereum client*—This acts as a runtime and contains four elements:
    - A virtual machine called *Ethereum Virtual Machine (EVM)*, capable of executing smart contract code generally written in a language called Solidity and compiled into EVM bytecode.

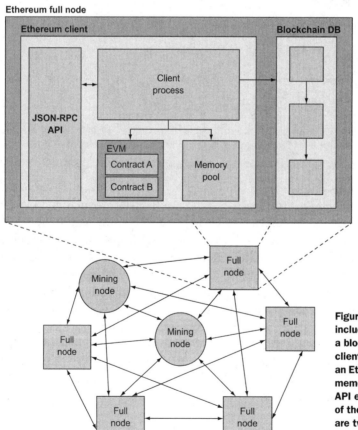

Figure 2.1   **An Ethereum node includes an Ethereum client and a blockchain database. The client contains a client process, an Ethereum Virtual Machine, a memory pool, and a JSON-RPC API exposing the functionality of the node externally. There are two types of nodes: full nodes and mining nodes.**

    – A *memory pool*, where the node stores transactions that it receives, such as a vote submitted by a voter from the client side, before it propagates them further into the network.

    – A *client process*, which coordinates the processing. It handles incoming messages and transactions, dispatches them to the EVM when appropriate, and stores transactions to, and retrieves them from, the memory pool. The client process also handles incoming blockchain blocks that the node receives from peer nodes and appends them to the local copy of the blockchain database.

    – A *JSON-RPC API*, which exposes the functionality of the client to other nodes and external users.

- A *blockchain database*—Apart from transaction data, such as votes submitted by voters, the blockchain also keeps a copy of the EVM bytecode of all smart contracts deployed on the network and holds their state. Mining nodes append new blocks to the blockchain regularly, every 15 seconds.

2.1.2 Revisiting the lifecycle of a transaction

Now that you know an Ethereum node hosts a JSON-RPC interface, an EVM, and a memory pool, I can explain to you, with the help of some diagrams (figures 2.2 to 2.4), what role they play during the transaction lifecycle.

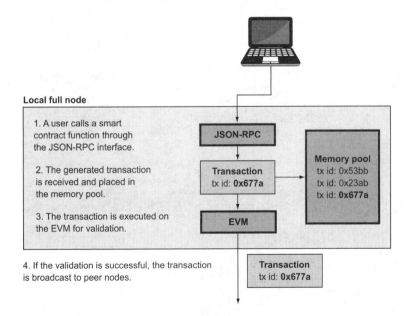

Figure 2.2   The lifecycle of a transaction. A voting transaction is created when a function is invoked on a smart contract on a chosen Ethereum node through the JSON-RPC interface. The node places the transaction in the memory pool and executes it on the EVM for validation. If the validation is successful, the transaction is broadcast to peer nodes until it reaches a mining node; otherwise, it dies out.

A transaction is generated when a function is invoked on a smart contract of the chosen Ethereum node through the JSON-RPC interface. (See figure 2.2.)

1 A full node receives the transaction from a peer node and places it in the memory pool. (See figure 2.2.)

2 The full node executes the transaction on the EVM for validation. (See figure 2.2.)

3 If the validation is successful, the node broadcasts the transaction to its peer nodes. If the validation is unsuccessful, the node doesn't propagate the transaction further, and it dies out.

4 A mining node places the transaction received from a peer node in the memory pool. (See figure 2.3.)

5 The mining node picks transactions deemed to be profitable from the memory pool, executes them on the EVM, and tries to add them onto a new block. (See figure 2.3.)

6 If the block created is added successfully to the blockchain, the mining node removes the related transactions from the memory pool. (See figure 2.3.)

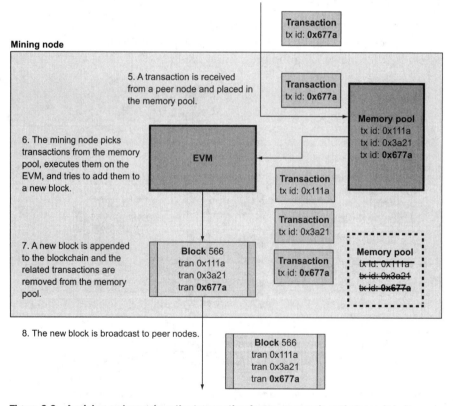

Figure 2.3 A mining node receives the transaction from a peer node and places it in its memory pool. The node later picks it and executes it on the EVM, among other transactions, to place it on a new block. If the block is appended on the blockchain, the transaction is removed from the memory pool and the block is broadcast to peer nodes.

7 The node broadcasts the new block to peer nodes. (See figure 2.3.)

8 A full node receives the new block from a peer node. (See figure 2.4.)

9 The full node executes all the block transactions on the EVM for validation. (See figure 2.4.)

10 The node removes all the associated transactions from its memory pool if the block has been validated successfully. (See figure 2.4.)

11 The node broadcasts the block to peer nodes. (See figure 2.4.)

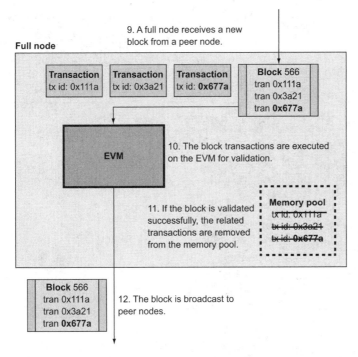

Figure 2.4 The full node's process, from when it receives the new block to when it processes all its transactions on the EVM for validation, then, if validation is successful, removes the related transactions from the memory pool and propagates the block further into the network

2.1.3 *Development view: Deploying the voting smart contract*

By now, you should have a good idea of both what a decentralized application looks like and how a transaction flows throughout the system. You might still be wondering, though, when and how a smart contract gets propagated throughout the network. It turns out that the server-side contract propagation process is similar to that of a standard transaction, such as the voting transaction analyzed in the previous chapter in figure 1.8.

An Ethereum smart contract, such as the voting smart contract of the voting Dapp, is code written in the Solidity language. A smart contract developer compiles the code into EVM bytecode and then deploys it across the P2P network through a contract deployment transaction, which executes on a local Ethereum node and then propagates throughout the network. During its propagation throughout the network, a mining node processes the deployment transaction and stores its EVM bytecode on the blockchain, as illustrated in figure 2.5.

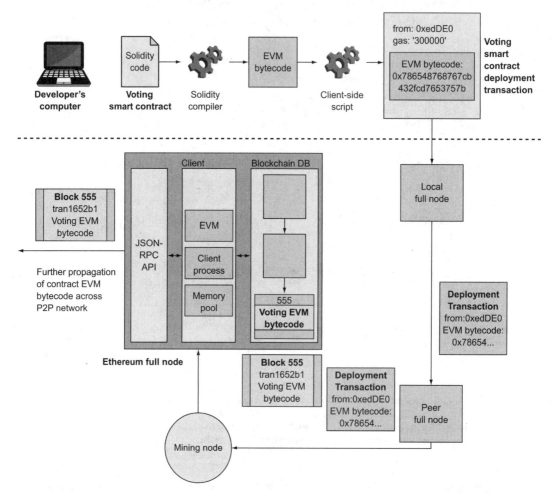

Figure 2.5   A developer writes the voting smart contract in the Solidity language, then compiles it into EVM bytecode and inserts it into a contract deployment transaction. This is pushed to the local Ethereum node and propagated throughout the network. It's then mined and appended to the blockchain.

You might have noticed, while going through the static, dynamic, and development views of a Dapp, in these two initial chapters, that I've mentioned languages and JavaScript libraries that might be unfamiliar to you. You shouldn't be particularly worried about the amount of technology you'll have to learn. You can implement a Dapp based on the Ethereum blockchain with languages much like those used in centralized apps you're already familiar with. The client side of a Dapp is generally based on standard HTML5 + JavaScript; the communication layer between the UI and the server side is based on a JavaScript library called Web3 that's executed on the client side; and you can implement server-side smart contracts in Solidity, which is a flavor of JavaScript.

Your journey through this book will continue, as shown in figure 2.6, from the server side, which is the core of decentralized applications, and you'll write smart contracts in Solidity. Then you'll learn how to interact with a smart contract remotely through the Web3.js JavaScript library. Finally, you'll implement a web-based UI, built on HTML and JavaScript.

Server-side smart contracts	Client-side to server-side communication	Client-side web UI
Solidity	JavaScript + Web3.js	HTML + JavaScript

Progress through book

Figure 2.6   You'll progress from writing smart contracts in Solidity, to interacting with smart contracts remotely through the Web3.js JavaScript library, to building a web UI in HTML and JavaScript.

In summary, with some knowledge of JavaScript, or any C-like language, it isn't difficult to transition from centralized to decentralized application development. But during that transition, it's important to fully understand the technologies underlying decentralized applications, because they're rather different from the technologies that centralized applications are built on. We'll explore that in the next section.

2.2   What technologies make Dapps viable?

As you know, a Dapp is based on business logic encapsulated into smart contracts that are executed against a distributed database called blockchain. Blockchain technology is based, in turn, on public key cryptography, cryptographic hash functions, and the concept of consensus, which you can implement using *proof of work* and *proof of stake* algorithms, among other ways.

You might be feeling like I keep opening more and more Russian dolls, and this might never end, but please don't get frustrated! Cryptography is the lowest level I'm going to cover, I promise.

2.2.1   Blockchain technologies

In the next several sections, I'll explain briefly all the cryptographic terms I've just mentioned so you can form a mental model of how a blockchain database works before we proceed further. Public key cryptography is the lowest technological block underlying the blockchain, so let's start from there.

PUBLIC KEY CRYPTOGRAPHY

Public key cryptography is an encryption methodology based on a pair of keys: a *private key*, usually generated randomly, which is known only to its owner, and a *public key*, known to everyone, generated from an algorithm that takes the private key as an input. Figure 2.7 illustrates how private and public keys are generated.

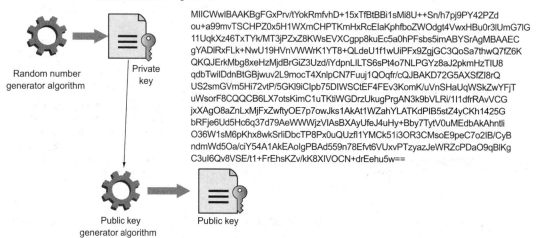

MIGeMA0GCSqGSIb3DQEBAQUAA4GMADCBiAKBgFGxPrv/tYokRmfvhD+15xTfBtBB
i1sMi8U++Sn/h7pj9PY42PZdou+a99mvTSCHPZ0x5H1WXmCHPTKmHxRcElaKphfb
oZWOdgt4VwxHBu0r3lUmG7IG11UqkXz46TxTYk/MT3jPZxZ8KWsEVXCgpp8kuEc5
a0hPFsbs5imABYSrAgMBAAE=

MIICWwIBAAKBgFGxPrv/tYokRmfvhD+15xTfBtBBi1sMi8U++Sn/h7pj9PY42PZd
ou+a99mvTSCHPZ0x5H1WXmCHPTKmHxRcElaKphfboZWOdgt4VwxHBu0r3lUmG7IG
11UqkXz46TxTYk/MT3jPZxZ8KWsEVXCgpp8kuEc5a0hPFsbs5imABYSrAgMBAAEC
gYADIRxFLk+NwU19HVnVWWrK1YT8+QLdeU1f1wUiPFx9ZgjGC3QoSa7thwQ7fZ6K
QKQJErkMbg8xeHzMjdBrGiZ3Uzd/iYdpnLILTS6sPt4o7NLPGYz8aJ2pkmHzTIU8
qdbTwilDdnBtGBjwuv2L9mocT4XnlpCN7Fuuj1QOqfr/cQJBAKD72G5AXSfZI8rQ
US2smGVm5Hi72vtP/5GKl9iClpb75DIWSCtEF4FEv3KomK/uVnSHaUqWSkZwYFjT
uWsorF8CQQCB6LX7otsKimC1uTKtiWGDrzUkugPrgAN3k9bVLRi/1l1dfrRAvVCG
jxXAgO8aZnLxMjFxZwftyOE7p7owJks1AkAt1WZahYLATKdPIB5stZ4yCKh1425G
bRFje6Ud5Hc6q37d79AeWWWjzVIAsBXAyUfeJ4uHy+Bby7TytV0uMEdbAkAhntli
O36W1sM6pKhx8wkSrliDbcTP8Px0uQUzfl1YMCk51i3OR3CMsoE9peC7o2IB/CyB
ndmWd5Oa/ciY54A1AkEAolgPBAd559n78Efvt6VUxvPTzyazJeWRZcPDaO9qBlKg
C3ul6Qv8VSE/t1+FrEhsKZv/kK8XIVOCN+drEehu5w==

Random number
generator algorithm

Private
key

Public key
generator algorithm

Public key

Figure 2.7 A private key is generated with a random number generator. It's then fed to an algorithm that generates a public key.

To better visualize it, think of the private key as the physical key of your mailbox (only you have a copy of it) and the public key as your postal address (everyone knows it), as shown in figure 2.8.

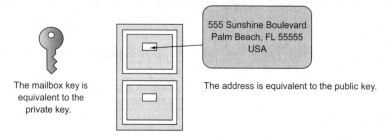

555 Sunshine Boulevard
Palm Beach, FL 55555
USA

The mailbox key is
equivalent to the
private key.

The address is equivalent to the public key.

Figure 2.8 To understand the purpose of private and public keys, you can think of the public key as your postal address, known by everybody, and the private key as the key to your mailbox, only owned by you.

The private key has two main purposes, as illustrated in figure 2.9:

- It allows the decryption of data that has been encrypted using the public key.
- It allows someone to digitally sign a document. They can produce the signature only if they know the private key, but anyone who knows the public key can verify the signature. As you'll see, the authenticity of smart contract transactions relies on digital signatures.

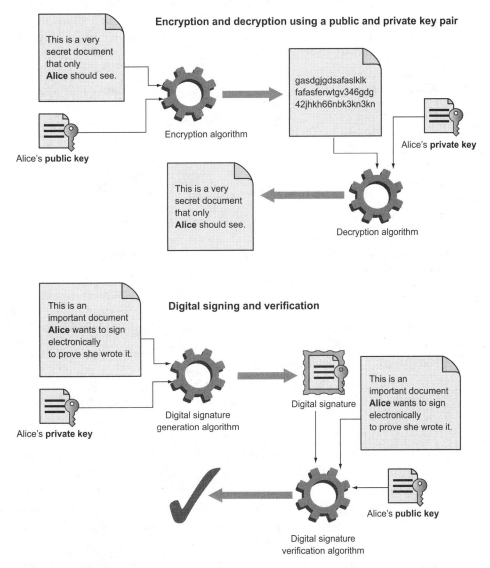

Figure 2.9   You can use a private key to decrypt a document that has been encrypted with the related public key, as you can see in the top diagram. As shown in the bottom diagram, a private key also allows someone to sign a document digitally to prove provenance. The generated digital signature can then be verified against the document and the related public key.

In the context of a blockchain platform, cryptocurrency is generally stored against an account that is identified by a public key but can be operated only if you know the private key. If the private key is forgotten or lost, no one can use the account anymore, and its funds are considered lost.

CRYPTOGRAPHIC HASH FUNCTIONS

A *hash function* is any function that can map data of arbitrary size to data of fixed size. The fixed size data is called hash or digest. To give an example, you can design a hash function so that it always generates a 64-bit hash from a file or string of any size. Whether its size is 10 KB or 10 GB, a 64-bit hash will be generated, as illustrated in figure 2.10.

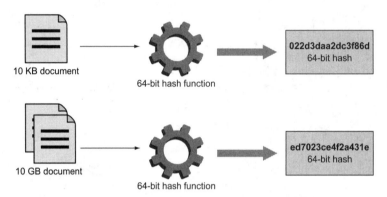

Figure 2.10   A hash function produces a hash of a fixed size (64 bits in this example) given an input of any size.

A *cryptographic hash function* is a hash function that has five additional properties:

- *It's deterministic.* The same input will always generate the same hash.
- *It's quick to compute.*
- *It's a one-way function, unfeasible to invert.* This means that the only way to deduce the original data from its hash would be to try, by brute force, to obtain the same hash by applying the function to an enormous number of input data sets.
- *It should be almost impossible to obtain the same hash from two different sets of input data.* Although a small chance exists that two inputs might produce the same hash, it's impossible to determine them a priori, without applying the function to an enormous number of inputs, as suggested in the previous point.
- *A slight change in the input data should produce substantially different hash values.* Consequently, also because of what I said in the previous point, unless you're applying the cryptographic hash function to the same input, you won't be able to *intentionally* get the same hash or even a close one.

Given these properties, think about the following scenario. Imagine you're writing a check for $30 to pay for the latest blockchain book from your local bookstore. I know, checks are almost no longer used and, if you're a young reader, you might never have seen one! Please bear with me for a moment.

You filled out and signed the check, and you're on your way to the bookstore, when, while on your mobile phone chat app, you trip over a curb. You don't realize the check falls on the road and a gust of wind takes it away. You're so unlucky that it ends up in the hands of Jack Forger, a local petty criminal. He knows how to remove ink, and he quickly replaces the amount and recipient as shown in figure 2.11.

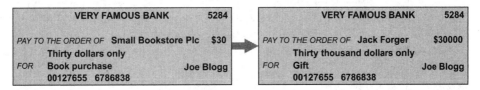

Figure 2.11   A physical check forged by reusing the original signature and altering the recipient and amount

Jack then goes to a bank and successfully cashes the check for $30,000. The criminal had your handwritten signature and was able to replace the name of the recipient and the amount. Let's see how a digital signature on an electronic check would avoid this unpleasant situation.

The digital signature on an electronic check would be a cryptographic hash produced using as the input the details of your check, the amount you're paying, and the recipient, together with a private key associated with your bank account (the equivalent of your handwritten signature), as illustrated in figure 2.12.

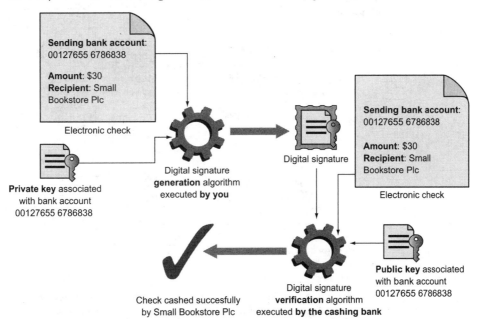

Figure 2.12   An e-check can be secured with a digital signature generated with the private key associated with the sending bank account and the details of the check. It can be verified by checking the digital signature against the public key associated with the sender bank account and the check details.

When someone presents this kind of electronic check to a bank, together with the public key associated with your bank account, the bank can verify that the digital signature matches the details of the check (amount and recipient) and has been produced using your private key. That's how the bookstore owner will be able to cash your check.

Because the digital signature is a cryptographic hash, that exact signature can only be produced from the specific details you used when filing the electronic check. If someone tried to hijack the electronic check—let's say a group of skilled hackers—changing the amount and, most importantly, the recipient would be pointless for two reasons:

1 A new amount or recipient would generate a completely different digital signature, so the bank wouldn't recognize the current one as valid, as shown in figure 2.13.
2 If the hackers attempted to generate a new digital signature with new check details, they couldn't generate one that could be associated with the public key of your bank account because they don't know your private key.

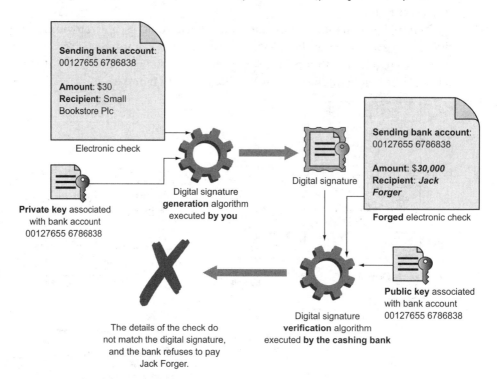

Figure 2.13 An attempt at forging an e-check secured by a digital signature is unsuccessful because the new original digital signature doesn't match the altered check details.

Blockchain transactions are much like the electronic check described here:

- They originate from an account identified by a public key.
- They contain transaction details, such as an amount of cryptocurrency and the recipient, also identified by a public key.
- They carry a digital signature proving the transaction details have been entered by the owner of the sender account through their private key.

Blockchain transactions don't have to carry cryptocurrency; they can carry any data. The crucial point is that by carrying a digital signature, they can prove they've been genuinely sent by the sender.

Cryptographic hash functions aren't only useful for digital signatures. If you're interested in finding out more, read in the sidebar how you can use them to protect a seller from malicious buyers.

Protecting a seller from malicious buyers with a commit-reveal scheme

Cryptographic hash functions can be handy in various situations. Do you remember the decentralized e-commerce application I described at the beginning of chapter 1? If you're reading this book with the mindset of a seller, you might have found the solution not as convincing as when seen through the eyes of a buyer. For example, there seems to be nothing, in the solution presented, preventing the user from accepting the goods and then not authorizing the payment to the seller. That's disappointing! Don't despair: cryptographic hash functions to the rescue!

You could make the application more secure for sellers if you required the buyer to generate a secret code, for instance a secret phrase or a random number, and then supply its cryptographic hash to the seller during the confirmation of the order. You could view this hash as a sort of keylock for the payment. When delivery comes, the courier would hand the goods over only upon receipt of the secret code, which, when supplied to the e-commerce Dapp, would generate the expected initial hash code and, as a physical key into its associated keylock, would unlock the payment.

This way of initially providing a hash of the original information and then revealing the full information in a second stage is called a *commitment scheme* or *commit-reveal scheme*, and it has two phases:

1 The commit phase, during which a cryptographic hash of the original information produced with a disclosed algorithm is committed to the other party

2 The reveal phase, during which the full information is revealed, and it's verified against the committed hash to prove the revealed information is indeed associated with the hash

This powerful idea of proving the knowledge of some information without revealing the information itself had already been used in the 16th century by Galileo, who initially published his discovery of the phases of Venus in an anagram of the original paper, before finalizing his research. Hooke and Newton later used a similar technique to conceal the details of their discoveries, while at the same time being able to claim they were the first to make such discoveries.

In the rest of the book, you'll see how this idea is used to secure decentralized applications.

Congratulations, you've completed the Cryptography 101 course! I hope it wasn't too painful. You now have the necessary tools to understand how a blockchain works. Now we'll enter the blockchain.

BLOCKCHAIN

A blockchain is a distributed database that holds records called blocks. Figure 2.14 illustrates the structure of a typical blockchain.

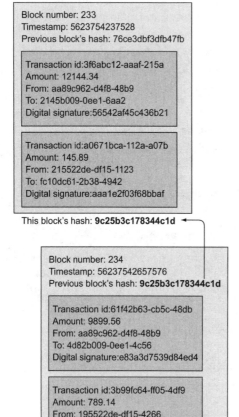

Figure 2.14   **A blockchain is a sequence of blocks, each containing a sequence number, a timestamp, and a list of transactions, each individually digitally signed. Each block also references the cryptographic hash of the previous block.**

A block includes a list of transactions, which are digitally signed to prove their provenance. Most blockchains digitally sign transactions with an *elliptic curve digital signature algorithm* (ECDSA), based on elliptic-curve cryptography, rather than a traditional digital signature algorithm (DSA), because ECDSA is harder to break and uses smaller keys to guarantee the same level of security. Each block contains a timestamp and a link to a previous block based on its cryptographic hash. It also contains a cryptographic hash summarizing the full content of the block, including the hash of the previous block. In this way, the blockchain holds both the current state (the latest block) and the full history of all the transactions that have been stored on it since its inception.

This structure guarantees transactions can't be tampered with or modified. A transaction recorded in a block can't be altered retroactively because to modify it, the hash of the block containing it would have to be regenerated, and this wouldn't match the existing one already referenced by subsequent blocks, as shown in figure 2.15.

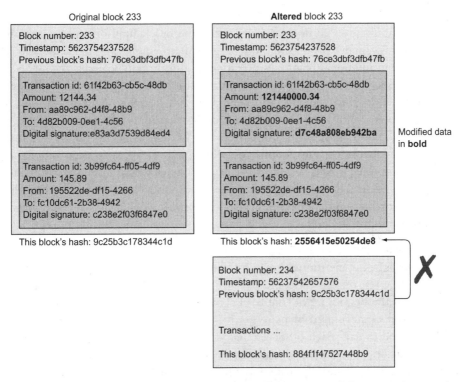

Figure 2.15   An attempt at altering the contents of a block, for example its transactions, won't be successful: the new hash generated from the altered block details won't match the original block's hash already directly referenced in the next block and indirectly referenced in the subsequent blocks.

NOTE   If two transactions contradict each other—for instance, each of them tries to transfer all the funds of the same account to a different destination account (known as a "double-spend attack")—miners will execute only the first one, recognized in the Ethereum network through a globally accessible sequence number. They will reject the second one, and it will never appear on a consolidated block. Satoshi Nakamoto of Bitcoin was the first to solve the double-spend problem. Every blockchain has a solution for it; otherwise, it wouldn't be viable.

The blockchain structure I've described is, in fact, a simplified version of real-world blockchain data structures such as the Merkle tree used by Bitcoin or the Patricia tree used in Ethereum. A blockchain is managed autonomously through a P2P network that facilitates fault tolerance and decentralized consensus by processing all transactions independently on each node. Given these characteristics, blockchains are particularly suitable for recording permanently the history of events. This is useful for identity management, transaction processing, and provenance tracking, to name a few use cases.

MINING

To encourage the P2P network supporting the blockchain to process its transactions continuously, active processing nodes, also called *mining nodes* or *miners*, are rewarded for the computational resources provided, and indirectly to cover the associated electricity costs, through the *consensus* mechanism. Every few seconds, one successful miner is entitled to generate and keep a certain number of tokens of the cryptocurrency supported by the platform. Such cryptocurrency has economic value, as it can be used to purchase services on the network, but it also can be exchanged for conventional currencies, such as dollars, yen, euros, and so forth. In the case of the Bitcoin blockchain, they'll be given several Bitcoin tokens, worth around $2,000 each at the time of writing. The tokens given by the Ethereum blockchain are called Ether, and they're worth around $200 each at the time of writing. Let's now look at how the consensus mechanism works.

CONSENSUS

Consensus is, as I mentioned earlier, the mechanism by which participant nodes of the network agree on the outcome of a transaction. In the consensus definition I presented at the beginning of chapter 1, I also emphasized that consensus is distributed, because it's determined by many participants, and trustless, because the participants don't need to trust each other. In fact, consensus isn't reached on individual transactions but on new blockchain blocks. Each participant verifies independently that a new block is valid and, if satisfied, propagates it further to the rest of the network.

What happens in practice is that if most participants have accepted the block as valid and it has propagated successfully throughout the network, miners will use such a block as the latest valid block, and the rest of the blockchain will be built on it. If a malicious miner appended an incorrect block to the blockchain and it propagated to its peer nodes, these nodes would reject the new block, and the malicious chain would die out immediately. The same would happen if a full node tried to modify a block before propagating it to its peers.

As you can see, the key step of the consensus mechanism is the verification of the latest block by a participant node. After verifying the digital signature of the individual transactions present on a block, a participant node verifies that the hash of the block is valid. Such hash is produced by miners according to an agreed protocol. The earlier versions of Ethereum used an algorithm called *Ethash*, based on a Proof of Work protocol. Future versions will be based on a Full of Stake protocol called *Casper*. I'll explain both protocols.

PROOF OF WORK

As you saw earlier, a block contains a cryptographic hash summarizing the full content of the block, including its metadata and transactions data, and an additional piece of data of a fixed length, such as 32 bits, called *nonce*. The objective of the Proof of Work (PoW) protocol is that miners must find a nonce such that the hash generated fits a certain constraint, for instance, having many leading zeros. Constraining a 64-bit unsigned integer hash to have 13 leading zeros when represented in hexadecimal format, as in the example of figure 2.16, reduces the number of valid hashes from the theoretical maximum number of 18,446,744,073,709,551,615 to 4,095.

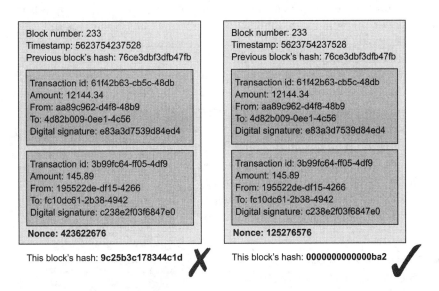

Figure 2.16 Proof of Work: generation of an unsuccessful and a successful block hash

Because of the properties of hash functions you saw earlier, the only way a miner can find such a nonce is by trying many possible values until the constraint on the hash has been met. In the example I just gave, every such attempt will only have a roughly 0.00000000000002% chance of being successful. When a satisfactory hash has been found, the miner is entitled to append the new block being processed to the blockchain and claim the token reward. As you can understand, this way of producing a valid hash is CPU-intensive, energy-consuming, and, consequently, economically expensive. The main reason for such an expensive algorithm is to dissuade malicious participants from appending new incorrect blocks or modifying preexisting blocks and making them look like genuine blocks. The amount of energy (and money) necessary to perform such actions would make them unviable. In the sidebar in section 3.3.4, I'll give you an idea of the hardware most miners use.

PROOF OF STAKE

Proof of Work, which the Bitcoin network also uses, has been widely criticized for the immense amount of energy consumed (or rather, wasted?) by the competing miners. It has been estimated that the Bitcoin network alone will consume as much electricity as Bulgaria by 2020.

To tackle this problem, Vitalik Buterin, one of the Ethereum founders, has proposed an alternative approach based on a Proof of Stake. This is based on a pool of *validators* that vote on the validity of new blockchain blocks. To join the validator pool, which is open to anyone, a node must commit an Ether deposit that will be held until the node leaves the pool. Votes expressed by each node are weighted on the amount of the deposit committed (which equates to the stake of a node in the pool). Under this scheme, a validator profits from transaction fees that the transaction senders pay. If a validator cheats, the associated Ether deposit is deleted from the network and the owner is banned from rejoining, which acts as a deterrent against manipulation.

You've now covered all the general cryptographic techniques underlying blockchain databases. If you'd like to learn more about the subject, I encourage you to read *Grokking Bitcoin* by Kalle Rosenbaum) (Manning, 2019). Let's now examine more recent technologies that have simplified Dapp development.

THE MERKLE TREE AND MERKLE ROOT

The blockchain structure I've shown in the previous diagrams is a simplified representation of a real one. Generally, a miner places in the block two parts: a *header* and a *body*, as shown in figure 2.17. The body contains all the transactions included in the block. The header contains the block metadata you saw earlier, such as the block number, timestamp, previous block hash, and PoW nonce. It also contains the *Merkle root* of the *transactions Merkle tree* that the miner calculates.

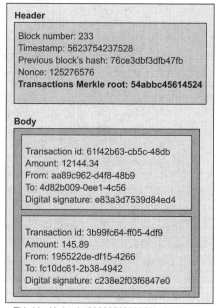

Figure 2.17   The structure of a block, including a header containing metadata, such as the block number, timestamp, previous block hash, and Merkle root of the transactions Merkle tree, and a body containing the transactions collection

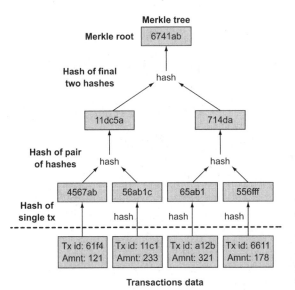

Figure 2.18   A Merkle tree. Individual transactions are located at the bottom; the tree's leaves are the hashes of the individual transactions; and the next row up is made of the hashes of the tree's leaves. The top row, which is the hash of the hashes below, ends the tree: this is the Merkle root.

The transactions Merkle tree, as shown in figure 2.18, is a tree structure built as follows:

- The block's transactions are placed at the bottom of the tree, arranged in pairs.
- Each transaction is hashed, and each of these hashes becomes a leaf of the Merkle tree.
- A hash is calculated for each pair of contiguous hashes.
- The hashing of contiguous hashes is repeated until only two hashes remain. The hash of these two final hashes is the *Merkle root*.

The Merkle root is therefore a single hash summarizing all of the transactions contained in the block in a way that guarantees their integrity. The advantage of having the Merkle root on the block header is that a client can synchronize the blockchain in a faster way by retrieving the block headers, rather than the entire transaction history, from the network peers. This is generally called *light synchronization*.

2.2.2   Ethereum technologies

Although smart contracts can be implemented, with some difficulty, on early blockchain systems such as Bitcoin, they can be more easily written and executed on later blockchain platforms, such as Hyperledger, Nxt, and Ethereum, that have been designed with the main purpose of simplifying their development. For this reason, later blockchain platforms are considered part of the so-called *smart blockchain* or *blockchain 2.0* wave. Let's now examine briefly the main innovations that Ethereum has introduced: an improved blockchain design, the EVM, and smart contracts.

THE ETHEREUM BLOCKCHAIN

In the previous section, you learned about the blockchain and a more efficient structure that allows quicker client synchronization based on a block header containing a block's metadata and a body containing the transactions. The Ethereum blockchain improves the design further. First of all, transactions are hashed in a more compact and efficient (yet still cryptographically authenticated) structure called a *Merkle-Patricia trie* (see sidebar for more details). Secondly, the block header (generated as usual by the miner) also contains, in addition to the Merkle-Patricia root of the transactions, the Merkle-Patricia root of the receipts, which are the transaction outputs, and the Merkle-Patricia root of the current blockchain state, as shown in figure 2.19.

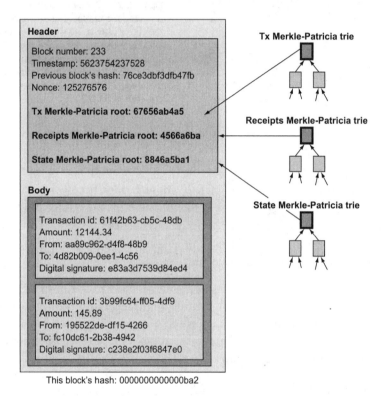

This block's hash: 0000000000000ba2

Figure 2.19   An Ethereum improved block header. The header of a block of the Ethereum blockchain contains the root of the transactions Merkle-Patricia trie, which is a more compact and efficient structure than a Merkle tree. In addition, it contains the Merkle-Patricia root of receipts (which are the transactions effects) and the blockchain state.

As Vitalik Buterin explained in his blog post "Merkling in Ethereum,"[1] with these three Merkle-Patricia tries, a client can efficiently check, in a verifiable way, the following:

---

[1]   See Vitalik Buterin, "Merkling in Ethereum," Ethereum Blog, November 15, 2015, http://mng.bz/QQYe.

- Whether a certain transaction is included in a certain block
- What the output of a transaction would be
- Whether an account exists
- What the balance of an account is

The Merkle-Patricia trie

A *trie*[2] (or *prefix tree*) is an ordered data structure you use to store a dynamic set, where the keys are usually strings. The root of a trie is an empty string, and then all the descendants of a node have the common prefix of the string associated with that node, as you can see in the figure.

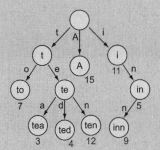

Trie structure (Credit: Booyabazooka (based on a PNG image by Deco). Modifications by Superm401. - own work (based on PNG image by Deco))

The Merkle-Patricia trie is a data structure that combines a trie and Merkle tree. It improves the efficiency of a Merkle tree (named after Ralph Merkle) by storing the node keys using the *PATRICIA* algorithm (*practical algorithm to retrieve information coded in alphanumeric*), designed by D. R. Morrison in 1968. You can read about the Patricia algorithm on the Lloyd Allison Algorithm Repository.[3] The Ethereum Merkle-Patricia trie is described in detail, with code examples, in the Ethereum wiki.[4]

When a full node receives a new block, the transactions contained in the body are processed as follows:

- The transactions are arranged in a transaction Merkle-Patricia trie specific to the new block.
- Transactions are executed on the EVM. This action generates transaction receipts, which are arranged in a receipts Merkle-Patricia trie specific to the new block. It also alters the global state trie, of which only one instance exists on each node.

If the roots of the new transaction trie, receipt trie, and modified state trie match those in the header, the block is considered validated. Then the new and altered tries

---

[2] See the "Trie" Wikipedia page at https://en.wikipedia.org/wiki/Trie for more information on this data structure.

[3] http://www.allisons.org/ll/AlgDS/Tree/PATRICIA/.

[4] https://github.com/ethereum/wiki/wiki/Patricia-Tree.

are stored on the full node in a respective key-value store based on LevelDB, an open source NoSQL database developed by Google. Note the following in figure 2.20:

- The *transaction store* contains a transaction trie per block, and each trie is immutable. The key of this store is the transaction hash (keccak 256-bit hash).
- The *receipts store* contains a transaction trie per block, and each trie is immutable. The key of this store is the hash of the receipts of a transaction (keccak 256-bit hash).
- The *state store* contains a single *state trie* that represents the latest global state and is updated each time a new block is appended to the blockchain. The state trie is account-centric, so the key of this store is the account address (160 bytes).

A major benefit of the Ethereum blockchain design is that it allows three types of synchronization:

- *Full*—Your client downloads the entire blockchain and validates all blocks locally. This is the slowest option, but you'd be confident of the integrity of the local blockchain copy.
- *Fast*—Your client downloads the entire blockchain, but validates only the 64 blocks prior to the start of the synchronization and the new ones.
- *Light*—Your client retrieves the current state trie of the blockchain from a peer full node and stores it locally. It doesn't retrieve any historic blocks from peers, and it receives only the new ones, so you don't have to wait long. This will allow you to get up and running quickly.

NOTE   Although in this section I've covered the physical design of the Ethereum blockchain in some detail because it's important you understand how transactions and state are maintained, in the rest of the book I'll use simplified logical diagrams in which I'll represent a block as a collection of transactions.

ETHEREUM VIRTUAL MACHINE

The *Ethereum Virtual Machine (EVM)* is similar in purpose to the Java Virtual Machine (JVM) or the .NET Common Language Runtime (CLR). It runs on each node of the Ethereum P2P network. It's Turing complete, which means it can run code of any complexity. It can access blockchain data, both in read and write mode. The EVM executes code only after its digital signature has been verified and constraints based on the current state of the blockchain are satisfied.

SMART CONTRACT

A *smart contract,* or simply *contract,* encapsulates the logic of a decentralized application. As I mentioned earlier, an Ethereum smart contract is written in a high-level language, such as Solidity or Serpent, and is compiled into EVM bytecode. It gets deployed on each node of the P2P network and is executed on the EVM.

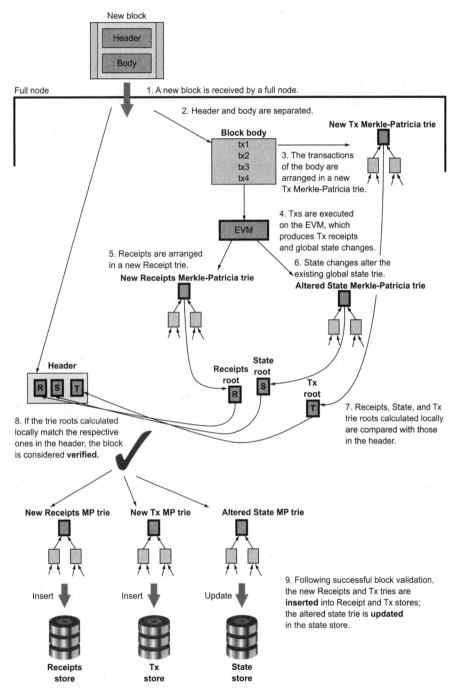

Figure 2.20 Detailed block processing in an Ethereum node. When a full node receives a new block, it separates the header and the body. It then creates a local transactions trie and a local receipts trie and updates the existing state trie. The new and updated tries are then committed in the respective stores.

NEXT GENERATION BLOCKCHAIN

Thanks to the EVM, Ethereum is a *programmable blockchain*. Therefore, you can develop any type of decentralized application on it, not only cryptocurrencies, as was the case for earlier blockchains. Because of this programmability, Ethereum is considered a generalized or next generation blockchain. Some go as far as thinking smart blockchain platforms will be the foundation of a new generation of the internet, a Web 3.0 (although this exact version of the web is also used by the "semantic web" community), which will be characterized by more empowered users.

2.3   *Ethereum's history and governance*

Before closing the chapter, I'd like to share how Ethereum was created and how it evolved after the initial release. In the next few chapters, you'll start using several components of the Ethereum platform. Before you do so, it's important you understand how these components came about and what the process is for proposing and agreeing on changes. You'll realize decentralization isn't only a technical aspect of Ethereum; it's almost a philosophy that also permeates its governance.

2.3.1   *Who created Ethereum?*

Ethereum is the brainchild of Vitalik Buterin, an early follower of bitcoin and cryptocurrency technology since 2011, when he also cofounded Bitcoin magazine. After researching the possibility of generalizing blockchain technology for building any application, in November 2013 he wrote the *Ethereum White Paper* (https://github.com/ethereum/wiki/wiki/White-Paper), in which he laid out the design of the Ethereum protocol, together with the first details of the smart contract infrastructure. Among the first people who engaged with Vitalik's vision were Gavin Wood, who contributed to the shaping of the protocol and became the lead developer of the C++ client, and Jeffrey Wilcke, who became the lead developer of the Go client. After only a few months of work, in January 2014, Vitalik announced the Ethereum initiative on bitcointalk[5] and received considerable response. Soon afterwards, in April 2014, Gavin wrote the *Ethereum Yellow Paper*,[6] which specifies the design of the Ethereum virtual machine. To accelerate the development of the platform, in July 2014 Ethereum raised around $18.4M through an Ether crowdsale, which was legally backed by the Ethereum Foundation, set up in Switzerland only one month earlier with the mission to do the following (quoting the official website at https://www.ethereum.org/foundation):

> *...promote and support Ethereum platform and base layer research, development and education to bring decentralized protocols and tools to the world that empower developers to produce next generation decentralized applications (Dapps), and together build a more globally accessible, more free and more trustworthy Internet.*

---

[5] See Vitalik Buterin, "Welcome to the Beginning," https://bitcointalk.org/index.php?topic=428589.0.
[6] See "About the Ethereum Foundation," https://github.com/ethereum/yellowpaper.

Table 2.1 summarizes Ethereum's timeline since its inception to the time of writing of this book.

Table 2.1 Ethereum timeline from inception to summer 2018

Sep 2011	Vitalik Buterin cofounds Bitcoin magazine with Mihai Alisie.
Nov 2013	Vitalik publishes the Ethereum White Paper, presenting the design of the Ethereum protocol and the smart contract infrastructure.
Dec 2013	Gavin Wood contacts Vitalik, and they start detailed design discussions.
Jan 2014	Vitalik makes the official Ethereum announcement on bitcointalk.
Apr 2014	Gavin wood publishes the Ethereum Yellow Paper, which specifies the Ethereum virtual machine (EVM).
Jun 2014	The Ethereum Foundation is set up in Switzerland.
Jul 2014	Ethereum raises $18.4M through an Ether crowdsale.
Aug 2014	Vitalik Buterin, Gavin Wood, and Jeffrey Wilcke set up ETH DEV, a nonprofit organization focused on the development of the core Ethereum protocol and infrastructure, which managed the development of various proofs of concept throughout 2014.
Nov 2014	ETH DEV organizes DEVCON-0, the first Ethereum developer conference, in Berlin, where the entire Ethereum project team meets for the first time.
Jan 2015	The Go Ethereum team meets in Amsterdam, where Whisper Dapp and Mist prototypes are presented.
Jul 2015	Mainnet release 1.0, codenamed Frontier, and the stable beta of Ethereum Wallet are released.
Nov 2015	In London, 400 people attend DEVCON-1, where more than 80 talks on each part of the Ethereum ecosystem are given.
Mar 2016	The project releases Mainnet release 2.0, codenamed Homestead.
Jul 2016	An unplanned Ethereum fork occurs following a DAO attack, and a split takes place between Ethereum and Ethereum Classic. (See the sidebar.)
Oct 2017	The project releases Mainnet release 3.0, codenamed Byzantium.
Jun 2018	The project releases the Proof of Stake (PoS) Testnet release, codenamed Casper.

If you're interested in knowing more about the history of Ethereum, the official documentation has a page[7] dedicated to it. But you can get a firsthand and more engaging account of the main events that took place around Ethereum's creation in the blog posts "Cut and Try: Building a Dream,"[8] by Taylor Gerring (a core Ethereum developer), and "A Prehistory of the Ethereum Protocol,"[9] by Vitalik Buterin himself.

---

[7] See "History of Etherum," Ethereum Homestead, http://mng.bz/XgwM.
[8] See Taylor Gerring, "Cut and Try: Building a Dream," February 9, 2016, http://mng.bz/y1BE.
[9] See Vitalik Buterin, "A Prehistory of the Ethereum Protocol," http://mng.bz/MxRm.

The DAO attack and the split between Ethereum and Ethereum Classic

The DAO (which stands for decentralized autonomous organization) was one of the first mainstream Dapps in the Ethereum space. It was a decentralized venture capital fund. The DAO token holders were meant to vote on all investment decisions. While the DAO smart contract was still being developed, tokens were sold to investors through a crowdsale, a sort of decentralized crowdfunding application. (You'll read more about crowdsales in chapters 6 and 7.) This funding campaign, which took place in May 2016, managed to collect over 12M Ether, which at the time was worth around $150M (with Ether trading at $11).

One of the features of the DAO contract was that groups of DAO token holders unhappy with decisions that the qualified majority made (investment decisions were approved with 20% of the votes) could split from the main DAO and create their own Child DAO, where they'd start to vote on different investment proposals. In June 2016, this feature, which had been identified by some community members as potentially weak from a security point of view, was exploited by a hacker, who managed to gain control of 3.5M Ether (worth around $50M at that time) through a recursive call that kept withdrawing funds.

Luckily, the Child DAO creation feature required funds to be withheld for 28 days before they could be transferred out to another account, so the hacker couldn't steal them immediately. This gave the DAO developers and the Ethereum community some time to propose solutions to prevent the theft. Finally, after a failed soft fork of the blockchain that would have blacklisted any transaction coming out of the DAO, the community voted for a hard fork, including a smart contract designed to return the stolen funds to the original owners. Although the majority had voted for the hard fork, some members of the community argued that the hard fork had broken various principles of the Ethereum white paper, mainly the promise that smart contract code is implicitly law and the guarantee that the blockchain is immutable. They consequently decided to keep the original blockchain running, and this was renamed Ethereum Classic.

You can find many articles and blog posts on the DAO attack, ranging in complexity from the technical to the high-level. Given that you don't yet have a strong technical foundation in this area, if you want to learn more about this, I recommend you have a look at "The DAO, The Hack, The Soft Fork and The Hard Fork,"[10] which describes in detail what happened without getting too much into the technical side. You'll be able to understand the DAO attack better after having read chapter 15 on security, but I cover it specifically because most of the techniques used are beyond the scope of this book. Nevertheless, if at that point you're eager to jump to the technical details of the hack, I recommend the brilliant "Analysis of the DAO Exploit."[11]

---

[10] See Antonio Madeira, "The DAO, The Hack, The Soft Fork and The Hard Fork," July 26, 2016, http://mng.bz/a7NY.

[11] See Phil Daian, "Analysis of the DAO exploit," Hacking, Distributed, June 18, 2016, http://mng.bz/gNrn.

2.3.2 *Who controls Ethereum's development?*

After the Frontier release back in July 2015, the hot topic of Ethereum governance started to gather momentum within the Ethereum Foundation, as well as across the wider Ethereum community. Key questions, such as "Who controls Ethereum's development," "How do changes get proposed," and "Who approves them and how" got debated openly so that early adopters could be encouraged to use and trust the platform.

Blockchain governance is about the rules and processes that participants must follow for making changes to the platform, and about how the rules and processes themselves should get defined. In short, it's about who decides on changes and how the decisions get approved and followed.

ETH DEV, the nonprofit organization leading Ethereum development, gathers proposals in the Ethereum Improvement Proposals (EIPs, https://eips.ethereum.org/) repository.[12] This is based on established processes also followed by other open source projects—Python Improvement Proposals (PIPs) and Bitcoin Improvement Proposals (BIPs) are classic examples. Proposals are initially studied and Proofs of Concept (PoCs) often follow.

If a proposal gathers enough momentum (it's considered interesting by the core Ethereum developers), it progresses to *Draft* status and might be debated further among the wider community at developer conferences or official online forums. If an informal consensus is reached, the proposal can progress immediately to *Accepted* or *Rejected* status. Accepted proposals get scheduled for future platform releases, and more effort is consequently put into them. Obviously, there's always the risk that the participants won't all agree with the proposal or its implementation, so the proposal is considered implicitly accepted only after most participants have adopted it.

Occasionally, some proposals cause heated debate in the wider community. In those cases, the decision isn't clear-cut, and they go through formal on-chain voting. When it comes to on-chain voting, one of the following two competing models is generally followed:

- *Loosely coupled on-chain voting (aka informal governance)*—The community leaders (for example the Ethereum Foundation and ETH DEV) signal how to vote. Participants vote on-chain through a dedicated smart contract that weights their preference based on how much Ether they own. (This voting is often referred to as *coinvoting*.) The proposal is then implemented if the outcome of the voting is favorable. Although the vote is ethically binding, developers or other key participants, such as miners, might always decide not to implement or adopt the winning proposal, at risk of being stigmatized by the community.
- *Tightly coupled on-chain voting (a.k.a on-chain governance)*—The proposal gets fully implemented before the vote takes place, generally by a group of developers

---

[12] See the EIPs page on GitHub at https://github.com/ethereum/EIPs.

backing it, and then a smart contract switches on the functionality in the production network only following successful on-chain voting. This model is often favored by purists, who argue the technical analysis shouldn't be influenced by politics until the last stage.

Tightly coupled on-chain voting has been introduced in various blockchain platforms and has become somewhat fashionable. But like other established blockchain platforms, such as Bitcoin and Zcash, Ethereum tends to follow the principle of loosely coupled voting, openly supported by Vitalik Buterin in his blog post "Notes on Blockchain Governance."[13]

As you can see, Ethereum governance is relatively informal and centralized, as core developers seem to have more decision-making weight than the wider community. The argument is that if everything went through formal voting, the platform would evolve too slowly. If you're interested in reading more on Ethereum governance, I recommend the following articles:

- "Ethereum Is Throwing Out the Crypto Governance Playbook"[14]
- "Experimental Voting Effort Aims to Break Ethereum Governance Gridlock"[15]
- "A user's perspective and introduction to blockchain governance"[16]

Summary

- An Ethereum node hosts an Ethereum client and a copy of the blockchain.
- An Ethereum client contains
  - a virtual machine called Ethereum Virtual Machine (EVM), capable of executing smart contract bytecode
  - a memory pool, where transactions received by the node get stored before being propagated further into the network
  - a JSON-RPC API, which exposes the functionality of the client to other nodes and external users
  - a client process, which coordinates the processing
- An Ethereum smart contract is code written in the Solidity language and compiled into EVM bytecode.
- An Ethereum smart contract is deployed across the P2P network through a contract deployment transaction, pushed to a local Ethereum node, and then propagated throughout the network.

---

[13] See Vitalik Buterin, "Notes on Blockchain Governance," December 17, 2017, https://vitalik.ca/general/2017/12/17/voting.html.

[14] See Rachel Rose O'Leary, "Ethereum Is Throwing Out the Crypto Governance Playbook," Coindesk, March 14, 2018, http://mng.bz/edwZ.

[15] See Rachel Rose O'Leary, "Experimental Voting Effort Aims to Break Ethereum Governance Gridlock," Coindesk, May 23, 2018, http://mng.bz/pgQ0.

[16] See Richard Red, "A user's perspective and introduction to blockchain governance," Medium, http://mng.bz/O2VO.

- A blockchain is a sequence of blocks, each containing a sequence number, a timestamp, and a list of transactions, each individually digitally signed. Each block includes a copy of the cryptographic hash of the previous block and the nonce, which generates the hash of the current block.
- The main innovation introduced by Ethereum with respect to previous blockchain implementations is the EVM and the concept of the smart contract.
- Ethereum follows an informal governance model, where proposals go through the Ethereum Improvement Proposals (EIPs) process: they get analyzed by the core Ethereum developers, are often tried through Proofs of Concept (PoCs), and ultimately get accepted or rejected.
- Occasionally, when an EIP causes heated debate, it gets formally voted on-chain by the participants, but, even if the vote is favorable, a proposal is considered practically accepted only when the majority of the participants have adopted it.

The Ethereum platform

This chapter covers

- Interacting with Ethereum through the Ethereum wallet
- Understanding the characteristics of Ethereum smart contracts
- Interacting with Ethereum through the Go Ethereum (geth) client
- Understanding and managing accounts

The previous chapter introduced Dapps and the underlying concepts and technologies, among which is Ethereum. In this chapter, I'll cover Ethereum in much greater depth, so you'll get the foundation you need to develop Dapps on this platform effectively. I'll begin by presenting the Ethereum wallet, a UI tool you'll use to start interacting with the Ethereum P2P network by transferring some Ether, the Ethereum cryptocurrency. Then you'll get a wide overview of smart contracts, the key technology that Ethereum introduced.

After learning about Go Ethereum, one of the many clients available on the platform, and once you understand the purpose of accounts, you'll move to the next level and start interacting with the Ethereum network through Go Ethereum in several ways: with commands entered into the operating system shell, with instructions entered into the Go Ethereum console, and with HTTP requests. At that point, you should have acquired enough familiarity with the platform to progress with confidence through the rest of the book. It'll be a dense but rewarding chapter. Let's get started.

3.1 Connecting to Ethereum through the wallet

The Ethereum network offers two main graphical user interfaces:

- *Mist*—A browser for Ethereum Dapps
- *Ethereum wallet*—A specific version of Mist with a single Dapp bundled in it

You'll learn about Mist in a later chapter. For the moment, we'll focus on the Ethereum wallet. The main purpose of the wallet is to store, receive, and transfer Ether, the Ethereum cryptocurrency. It's similar to a Bitcoin wallet, if you've ever handled bitcoins, and you'll initially use it to transfer Ether so that you can start to interact with the platform in the simplest way. It's also a useful tool to learn how to deploy smart contracts and interact with them on one of the public Ethereum networks.

3.1.1 Getting started with the Ethereum wallet

When you open the download page (https://github.com/ethereum/mist/releases), you'll find various versions of Mist and the Ethereum wallet. Pick the version of the Ethereum wallet corresponding to your operating system and download the related zip file. (I've picked Ethereum-Wallet-win64-0-11-1.zip.) After unzipping it, you can run the executable Ethereum Wallet.exe directly. The first time you launch it, it'll default to the main network. In this chapter, you'll work against the public test Ropsten network instead. To select it, you must pick it from the top menu, as shown in figure 3.1: Develop > Network > Ropsten. You also can select the Ropsten network through the Alt+Ctrl+2 shortcut.

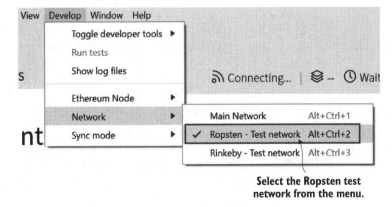

Select the Ropsten test
network from the menu.

Figure 3.1 Choosing the test Ropsten network from the Develop > Network > Ropsten menu option or through the Alt+Ctrl+2 shortcut

After you select the Ropsten network, the wallet will start to synchronize with the related blockchain. By default, the synchronization mode is Light, which, as you saw in the previous chapter, downloads the current state trie from a peer full node, so you don't have to wait long (minutes). This will allow you to get up and running quickly. But if you want to perform write operations, such as transferring Ether or deploying smart contracts, which is what you'll be doing, you must get a full copy of the block-chain—you can choose between Fast and Full. (Go back to the previous chapter if you don't remember how these sync modes work.) Here's a rough estimate of what to expect when you're synchronizing the Ropsten blockchain locally:

- *Fast*—Uses roughly 1 GB of disk space and takes two to four hours
- *Full*—Uses roughly 100 GB of disk space and can take up to a day or two

Once you're synchronized, you'll be able to see synchronization details at the top of the screen, including the name of the network you're connected to, the latest block number, and the number of seconds passed since receiving the last block, as shown in figure 3.2.

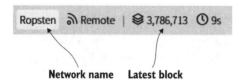

Figure 3.2   You can see synchronization details, including the name of the network and the latest block number, at the top of the screen.

WARNING   To perform the operations I'll cover in this chapter and the next, you *must choose Fast or Full* synchronization; otherwise, you won't be able to transfer Ether or deploy a contract through the wallet. To be able to execute a transaction, you must have a full local copy of the blockchain. If the wallet appears unresponsive after a while and you don't notice any progress in the synchronization, it might be because the wallet hasn't managed to connect to any peer nodes. In that case, close it down and try to synchronize the Ropsten blockchain through the geth client. If you need to do this, read about geth in section 3.3, and then synchronize it to Ropsten as explained in chapter 8, section 8.1.

At this point, you're ready to create accounts. Click the Wallets tab, which will bring you to the Accounts Overview screen, and then click the Add Account button, which has a plus symbol next to it, as you can see in figure 3.3.

You'll see a small dialog box asking for a strong password. (Make sure you stretch the dialog from the bottom-right corner until you see the OK button.) After entering a password (twice), you'll be reminded to back up your keyfiles (more on this later) and password.

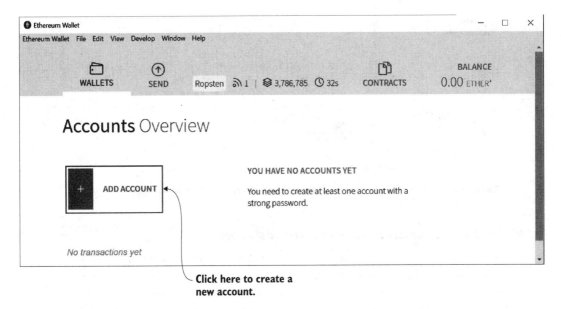

Figure 3.3 Accounts overview screen. You can create an account by clicking Add Account.

WARNING Manage your passwords carefully. If you forget your password, you won't be able to click any "I Forgot My Password" button. Losing your password means losing the Ether stored in the account. This isn't a major problem when pointing to a test network, because Ether has no value there. But, especially when moving to the production network, you should get into the habit of choosing a strong password and keeping a copy of it somewhere secure. Better safe than sorry!

NOTE If you're using the Ethereum wallet for Mac OS or LINUX, the interface is slightly different, screenshots won't match what you see, and my descriptions might not work to the letter. Also, the default network shown might be different. But you should be able to find alternative ways to perform the operations I describe.

After the wallet has generated the account, on the Accounts Overview screen you'll see *Account 1* with the related hexadecimal address and a balance of zero Ether. I'll cover accounts in more detail later; for now, create one more account in the same way, and you now should see two accounts on the screen, as shown in figure 3.4. Now that you have a couple of accounts (feel free to create more), you can try out some common operations with the wallet.

Figure 3.4   Account details shown on the Accounts Overview screen after their creation

3.1.2 *Performing common operations with the wallet*

With a balance of zero Ether (the Ethereum cryptocurrency) on all your accounts, you won't be able to go too far, because as you'll learn, to execute transactions on the network, you must pay transaction costs in Ether. Because it isn't possible to buy Ether in the test network, you'll have to generate it somehow. One way is through mining.

MINING

Mining is the process through which new transactions get consolidated into blocks of the blockchain. Many participants in the Ethereum network run special mining nodes through which they hope to be rewarded in Ether tokens and be compensated for the computational power they provide to the network. Although mining Ether in the real public network is challenging and requires specialized hardware based on advanced GPU chipsets, it's easy to generate Ether in the test network with "plain CPU" mining through the wallet menu:

Develop > Start Mining (Testnet only)

> **NOTE**   The menu option Develop > Start Mining will appear only after the blockchain has been entirely synchronized in Fast or Full mode.

The CPU of your machine will get busy, and after a few minutes you should have accumulated enough Ether to get going.

If for any reason mining is taking too long, an alternative way to fund your Ropsten accounts is through the so-called *faucet*. The following URL can send your addresses free test Ether: http://faucet.ropsten.be:3001/donate/<destination address>, for example, http://faucet.ropsten.be:3001/donate/0x8713Cb74c7DB911f2056C8DD2bA5036-7eeEa11D0. After a few seconds, your destination address should receive 1 Ether, as you can see in figure 3.5. You can check the status of the Ether transfer from the faucet by entering your address in the text box at the top of the Ropsten Etherscan webpage: https://ropsten.etherscan.io/. If faucet.ropsten.be isn't working as expected or you keep getting gray-listed, try https://faucet.kyber.network/. Alternatively, try Google ropsten faucet.

Figure 3.5   Account balances after using the faucet facility

TRANSFERRING ETHER

Now you can try to move some Ether between accounts. It's easy. First, go to the Send screen. Select the source (Account 1) and target account addresses (copy the address of Account 2 from the Accounts Overview screen), then select the amount of Ether you want to transfer—for example, 0.5 Ether. Finally, after deciding on a transaction fee, click Send Transaction. Don't worry too much about this for now; we'll examine transaction fees later.

You'll be prompted to enter a password, as shown in figure 3.6. Enter the password of the source account (Account 1) to digitally sign the transaction and subsequently prove that the account owner is sending it, and then click Send Transaction. You've now completed your first Ether transaction!

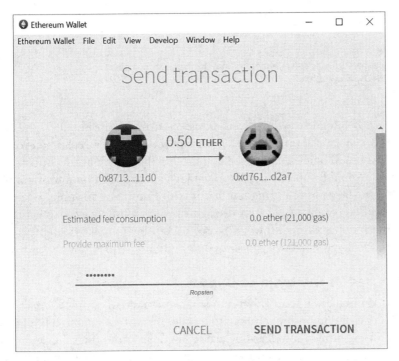

Figure 3.6   Password entry screen for moving Ether between accounts. You're required to enter the password of the sending account when transferring Ether with the Ethereum wallet, to digitally sign the transaction and consequently prove it's genuinely the account owner who's sending the Ether.

To check the status of the transaction, go back to the Accounts Overview screen and click Latest Transactions at the bottom of the screen. Clicking on the related link will allow you to drill down into further details, such as those shown in the screenshot in figure 3.7.

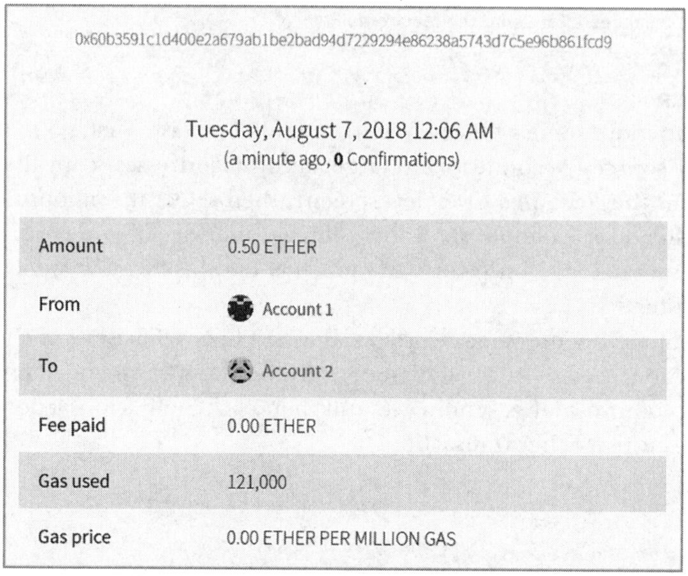

0x60b3591c1d400e2a679ab1be2bad94d7229294e86238a5743d7c5e96b861fcd9

Tuesday, August 7, 2018 12:06 AM
(a minute ago, **0** Confirmations)

Amount	0.50 ETHER
From	Account 1
To	Account 2
Fee paid	0.00 ETHER
Gas used	121,000
Gas price	0.00 ETHER PER MILLION GAS

Figure 3.7   Summary transaction information from the Transactions panel of the Accounts Overview screen

You can get a better idea of how your transaction has contributed to the Ropsten blockchain by checking it on *Etherscan*, a website reporting the real-time evolution of the Ethereum blockchain. Use this URL to access the test network: https://ropsten .etherscan.io/. You'll be able to get detailed block and transaction information.

Now that you've acquired some familiarity with Ethereum, it's time to learn more about one of the greatest innovations that this platform introduced: smart contracts. Once you grasp how smart contracts work, you'll be able to make further progress on SimpleCoin, the cryptocurrency you started to build in the previous chapter.

3.2   *Smart contracts: The brain of Dapps*

As I described in chapter 1, an Ethereum smart contract, or simply *contract*, is a software artifact containing business rules and a state. It's written in a high-level language such as Solidity, compiled into EVM bytecode, deployed onto the Ethereum network, and stored on its blockchain against a specific account generated at deployment.

As shown in figure 3.8, a contract receives transaction messages from a user account (or from other contracts) and executes its logic on the Ethereum Virtual Machine (EVM). This might optionally involve sending messages to other contracts,

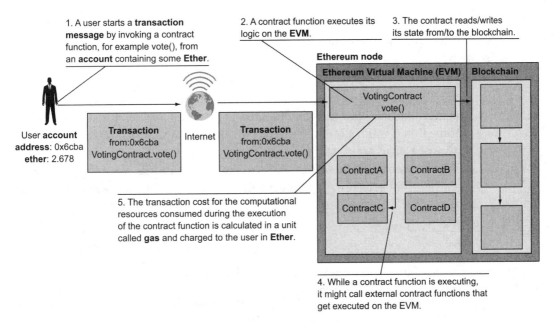

Figure 3.8 An Ethereum contract receives a transaction message from a user account. Its logic is executed on the Ethereum Virtual Machine (EVM); then the successful miner calculates the cost for the computational and network resources used, in a unit called *gas*, and charges the user account in Ether.

reading state from the blockchain, or writing state to the blockchain (specifically from/to the State Merkle-Patricia trie). The account sending the message to the contract gets charged (in Ether) by the successful mining node for computation and network resources consumed during the processing of the requested operation. The amount of such computation and resources is calculated in a unit called *gas*, as you'll see in section 3.2.3, so it's common to say that a transaction consumes a certain amount of gas (rather than resources).

If you want to understand smart contracts, how they get instantiated by users and by other contracts, and especially how they get executed, you need to go in greater detail through various concepts I've only touched on so far:

- Accounts
- Ether and gas
- Transaction messages
- The Ethereum Virtual Machine

I'll start by telling you more about the various types of accounts.

3.2.1   Accounts

You've already come across the concept of *accounts* a few times. Accounts are available in two types:

- *Externally owned accounts (EOA)* (or simply *External Accounts*)—These are also known informally as *user accounts*. They're publicly identifiable from their public key, but they can only be operated by knowing the private key. If you buy some Ether, you'd store it in this type of account. Also, you'd start a transaction against a smart contract from an EOA.
- *Contract accounts*—These are the accounts that contracts are executed under. The account address is generated at deployment time, and it identifies the location of the contract in the blockchain.

Both EOAs and contract accounts hold data in the form of a key-value store and an Ether balance. Table 3.1 compares the main properties of EOAs and contract accounts.

Table 3.1   Comparison between an EOA and a Contract Account

Property	Externally owned account	Contract account
Has Ether balance	Yes	Yes
Can start transaction message	Yes	No
Can start call message	No	Yes
Has code	No	Yes

3.2.2   Ether

I've mentioned Ether casually a few times, so it's probably time you learned more about it. Ether is the cryptocurrency that the Ethereum blockchain supports. Its main purpose is to represent monetary value for services and goods traded over the platform.

Ether is also used to pay for transaction fees. These are, as mentioned in section 3.2 and covered more in section 3.2.3, calculated in a unit called gas, which measures computational resources that a transaction consumes. But these fees are settled in Ether (calculated from the price of a unit of gas, expressed in Ether). Miners charge transaction fees to get compensated for the computational power they provide the network while appending new transaction blocks to the blockchain.

Ether comes in various denominations, which are all defined, as you can see in table 3.2, as a multiple of Wei, the smallest Ether denomination.

Table 3.2   Ether denominations and values in Wei

Unit	Wei value	Wei
Wei	1 Wei	1
Kwei (Babbage)	1e3 Wei	1,000

Table 3.2   Ether denominations and values in Wei

Unit	Wei value	Wei
Mwei (Lovelace)	1e6 Wei	1,000,000
Gwei (Shannon)	1e9 Wei	1,000,000,000
Microether (Szabo)	1e12 Wei	1,000,000,000,000
Milliether (Finney)	1e15 Wei	1,000,000,000,000,000
Ether	1e18 Wei	1,000,000,000,000,000,000

Figure 3.9 summarizes the Ether lifecycle, which goes through the following steps:

1 Minting Ether
2 Transferring Ether
3 Storing Ether
4 Exchanging Ether

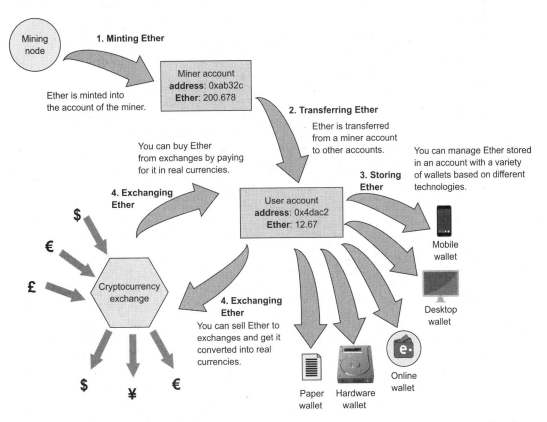

Figure 3.9   The Ether lifecycle. Ether is minted by miner nodes into miner user accounts. Then it's transferred to EOAs (also known as user accounts). From there, it can be stored on various wallets. Ultimately, it can be converted to real currency, such as USD, EUR, YEN, GBP, and others, through cryptocurrency exchanges.

MINTING ETHER

If you're unfamiliar with cryptocurrencies, you must be wondering how Ether is minted and exchanged. Ether is generated through the mining process, during which miners compete to group and append transactions into new blockchain blocks, as I discussed in section 1.1.2. When successful, a miner gets rewarded with a certain number of Ether coins. Blocks are added to the Ethereum blockchain every 15 seconds or so, and the money supply increases accordingly.

TRANSFERRING ETHER

Once Ether has been generated, it's allocated to the miner's external account. Miners can then transfer Ether to other external accounts or contract accounts, either through the Ethereum wallet or programmatically, as you'll see later.

EXCHANGING ETHER

Because Ether is valuable, it doesn't generally get transferred for free between accounts. It's often transferred in return for goods and services traded through smart contracts, but also in return for conventional currency, such as US dollars, euros, pounds, yen, and so on. Although it's possible to buy Ether from individual owners and pay them an agreed amount of conventional currency, it's more effective to handle such transactions using cryptocurrency exchanges. Two main types of exchanges are available: centralized, such as Kraken, Coinbase, and Coinsquare, and decentralized, such as EtherEx. Each exchange is generally biased toward a specific real-world currency.

STORING ETHER

Once someone acquires Ether, whether through mining, smart contract trading, or exchange-based trading, it's allocated to an account. You can manage accounts using many methods, each with a different trade-off between convenience and security. The most convenient one is generally through desktop or online wallets, which allow you to transfer Ether easily. The most secure one is through cold or paper storage, which means generating the private key offline and holding it literally on a piece of paper. Hardware wallets present another high-security option and are conceptually similar to paper wallets because they can be considered offline. The main difference is that the account owner stores the private key on a small electronic device similar to a USB key. Table 3.3 summarizes the different options.

Table 3.3 Wallet types and their characteristics

Wallet type	Convenience	Security	Examples
Desktop wallet	High	High	Ethereum wallet, Exodus
Mobile wallet	High	Low	Jaxx
Online wallet	High	Medium	MyEtherWallet, Coinbase, Kraken
Hardware wallet	Medium	Very high	Trezor, Ledger Nano, KeepKey
Paper storage	Low	Very high	EthAddress

I've mentioned that transaction fees are charged in Ether but calculated in a unit called gas. Let's see what gas is and how it's related to transaction costs.

3.2.3 Gas

Gas is the unit of measure for transaction fees charged on the Ethereum platform. The amount of gas used to complete a transaction depends on the amount of computational resources that the EVM spends while running the transaction. Specifically, it depends on the exact low-level EVM instructions that have been executed during the transaction. Table 3.4 gives an idea of the amount of gas charged for the most common EVM operations.

Table 3.4 Gas cost for simple EVM operations

Operation	EVM op code	Gas cost
Addition, subtraction	ADD, SUB	3
Multiplication, division	MUL, DIV	5
Comparison	LT, GT, SLT, SGT	3
Load word from memory	MLOAD	3
Store word to memory	MSTORE	3
Load word from storage	SLOAD	200
Storing word into storage	SSTORE	>5000
Contract creation	CREATE	32000

The main reason the execution of a transaction is charged in units of gas, and indirectly in units of computational work, is to prevent denial of service (DoS) attacks by unscrupulous participants who might want to disrupt the network. To launch a DoS attack, a malicious participant would have to spam the network with a high number of transactions, each performing a large amount of computational work; for instance, an infinite loop. The amount of gas corresponding to this work would be high, and it would have to be paid in a correspondingly high amount of Ether—it's unlikely anyone would pay to disrupt a service!

Most smart contract development IDEs give an idea of the total amount of gas required to complete a transaction. For example, in the screenshot in figure 3.10, you

```
[vm] from:0xca3...a733c, to:browser/SimpleCoin.sol:SimpleCoin.transfer(address,uint256) 0x692...77b3a, value:0 wei, data:0xa90...00014,   [Details]  [Debug]
1 logs, hash:0xa43...3f1b8
```

status	0x1 Transaction mined and execution succeed
from	0xca35b7d915458ef548ade6068dfe2f44e8fa733c
to	browser/SimpleCoin.sol:SimpleCoin.transfer(address,uint256) 0x692a70d2e424a56d2c6c27aa97d1a86395877b3a
gas	3000000 gas
transaction cost	36480 gas
execution cost	13608 gas

Figure 3.10 Transaction costs for the execution of the `SimpleCoin` transfer function

can see a gas estimate for the execution of the transfer function of the `SimpleCoin` contract from the last section of chapter 1, obtained by clicking the Details button on the output panel.

Transaction fee costs are calculated according to this formula: transaction fees (in Ether) = number of units of gas consumed * price per unit of gas (in Ether). Let's break it down:

- The EVM determines the *number of units of gas consumed* while running the transaction, and that depends on the computational cost of the code being run during the transaction.
- The sender of the transaction decides the *price of a unit of gas* (in Ether). The higher it is, the more likely it is that miners will include the transaction in the block they're processing. Miners prioritize transactions that are likely to pay high fees, so if a transaction is expected to consume a relatively low amount of gas, the sender will have to set a relatively high gas price to guarantee quick processing.
- The transaction sender sets a *limit* for *the maximum amount of gas* that a transaction should consume. This protects the sender from higher-than-expected transaction costs due to execution of the code in a way different from what was intended; for instance, if the developer introduces a bug that causes an infinite loop. Such limits should be relatively close to the estimated amount of gas needed to complete the transaction.

While a transaction is being executed, the EVM consumes its gas. Two outcomes are possible at the end of the transaction:

1 *The transaction completes successfully.* In this case, the unused gas is returned to the sender.
2 *The amount of gas available ends before the completion of the transaction.* In this case, the EVM throws an *end of gas exception,* and the transaction is rolled back.

You might be wondering who pockets the transaction fee. Given either of the two transaction outcomes, the miner who has processed the transaction receives the fee. For the first outcome, they earn the fee by including the transaction in a new block that has been successfully appended to the blockchain. For the second outcome, even though the EVM throws an exception, the miner still charges the gas in Ether, and they collect the related transaction fee as usual. In short, a successful miner is rewarded by minting new Ether and getting transaction fees from the transaction senders. In the early stages of the Ethereum platform, most of a miner's profits came from minting.

3.2.4 *Calls and transactions*

Accounts interact with each other through two types of messages: calls and transactions.

CALLS

A call is sent through a message that doesn't get stored on the blockchain and whose execution has the following characteristics:

- It can only perform read-only operations, which don't alter the state of the blockchain.
- It doesn't consume any gas, and consequently, it's free.
- It's processed synchronously.
- It immediately returns a return value.
- It doesn't allow transferring Ether to the contract account.

Typical calls are direct invocations of contract member variables, including mappings, and invocations of so-called *constant functions*, which don't alter contract state. You performed calls, for example, when you checked account balances of SimpleCoin, the basic cryptocurrency you started to build at the end of chapter 1.

TRANSACTIONS

A transaction, which I introduced to you in the Dapp dynamic view in chapter 1, is sent through a message that gets serialized and stored on the blockchain during the mining process. It contains the following fields:

- *Sender address*
- *Recipient address*
- *Value*—Amount of Ether to be transferred (in Wei), in case the message is being used to transfer Ether (optional)
- *Data*—Input parameters, in case the message is being used as a function call (optional)
- *StartGas*—Maximum amount of gas to be used for the execution of the message. If this limit is exceeded, the EVM throws an exception and rolls back the state of the message.
- *Digital signature*—Proves the identity of the transaction sender
- *GasPrice*—The price of a unit of gas (expressed in Ether) the transaction initiator is willing to pay, as discussed in the gas section

You executed transactions when you performed SimpleCoin transfers. The execution of a transaction has the following characteristics:

- It can perform write operations, which alter the state of the blockchain.
- It consumes gas, which must be paid for in Ether.
- It's processed asynchronously: it gets executed through mining and then gets appended on a new blockchain block, which gets broadcast throughout the network.

- It immediately returns a transaction ID, but not a return value.
- It allows transferring Ether to the contract account. (The Ether transfer becomes part of the transaction itself.)

By now you know contracts are executed on the EVM on each node of the Ethereum network. I'll provide a quick overview of how the EVM works.

3.2.5   *The Ethereum Virtual Machine*

The Ethereum Virtual Machine (EVM) is a stack-based abstract computing machine, similar in purpose to the Java virtual machine (JVM) and to the .NET Common Language Runtime (CLR). It enables a computer to run an Ethereum application and has two memory areas:

- *Volatile memory,* or simply *memory.* This is a word-addressed byte array, which gets allocated to a contract at every message call. Reads access 256-bit words, whereas writes can be performed on a width of 8 or 256 bits.
- *Storage.* This is a key-value store where both key and value have a width of 256 bits. Storage is allocated to each account and is persisted on the blockchain. A contract account can access only its own storage.

EVM opcodes cover operations including Boolean, bitwise, and arithmetic comparisons and jumps (both conditional and unconditional). These are the main opcodes handling contract creation and calls:

- CREATE—This performs the creation of a new contract instance.
- CALL—A contract sends a message to itself or other contracts through this operator.
- DELEGATECALL—This operator allows the calling contract to send a message to an external contract but execute the related code in the context of the caller. This operator is especially useful for the creation of libraries of shared code that multiple contracts can access.

The EVM is completely sandboxed: a contract can't access network or filesystem resources. It can only access other contracts. A more in-depth explanation of the EVM is outside the scope of this book. The best reference for understanding its design is Gavin Wood's so-called *Yellow Paper:* http://gavwood.com/paper.pdf.

At this point, you've consolidated your knowledge on smart contracts. Now it's time to take a step further and connect to the Ethereum network through a proper client: the Go Ethereum client.

3.3   *Connecting to Ethereum with geth*

Before you start installing a client, I'd like to give you a more detailed overview of the Ethereum network, which I started introducing in chapter 1. It'll help you understand the wider context that a client fits in.

You already know the Ethereum network is a peer-to-peer (P2P) network, which means there's no central master or server node coordinating them. Consequently, all nodes are clients to each other. Nodes are designed to work and communicate with each other in exactly the same way, according to a predefined protocol called Wire, described in the Yellow Paper. This means all nodes must be able to append new transaction blocks to the blockchain (if mining is activated) and verify them while blocks get propagated throughout the network.

From an implementation point of view, the network contains two broad categories of nodes:

- *Miners*—They process the latest transactions and consolidate them into the blockchain in exchange for transaction fees and a mining reward (in Ether) if they manage to execute the consensus algorithm successfully. In that case, they propagate the blocks they've consolidated onto the blockchain to other peers of the network. Because these nodes generate new blocks, they're considered producers (although they're technically also still consumers).
- *Full nodes*—They mainly verify the validity of the blocks they've received from neighboring peers and keep propagating them to the rest of the network. Therefore, they're considered consumers.

Mining nodes run on clients optimized for processing transactions, generating blocks, and executing the Proof of Work algorithm efficiently, to get rewarded relatively frequently. Mining implementations, such as *ethminer*, have been written in C++ and use GPU libraries such as NVIDIA's CUDA. Consequently, they run on GPU hardware that can deliver superior performance.

On the other hand, full nodes don't have performance requirements, so standard clients have been implemented in various languages. Table 3.5 summarizes the main client implementations available to date, ordered by popularity, as reported in Ethernodes (https://ethernodes.org/network/1).

Table 3.5 Ethereum client implementations by language

Client	Language
Go Ethereum (geth)	Go
Parity	Rust
Cpp-ethereum (eth)	C++
Ethereum(J)	Java
Pyethapp	Python
ethereumjs-lib	JavaScript
ruby-ethereum	Ruby
ethereumH	Haskell

Each client comes with a console, and some of them also include a graphical browser or a wallet. While working with this book, you'll use Go Ethereum, also known as geth, which is the most popular client, installed on over 70% of the network nodes.

3.3.1 Getting started with geth

The download page for the Go Ethereum website, https://ethereum.github.io/go-ethereum/downloads/, shows releases for all major operating systems: Android, iOS, Linux, MacOS, and Windows. Various installation formats are available for some of the supported operating systems. For example, for Windows, you can choose between the 32- and 64-bit version and whether to download only the executable (Archive option) or the full installer (Installer option). I've picked the 64-bit Geth & Tools 1.8.13 archive.

Once you've installed or uncompressed the relevant file, you can run the geth executable. If you have the Ethereum wallet open, close it before starting geth, because they use the same port number! If you run geth with no parameters, it'll start to synchronize in Full mode with the public production network, also known as MAINNET, as shown in the screenshot in figure 3.11.

Figure 3.11 **geth synchronizing with the MAINNET network at startup**

After geth has synchronized the full blockchain (this could take from hours to days, depending on your hardware and internet connection), the console will start to slow down and show blocks being added to the blockchain in real time.

NOTE As for the wallet, you can synchronize geth in Light or Fast mode—for example, `C:\program files\geth>geth --syncmode "light"`—if you prefer to get up and running more quickly (in minutes as opposed to hours or even days) and don't mind not having downloaded the full blockchain locally.

You can interact with geth in two ways:

- Through the user-friendly geth interactive JavaScript console
- Through low-level JSON-RPC calls over HTTP

I'll present both techniques to you. Let's start with the simpler tool: the interactive JavaScript console.

3.3.2   *A first look at the geth interactive console*

geth comes with an interactive console that accepts JavaScript instructions. It implicitly references Web3.js, a JavaScript implementation of Web3, the official high-level library for interacting with Ethereum clients. This console is similar in purpose to read-eval-print loop (REPL) consoles for programming language IDEs. I'll cover Web3 extensively in the next few chapters. For the moment, let's get a quick feel for it.

First, open the interactive console. You've got two possible ways to start it up:

- If no geth clients are running on the same machine, run the geth executable with the console command:

```
C:\program files\geth> geth console
```

- If a geth client is already running on the machine, attach to a running geth process with the attach command:

```
C:\program files\geth> geth attach ipc:\\.\pipe\geth.ipc
```

You have a running geth process, so you'll go for the second option.

> **NOTE**   In this book, I'm assuming you use Windows, as over 60% of the nodes of the Ethereum network run on this operating system. Consequently, I'll show shell commands with a Windows command prompt format. Also note that after successful execution of instructions in the console, you might see *undefined* right before or after the correct results. You can ignore it.

DISPLAYING VERSION INFORMATION

First of all, you can query the console for version information. A Web3 object named web3 is implicitly instantiated when opening the console, so you can access version information in this way by typing

```
> web3.version
```

and you'll see something like

```
{
  api: "0.20.1",
  ethereum: "0x3f",
  network: "1",
  node: "Geth/v1.8.13-stable-225171a4/windows-amd64/go1.10.3",
  ...
```

As you can see, the version property is an object that contains many subproperties. If you want, you can be specific and query an individual property of the version object:

```
> web3.version.api
```

and you'll see something like

```
"0.20.1"
```

Because the console accepts JavaScript instructions, it's possible to assign the values of Web3 properties and subproperties to variables and then display them through the console object:

```
> var apiVersion = web3.version.api
> var nodeVersion = web3.version.node
> console.log('Api version: ' + apiVersion)
> console.log('Node version: ' + nodeVersion)
```

CHECKING CONNECTIVITY

You can get some client connectivity information from the web3.net object. (You can omit the web3 namespace because it's implicitly referenced.) If you type

```
> net
```

you'll see something like

```
{
  listening: true,
  peerCount: 2,
  version: "3",
  getListening: function(callback),
  getPeerCount: function(callback),
  getVersion: function(callback)
}
```

As for the version object, you can directly access individual properties of the net object as follows:

```
> console.log('this geth instance is listening for network connections : ' +
      web3.net.listening)
> console.log('number of peers connected to this geth instance: ' +
      web3.net.peerCount)
```

If you want to get more detailed information about your node, you can use the web3.admin object and call

```
> admin.nodeInfo
```

and you'll see something like

```
{
  enode: "enode://90946319e42ef4d4670c1d7...,
  id: "90946319e42ef4d467...,
  ip: "::",
  listenAddr: "[::]:30303",
  name: "Geth/v1.8.13-stable-225171a4/windows-amd64/go1.10.3",
  ...
```

The peers property gives you detailed information about the peers you're connected to:

```
> admin.peers
```

will yield something like

```
[{
    caps: ["eth/62", "eth/63"],
    id: "0b64924d478abaf6900ffe...",
    name: "Geth/v1.6.1-stable-021c3c28/linux-amd64/go1.8.1",
    network: {
      localAddress: "192.168.1.108:53557",
      remoteAddress: "136.144.129.222:30303"
    },
...
```

ACCESSING THE BLOCKCHAIN

The web3.eth object retrieves real-time information about the client and the block-chain. Look at the console of the geth process currently running. You should see how new blocks are getting appended to the blockchain in real time. Take note of the block number of a recently appended block, and then switch back to the JavaScript console.

You can get the most recent block number through the eth.blockNumber property:

```
> var latestBlockNum = eth.blockNumber
> console.log('Latest block #: ' + latestBlockNumber)
```

Then you can display summary information about this block by calling

```
> eth.getBlock(latestBlockNum)
```

and you'll see something like

```
{
  difficulty: 64344784,
  extraData: "0xd7830106078467657...",
  gasLimit: 4723091,
  gasUsed: 262264,
  hash: "0x8196edb66315b460f0bd4b9bdfa884...",
  nonce: "0x2ac78a350ec95787",
  number: 1732206,
...
```

You also can drill down at transaction level. You can get the first transaction stored in the latest block in this way:

```
> eth.getTransactionFromBlock(latestBlockNum, 0)
```

You'll see something like

```
{
  blockHash: "0x8196edb66315b460f0bd4b9bdfa88...",
  blockNumber: 1732206,
```

```
    from: "0x392fd4954de442bb6c4d57f1923b4708642d3408",
    gas: 210000,
    gasPrice: 120000000000,
    hash: "0x4eb5ae8d7b7919f92d1dd02fcc407d6...",
...
```

I encourage you to have a look at the content of the whole `eth` object:

```
> eth
```

PERFORMING ETHER CONVERSIONS

The Web3 API offers some useful functions to convert any Ether denomination from/to Wei. You can convert a Wei amount to a specific denomination:

```
> var amountInWei = 12000000
> var amountInSzabo = web3.fromWei(amountInWei, 'szabo')
> console.log(amountInWei + ' Wei is equivalent to '  + amountInSzabo + '
    szabo')
12000000 Wei is equivalent to 0.000012 szabo
```

And you can convert a specific denomination into Wei:

```
> var amountInEther = 12
> var amountInWei = web3.toWei(amountInEther, 'Ether')
> console.log(amountInEther + ' Ether is equivalent to '  + amountInWei + '
    Wei')
12 Ether is equivalent to 12000000000000000000 Wei
```

3.3.3 *A first look at JSON-RPC*

Now that you've learned the basics of the JavaScript console, you can try to interact with geth by performing a few JSON-RPC calls. geth offers a remote procedure call (RPC) interface that allows you to access node functionality and blockchain data to a much finer degree of control than that offered by the Web3 API. In fact, Web3 is built on top of the RPC layer, which is the lowest level API exposed by the Ethereum platform, as shown in figure 3.12.

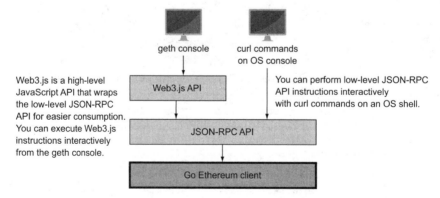

Figure 3.12 Comparison between accessing geth through Web3.js and JSON-RPC

The RPC interface has been designed against the JSON-RPC 2.0 standard, and consequently it sends and receives data in JSON format. You can find more information on JSON-RPC in the sidebar.

If you want to communicate with geth directly through JSON-RPC, you have to do two things:

1 Stop any instance of geth running in a standard operating system command shell or in a geth console.

2 Start geth in RPC mode using the `--rpc` and `--rpcapi` options:

```
C:\program files\geth>geth --rpc --rpcapi "eth,net,web3,personal"
```

When you launch geth in RPC mode, it's accessible through an HTTP server that accepts HTTP requests, by default on

```
http://localhost:8545
```

JSON-RPC

JSON-RPC is a lightweight remote procedure call that uses JSON as a data format.

You invoke an RPC call by sending a request object to a server, typically over HTTP, or in any other way, such as socket or even messaging, because the transport layer isn't part of the protocol.

The request object must contain the following members:

- `jsonrpc`—This sets the protocol version, currently 2.0.
- `method`—Name of the remote procedure to be called.
- `params`—Array with procedure parameters.
- `id`—A call identifier, typically a string or integer. It must be not null.

After the server processes the call, it replies with a response object, which contains the following members:

- `jsonrpc`—This sets the protocol version, currently 2.0.
- `result`—This field is present if the response is successful; it isn't included if errors occur.
- `error`—This field is present if errors occur; it isn't included if the response is successful.
- `id`—Same as specified in the request.

You'll perform JSON-RPC calls to geth's HTTP server using the cURL console command. To help you appreciate the differences between the Web3 API and the JSON-RPC API, I'll show you how to execute in cURL the same operations you performed in Web3 through the interactive console.

NOTE   cURL is available in most operating systems, including Windows (version 7 and 10) and Linux. Alternatively, you can either download from the internet an open source version of cURL or perform HTTP requests through a graphical tool such as Postman, if you prefer.

DISPLAYING VERSION INFORMATION

You can retrieve version information about the geth client with this call:

```
C:\>curl -H "Content-Type: application/json" -X POST --data
{\"jsonrpc\":\"2.0\",\"method\":\"web3_clientVersion\",\"params\":[],\"id\":2
3} http://localhost:8545
```

```
{"jsonrpc":"2.0","id":23,"result":"Geth/v1.6.5-stable-cf87713d/windows-
amd64/go1.8.3"}
```

(If you're using Windows, you must escape JSON double quotes, as explained in the sidebar.) The result is equivalent to what you got from web3.version.node.

---

cURL JSON escaping on Windows

cURL operations must escape the double-quote symbol " with \" in the JSON POST data, in certain versions of Windows. For example, in a command shell in Windows, you perform the request this way:

```
C:\>curl -H "Content-Type: application/json" -X POST --data
{\"jsonrpc\":\"2.0\",\"method\":\"web3_clientVersion\",\"params\":[],\"i
d\":23} http://localhost:8545
```

And in Linux:

```
$curl -H "Content-Type: application/json" -X POST --data
'{"jsonrpc":"2.0","method":"web3_clientVersion","params":[],"id":23}'
http://localhost:8545
```

CHECKING CLIENT CONNECTIVITY

You can get connectivity information by performing several calls. For instance, to check whether the client is actively listening for network connection, you must execute this request:

```
C:\>curl -H "Content-Type: application/json" -X POST --data
{\"jsonrpc\":\"2.0\",\"method\":\"net_listening\",\"params\":[],\"id\":23}
http://localhost:8545
```

And you'll get

```
{"jsonrpc":"2.0","id":23,"result":true}
```

The result is equivalent to web3.net.listening.

To get the number of peers connected to the client, you must execute this call:

```
C:\>curl -H "Content-Type: application/json" -X POST --data
{\"jsonrpc\":\"2.0\",\"method\":\"net_peerCount\",\"params\":[],\"id\":23}
http://localhost:8545
```

And you'll get

```
{"jsonrpc":"2.0","id":23,"result":"0x6"}
```

The result, which contains numbers encoded in hexadecimal format, as explained in the sidebar, is equivalent to web3.net.peerCount.

Numbers through JSON-RPC

Ethereum's JSON-RPC interface handles numbers differently than the official JSON-RPC 2.0 specification does. Numbers sent and returned through JSON-RPC must be encoded in hexadecimal format. Doing so makes sure each client implementation parses and processes large numbers appropriately, independent of the support for large numbers that the underlying language in which the client has been coded provides.

Hexadecimal encoding should include a 0x prefix and at least one valid digit with no leading zeros, as shown here:

0x4d2 ⊲——| **This is equivalent to 1234 in decimal.**

Here are some examples of how numbers should be encoded into hexadecimal format:

Decimal format	Hexadecimal format
0	0x0
9	0x9
1234	0x4d2

And here are some examples of incorrectly encoded numbers:

Incorrect hex encoding	Reason
0x	No digit has been specified after the 0x prefix.
42d	No 0x prefix has been specified.
0x042d	Leading 0 digits aren't allowed.

ACCESSING THE BLOCKCHAIN

You can get the latest blockchain block number this way:

```
C:\>curl -H "Content-Type: application/json" -X POST --data
{\"jsonrpc\":\"2.0\",\"method\":\"eth_blockNumber\",\"params\":[],\"id\":23}
http://localhost:8545
```

And you'll get

```
{"jsonrpc":"2.0","id":23,"result":"0x1a705d"}
```

Once you have the latest block number, you can inspect it by calling (replacing the block number in params with the one from your result):

```
C:\>curl -H "Content-Type: application/json" -X POST --data
{\"jsonrpc\":\"2.0\",\"method\":\"eth_getBlockByNumber\",\"params\":[\"0x1a70
5d\",true],\"id\":23} http://localhost:8545
```

And you'll get

```
{"jsonrpc":"2.0","id":23,"result":{"difficulty":"0x3e37031","extraData":"0xd6
    83010700846765746885676...","gasLimit":"0x47e7c4","gasUsed":"0x323db6","
    hash":"0x0d6ae4b07a731834f5ca0d18859...",...
"miner":"0x22d1d502356c1c2d...","nonce":"0x3b886846920d3c81","number":"0x1a70
    5d","parentHash":"0x90fbbacbf8945fb8d4..."
...
```

Then you can inspect the first transaction of the block you retrieved in a way equivalent to how you did in Web3 through the interactive console (again, putting the block number you got in results into params):

```
C:\>curl -H "Content-Type: application/json" -X POST --data
{\"jsonrpc\":\"2.0\",\"method\":\"eth_getTransactionByBlockNumberAndIndex\",\
"params\":[\"0x1a705d\",\"0x0\"],\"id\":23} http://localhost:8545
```

And you'll get

```
{"jsonrpc":"2.0","id":23,"result":{"blockHash":"0x0d6ae4b07a731834f5ca0d1885.
..","blockNumber":"0x1a705d","from":"0xcaf4a30e5fef5c0a...","gas":"0x47b760",
"gasPrice":"0x1bf08eb000","hash":"0x9acf62392d266086ec8..."
...
```

The result object is similar to that returned by the Web3 eth.getTransactionFrom-Block call.

In the rest of the book, you'll be interacting with geth mainly through Web3.js, but occasionally I'll show you how to perform equivalent operations in JSON-RPC. If you're interested in learning more about the JSON-RPC API, consult its wiki at https://github.com/ethereum/wiki/wiki/JSON-RPC.

3.3.4 *Mining with the geth console*

You can't consider a section on Ethereum clients to be complete before at least mentioning how to perform mining through a client. You already performed some mining through the Ethereum wallet at the beginning of this chapter, to load your test accounts with Ether.

As you can imagine, performing operations through the wallet hides what happens under the hood. For example, have you asked yourself why the Ether you mined got assigned to account1? That happened because the *etherbase* account, which is the account associated with the miner thread, is set by default to eth.accounts[0]. But after restarting geth and reopening the geth console in attach mode, as you did previously (in case you shut it down), you can reconfigure the etherbase account to eth.accounts[1], if you prefer, through the implicitly instantiated miner object, as follows:

```
C:\program files\geth> geth attach ipc:\\.\pipe\geth.ipc

> miner.setEtherbase(eth.accounts[1])
```

Regardless of whether your etherbase account is eth.accounts[0] or you've reconfigured it to eth.accounts[1], you can start mining as follows:

```
> miner.start()
```

At this point, the CPU of your machine will go to nearly 100%. Then you can stop mining:

```
> miner.stop()
```

In the unlikely event you've mined some Ether, this will now be assigned to your eth.accounts[1], or to eth.accounts[0] if you decided not to reconfigure it.

When you kicked off mining on the geth interactive window with miner.start(), you might have noticed output similar to the following:

```
INFO [09-29|18:08:23] Imported new chain segment               blocks=1
    txs=20  mgas=4.401    elapsed=25.066ms  mgasps=175.592 number=1732751
    hash=fa5a62...050eb5
INFO [09-29|18:08:25] Updated mining threads                   threads=0
INFO [09-29|18:08:25] Transaction pool price threshold updated
    price=18000000000
INFO [09-29|18:08:25] Starting mining operation
INFO [09-29|18:08:25] Commit new mining work                   number=1732752
    txs=5    uncles=0 elapsed=7.017ms
INFO [09-29|18:08:27] Generating DAG in progress               epoch=57
    percentage=0 elapsed=922.455ms
INFO [09-29|18:08:28] Generating DAG in progress               epoch=57
    percentage=1 elapsed=1.846s
INFO [09-29|18:08:29] Generating DAG in progress               epoch=57
    percentage=2 elapsed=2.772s
```

```
INFO [09-29|18:08:30] Generating DAG in progress            epoch=57
    percentage=3 elapsed=3.753s
INFO [09-29|18:08:31] Imported new chain segment            blocks=1
    txs=0    mgas=0.000    elapsed=6.016ms    mgasps=0.000    number=1732752
    hash=c98db8...2d044c
INFO [09-29|18:08:31] Commit new mining work               number=1732753
    txs=6    uncles=0 elapsed=22.058ms
INFO [09-29|18:08:31] Generating DAG in progress            epoch=57
    percentage=4 elapsed=4.724s
INFO [09-29|18:08:31] Imported new chain segment            blocks=1
    txs=5    mgas=3.693    elapsed=21.056ms    mgasps=175.370 number=1732752
    hash=f4432f...8bae81
```

You might wonder what DAG is and why it takes such a long time to compute. DAG stands for directed acyclic graph, and it's the data structure underlying *Ethash*, the Proof of Work (PoW) algorithm for mining on the Ethereum platform. DAG requires a relatively high amount of memory, so Ethash is considered a memory-intensive PoW algorithm. It consequently discourages mining through application-specific integrated circuit (ASIC) hardware, which is effective only for CPU-intensive PoW algorithms, such as the one used on the Bitcoin network. The Ethash algorithm encourages mining instead through commodity hardware, such as a GPU chipset (explained more in sidebar).

Mining is a specialized topic outside the scope of this book. If you're interested in learning more about Ethash, I encourage you to consult the official notes at http://mng.bz/WaOw.

Now that you've experienced mining firsthand, you might ask yourself what happens if you have the luck to append a new block to the blockchain, get the related Ether reward in your etherbase account, and then decide to quit your mining activity by shutting down your node. Would the block you've created and appended to the blockchain still be valid, even if you've disappeared from the network? Would the transactions included in the block still be valid? Would you still be able to transfer the Ether in your etherbase account to another account?

The answer to all these questions is yes. Remember that the blockchain validation process, performed continuously by all active full nodes, only cares about the cryptographic consistency between a block hash and the public address of the miner who has generated the block, in the same way it cares about the consistency between a transaction hash and the public address of the account that has generated it. So whether the node that created a new block is active or inactive is as irrelevant to the block (and transaction) history as whether your computer is on or off after having transferred some Ether from an account of your desktop Ethereum wallet to another account.

GPU mining

If you want to try your luck and hope to get rich by generating Ether on the public production network with CPU mining, as you've done so far in the test network, I hate to break the news, but you're more likely to get rich by winning the lottery. As you saw in chapter 1, the execution of the PoW algorithm is successful only if the hash obtained combining the block information and a nonce has certain characteristics—for example, a high number of leading zeros. PoW algorithms are designed so that you must try millions of nonce values before hitting the lucky one that generates a valid hash. Consequently, mining successfully means being able to generate more hashes per second than other miners.

With the best CPU chipset, you'll be able to generate at most 1 megahash per second (Mh/s), where megahash means one million hashes. With good GPU chipsets, you might be able to generate up to 30 Mh/s—nearly 30 times the hashing capability of a standard CPU. Also consider that mining pools, which are organizations that pool various GPU miners together so they can share resources and rewards, can generate up to 30 Th/s (30 trillion hashes per second), which means up to 30 million times what a CPU is able to generate during the same time. Finally, consider that in the Ethereum space, around 40 mining pools have a hash rate ranging between 30 Gh/s and 30 Th/s.

Now you can understand why your chances of generating Ether using a CPU alone are slim. You might find this stark reality disappointing, and you might even think that the huge influence of mining pools on the mining process might bring into question Ethereum's credibility, as far as decentralization is concerned. Many Ethereum participants believe that as long as many mining pools are competing, decentralization should be guaranteed. Also consider that the new consensus algorithm being implemented, Stake of Work, introduced in the previous chapter, might change completely how power is concentrated (or hopefully spread) in the Ethereum network. Here's a quick summary of the hash rate that different hardware can achieve:

Hardware	Hashrate
Single CPU	1 Mh/s
Single GPU	30 Mh/s
GPU rig (10xGPUs)	300 Mh/s
Mining pool	30,000,000 Mh/s

3.3.5 Other clients

Although Go Ethereum is the most popular client, other implementations offer various benefits with respect to geth:

- *Parity*, written in Rust, is the second most popular Ethereum client, and it's regarded as the fastest, lightest, and most secure implementation. It comes with a console and a built-in wallet.

- *cpp-ethereum*, written in C++ and known as *eth*, is another fast implementation, third in popularity, and well regarded for its portability. *Ethminer*, a specialized mining client, is a fork from cpp-ethereum.
- *pyethapp*, written in Python, is built on two core components: *pyethereum* provides EVM, blockchain, and mining functionality, whereas *pydevp2p* supports access to the P2P network and node discovery mechanisms. Python developers especially appreciate this implementation for its extensibility.

You've learned about various components and tools of the Ethereum platform. Before leaving this chapter, you'll reinforce your understanding of accounts, a key concept you must get familiar with to work effectively with Ethereum.

3.4   *Managing accounts with geth*

At the beginning of this chapter, while covering smart contracts, I touched briefly on accounts. I also helped you create some accounts through the Ethereum wallet UI so you could use them to transfer some Ether around. Armed with the geth console, you can now deepen your knowledge of accounts by creating them and interacting with them programmatically.

3.4.1   *Ethereum accounts*

As you know, the Ethereum platform supports two types of accounts:

- *Externally owned accounts (EOAs)*—These impersonate end users, as well as miners and autonomous agents.
- *Contract accounts*—These impersonate contracts.

For the rest of this chapter, we'll deal only with EOAs, which I'll call *accounts*.

As with most blockchain systems, the security of the Ethereum platform is based on public key cryptography. An account is therefore identified by a private/public key pair. The account's address is represented by the last 20 bytes of the public key.

The private/public key pair associated with an account is stored in a text *keyfile*. The public key is visible in plain text, whereas the private key is encrypted with the password introduced at account creation. Account keyfiles are in the *keystore* folder within the Ethereum node's data directory:

- Windows: C:\Users\username\%appdata%\Roaming\Ethereum\keystore
- Linux: ~/.ethereum/keystore
- Mac: ~/Library/Ethereum/keystore

TIP   It's strongly recommended that you back up the keystore folder on a regular basis and keep a copy of the passwords you've introduced when creating each account in a secure place. Sorry if I keep pestering you with this, but if you haven't noticed, I do want to make a point of how sensitive key and password details are in the blockchain world!

Account portability

You can't use an account that you've created on the public production network on a test network, for example Ropsten, and vice versa. This is because the keystore of each network is different and is located in a separate folder within the Ethereum folder:

- Main prod network keystore: ~/.ethereum/keystore
- Rinkeby test network keystore: ~/.ethereum/rinkeby/keystore
- Ropsten test network keystore: ~/.ethereum/testnet/keystore

You can create accounts and interact with them through four different avenues:

- The Ethereum wallet, as you saw earlier in this chapter
- geth commands
- Web3 on the geth console
- JSON-RPC calls

You've already seen how to manage accounts with the Ethereum wallet. In the next several sections, you'll manage accounts through geth commands and the geth console. You'll also get a quick feel for how to perform some operations on accounts through the JSON-RPC API.

3.4.2 *Managing accounts with the geth command*

You can manage an account easily through your operating system console by entering specific geth commands from the directory of the geth executable (or from any directory if geth is in your PATH global variable).

CREATING A NEW ACCOUNT

You can create a new account manually or using a plain text file:

1 Manual creation
   a To create a new account, enter

   ```
   C:\program files\geth>geth account new
   ```

   b You'll be prompted to enter a password twice, and then you'll be shown the address of the account you created:

   ```
   Your new account is locked with a password. Please give a password.
     Do not forget this password.
   Passphrase:
   Repeat passphrase:
   Address: {47e3d3948f46144afa7df2c1aa67f6b1b1e35cf1}
   ```

TIP Get into the habit of choosing strong passwords or generating them through a strong password generator. I'm repeating myself; I know, I know! But this is important, believe me!

2 Text file creation

    a To avoid having to enter the password manually, you can store it in plain text in a text file.

    b Execute the geth account command as follows:

```
C:\program files\geth>geth --password passworddirectory/passwordfile
    account new
```

TIP As you can understand, although placing a password in a plaintext file might be acceptable in a test environment, this way of creating an account might pose much greater risks in a production environment, where you must make sure access to the password file is tightly restricted.

LISTING ACCOUNTS

Once you've created an account, you can verify it's indeed present in your node by executing the following command:

```
C:\program files\geth>geth account list
```

You'll see the accounts you created through the geth account command and the geth console:

```
Account #0: {edde06bc0e45645e2f105972bdefc220ed37ae10}
    keystore://C:\Users\rober\AppData\Roaming\Ethereum\keystore\UTC--2017-
    06-24T08-49-46.377533700Z--edde06bc0e45645e2f105972bdefc220ed37ae10
Account #1: {4e6c30154768b6bc3da693b1b28c6bd14302b578}
    keystore://C:\Users\rober\AppData\Roaming\Ethereum\keystore\UTC--2017-
    06-24T13-26-18.696630000Z--4e6c30154768b6bc3da693b1b28c6bd14302b578
Account #2: {70e36be8ab8f6cf66c0c953cf9c63ab63f3fef02}
    keystore://C:\Users\rober\AppData\Roaming\Ethereum\keystore\UTC--2017-
    06-24T18-21-36.890638200Z--70e36be8ab8f6cf66c0c953cf9c63ab63f3fef02
Account #3: {c99048e9b98d3fcf8b5f0d5644794b562f9a2ea4}
    keystore://C:\Users\rober\AppData\Roaming\Ethereum\keystore\UTC--2017-
    06-24T18-21-47.794428600Z--c99048e9b98d3fcf8b5f0d5644794b562f9a2ea4
...
```

UPDATING ACCOUNTS

After geth creates and saves an account in a keyfile in the keystore folder, a subsequent geth release might implement a new keyfile format. In that case, it becomes necessary to update the account. Another reason you might want to update an account is because you want to change the password.

    You can update account 47e3d3948f46144afa7df2c1aa67f6b1b1e35cf1 you created earlier with the following geth command (obviously replace with your account number):

```
C:\program files\geth>geth account update
    47e3d3948f46144afa7df2c1aa67f6b1b1e35cf1
```

You'll be prompted to enter the existing password, to unlock the account, and subsequently a new password, which you'll have to type twice, as usual. You'll then be shown the new address of the account:

```
Unlocking account 47e3d3948f46144afa7df2c1aa67f6b1b1e35cf1 | Attempt 1/3
Passphrase:
INFO [09-30|08:36:25] Unlocked account
    address=0x47e3d3948f46144afa7df2c1aa67f6b1b1e35cf1
Please give a new password. Do not forget this password.
Passphrase:
Repeat passphrase:
```

The geth account update command offers the same --password option that the geth account new command provides. But in this case you can also use it to unlock the account for the purpose of converting it into a new keyfile format.

3.4.3 *Managing accounts with Web3 on the geth console*

Let's repeat some of the earlier account management operations through the interactive console.

CREATING A NEW ACCOUNT

Go back to the interactive geth console. You can create accounts using the web3.personal object:

```
> personal.newAccount()
```

As for the geth account command, you'll be asked to enter a password twice, and then you'll be shown the account address:

```
Passphrase:
Repeat passphrase:
"0x70ff99d4bc8054b2e09269bcbfdddf8e1ae7d155"
```

LISTING ACCOUNTS

You can list accounts with the interactive console by displaying the value of the account property of the web3.eth object. You'll get the same result set you obtained with the geth account list command:

```
> eth.accounts
```

will yield something like

```
["0xedde06bc0e45645e2f105972bdefc220ed37ae10",
    "0x4e6c30154768b6bc3da693b1b28c6bd14302b578",
    "0x70e36be8ab8f6cf66c0c953cf9c63ab63f3fef02",
    "0xc99048e9b98d3fcf8b5f0d5644794b562f9a2ea4",
...
```

You also can directly reference a specific account of the eth.accounts array:

```
> eth.accounts[0]
```

This will yield something like

```
"0xedde06bc0e45645e2f105972bdefc220ed37ae10"
```

CHECKING AN ACCOUNT'S ETHER BALANCE

You can check the amount of Ether stored in an account using the following call, which returns it in Wei:

```
> var balanceInWei = eth.getBalance(
"0x407d73d8a49eeb85d32cf465507dd71d507100c1")
```

Then you can convert it to Ether as usual:

```
> var balanceInEther = web3.fromWei(balanceInWei, "Ether")
```

TRANSFERRING ETHER BETWEEN ACCOUNTS

You can try transferring 0.0025 Ether from accounts[1] to accounts[2]. First of all, check the current balances of these accounts, as you saw earlier:

```
> var balanceAcc1 = eth.getBalance(eth.accounts[1]);
> var balanceAcc2 = eth.getBalance(eth.accounts[2]);
> console.log('Balance account 1: ' + balanceAcc1 + '; Balance account 2: ' +
    balanceAcc2);
Balance account 1: 1938331059000000000; Balance account 2:
    1000741600000000000
```

Before transferring Ether from a certain account, for example accounts[1], you must unlock it:

```
> personal.unlockAccount(eth.accounts[1]);
```

As usual, you'll be asked to enter the password associated with this account:

```
Unlock account 0x4e6c30154768b6bc3da693b1b28c6bd14302b578
Passphrase:
true
```

Then, you can transfer Ether between accounts with the web3.eth.sendTransaction function, which takes an amount in Wei, as follows:

```
> var sender = eth.accounts[1];
> var recipient = eth.accounts[2];
> var amount = web3.toWei(0.0025, "Ether");
> eth.sendTransaction({from:sender, to:recipient, value: amount});
"0xf1c342c668bcd1d59f3e95cfaf08acc6d7cda8adae02da05ceb76c8c3c137eef"
```

The value returned is the hash of the transaction sent.

After a couple of minutes, recheck the balances:

```
> console.log('Balance account 1: ' + eth.getBalance(eth.accounts[1]) + ';
    Balance account 2: ' + eth.getBalance(eth.accounts[2]));
Balance account 1: 1933311059000000000; Balance account 2:
    1003241600000000000
```

If the balance hasn't been updated yet, it's because the transaction hasn't been mined yet.

3.4.4 Managing accounts with JSON-RPC

I'll give you a quick example of how to perform account management operations in JSON-RPC. Open a new OS shell and you can list your accounts with the following JSON-RPC call:

```
C:\>curl -H "Content-Type: application/json" -X POST --data
{\"jsonrpc\":\"2.0\",\"method\":\"eth_accounts\",\"params\":[],\"id\":23}
http://localhost:8545
```

This will yield something like

```
{"jsonrpc":"2.0","id":23,"result":["0xedde06bc0e45645e2f105972bdefc220ed37ae1
0","0x4e6c30154768b6bc3da693b1b28c6bd14302b578","0x70e36be8ab8f6cf66c0c953cf9
c63ab63f3fef02","0xc99048e9b98d3fcf8b5f0d5644794b562f9a2ea4",...
```

3.5 Revisiting SimpleCoin's contract

We've covered quite a lot of ground in this chapter. If you've followed me up to this point, congratulations: you've completed the introduction to Ethereum covering the Ethereum wallet and the Go Ethereum client. You've also started interacting with the platform in many ways—through the geth commands, through Web3 instructions on the geth interactive console, and through direct JSON-RPC requests.

It's been an intense ride. I bet you're eager to get back to some coding! Let's revisit your initial implementation of SimpleCoin, the basic cryptocurrency I introduced at the end of chapter 1, and try to improve it.

Reenter the SimpleCoin code you saw in the previous chapter into Remix (http://remix.ethereum.org), as shown in the following listing. As usual, ignore warnings for the moment: they'll disappear as you improve the code in the next chapters.

Listing 3.1 SimpleCoin contract as you left it in chapter 1

```
pragma solidity ^0.4.0;

contract SimpleCoin {

  mapping (address => uint256) public coinBalance;

  constructor() public {
    coinBalance[0x14723A09ACff6D2A60DcdF7aA4AFf308FDDC160C] = 10000;
  }
```

```
function transfer(address _to, uint256 _amount) public {
  coinBalance[msg.sender] -= _amount;
  coinBalance[_to] += _amount;
}
}
```

This code is rudimentary. Even if you don't know the Solidity language yet, you can see a hardcoded value in the constructor and a lack of input validation in the transfer function. You can improve the code in several ways. First of all, you can parameterize the constructor so the initial money supply doesn't get allocated to the address of an arbitrary test account, but to the address of the contract owner's account. Then you can introduce some checks in the transfer function to prevent incorrect transfers. Finally, you can set things up so that when tokens get transferred, an event can be raised, and then clients of the smart contract can be notified or react to it.

3.5.1 *Improving SimpleCoin's contract*

You'll improve both the constructor and the transfer function. You can start from the constructor.

PARAMETERIZING THE CONSTRUCTOR

Rewrite the constructor as follows:

```
constructor(uint256 _initialSupply) public {
  coinBalance[msg.sender] = _initialSupply;
}
```

You've already come across the special property msg.sender, whose value is the address of the message sender (or function caller). When it comes to the constructor, the message sender is the account that instantiates the contract, which consequently becomes its owner. As a result, when the constructor gets called, the amount of tokens specified in the _initialSupply parameter gets allocated to the contract owner.

MAKING TRANSFERS MORE ROBUST

Rewrite the transfer function as shown in the following listing.

Listing 3.2   A more robust transfer function with checks on the input

```
function transfer(address _to, uint256 _amount) {
  require(coinBalance[msg.sender] >= _amount);
  require(coinBalance[_to] + _amount >=
    coinBalance[_to]);
  coinBalance[msg.sender] -= _amount;
  coinBalance[_to] += _amount;
}
```

Checks that the sender account has an amount of coins equal to or larger than what you're trying to transfer

Checks that an arithmetic overflow hasn't been produced on the recipient's balance during the transfer operation. (This can happen if the balance, because of the amount received from the sender, becomes bigger than uint256.)

The `require` special function throws an exception if the condition isn't met. You can also throw the exception directly with the `throw` keyword, but this way of validating input is being deprecated. For example

```
require(coinBalance[msg.sender] > _amount);
```

could have been previously written as

```
if (coinBalance[msg.sender] < _amount) throw;
```

RAISING AN EVENT

A contract can declare one or more events that can be raised in any of its functions. A client that's monitoring the state of a contract can handle an event. For instance, you can declare an event that notifies that a transfer of SimpleCoin tokens has taken place:

```
event Transfer(address indexed from, address indexed to, uint256 value);
```

You'll raise this event at the bottom of the transfer function:

```
function transfer(address _to, uint256 _amount) {
    ...

    emit Transfer(msg.sender, _to, _amount);
}
```

3.5.2 *Trying out the amended code*

The amended `SimpleCoin` contract will now look like the following listing.

Listing 3.3 `SimpleCoin` **with parameterized constructor, input validation, and event**

```
pragma solidity ^0.4.0;

contract SimpleCoin {
    mapping (address => uint256) public coinBalance;

    event Transfer(address indexed from, address indexed to, uint256 value);

    constructor(uint256 _initialSupply) public {
        coinBalance[msg.sender] = _initialSupply;
    }

    function transfer(address _to, uint256 _amount) public {
        require(coinBalance[msg.sender] > _amount);
        require(coinBalance[_to] + _amount >= coinBalance[_to] );
        coinBalance[msg.sender] -= _amount;
        coinBalance[_to] += _amount;
        emit Transfer(msg.sender, _to, _amount);
    }
}
```

TRYING OUT THE AMENDED CONSTRUCTOR

Reopen Remix if you closed it, and copy the code in listing 3.3 into the editor. Then pick a test account address from the Transaction Origin drop-down list; for example, 0x4b0897b0513fdc7c541b6d9d7e929c4e5364d2db. This will be the account executing the constructor, and it'll consequently become the contract owner.

   Click the Run tab on the right panel. You can now enter the initial supply of SimpleCoin tokens next to the Deploy button, say 10,000, and then click Deploy. As usual, the coinBalance and transfer buttons will appear on the lower part of the screen, as in the previous chapter, as shown in the screenshot in figure 3.13.

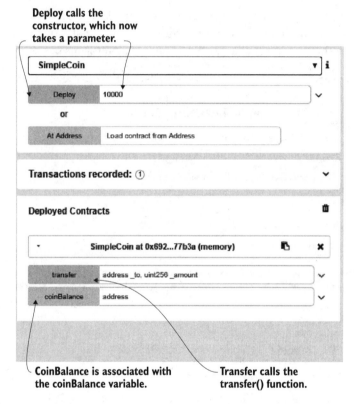

Figure 3.13   The Deploy operation now accepts the constructor input. After you instantiate the contract by clicking Deploy, the CoinBalance and Transfer buttons appear.

You can check the contract owner's address balance in the coinBalance mapping. As expected, you'll get 10,000. You can also double-check that the balances of the other addresses are zero, as shown in table 3.6.

Table 3.6 The balances of the SimpleCoin accounts

Account address	Account balance
0xca35b7d915458ef540ade6068dfe2f44e8fa733c	0
0x14723a09acff6d2a60dcdf7aa4aff308fddc160c	0
0x4b0897b0513fdc7c541b6d9d7e929c4e5364d2db	10,000
0x583031d1113ad414f02576bd6afabfb302140225	0
0xdd870fa1b7c4700f2bd7f44238821c26f7392148	0

TRYING OUT THE AMENDED TRANSFER FUNCTION

Try to transfer some SimpleCoin tokens from an account that doesn't have any; for example, 0x583031d1113ad414f02576bd6afabfb302140225. Select this address from the Transaction Origin drop-down list and enter the following comma-delimited value into the transfer text box:

```
"0xdd870fa1b7c4700f2bd7f44238821c26f7392148", 150
```

After clicking Transfer, you'll get the following error message, thanks to the `require` check you added earlier:

```
transact to browser/SimpleCoin.sol:SimpleCoin.transfer errored: VM error:
    invalid opcode.
  The constructor should be payable if you send value.
  The execution might have thrown.
  Debug the transaction to get more information.
```

Now try to transfer 150 tokens from the contract owner's account to the same recipient you just tried. You need to select the account starting with 0x4b0897b on the Transaction Origin drop-down list and reenter the following comma-delimited value into the transfer text box:

```
"0xdd870fa1b7c4700f2bd7f44238821c26f7392148", 150
```

The operation will now be successful, as you can see in the output on the left side of the screen shown in figure 3.14.

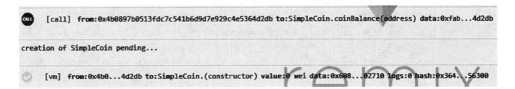

Figure 3.14 Output of successful transfer operation

If you click the arrow next to Debug, you can verify in the logs property that the Transfer event has been raised at the end of the function call:

```
[
  {
    "event": "Transfer",
    "args": [
      "0000000000000000000000004b0897b0513fdc7c541b6d9d7e929c4e5364d2db",
      "000000000000000000000000dd870fa1b7c4700f2bd7f44238821c26f7392148",
      "150"
    ]
  }
]
```

After rechecking all the balances, the results should match table 3.7.

Table 3.7   **The new balances of the SimpleCoin accounts**

Account address	Account balance
0xca35b7d915458ef540ade6068dfe2f44e8fa733c	0
0x14723a09acff6d2a60dcdf7aa4aff308fddc160c	0
0x4b0897b0513fdc7c541b6d9d7e929c4e5364d2db	9,850
0x583031d1113ad414f02576bd6afabfb302140225	0
0xdd870fa1b7c4700f2bd7f44238821c26f7392148	150

Congratulations! You've completed this exercise. The improvements you've made weren't particularly challenging, but making them should have helped you gain more familiarity with contracts.

3.5.3   *How does the coin transfer execute in the Ethereum network?*

You might have understood the Solidity code that performs the coin transfer but...if this transfer was taking place on a real Ethereum network rather than on the Remix JavaScript EVM emulator, would you know where within the network it would be executed? And would you know what effect a transfer of SimpleCoin tokens would have on the blockchain? You can get the answers to these questions by looking at the diagram in figure 3.15. I've adapted it for SimpleCoin from the transactional view you saw in figure 1.8 (chapter 1).

You'll see other transaction lifecycle diagrams similar to this for all Dapps I'll cover in the book. The lifecycle of an Ethereum transaction will be cemented in your head progressively throughout the book, until it becomes second nature to you.

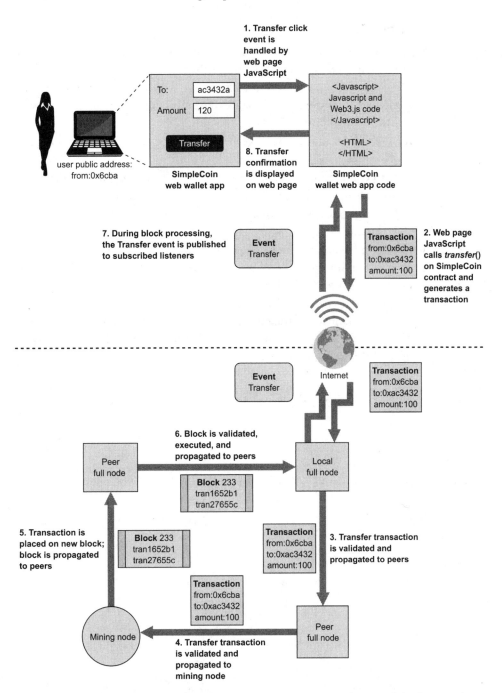

Figure 3.15 The lifecycle of a SimpleCoin transfer transaction. A transfer transaction is created when a SimpleCoin wallet invokes the `transfer()` function on the `SimpleCoin` smart contract on a local node of the Ethereum network. This is then validated and propagated throughout the network until it's included on a new blockchain block by a mining node. The new block is then propagated throughout the network, and finally it gets back to the local node.

Summary

- The Ethereum wallet is a GUI that allows you to interact with the platform by creating accounts and transferring Ether intuitively.
- The most popular Ethereum client is Go Ethereum, also known as geth. It comes with an interactive console that references Web3.js, a high-level interface to Ethereum clients.
- It's possible to interact with geth, for instance to create accounts, through various avenues:
  - geth commands executed in the operating system command shell
  - Web3.js instructions executed in the geth interactive console
  - HTTP JSON-RPC commands executed through cURL or a UI tool such as Postman
- Ethereum smart contracts, or just *contracts*, are written in a high-level language such as Solidity, compiled into EVM bytecode, deployed on the Ethereum network, and stored in the blockchain.
- It's possible to communicate with contracts using calls, transactions, and events. A transaction involves the consumption of computational and network resources, which is calculated in a unit called gas and settled in Ether, the cryptocurrency of the Ethereum platform.

Deploying your first smart contract

4

This chapter covers

- Deploying a contract onto the Ethereum network
- Interacting with the contract over the network
- Nodeless contract deployment and interaction with MetaMask

In the first two chapters, you started building SimpleCoin, your basic cryptocurrency. You did so in the Remix IDE and tried out its minimal functionality through its JavaScript-based EVM emulator. The experience was useful to help you understand from a conceptual point of view what a smart contract looks like and how to activate and interact with it. But SimpleCoin still looks like a bit of code running in an IDE. Now that you're becoming familiar with the Ethereum platform, you may be wondering, "Wouldn't it be nice to see SimpleCoin in action in a more realistic environment?" That's exactly what you'll be doing in this chapter.

You'll deploy the `SimpleCoin` contract onto the Ethereum network, and then you'll interact with it in a couple of ways. First, you'll go through the Ethereum wallet, which requires you to import a copy of the blockchain locally, and then you'll go through MetaMask, a third-party tool that allows you to connect to the Ethereum network without accessing an Ethereum client or the wallet.

4.1 *Deploying a contract onto the network*

You're probably used to deploying centralized applications on servers. If you've ever developed a web application, for example, you might have initially developed all the layers on your desktop computer. Then, after the application was mature enough for users or testers to test it, you deployed its components into the user acceptance testing (UAT) environment on one or more servers. A typical deployment for a web application might include

- One web server that hosts static and dynamic web pages
- One or more application servers that host the services the web pages use
- One or more database servers that persist the data that the services use

The deployment of a decentralized application is quite different. Even a simple decentralized application consisting of only one smart contract, like your SimpleCoin application, would get deployed across the entire Ethereum network. As you might recall from the development view I introduced in chapter 2, section 2.1.3., a smart contract gets deployed as a special transaction whose payload is compiled EVM bytecode. You submit the deployment transaction through a local node, which propagates it throughout the Ethereum network until it hits mining nodes. The smart contract only gets deployed after a mining node has successfully processed the deployment transaction containing the contract EVM bytecode to a new block that gets appended to the blockchain. That block is then replicated throughout the Ethereum network, as shown in figure 4.1.

You have two options for deploying contracts onto the network:

- Manually, through the Ethereum wallet
- Through terminal commands, on geth's interactive console

In this chapter, you'll deploy the SimpleCoin contract manually. By doing so, you'll go through the deployment process in a visual and intuitive way that will help you learn quickly.

Once you get used to deploying contracts through the Ethereum wallet, you'll be ready for the next step: command-based deployment. Though it may seem slightly intimidating at first, deploying contracts through geth's console is a useful exercise because it helps you understand the platform more thoroughly. You'll explore this in the next several chapters. For now, I'll quickly recap what you know:

- *The mechanisms to trigger deployment*—You know that you can deploy contracts manually through the Ethereum wallet or by using commands on geth's console. (You'll see these in action soon.)
- *What happens during deployment*—The contract's bytecode gets stored on the blockchain following the execution of its deployment transaction.

But what exactly is the Ethereum network? I'll answer that question in the next section.

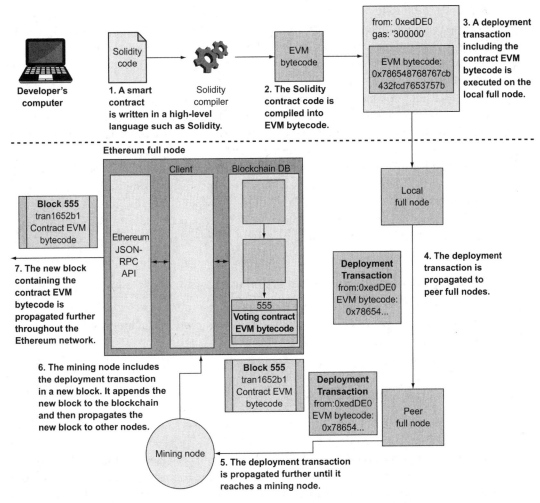

Figure 4.1 A contract written in a high-level language such as Solidity is compiled into EVM bytecode and deployed to the network through a deployment transaction containing the contract EVM bytecode, which is executed through a local full node of the network. The deployment transaction is propagated throughout the network; then it's processed by a mining node and included in a new block that gets replicated throughout the network. It's like any other transaction, except that what's being stored on the blockchain isn't Ether or data but EVM bytecode.

4.1.1 Ethereum public networks

When you connected to Ethereum in the previous chapter, you might not have noticed that you connected to two different networks:

- From the Ethereum wallet, you connected to *Ropsten*, a public test network.
- From geth, you connected to *Mainnet*, the public production network.

Ropsten is the public test network that Ethereum provides for mining based on proof of work (PoW), which is the current algorithm used in the public production network. If you followed the instructions I gave you, your Ethereum wallet is already pointing to the Ropsten network, and you only have fake Ether in your accounts, which you generated through CPU mining.

If you left your geth client running from the previous chapter, it's pointing to *Mainnet*, the production network. Ether moved between accounts in this network is real. You should use this network only to perform transactions against production Dapps; you should avoid it during development.

Another public test network called *Kovan* is available, and it supports mining performed with a new algorithm called Proof of Authority. So far, this has only been implemented in the Parity client, so it's outside the scope of this book.

In the next section, you'll deploy the `SimpleCoin` contract to Ropsten through the wallet. As a result, you don't need to make any environmental configuration changes yet.

4.1.2 *Deploying SimpleCoin with the Ethereum wallet*

Start up the Ethereum wallet—make sure the sync mode is Fast or Full and wait until it's fully synchronized—and open the Contracts screen by clicking Contracts on the top bar, near the top-right corner. You'll see two main options:

- *Deploy New Contract*—You can deploy a new contract by supplying its Solidity code.
- *Watch Contract*—You can reference a contract that already has been deployed so you can interact with it.

Click Deploy New Contract. When the Deploy Contract screen opens, you can decide which account will become the contract owner. Choose Account 1, and then click the Solidity Contract Source Code tab at the bottom of the screen and paste the Simple-Coin code from the end of chapter 3, as shown in the following listing. (Make sure the constructor and functions are declared as *public* to be compiled in the wallet; I'll explain function access modifiers such as public in chapter 5.)

Listing 4.1   Latest version of `SimpleCoin` (from chapter 3)

```solidity
pragma solidity ^0.4.0;

contract SimpleCoin {
    mapping (address => uint256) public coinBalance;

    event Transfer(address indexed from, address indexed to, uint256 value);

    constructor(uint256 _initialSupply) public {
        coinBalance[msg.sender] = _initialSupply;
    }

    function transfer(address _to, uint256 _amount) public {
        require(coinBalance[msg.sender] > _amount);
```

```
require(coinBalance[_to] + _amount >= coinBalance[_to] );
coinBalance[msg.sender] -= _amount;
coinBalance[_to] += _amount;
emit Transfer(msg.sender, _to, _amount);
    }
}
```

Once you've pasted the code, the wallet will compile it into EVM bytecode, and a drop-down list will appear on the right-hand side. Pick Simple Coin from the list and enter 10000 as the constructor parameter. Finally, click Deploy at the bottom of the screen, as shown in figure 4.2.

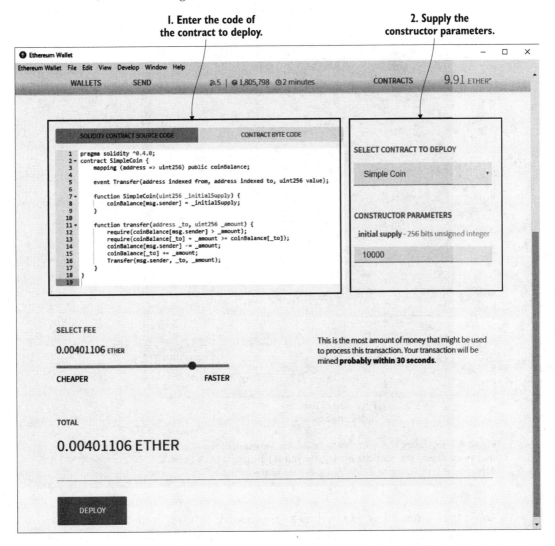

Figure 4.2 After you enter the Solidity code of a contract, the wallet compiles it into EVM bytecode. Supply the contract parameters, click Deploy, and a new dialog box will confirm the deployment transaction.

A new dialog box will appear, as shown in figure 4.3. You'll be asked to enter the password and to send the deployment transaction. Remember: you need Ether in your account to be able to submit the transaction! Once you send the deployment transaction, you can check its status in the Latest Transactions section of the wallet main screen. There you can see that the deployment transaction is treated like any other transaction.

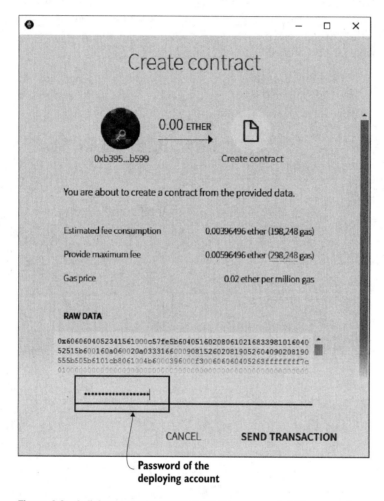

Figure 4.3 A dialog box asks you to enter the password of the account that you'll deploy the contract from. After you supply it and click Send, a deployment transaction is generated and sent to the network.

Once the contract has received all the necessary network confirmations, which you can view in the Latest Transactions panel (see figure 4.4), go back to the Contracts screen. You'll see Simple Coin with a balance of zero Ether (figure 4.5).

You can monitor deployment transaction confirmations in the Latest Transactions panel.

LATEST TRANSACTIONS

Filter transactions

Jun 18	**Created contract** Main account (Etherbase) → 🗋 Created contract at ● : Simple Coin 724a	5 of 12 Confirmations
Jun 17	**Transfer between accounts** Main account (Etherbase) → ● Account 2	15 hours ago

Figure 4.4 After a contract transaction has been submitted to the network, you can monitor its network confirmations in the Latest Transactions panel of the Contracts screen.

Contracts

+ **DEPLOY NEW CONTRACT**

CUSTOM CONTRACTS

To watch and interact with a contract already deployed on the blockchain, you need

● 🗋 : SIMPLE COIN 724A
0.00 ether
0x724A0e1c468aDd5BD03980553352b2F7e1AA058E

After the contract receives all confirmations, the deployed contract appears in the Contracts screen.

Figure 4.5 After the contract receives 12 confirmations, which makes it very likely the deployment transaction is permanently stored on the blockchain, a deployed contract appears in the Contracts panel.

> **DEFINITION**   *Transaction confirmations* indicate the depth of the transaction in the blockchain. A new confirmation is received as soon as a new block is appended to the blockchain after the block containing the transaction in question. The probability of a block reversal decreases exponentially as the number of confirmations increase, so a transaction is considered consolidated after 12 confirmations. (That means 12 blocks have been added to the blockchain after the block containing the transaction.)

Congratulations! You've deployed your first contract on the Ethereum network. Now you can interact with the contract, much as you did earlier with Remix. You can start by moving SimpleCoin tokens between accounts and verifying the expected balances.

4.2   *Interacting with the contract*

Before starting to move SimpleCoin tokens, go back to the wallet's main screen and add two more accounts. (Remember to take note of the related passwords.) These extra accounts will become handy when testing contract operations. I recommend you copy all the account addresses you have in your wallet to a temporary text file. Table 4.1 shows what it would contain in my case.

Table 4.1   Ethereum wallet account addresses

Account name	Account address
Main account	0xedDE06bC0e45645e2f105972BDefC220ED37Ae10
Account 2	0x4e6C30154768b6bc3Da693b1B28C6bd14302b578
Account 3	0x70e36bE8AB8f6Cf66C0C953cF9c63aB63f3FeF02
Account 4	0xc99048E9B98D3FcF8b5f0D5644794B562f9A2ea4

> **TIP**   To copy an address, select it, and then click Copy Address. Alternatively, you can use the usual Ctrl+C shortcut. Either way, the wallet will ask you to confirm you want to go ahead with this operation. (There is risk that malware may replace the address.)

Now go back to the Contracts screen and click SimpleCoin. At the top of the screen, just below the name of the contract, you'll see the contract address, which is the account address of the contract in the blockchain. You'll notice that the area associated with the `SimpleCoin` contract is logically divided into two parts: Read from Contract on the left and Write on Contract on the right. This arrangement is similar to the color codes you saw in Remix for read-only functionality (blue) and write functionality (red).

4.2.1 Checking coin balances

You can first check the coin balance of all accounts by entering the address of each account next to the coin balance textbox. The expected balances are shown in table 4.2.

Table 4.2 Expected account balances

Account address	Account balance
0xedDE06bC0e45645e2f105972BDefC220ED37Ae10	10,000
0x4e6C30154768b6bc3Da693b1B28C6bd14302b578	0
0x70e36bE8AB8f6Cf66C0C953cF9c63aB63f3FeF02	0
0xc99048E9B98D3FcF8b5f0D5644794B562f9A2ea4	0

What happens if you try to check the balance of an invalid address? For example, replace the last digit of the main account (starting with 0xedDE06bC) with an 8 and try to check the coin balance. You won't be allowed to enter such an address because the wallet will consider its checksum invalid. But you will be allowed to enter any valid Ethereum address, even if it's not associated with your accounts. (You can grab some to try from https://etherscan.io/.)

4.2.2 Transferring coins

Now you can move some coins around. You can start with a transfer of 150 Simple-Coins from the Main Account to Account 3. This is the same operation you performed on Remix in the previous chapter. Pick Transfer from the Select Function drop-down in the Write to Contract panel. All the input fields required for the coin transfer will appear, as in figure 4.6.

Pick the Main Account from the Execute From list, then set the address of Account 3 in the To field and an amount of 150. After you click Execute, you'll be asked to enter the password of the Main account to digitally sign the transaction.

If you select the Watch Contract Events box in the Latest Events pane, you'll soon see the details of the transaction you've sent. At this point, you can recheck the balances of all addresses. The expected balances are shown in table 4.3.

Table 4.3 Expected updated account balances

Account address	Account balance
0xedDE06bC0e45645e2f105972BDefC220ED37Ae10	9,850
0x4e6C30154768b6bc3Da693b1B28C6bd14302b578	0
0x70e36bE8AB8f6Cf66C0C953cF9c63aB63f3FeF02	150
0xc99048E9B98D3FcF8b5f0D5644794B562f9A2ea4	0

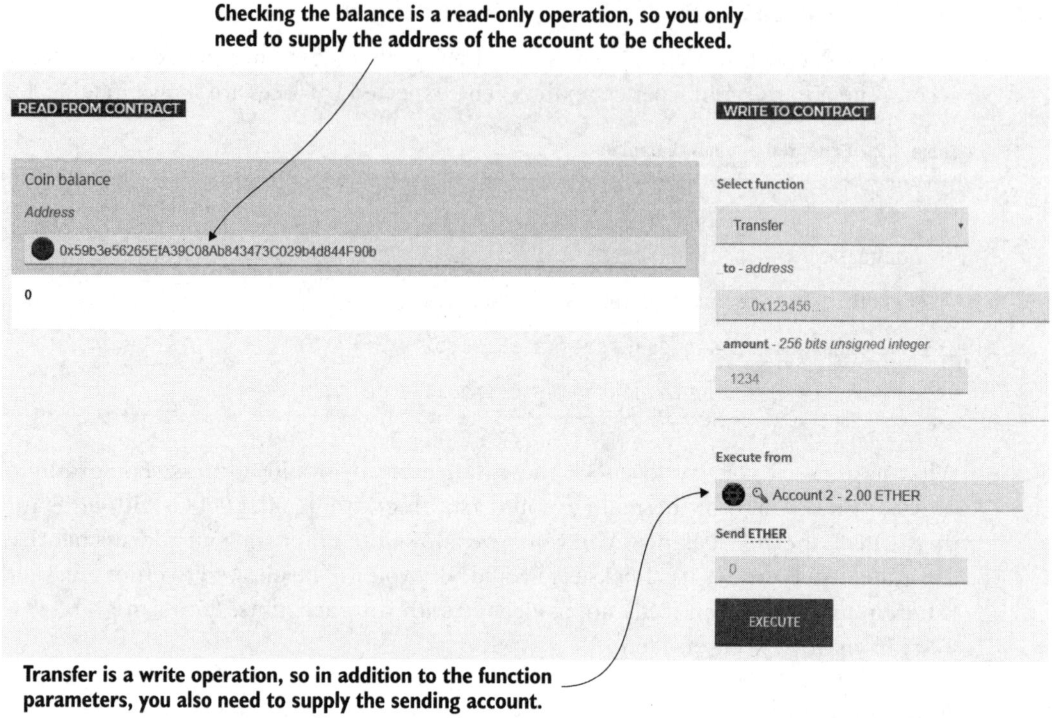

Checking the balance is a read-only operation, so you only need to supply the address of the account to be checked.

Transfer is a write operation, so in addition to the function parameters, you also need to supply the sending account.

Figure 4.6   Checking the SimpleCoin balance is a read-only operation, so you only need to specify the input address. Transferring coins is a write operation. As seen here, you have to specify the number of coins to be transferred, the destination address, and the sending account.

Now try to move 50 coins from Account 3 to Account 2 and recheck the balances after the transaction has appeared in the Latest Events panel. You'll notice that the only accounts listed in the Execute From drop-down list are the Main Account and Account 2. This is because the wallet doesn't allow you to execute a transaction from an account with no Ether in it.

As you saw in chapter 2, the executing account must pay a transaction fee calculated in gas but settled in Ether to perform a transaction. For Accounts 3 and 4 to be useful, you must send some Ether to them from the Main Account. You can perform this Ether transfer from the Send screen, as you did in the previous chapter when you set up Account 2. As usual, you can monitor the Ether transfer transactions on the Latest Transactions panel and wait for them to complete. Once all accounts own some Ether, you're ready to perform a transaction.

Go back to the `SimpleCoin` contract screen and pick the transfer function again. The Execute From drop-down list will now show all the accounts, so you can pick Account 3. Enter the address of Account 2 in the To textbox and 50 in the Amount field. When you click Execute, you'll be asked for the password for Account 3, the sending account. After the transaction has been confirmed, recheck the balances. The new expected balances are shown in table 4.4.

Table 4.4   Updated account balances after second transfer

Account address	Account balance
0xedDE06bC0e45645e2f105972BDefC220ED37Ae10	9,850
0x4e6C30154768b6bc3Da693b1B28C6bd14302b578	50
0x70e36bE8AB8f6Cf66C0C953cF9c63aB63f3FeF02	100
0xc99048E9B98D3FcF8b5f0D5644794B562f9A2ea4	0

TRYING TO TRANSFER UNAVAILABLE COINS

As you'll remember, the code of the SimpleCoin `transfer` function performs some checks before modifying the balances of the sender and recipient addresses. It prevents an account from attempting to transfer unavailable coins by throwing an error. You can see what happens if you try to do so through the wallet. For example, try to move 200 coins from Account 4 to Account 3. As expected, you'll get an error message indicating the transaction will fail, as shown in figure 4.7.

You might be surprised that the error message is thrown before the transaction has even been sent out. This happens because the wallet verifies transactions locally, before sending, as any node would do. If an error is returned, the wallet doesn't propagate the transaction to the network, and you receive an error message immediately.

Well done! You've fully, manually, tested `SimpleCoin` on the public test network.

So far, this chapter has given you an idea of how to deploy a smart contract to a public network without having to run a full Ethereum node. You performed it through the Ethereum wallet, which, under the hood, still connects to a fully synchronized copy of the blockchain. But you might be wondering whether you can achieve the same thing without having a local synchronized copy of the blockchain. The answer is yes. As we'll explore in the next section, you can connect to a set of publicly accessible nodes exposed by a Chrome plugin called Metamask.

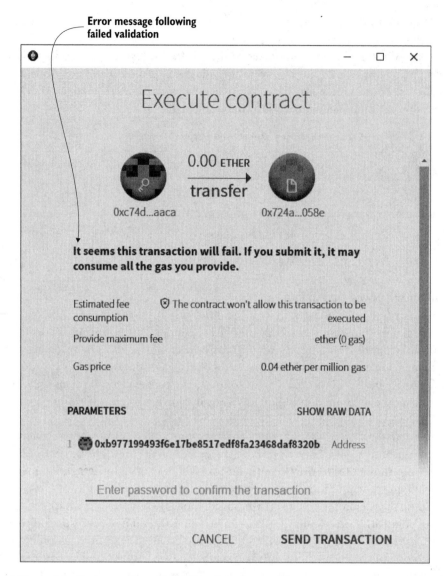

Figure 4.7   If a transaction generated from a write operation, such as
`SimpleCoin.transfer()`, **fails validation checks, it can't be sent to the network.**

4.3   *Nodeless deployment through MetaMask*

MetaMask is a Chrome extension that connects you to an external set of Ethereum
nodes, as you can see in figure 4.8. It allows you to deploy a contract to a public network and interact with it without having to install and maintain any Ethereum software. As an alternative, if you don't want to use Chrome, you can download the Brave
browser and install MetaMask as an extension. MetaMask is especially handy if you

don't develop smart contracts continuously and don't want the inconvenience of having to update the wallet or Go Ethereum client and resynchronize the blockchain every time you resume your development.

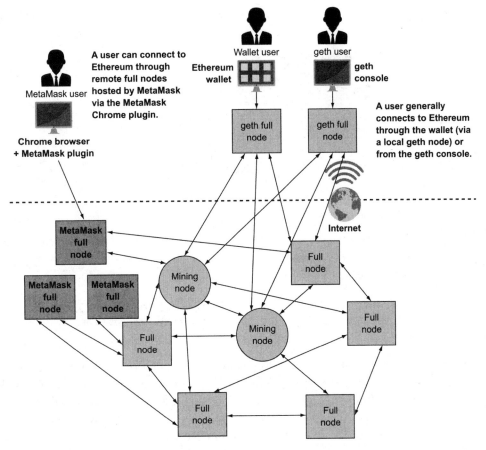

Figure 4.8   When connecting to Ethereum through the Ethereum wallet or the Go Ethereum client console, you do so through a local node. When connecting to Ethereum through Metamask, you do so through a remote node.

In the next section, you'll install MetaMask. Then you'll redeploy SimpleCoin to Ropsten through MetaMask and interact with it, completely bypassing your local geth client and Ethereum wallet.

4.3.1   Installing MetaMask

You can install the MetaMask chrome extension from this url: http://mng.bz/8JzB. After adding the extension, you should see the MetaMask icon next to the browser address bar.

You can now start to set up a MetaMask wallet by clicking on the MetaMask icon. You'll be invited to accept a privacy notice and terms and conditions (at your own risk). Then you'll be asked to create a new password, as shown in figure 4.9.

Figure 4.9   Creation of a password to secure the MetaMask wallet

Enter your new (possibly secure) password and click Create. You'll be advised to copy and securely store the system-generated 12-word recovery passphrase. The wallet will be created after you confirm you've done so, and at that point you'll see on the top left, next to the MetaMask icon, the name of the network you're connected to. Initially, you're connected to Main Ethereum Network, as shown in figure 4.10.

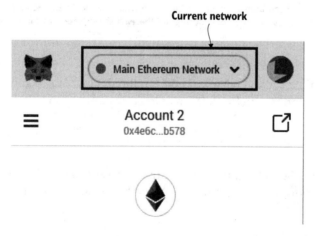

Figure 4.10   MetaMask initially points to Main Ethereum Network.

Given that you'll deploy `SimpleCoin` onto a test network, change your current network by clicking Main Ethereum Network and selecting the Ropsten Test Network from the drop-down list, as shown in figure 4.11.

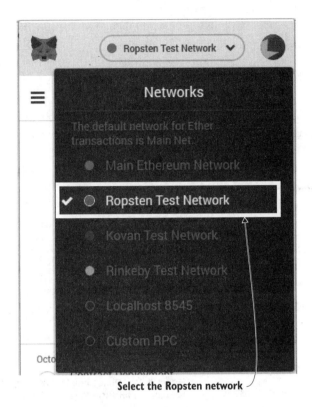

Select the Ropsten network

Figure 4.11 It's possible to connect to various Ethereum networks through MetaMask.

You'll notice the default account has nothing to do with any of the accounts you have in your Ropsten Ethereum wallet. And this default test account hasn't got any Ether, so you won't be able to do much with it. To import some of your existing Ropsten accounts, which already contain Ether, click the menu icon on the top right, and then select Import. In the Import dialog box, you'll see a Select Type drop-down list. Select JSON File, as shown in figure 4.12.

Now you have to supply the JSON file containing the private key of your existing Ropsten account. Remember, the key pairs of your Ropsten account are held in the testnet keystore, which, depending on your OS, you can find in one of the locations shown in table 4.5.

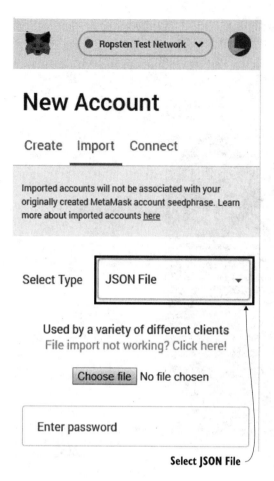

Figure 4.12   Dialog box for importing accounts from JSON files

Select JSON File

Table 4.5   Testnet keystore locations

System	Keystore path
Windows	`C:\Users\username\%appdata%\Roaming\Ethereum\testnet\keystore`
Linux	`~/.ethereum/testnet/keystore`
Mac	`~/Library/Ethereum/testnet/keystore`

The testnet keystore folder should contain a list of files whose names contain the timestamp and the account address they refer to:

- `UTC--2017-06-24T08-49-46.377533700Z--`
  `edde06bc0e45645e2f105972bdefc220ed37ae10`

- UTC--2017-06-24T13-26-18.696630000Z--4e6c30154768b6bc3-da693b1b28c6bd14302b578
- UTC--2017-06-24T18-21-36.890638200Z--70e36be8ab8f6cf66c0c953cf9c63ab63f3fef02
- UTC--2017-06-24T18-21-47.794428600Z--c99048e9b98d3f-cf8b5f0d5644794b562f9a2ea4

Although the file extension isn't present, these are JSON files. For example, the second file on the list refers to account 4e6c30154768b6bc3da693b1b28c6bd14302b578. If you open the file with a text editor, such as Notepad in Windows, you should see JSON content similar to this:

{"address":"4e6c30154768b6bc3da693b1b28c6bd14302b578","crypto":{"cipher":"aes
-128-ctr","ciphertext":"bc7569458b99dcbbdcb0cf46402eeb83875baa6302d27e887a6d4
e2d6e31771f","cipherparams":{"iv":"f0838a98d39d532e8d96e9f7cc799712"},"kdf":"
scrypt","kdfparams":{"dklen":32,"n":262144,"p":1,"r":8,"salt":"fb2dbd4f24553c
585025417b691ef11784cf6ae90aa412b73e4965ba3d4f2772"},"mac":"36ba647b1d2ff7a3d
8ca6b32731593caee920dcc19d14e91915cb98a7a244c2c"},"id":"32bb1449-60f5-4cd0-
a4d2-4608fa9fc1c3","version":3}

In the MetaMask Import Account dialog box, click Choose File, navigate to your testnet keystore, and then pick the file related to the account you want to import. You must supply the password you entered when creating this account, and then click Import. After a few seconds, you should see the details of the account you've imported, including the Ether contained in it, as shown in figure 4.13. Once you've imported a couple of your existing Ropsten accounts, you can proceed to the deployment of SimpleCoin.

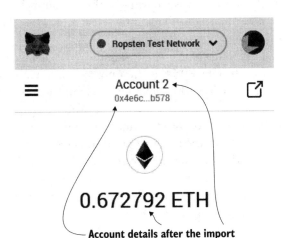

Figure 4.13 After you import an account from the keystore, all its details appear on MetaMask.

4.3.2   *Deploying SimpleCoin through MetaMask*

To deploy SimpleCoin, first open Remix and enter the latest version of SimpleCoin, the same one you entered into the wallet, shown earlier in listing 4.1. Now pick the Injected Web3 option in the Environment drop-down list in the Run tab of the right-hand side panel, as shown in figure 4.14.

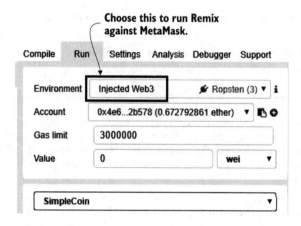

Figure 4.14   The screenshot shows how you can configure Remix to use external MetaMask nodes (rather than the local JavaScript Virtual Machine emulator) by selecting Injected Web3 in the Environment drop-down list.

Remix will detect MetaMask, and it'll use one of the MetaMask nodes rather than the local JavaScript EVM emulator. If no account is showing in the Account drop-down list, refresh the Remix webpage and the account currently selected in MetaMask will be selected.

You can trigger SimpleCoin's deployment by clicking the red Deploy button. Account 2, whose address starts with 0x4e6c30154, is the only option available and is currently selected in the Account drop-down list box. That account will deploy the contract.

After you click Deploy, you'll see a dialog box summarizing information on the executing account and transaction costs for the deployment transaction. You'll also be asked to confirm you want to go ahead with it, as you can see in figure 4.15.

Figure 4.15 After configuring Remix to point to external Metamask nodes and starting the deployment of a contract (such as `SimpleCoin`), you get a (deployment) transaction confirmation dialog box from Metamask. This shows information on the account executing the deployment transaction and on transaction costs. The dialog box also asks the user to confirm whether to go ahead with the deployment of the contract.

Confirm you want to go ahead with the deployment transaction.

After clicking Confirm, you can check the transaction status in the bottom area of the Metamask wallet. The status will move from Submitted to Confirmed, as shown in figure 4.16.

If you click the label Transaction Number while the contract is in status Submitted, and then after it has moved to Confirmed, you'll see the transaction details from the Etherscan website, as shown in figure 4.17. As you can see, Etherscan also shows the destination address (starting with 0x0c9189e4d6) of the contract.

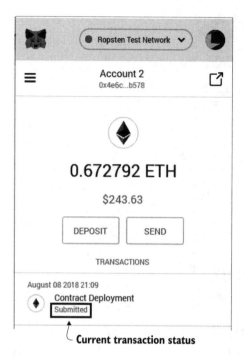

Figure 4.16   It's possible to monitor the status of the deployment transaction in the bottom area of the Metamask wallet. This will change from Submitted to Confirmed.

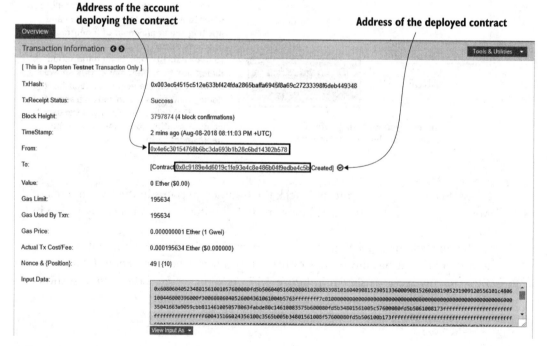

Figure 4.17   Transaction details from the Etherscan website, invoked when clicking the (Submitted or Confirmed) status on the MetaMask wallet

If you move back to Remix, you'll see some deployment details below the Deploy button, including the deployment address, which is the same one you saw on the Etherscan page. You can grab the address by clicking the Copy Address link, as shown in figure 4.18.

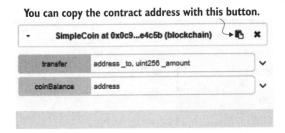

Figure 4.18 After the completion of the deployment transaction, the contract address is shown in Remix, below the Deploy button.

Well done! You've redeployed `SimpleCoin` on Ropsten through MetaMask. Now you can see how you can interact with it through MetaMask.

4.3.3 Interacting with SimpleCoin through MetaMask

Figure 4.18 also shows that after deploying `SimpleCoin`, Remix displays two buttons: CoinBalance and Transfer. These are exactly the same buttons that appeared when you created the contract for the first time on the JavaScript VM, back in chapter 1. This time, though, you'll be interacting with a contract instantiated on a real network.

The first operation you can perform is to check the token balance of Account 2, the account that deployed the contract. Enter "0x4e6c30154768b6bc3da693b1b28-c6bd14302b578" (remember, as usual, to surround the address with double quotes) and click CoinBalance. You'll immediately get 10,000, as expected. As with checking balances through the Ethereum wallet, this operation is read-only and doesn't produce a transaction. Consequently, you don't need to authorize it.

Now move 250 tokens from Account 2 to Account 3. Enter this into the Transfer text box:

```
"0x70e36bE8AB8f6Cf66C0C953cF9c63aB63f3FeF02", 250
```

Click Transfer. This is a write operation, so the MetaMask transaction confirmation dialog box pops up, as shown in figure 4.19. You can authorize it from Account 2. Click Confirm and follow the transaction status in the MetaMask dialog box.

If you click on the transaction number icon, you'll see the transaction details in Etherscan. You can now go back to Remix and check the transaction details there as well.

Figure 4.19   To transfer SimpleCoin tokens, which is a contract-state write operation, the sending account needs to be authorized. Subsequently, the MetaMask transaction confirmation dialog box is shown to get user confirmation.

Confirm the transaction with this button.

Both Etherscan and Remix confirm that the move of 250 SimpleCoin tokens from Account 2 to Account 3 has been successful, but you can double-check the new balances of these accounts with the coinBalance function, which should match those in table 4.6.

Table 4.6   Account balances after transferring 250 tokens

Account address	Account balance
0x4e6C30154768b6bc3Da693b1B28C6bd14302b578	9,750
0x70e36bE8AB8f6Cf66C0C953cF9c63aB63f3FeF02	250

I'll stop here, but I'd encourage you to generate some error messages, for example by trying to move unavailable coins, as you did previously with the Ethereum wallet. Doing so will allow you to confirm whether the contract also works correctly on MetaMask.

Summary

- You can deploy a contract onto the Ethereum network and interact with it using the Ethereum wallet.
- The Ethereum wallet communicates with Ethereum through a local geth instance.
- You can deploy a contract onto the Ethereum network and interact with it using MetaMask.

Part 2

Part 2 is all about smart contracts. This innovative technology has allowed Ethereum to move from single-purpose blockchains, supporting only cryptocurrencies, to multipurpose blockchains you can use to develop any decentralized application.

Chapter 5 introduces Solidity, the most popular language for writing smart contracts on the Ethereum Virtual Machine. Chapter 6 describes the structure of a typical smart contract through a sample crowdsale. This includes a constructor, state variables, functions, and events. Toward the end of this chapter, you'll learn to generalize contract functionality through inheritance. Chapter 7 focuses on more advanced object-oriented features, such as abstract contracts and interfaces, which I introduce progressively so you can improve and extend the initial crowdsale application and make it more maintainable. This chapter also presents libraries, which provide another way to make contracts more maintainable. Chapter 8 explains how to deploy a smart contract to a public test network and interact with it through Web3, an Ethereum communication library; the Go Ethereum console; Node.js; and a web user interface. It also explains how to perform the same operations on a private network and on a mock network client, such as Ganache.

5

Programming smart contracts in Solidity

This chapter covers

- Understanding EVM languages
- Understanding the structure of a contract
- Learning core Solidity syntax

Thanks to SimpleCoin, the basic cryptocurrency you've been building, you've learned the basics of Solidity through example. By now, you know Solidity is a high-level EVM language that allows you to write contracts. You also know a smart contract (or, simply, contract) is equivalent to a class in other languages and contains state variables, a constructor, functions, and events. In this chapter, you'll learn Solidity's main language constructs in a more structured way and develop a progressively deeper understanding of the language.

This chapter lays the foundation for the next chapter, where you'll learn how to implement complex contracts and multicontract Dapps in Solidity. By the end of this chapter, you'll be able to improve and extend SimpleCoin's functionality with the knowledge you've acquired.

5.1 *EVM contract languages*

Before diving into Solidity, let's take a little step back and explore briefly some alternative EVM languages. Solidity isn't the only EVM high-level language for writing contracts. Although it's the most popular option among Ethereum developers, mainly because it's frequently upgraded, well maintained, and recommended in the official Ethereum documentation, other alternatives exist, namely LLL, Serpent, and Viper. Let's see what these languages look like and when it would make sense to use them instead of Solidity.

5.1.1 *LLL*

LLL, whose acronym stands for lovely little language, is a Lisp-like language (which LLL also stands for) that provides low-level functions close to the EVM opcodes and simple control structures (such as for, if, and so on). These functions allow you to write low-level contract code without having to resort to handwriting EVM assembly. If you've ever seen Lisp code or you're familiar with Clojure, you'll recognize the distinctive prefix notation and heavy parentheses used in the following LLL listing:

```
                              Instructs the LLL compiler          Declares a variable named
                              to evaluate expressions             value at memory location 0x00
                              below this line in order
(seq       ◁──┘
   (def 'value 0x00)
   (def 'dummy 0xbc23ecab)  ◁──            Declares a function called dummy
   (returnlll                              at memory location 0xbc23ecab
      (function dummy     ◁──┐
         (seq              ◁─┤  Defines a macro in the LLL compiler
            (mstore value(calldataload 0))  ◁──  to return the code below it
            (return value 32)))))  ◁──        Reads the location 0 of the
                                              data passed in when calling the
                          Returns 32 bytes from    function (call data) and stores
                          the variable value       it in a variable named value
```

Starts defining the function 'dummy'

This is roughly equivalent to the following Solidity code:

```
contract Dummy {
    function dummy(bytes32 _value) returns (bytes32) {
        return _value;
    }
}
```

> **WARNING** Strictly speaking, these two pieces of code aren't entirely equivalent because the LLL code doesn't check the function signature or prevent Ether transfer, among other things.

LLL was the first EVM language that the Ethereum core team provided because, given the similarity between how the stack-based Lisp language and the EVM work, it allowed them to deliver it more quickly than any other language. Currently, the main benefit of using LLL would be to get a more compact bytecode, which might be cheaper to run.

After the first public release of the platform, the focus shifted to higher-level languages that would provide a simpler syntax to contract developers. Serpent was the first to be developed.

5.1.2 *Serpent and Viper*

Serpent is a Python-like language that was popular for a few months after its release. It was praised for its minimalistic philosophy and for offering the efficiency of a low-level language through simple syntax.

If you're familiar with Python, these are the main limitations you'll find in Serpent:

- It doesn't provide list comprehensions (elegant syntax to create lists from existing sequences and lists) and complex data structures.
- It doesn't support first-class functions, therefore limiting your ability to use a functional programming style.

The following listing shows how `SimpleCoin` would look in Serpent:

```
def init():
    self.storage[msg.sender] = 10000

def balance_query(address):
    return(self.storage[address])

def transfer(to, amount):
    if self.storage[msg.sender] >= amount:
        self.storage[msg.sender] -= amount
        self.storage[to] += amount
```

Even if you don't know Python, you should be able to understand this code. The only variable you might be confused about is `self.storage`. This is a dictionary containing the contract state. It holds the equivalent of all the state variables in Solidity.

> **NOTE** A `dict` (or dictionary) is the Python implementation of a hash map (or hash table).

Serpent's popularity began to fade when the focus shifted to Solidity, which programmers started to maintain more regularly. A new experimental Python-like language, called Viper, is currently being researched and is publicly available on GitHub. Its aim is to provide a more extended type set than that offered by Serpent and easier bound and overflow checking on arithmetic operations and arrays. It will also allow you to write first-class functions, although with some limitations, and therefore write more functional code. The main benefit of using Viper is to get more compact and safer bytecode than you'd get from compiling Solidity.

Now that you have a better understanding of EVM languages, let's move back to Solidity. Open up Remix and enjoy the tour.

5.2   *High-level contract structure*

Before diving into the various aspects of Solidity, I'll present the high-level structure of a contract so you can appreciate the purpose of each language feature. This will also give you some context you can refer back to.

5.2.1   *Contract declarations*

The contract definition for `AuthorizedToken`, an example token similar to Simple-Coin, shown in the next listing, summarizes all the possible declarations that can appear on a contract. Don't worry if you don't fully understand this code: the point of this listing is to give you an idea of what all contract constructs look like.

Listing 5.1   High-level contract structure

```solidity
pragma solidity ^0.4.24;
contract AuthorizedToken {

    enum UserType {TokenHolder, Admin, Owner}          ⟵┐ Enum
                                                          definition

    struct AccountInfo {          ⟵┐ Struct
      address account;              │ definition
      string firstName;
      string lastName;
      UserType userType;
    }

    mapping (address => uint256)
      public tokenBalance;                    ⟵┐
    mapping (address => AccountInfo)           │
      public registeredAccount;               ⟵┤ State
    mapping (address => bool)                  │ variable
      public frozenAccount;                   ⟵┤ definitions
                                               │
    address public owner;                     ⟵┘

    uint256 public constant maxTranferLimit = 15000;

    event Transfer(address indexed from,
       address indexed to, uint256 value);     ⟵┐ Event
    event FrozenAccount(address target,         │ definitions
       bool frozen);                           ⟵┘

    modifier onlyOwner {               ⟵┐ Function
      require(msg.sender == owner);      │ modifier
      _;                                 │ definition
    }

    constructor(uint256 _initialSupply) public {    ⟵┐ Constructor
      owner = msg.sender;                             │ definition

      mintToken(owner, _initialSupply);
    }
```

Function definitions

```
    function transfer(address _to, uint256 _amount)
      public {  //#G
      require(checkLimit(_amount));
      //...
      emit Transfer(msg.sender, _to, _amount);
    }

    function registerAccount(address account,
      string firstName,
      string lastName, bool isAdmin) public onlyOwner {
      //...
    }

  function checkLimit(uint256 _amount) private
      returns (bool) {
      if (_amount < maxTranferLimit)
          return true;
      return false;
    }

    function validateAccount(address _account)
      internal
      returns (bool) {
      if (frozenAccount[_account] && tokenBalance[_account] > 0)
          return true;
      return false;
    }
```

Functions defined with modifiers

```
    function mintToken(address _recipient,
      uint256  _mintedAmount)
      onlyOwner public  {
      tokenBalance[_recipient] += _mintedAmount;
      emit Transfer(owner, _recipient, _mintedAmount);
      }

    function freezeAccount(address target,
      bool freeze)
      onlyOwner public  {
      frozenAccount[target] = freeze;
      emit FrozenAccount(target, freeze);
    }
}
```

In summary, these are the possible items you can declare:

- State variables
- Events
- Enums
- Struct types
- Functions
- Function modifiers

Let's go quickly through each of them. After we complete a high-level contract overview, we'll delve into each language feature.

STATE VARIABLES

State variables hold the contract state. You can declare them with any of the types that the language supports. Some types, such as mapping, are only allowed for state variables. The declaration of a state variable also includes, explicitly or implicitly, its access level.

EVENTS

An event is a contract member that interacts with the EVM transaction log and whose invocation is then propagated to clients subscribed to it, often triggering related call-backs. An event declaration looks more similar to a declaration of Java or C# events than a declaration of JavaScript events.

ENUMS

An enum defines a custom type with a specified set of allowed values. An enum declaration is similar to that of Java and C# enums.

STRUCT TYPES

A struct defines a custom type that includes a set of variables, each in general of a different type. A struct declaration is similar to that of a C struct.

FUNCTIONS

Functions encapsulate the logic of a contract, are altered by modifiers, have access to state variables, and can raise the events declared on the contract.

FUNCTION MODIFIERS

A function modifier allows you to modify the behavior of a function, typically to restrict its applicability to only certain input, in a declarative way. A contract might declare many modifiers that you might use on several functions.

5.3 *Solidity language essentials*

During this initial tour of Solidity, you'll get a firm foundation in the language by learning about most of its syntax and constructs:

- Data types
- The global namespace
- State variables
- Functions
- Function modifiers
- Variable declaration, initialization, and assignment
- Events
- Conditional statements

You'll explore more advanced object-oriented features and concepts in the next chapter.

Like most statically typed languages, Solidity requires you to explicitly declare the type of each variable, or at least needs the type to be inferred unequivocally by the compiler. Its data type system includes both value types and reference types, which I'll present in the next few sections.

5.3.1 Value types

A *value type* variable is stored on the EVM stack, which allocates a single memory space to hold its value. When a value type variable is assigned to another variable or passed to a function as a parameter, its value is copied into a new and separate instance of the variable. Consequently, any change in the value of the assigned variable doesn't affect the value of the original variable. Value types include most native types, enums, and functions.

BOOL

Variables declared as `bool` can have either a `true` or `false` value; for example

```
bool isComplete = false;
```

> **NOTE** Logical expressions must resolve to true or false, so trying to use integer values of 0 and 1 for false and true, as in JavaScript, C, or C++, isn't allowed in Solidity.

INTEGER TYPES

You can declare integer variables either as `int` (signed) or `uint` (unsigned). You also can specify an exact size, ranging from 8 to 256 bits, in multiples of 8. For example, `int32` means signed 32-bit integer, and `uint128` means unsigned 128-bit integer. If you don't specify a size, it's set to 256 bits. The sidebar explains how the assignment between variables of different integer types works.

Implicit and explicit integer conversions

Assignments between variables of different integer types is possible only if it's meaningful, which generally means the type of the receiving variable is less restrictive or is larger. If that's the case, an implicit conversion happens. The contract shown here, which you can enter into the Remix editor, shows some examples of valid and invalid assignments leading to implicit conversions when successful:

```
contract IntConversions {
    int256 bigNumber = 150000000000;
    int32 mediumNegativeNumber = -450000;
    uint16 smallPositiveNumber = 15678;

    int16 newSmallNumber = bigNumber;
    uint64 newMediumPositiveNumber =
        mediumNegativeNumber;
    uint32 public newMediumNumber =
        smallPositiveNumber;
    int256 public newBigNumber =
        mediumNegativeNumber;
}
```

Compile error because newSmallNumber is too small to contain bigNumber

Compiler error because uint64 can only hold positive numbers

smallPositiveNumber is implicitly converted from uint16 to uint32; newMediumNumber =15,678

mediumNegativeNumber is implicitly converted from int32 to int256; newBigNumber =-450,000

(continued)

To compile this code, remove the two lines that are causing errors, such as

```
TypeError: type int256 isn't implicitly convertible to expected type int16
```

Then instantiate the contract (click Deploy). Finally, get the values of `newMedium-Number` and `newBigNumber` by clicking the corresponding buttons.

When an implicit conversion isn't allowed, it's still possible to perform explicit conversions. In such cases, it's your responsibility to make sure the conversion is meaningful to your logic. To see an example of explicit conversions in action, add the following two lines to the IntConversions contract:

```
int16 public newSmallNumber =
    int16(bigNumber);
uint64 public newMediumPositiveNumber =
    uint64(mediumNegativeNumber);
```

The explicit conversion and assignment are successful, but newSmallNumber = 23,552.

The explicit conversion and assignment are successful, but newMediumPositiveNumber = 18,446,744,073,709,101,616.

Reinstantiate the contract (by clicking Create again), then get the value of `newSmall-Number` and `newMediumPositiveNumber` by clicking the corresponding buttons. The results of the explicit integer conversions aren't intuitive: they wrap the original value around the size of the target integer type (if its size is smaller than that of the source integer type) rather than overflowing.

The principles behind implicit and explicit conversions between integer types apply also to other noninteger types.

STATIC BYTE ARRAYS

You can declare byte arrays of a fixed size with a size ranging from 1 to 32—for example, `bytes8` or `bytes12`. By itself, `byte` is an array of a single byte and is equivalent to `bytes1`.

> **WARNING** If no size is specified, `bytes` declares a dynamic size byte array, which is a reference type.

ADDRESS

Address objects, which you generally declare using a literal containing up to 40 hexadecimal digits prefixed by 0x, hold 20 bytes; for example:

```
address ownerAddress = 0x10abb5EfEcdC09581f8b7cb95791FE2936790b4E;
```

> **WARNING** A hexadecimal literal is recognized as an address only if it has a valid checksum. This is determined by hashing the hexadecimal literal with the sha3 function (provided by the Web3 library) and then verifying that the

alphabetic characters in the literal are uppercase or lowercase, depending on the value of the bits in the hash at the same index position. This means an address is case-sensitive and you can't validate it visually. Some tools, such as Remix, will warn you if an address isn't valid but will still process an invalid address.

It's possible to get the Ether balance in Wei (the smallest Ether denomination) associated with an address by querying the `balance` property. You can try it by putting the following sample contract in Remix and executing the `getOwnerBalance()` function:

```
contract AddressExamples {
    address ownerAddress = 0x10abb5EfEcdC09581f8b7cb95791FE2936790b4E;

    function getOwnerBalance() public returns (uint)  {
        uint balance = ownerAddress.balance;
        return balance;
    }
}
```

You'll see the return value in the output panel at the bottom left of the Remix screen, after you click the Details button next to the output line corresponding to the function call. The address type exposes various functions for transferring Ether. Table 5.1 explains their purposes.

Table 5.1 Functions provided by the address type

Function	Purpose
transfer()	To transfer Ether in Wei—If the transaction fails on the receiving side, an exception is thrown to the sender and the payment is automatically reverted (although any spent gas isn't refunded), so no error handling code is necessary; transfer() can spend only up to a maximum of 2300 gas.
send()	To send Ether in Wei—If the transaction fails on the receiving side, a value of false is returned to the sender but the payment isn't reverted, so it must be handled correctly and reverted with further instructions; send() can spend only up to a maximum of 2,300 gas.
call()	To invoke a function on the target contract associated with the address (the target account is assumed to be a contract)—An amount of Ether can be sent together with the function call by specifying it in this way: call.value(10)("contractName", "functionName"); call() transfers the entire gas budget from the sender to the called function. If call() fails, it returns false, so failure must be handled in a similar way to send().

WARNING Because of security concerns, send() and call() are being deprecated, and it won't be possible to use them in future versions of Solidity.

This is an example of an Ether transfer using `transfer()`:

```
destinationAddress.transfer(10);    ⟵  Sends 10 Wei to
                                        destinationAddress
```

If sending Ether with `send()`, you must have error handling to avoid losing Ether:

```
if (!destinationAddress.send(10))
    revert();
```
⊲— If the send() operation fails, it returns false and must be handled, in this case by reverting the state and consequently the payment.

Another way of ensuring a transfer failure reverts the payment is by using the global `require()` function, which reverts the state if the input condition is false:

```
require(destinationAddress.send(10));
```
⊲— Reverts the payment if send fails and returns false

You can invoke a function on an external contract with `call()` as follows:

```
destinationContractAddress.call("contractName",
    "functionName");
```
⊲— Invokes an external contract function

You can send Ether during the external call as follows:

```
destinationContractAddress.call.value(10)(
    "contractName", "functionName");
```
⊲— Sends an amount of Ether expressed in Wei with the external call() by specifying it with value()

You must have handling for a failure of the external function call, as for `send()`, to ensure the state (including Ether payment) is reverted:

```
if (!destinationContractAddress.call.value(10)("contractName"
    , "functionName"))
    revert();
```
⊲— Reverts the state and consequently the payment

Chapter 15 on security will cover in detail how to invoke `transfer()`, `send()`, and `call()` correctly and how to handle errors safely.

ENUMS

An enum is a custom data type including a set of named values; for example:

```
enum  InvestmentLevel {High, Medium, Low}
```

You can then define an enum-based variable as follows:

```
InvestmentLevel level = InvestmentLevel.Medium;
```

The integer value of each enum item is implicitly determined by its position in the enum definition. In the previous example, the value of High is 0 and the value of Low is 2. You can retrieve the integer value of an enum type variable by explicitly converting the enum variable to an int variable as shown here:

```
InvestmentLevel level = InvestmentLevel.Medium;
...
int16 levelValue = int16(level);
```

Implicit conversions aren't allowed:

```
int16 levelValue = level;    ◁——— Doesn't compile
```

5.3.2 Reference types

Reference type variables are accessed through their reference (the location of their first item). You can store them in either of the following two data locations, which you can, in some cases, explicitly specify in their declaration:

- *Memory*—Values aren't persisted permanently and only live in memory.
- *Storage*—Values are persisted permanently on the blockchain, like state variables.

A third type of data location is available that you can't explicitly specify:

- *Calldata*—This is an area dedicated to holding the values of function parameters of external functions. Objects held in this area behave like objects stored in memory.

The following listing shows various reference type variables declared in different data locations.

> **Listing 5.2 Reference types with location declared implicitly or explicitly**

```
pragma solidity ^0.4.0;                      The data location of storageArray
contract ReferenceTypesSample {              implicitly defined as storage
    uint[] storageArray;        ◁

                                             The data location of fArray
                                             implicitly defined as memory
    function f(uint[] fArray) {}   ◁
    function g(uint[] storage gArray) internal {}   ◁        The data location
    function h(uint[] memory hArray) internal  {}   ◁        of gArray explicitly
}                                                             defined as storage
                              The data location of hArray
                              explicitly defined as memory
```

Before looking at code snippets focused on data locations, have a look at table 5.2, which summarizes the default data location of variables, depending on whether they're local or state variables, and of function parameters, depending on whether the function has been declared internal or external.

Table 5.2 Default data location of variables and function parameters

Case	Data location	Default
Local variable	Memory or storage	Storage
State variable	Only storage	Not applicable
Parameter of internal function	Memory or storage	Memory
Parameter of external function	Calldata	Not applicable

The behavior of reference type variables, specifically whether they get cloned or referenced directly when assigned to other variables or passed to function parameters, depends on the source and target data location. The best way to understand what happens in the various cases is to look at some code. The following code snippets all assume the `ReferenceTypesSample` contract definition given in listing 5.2.

The first case is the assignment of a state variable (whose data location is, as you know, the storage) to a local variable:

```
function f(uint[] fArray)  {
    uint[] localArray = storageArray;
}
```

localArray is defined implicitly in the storage and points directly to storageArray.

If `localArray` is modified, `storageArray` is consequently modified.

The next example is the assignment of a function parameter defined in memory to a local variable:

```
function f(uint[] fArray)  {
    uint[] localArray = fArray;
}
```

fArray is implicitly defined in memory.

localArray is defined in memory and points directly to fArray.

If `localArray` is modified, `fArray` is consequently modified.

The following example shows what happens if you assign a function parameter defined in memory to a storage variable:

```
function f(uint[] fArray)  {
    storageArray= fArray;
}
```

fArray is implicitly defined in memory.

storageArray stores a full copy of fArray.

If you pass a state variable to a function parameter defined in storage, the function parameter directly references the state variable:

```
function f(uint[] fArray)  {
    g(storageArray);
}
function g(uint[] storage gArray) internal {}
```

fArray is implicitly defined in memory.

During the call, gArray points directly to storageArray.

gArray is defined explicitly in storage.

If `gArray` is modified, `storageArray` is consequently modified.

If you pass a state variable to a function parameter defined in memory, the function parameter creates a local clone of the state variable:

```
function f(uint[] fArray)  {
    h(storageArray);
}
function h(uint[] memory hArray) internal {}
```

fArray is implicitly defined in memory.

During the call, hArray is assigned to a clone of storageArray.

hArray is defined explicitly in memory.

There are four classes of reference types:

- Arrays
- Strings
- Structs
- Mappings

Arrays can be static (of fixed size) or dynamic and are declared and initialized in slightly different ways.

STATIC ARRAYS

You must specify the size of a static array in its declaration. The following code declares and allocates a static array of five elements of type int32:

```
function f(){
    int32[5] memory fixedSlots;
    fixedSlots[0] = 5;
    //...
}
```

You can also allocate a static array and set it inline, as follows:

```
function f(){
    int32[5] memory fixedSlots = [int32(5), 9, 1, 3, 4];
}
```

> **NOTE** Inline arrays are automatically defined as to memory data location and are sized with the smallest possible type of their biggest item. In the inline static array example, imagine you hadn't enforced the item in the first cell as int32: int32[5] memory fixedSlots = [5, 9, 1, 3, 4]. In this case, the inline array would have been implicitly declared as int4[] memory, and it would have failed the assignment to the fixedSlots variable. Therefore, it would have produced a compilation error.

DYNAMIC ARRAYS

You don't need to specify the size in the declaration of dynamic arrays, as shown in the following snippet:

```
function f(){
    int32[] unlimitedSlots;
}
```

You can then append items to a dynamic array by calling the push member function:

```
unlimitedSlots.push(6);
unlimitedSlots.push(4);
```

If you need to resize a dynamic array, you must do so in different ways depending on whether its data location is memory or storage. If the data location is storage, you can reset its length, as shown in the following snippet:

```
function f(){
    int32[] unlimitedSlots;          ←─┤  Implicitly declares it with
    //...                                  storage data location
    unlimitedSlots.length = 5;       ←─┐
}                                        └  Resizes it by resetting its length
```

If the data location of a dynamic array is memory, you have to resize it with new, as shown in the following snippet:

```
function f(){
    int32[] memory unlimitedSlots;   ┐  Explicitly declares it with
    //...                          ←─┘  memory data location
    unlimitedSlots = new int32[](5); ←─┐
}                                        └  Resizes it with new
```

> **NOTE** As you saw earlier, bytes is an unlimited byte array and is a reference type. This is equivalent to byte[], but it's optimized for space, and its use is recommended. It also supports length and push().

If an array is exposed as a public state variable, its getter accepts the array positional index as an input.

STRING

string is in fact equivalent to bytes but with no length and push() members. You can initialize it with a string literal:

```
string name = "Roberto";
```

STRUCT

A struct is a user-defined type that contains a set of elements that in general are each of a different type. The following listing shows a contract declaring various structs that get referenced in its state variables. This example also shows how you can use enums in a struct.

Listing 5.3 Contract containing various struct definitions

```
contract Voting {

    enum UserType {Voter, Admin, Owner}

    enum MajorityType {SimpleMajority, AbsoluteMajority, SuperMajority
➥ , unanimity}

    struct UserInfo {
        address account;
        string name;
        string surname;
        UserType uType;
    }

    struct Candidate {
        address account;
```

```
        string description;
    }

    struct VotingSession {
        uint sessionId;
        string description;
        MajorityType majorityType;
        uint8 majorityPercent;
        Candidate[] candidates;
        mapping (address => uint) votes;
    }

    uint numVotingSessions;
    mapping (uint => VotingSession) votingSessions;

    //...
}
```

You can initialize a struct object as follows:

```
function addCandidate(uint votingSessionId,
address candidateAddress,
string candidateDescription) {
    Candidate memory candidate =
    Candidate({account:candidateAddress,
 description:candidateDescription});

    votingSessions[votingSessionId].candidates.push(candidate);
}
```

MAPPING

mapping is a special reference type that you can only use in the storage data location, which means you can declare it only as a state variable or a storage reference type. You might remember mapping is the Solidity implementation of a hash table, which stores values against keys. The hash table is strongly typed, which means you must declare the type of the key and the type of the value at its declaration:

```
mapping(address => int) public coinBalance;
```

In general, you can declare the value of any type, including primitive types, arrays, structs, or mappings themselves.

Contrary to hash table implementations of other languages, mapping has no containsKey() function. If you try to get the value associated with a missing key, it will return the default value. For example, your coinBalance mapping will return 0 when trying to get the balance of an address missing from the mapping:

```
int missingAddressBalance =
coinBalance[0x6C15291028D082...];              ⟵⎯⎯  missingAddressBalance == 0;
```

This completes your tour of data types. You've seen how to declare and instantiate value type and reference type variables. A certain set of variables are declared implicitly, and you can always access them from your contract. They're part of the so-called *global namespace* that we're going to explore next.

5.3.3 Global namespace

The global namespace is a set of implicitly declared variables and functions that you can reference and use in your contract code directly.

IMPLICITLY DECLARED VARIABLES

The global namespace provides the following five variables:

- `block` holds information about the latest blockchain block.
- `msg` provides data about the incoming message.
- `tx` provides transaction data.
- `this` is a reference to the current contract. You can use it to call internal functions as if they were defined `external` and therefore store the message call on the blockchain. (`internal` and `external` are function accessibility levels that I'll explain later, in the functions section.) If you use it by itself, it's implicitly converted to the address of the current contract.
- `now` is the time associated with the creation of the latest block, expressed as a Unix epoch.

Table 5.3 summarizes the functions and properties that global variables expose.

Table 5.3 Members of the main global variables

Global variable	Type	Member	Return type	Description
`block`	function	`blockhash(uint blocknumber)`	`bytes32`	Hash of given block (only available for last 256 blocks, as specified in the *Yellow Paper*, for simplicity of design and performance reasons)
	property	`coinbase`	`address`	Block's miner's address
	property	`gaslimit`	`uint`	Block's gas limit
	property	`number`	`uint`	Block's number
	property	`timestamp`	`uint`	Block's timestamp as UNIX epoch
`msg`	property	`data`	`bytes`	Full calldata body
	property	`sender`	`address`	Message sender (who is performing the current call)
	property	`gas`	`uint`	Remaining gas
	property	`value`	`uint`	Amount of Ether sent with the message, in Wei
`tx`	property	`gasprice`	`uint`	Transaction gas price
	property	`origin`	`address`	Transaction sender (who originated the full call chain)

Table 5.3 Members of the main global variables

Global variable	Type	Member	Return type	Description
now	property	N/A	uint	Although the name of this variable might lead you to believe that this might return the current time (perhaps as a UNIX epoch), now is in fact an alias for block.timestamp, which is the time at which the current latest block was created.

IMPLICITLY DECLARED FUNCTIONS

The following two functions, available from the global namespace, throw an exception and revert the contract state if the associated condition isn't met. Although they work exactly the same way, their intention is slightly different:

- require(bool condition)—This is used to validate function input. You've already seen it when validating the input of SimpleCoin.transfer().
- assert(bool condition)—This is used to validate contract state or function state.

You can also terminate the execution and revert the contract state explicitly by calling revert().

If you want to remove the current contract instance from the blockchain, for example because you've realized your contract has a security flaw that's being actively exploited by hackers, you can call selfdestruct(Ether recipient address). This will uninstall the current instance from the blockchain and move the Ether present at the associated account to the specified recipient address.

What does uninstalling a contract mean in the context of a blockchain? It means that the contract will be removed from the current state of the blockchain and will become unreachable. But its trace will remain in the blockchain history. The contract is considered fully removed only after the selfdestruct(recipient address) transaction has been mined and the related block has been propagated throughout the network.

> **WARNING** You should be aware that the recipient address has no way of rejecting Ether coming from a selfdestruct() call; the destruction of the contract and the crediting of the recipient account are a single atomic operation. As you'll see in a later chapter dedicated to security, this can be maliciously exploited to perform sophisticated attacks.

The global namespace also provides various cryptographic hash functions, such as sha256() (from the SHA-2 family) and keccak256() (from the SHA-3 family). More on those in a later chapter, but for now let's move on to state variables.

5.3.4 State variables

You already know state variables hold the contract state. What I haven't covered so far is the access level that you can specify when declaring them. Table 5.4 summarizes the available options.

Table 5.4   Access levels of a state variable

Access level	Description
public	The compiler automatically generates a getter function for each public state variable. You can use public state variables directly from within the contract and access them through the related getter function from external contract or client code.
internal	The contract and any inherited contract can access Internal state variables. This is the default level for state variables.
private	Only members of the same contract—not inherited contracts—can access private state variables.

The StateVariablesAccessibility contract in the following listing shows examples of state variable declarations, including their accessibility level.

Listing 5.4   Examples of state variables declared with various accessibility levels

> You can access frozenAccount only from within this contract, not from inherited contracts.

> isContractLocked is implicitly defined as internal, so it's accessible from within this contract and inherited contracts.

```
pragma solidity ^0.4.0;
contract StateVariablesAccessibility {
    mapping (address => bool)
    private frozenAccounts;
    uint isContractLocked;
    mapping (address => bool) public tokenBalance;

    ...
}
```

> tokenBalance is accessible externally, and the Solidity compiler automatically generates a getter function.

CONSTANT STATE VARIABLES

It's possible to declare a state variable as constant. In this case, you have to set it to a value that isn't coming from storage or from the blockchain in general, so values from other state variables or from properties of the block global variable aren't allowed.

This code shows some examples of constant state variables:

```
pragma solidity ^0.4.0;
contract ConstantStateVariables {
    uint constant maxTokenSupply = 10000000;
    string constant contractVersion ="2.1.5678";
    bytes32 constant contractHash =
        keccak256(contractVersion, maxTokenSupply);
    ...
}
```

> You can declare a value type or string state variable as constant.

> You can assign the result of a stateless built-in mathematical or cryptographic function to a constant state variable.

Although you've already come across functions, there are various aspects of functions that I haven't covered yet. I'll cover them in the next section.

5.3.5 Functions

You can specify function input and output parameters in various ways. Let's see how.

INPUT PARAMETERS DECLARATION

You declare input parameters in Solidity, as in other statically typed languages, by providing a list of typed parameter names, as shown in the following example:

```
function process1(int _x, int _y, int _z, bool _flag) {
...
}
```

If you don't use some of the parameters in the implementation, you can leave them unnamed (or anonymous), like the second and third parameter in the following example:

```
function process2(int _x, int, int, bool _flag) {
    if (_flag)
        stateVariable = _x;
}
```

You'll understand better the purpose of anonymous parameters in chapter 6, when you'll learn about abstract functions of abstract contracts and how to override them in concrete contracts. (Some overridden functions might not need all the parameters specified in the abstract function of the base abstract contract.)

> **NOTE** You might find, as I did initially, the naming convention for parameters a bit odd, because in other languages, such as Java or C#, you might have used an underscore prefix to identify member variables. In Solidity, an underscore prefix is used to identify parameters and local variables. But it seems this convention is fading away, and underscore prefixes might disappear altogether from Solidity naming conventions.

OUTPUT PARAMETERS DECLARATION

In Solidity, a function can in general return multiple output parameters, in a tuple data structure. You specify output parameters after the `returns` keyword and declare them like input parameters, as shown here:

```
function calculate1(int _x, int _y, int _z, bool _flag)
    returns (int _alpha, int _beta, int _gamma) {        ← Here, _alpha,
    _alpha = _x + _y;                                      _beta, and
    _beta = _y + _z;                                       _gamma are
    if (_flag)              No return                      declared as
        _gamma = _alpha / _beta;    statement is           returned
    else                            necessary to           parameters.
        _gamma = _z;                return the result
}                                   tuple to the caller.
```

NOTE   A tuple is an ordered list of elements, in general each of a different type. This is an example of a tuple: `23, true, "PlanA", 57899, 345`

As you can see in the code example, contrary to most languages, no `return` statement is necessary when you can write the logic in such a way that you've set all output parameters correctly before the execution of the function is complete. You can think of the output parameters as local variables initialized to their default value, in this case 0, at the beginning of the function execution. If you prefer, though, and if the logic requires you to do so, you can return output from a function using `return`, as shown here:

```
function calculate2(int _x, int _y, int _z, bool _flag)
    returns (int, int, int) {
    int _alpha = _x + _y;
    int _beta = _y + _z;
    if (_flag)
        return (_alpha, _beta, _alpha / _beta);

    return (_alpha, _beta, _z);
}
```

Only the types of the return tuple are declared.

You define and assign _alpha and _beta in the body of the function.

The result tuple is returned to the caller explicitly with a return statement.

FUNCTION ACCESS LEVELS

As for state variables, functions also can be declared with different access levels, as summarized in table 5.5.

Table 5.5 Access levels of a function

Access level	Description
`external`	An external function is exposed in the contract interface, and you can only call it from external contracts or client code but not from within the contract.
`public`	A public function is exposed in the contract interface, and you can call it from within the contract or from external contracts or client code. This is the default accessibility level for functions.
`internal`	An internal function isn't part of the contract interface, and it's only visible to contract members and inherited contracts.
`private`	A private function can only be called by members of the contract where it's been declared, not by inherited contracts.

The following contract code shows some function declarations, including the accessibility level:

```
contract SimpleCoin {
    function transfer(address _to, uint256 _amount)
        public {}

    function checkLimit(uint256 _amount) private
        returns (bool) {}
```

A public function, accessible internally and externally

A private function, only accessible from within this contract

```
function validateAccount(address avcount) internal
    returns (bool) {}
```
A private function, accessible from this and inherited contracts

```
function freezeAccount(address target, bool freeze)
    external {}
```
An external function, only accessible externally
```
}
```

INTERNAL FUNCTION INVOCATION

Functions can be invoked internally or externally. For example, a function can invoke another function directly within the same contract, as shown here:

```
contract TaxCalculator {
    function calculateAlpha(int _x, int _y, int _z)
        public returns (int _alpha)  {
        _alpha = _x + calculateGamma(_y, _z);
    }
```
This invocation results in a call: _y and _z are accessed directly through memory references.
```
    function calculateGamma(int _y, int _z)
        internal returns (int _gamma) {
        _gamma   = _y *3 +7* _z;
    }
}
```
This is an internal function, not accessible from outside the contract.

This way of invoking a function is known as a *call*. With a call, the body of the function accesses parameters directly through memory references.

EXTERNAL FUNCTION INVOCATION

A function can call a function of an external contract through the contract reference, as shown here:

```
contract GammaCalculator {
    function calculateGamma(int _y, int _z)
        external returns (int _gamma) {
        _gamma   = _y *3 +7* _z;
    }
}
```
GammaCalculator is an external contract with respect to TaxCalculator2.

```
contract TaxCalculator2 {

    GammaCalculator gammaCalculator;

    function TaxCalculator(address _gammaCalculatorAddress) {
        gammaCalculator = GammaCalculator(_
            gammaCalculatorAddress);
    }
```
gammaCalculator points to an instance deployed at address _gammaCalculatorAddress.

```
    function calculateAlpha(int _x, int _y, int _z)
        public returns (int _alpha) {
        _alpha = _x + gammaCalculator.calculateGamma(
            _y, _z);
    }
}
```
This is an external function invocation, which results in a 'transaction message' that gets stored on the blockchain.

In this case, parameters are sent to GammaCalculator through a *transaction message* that's then stored on the blockchain, as you can see in the sequence diagram in figure 5.1.

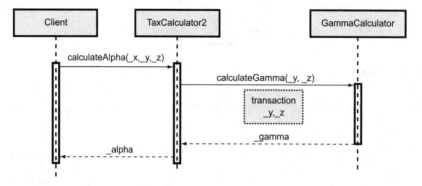

Figure 5.1 Sequence diagram illustrating an external function invocation. The calculateAlpha() function of the TaxCalculator2 contract calls the external calculateGamma() function on the GammaCalculator contract. Because the call is external, the function parameters are sent to the external contract through a transaction that's stored on the blockchain.

You can force a call to a public function to appear as an external invocation, and therefore execute through a transaction message, if it's performed through this, the reference to the current contract, as shown here:

```
contract TaxCalculator3 {
    function calculateAlpha(int _x, int _y, int _z)
        public returns (int _alpha) {
        _alpha = _x + this.calculateGamma(_y, _z);      ◁   The call on calculateGamma
    }                                                        through 'this' behaves as a
                                                             call on an external contract,
                                                             so a transaction message is
                                                             generated and this gets
                                                             stored on the blockchain.

    function calculateGamma(int _y, int _z)
        public returns (int _gamma) {          ◁    To be called through
        _gamma  = _y *3 +7* _z;                      this, you must declare
    }                                                calculateGamma as public.
}
```

CHANGING PARAMETERS ORDER AT FUNCTION INVOCATION

When invoking a function, you can pass the parameters in any order if you specify their name, as shown in the following listing:

```
contract TaxCalculator4 {
    function calculateAlpha(int _x, int _y, int _z)
        public returns (int _alpha) {
        _alpha = _x + this.calculateGamma(
            {_z:_z, _y:_y});               ◁    You can pass the parameters of
    }                                           calculateGamma in an arbitrary
                                                order, but in this case, you must
                                                also specify the parameter names.
    function calculateGamma(int _y, int _z)
        public returns (int _gamma) {
```

```
        _gamma  = _y *3 +7*_z;
    }
}
```

VIEW AND PURE FUNCTIONS

It's possible to declare a function as `view`, with the intent that it doesn't perform any action that might modify state, as defined in table 5.6. But the compiler doesn't check whether any state modification takes place, so the `view` keyword is currently used on functions mainly for documentation purposes.

Table 5.6　Actions that lead to a state modification

State modifying action
Writing to state variables
Raising events
Creating or destroying contracts
Transferring Ether (through `send()` or `transfer()`)
Calling any function not declared as `view` or `pure`
Using low-level calls (for example `call()`) or certain inline assembly opcodes

> **NOTE**　In earlier versions of Solidity, the `view` keyword was named `constant`. Many developers argued that `constant` was misleading because it wasn't clear whether it meant, as in other languages, that the function would return only constant results. So, although you can still use `constant` instead of `view`, the latter is recommended.

It's possible to declare a function as `pure`, with the intent that it doesn't perform any action that might modify state (as seen for `view` functions) or read state, as defined in table 5.7. As with `view` functions, the compiler doesn't check that `pure` functions don't modify or read state, so for now, the `pure` keyword has only a documentation purpose.

Table 5.7　Actions that can be interpreted as reading from state

State reading actions
Reading from state variables
Accessing account balance (through `this.balance` or `address.balance`)
Accessing the members of `block`, `tx`, and most of the members of `msg`
Calling any function not declared as `pure`
Using certain inline assembly opcodes

The code in the following listing highlights in bold, functions of listing 5.1 that you can declare as view or pure.

Listing 5.5   Functions you can declare as `view` or `pure`

```
pragma solidity ^0.4.24;
contract AuthorizedToken {

    //...

    mapping (address => uint256) public tokenBalance;
    mapping (address => bool) public frozenAccount;

    address public owner;
    uint256 public constant maxTranferLimit = 50000;

    //...

    function transfer(address _to, uint256 _amount) public {
        require(checkLimit(_amount));
        //...
        tokenBalance[msg.sender] -= _amount;
        tokenBalance[_to] += _amount;
        Transfer(msg.sender, _to, _amount);
    }

    //...

    function checkLimit(uint256 _amount) private pure
        returns (bool) {
        if (_amount < maxTranferLimit)
            return true;
        return false;
    }

    function validateAccount(address _account) internal view
        returns (bool) {
        if (frozenAccount[_account]
            && tokenBalance[_account] > 0)
            return true;
        return false;
    }

    //...

    function freezeAccount(address target, bool freeze)
        onlyOwner public {
        frozenAccount[target] = freeze;
        FrozenAccount(target, freeze);
    }
}
```

Doesn't alter state variable, so you can declare this function as view

Alters the state variable tokenBalance, so you can't declare transfer() as view or pure

Doesn't read or alter state, so you can declare this function as pure

Alters state variable frozenAccount, so you can't declare freezeAccount() as view or pure

PAYABLE FUNCTIONS

You declare a function as payable if you want to allow it to receive Ether. The following example shows how to declare a function as payable:

```
contract StockPriceOracle {
    uint quoteFee = 500;                                    Quote price in Wei, which
    mapping (string => uint) private stockPrices;           the caller must send when
                                                            invoking getStockPrice()
    //...

    function getStockPrice(string _stockTicker)            Checks the Ether amount
        payable returns (uint _stockPrice) {               sent (in Wei) to cover the
        if (msg.value == quoteFee)                         fee for the service to verify
        {                                                  it's correct
            //...
            _stockPrice = stockPrices[_stockTicker];
        }
        else                        If the fee sent is incorrect,
            revert();               reverts the transaction and
    }                               the sender isn't charged
}
```

The following code shows how to send Ether together with the input when calling the getStockPrice() function:

```
address stockPriceOracleAddress = 0x10abb5EfEcdC09581f8b7cb95791FE2936790b4E;
uint256 quoteFee = 500;
string memory stockTicker = "MSFT";

if (!stockPriceOracleAddress.call.value(quoteFee)       Sends Ether while
    (bytes4(sha3("getStockPrice()")),                   invoking an external
    _stockTicker))                                      function with call()
        revert();              If call() fails, it returns false, and
                               the state is reverted with revert();.
```

FALLBACK FUNCTION

A contract can declare one unnamed (or anonymous) payable function that can't have any input or output parameters. This becomes a *fallback* function in case a client call doesn't match any of the available contract functions, or in case only plain Ether is sent to the contract via send(), transfer(), or call().

The gas budget transferred to the fallback function is minimal if you call the fallback function by send() or transfer(). In this case, its implementation must avoid any costly operations, such as writing to storage, sending Ether, or calling internal or external functions that have complex or lengthy logic. A send() or transfer() call on a nonminimal fallback implementation is likely to run out of gas and fail almost immediately. You must avoid this situation because it puts Ether at risk of getting lost or even stolen, as you'll see in the chapter dedicated to security.

The following code shows the classic *minimal fallback* function implementation, which allows incoming `send()` and `transfer()` calls to complete an Ether transfer successfully:

```
contract A1 {
    function () payable {}
}
```

You also can implement a fallback function so that it prevents the contract from accepting Ether if it isn't meant to:

```
contract A2 {
    function () payable  {
        revert();
    }
}
```

> **WARNING** As you'll see in the chapter dedicated to security, the fallback function offers malicious participants various ways of attacking a contract, so if you decide to provide a fallback, you must learn how to implement it correctly.

GETTER FUNCTIONS

As I mentioned earlier, the compiler automatically generates a getter function for each public state variable declared in the contract. The getter function gets the name of the state variable it exposes. For example, given the usual contract

```
contract SimpleCoin {
    mapping (address => uint256) public coinBalance;
    //...
}
```

you can consult the balance of an account as follows:

```
uint256 myBalance = simpleCoinInstance.coinBalance(myAccountAddress);
```

A getter function is implicitly declared as `public` and `view`, so it's possible to invoke it from within the contract through `this`, as shown in the following code:

```
contract SimpleCoin {
    mapping (address => uint256) public coinBalance;
    //...

    function isAccountUsed(address _account)
        internal view returns (bool) {
        if (this.coinBalance(_account) > 0)    ◁
            return true;
        return false;
    }
}
```

This check is performed with a getter, but you could have it performed by accessing the mapping directly: this.coinBalance[_account], the only difference being parentheses versus square brackets.

You can alter the behavior of functions with function modifiers. Keep reading to see how.

5.3.6 *Function modifiers*

A function modifier alters the behavior of a function by performing some pre- and postprocessing around the execution of the function using it. As an example of a pre-processing modifier, the code in listing 5.6 shows onlyOwner, a typical modifier that allows the function to be called only if the caller is the contract owner, which is the account that instantiated the contract. isActive is a parameterized modifier that checks if the input user account isn't frozen.

> **Listing 5.6 Example of a contract with function modifiers**

```
contract FunctionModifiers {
    address owner;
    address[] users;
    mapping (address => bool) frozenUser;

    function FunctionModifiers () {        Sets the contract owner
        owner = msg.sender;            ◁── address at instantiation
    }
                                           Modifier definition
    modifier onlyOwner {           ◁──┘
        require(msg.sender == owner);
        _;
    }

    modifier isActive(address _account) {
        require(!frozenUser[_account]);
        _;
    }

    function addUser (address _userAddress)
        onlyOwner public {          ◁── Associates a modifier with
        users.push(_userAddress);       a function in this way
    }

    function refund(address addr)
        onlyOwner isActive(addr) public {   ◁── A function can have
        //...                                    more than one modifier.
    }
}
```

From a certain point of view, you can look at a modifier as an implementation of the classic *decorator* design pattern, as it adds behavior to a function without modifying its logic. As for decorators, you can chain modifiers, and you can attach several of them to a function, as shown in the refund() function, which can execute only if the caller is the contract owner and the user account isn't frozen:

```
function refund(address addr) onlyOwner isActive(addr) public {
    //...
}
```

> **WARNING** Modifiers get called in the reverse order from how they've been placed on the function definition. In the example, isActive is applied first and onlyOwner second.

5.3.7 *Variable declaration, initialization, and assignment*

Earlier, I explained how the calling code respectively sets and handles the input and output function parameters. I also illustrated relatively complex cases, such as how you can assign multiple variables from tuple results. In this section, I'll present more information about the declaration, initialization, and assignment of local function variables. Some of the considerations also apply to state variables.

IMPLICIT INITIALIZATION

Contrary to most statically typed languages, which force the developer to explicitly initialize variables, when you declare a variable in Solidity, it's implicitly initialized to its default value, corresponding to its bits being all set to zero, as summarized in table 5.8.

Table 5.8 Default values of solidity types

Type	Default value	Example
int and uint (all sizes)	0	int32 a; //0
bool	false	bool flag; //false
bytes1 to bytes32	All bytes set to 0	bytes4 byteArray; // 0x00000000
Static array	All items set to zero value	bool [3] flags; // [false, false, false]
bytes	Empty byte array	[]
Dynamic array	Empty array	int [] values; // []
string	Empty string	""
struct	Each element set to the default value	

> **NOTE** As explained in table 5.8, initialized variables are set to a zero-like value. There is no null value in Solidity.

DELETE

You can reinitialize the value of a variable to its default value, as shown in table 5.8, by calling delete on it, as shown in the following code:

```
contract DeleteExample {
    function deleteExample() returns (int32[5]) {
        int32[5] memory fixedSlots = [int32(5), 9, 1, 3, 4];
        //...
        delete fixedSlots;          ⟵  Implicitly reinitializes fixedSlots
        return fixedSlots;             to [int32 (0), 0, 0, 0, 0]
    }
}
```

You can execute this in Remix. Make sure you check the final value of `fixedSlots` in the output panel on the bottom left, as usual.

IMPLICITLY TYPED DECLARATION

You can declare the type of a variable implicitly with var if this can be inferred from an explicit initialization, as shown in this code:

```
contract TaxCalculator {
    function calculateAlpha(int _x)
        public returns (int _alpha)  {
        var _gammaParams =  [int(5), 9];        ◄——    Implicitly declares
        var _gamma = calculateGamma(_gammaParams[0],     _gammaParams as int32 [2]
          _gammaParams[1]);        ◄——┐
        _alpha = _x + _gamma;             Implicitly declares
    }                                     _gamma as int

    function calculateGamma(int _y, int _z)
        private returns (int _gamma) {
            _gamma  = _y *3;
    }
}
```

> **NOTE** Implicitly typed variable declaration with var doesn't mean Solidity supports dynamic typing. It means you can perform the type declaration implicitly rather than explicitly, but still at compile time.

Multiple implicitly typed declarations are also possible when *destructuring* a tuple returned from a function to multiple variables. For example, given the following `calculate()` function

```
contract Calculator {
    function calculate(uint _x)
        public returns (uint _a, uint _b,        Returns a tuple
          bool _ok) {        ◄——                 including three items
        //...
        _a = _x * 2;
        _b = _x** 3;                     ┌  Sets the tuple
                                         │  items within the
        _ok == (_a * _b) < 10000;        └  function body
    }
}
```

it's possible to *destructure* the tuple result into three variables, as follows:

```
var (_alpha, _beta, _success) =        Assigns the tuple returned by
    calculatorInstance.calculate(5);   ◄——  calculate() to three variables
```

> **NOTE** *Destructuring* means decomposing a tuple into its individual constituents, which are then assigned to separate variables.

TUPLE ASSIGNMENT

When assigning a tuple to several implicitly or explicitly typed variables, the assignment will work if the number of items in the tuple is at least equal to the number of variables on the left-hand side of the assignment. This code shows examples of correct and incorrect assignments, given the `calculate()` function defined earlier:

```
var (_alpha, _beta, ) =
    calculatorInstance.calculate(5);      ◁─┘ Ignores the _ok flag
                                               but will be successful
var (_alpha, _beta, _gamma, _ok) =
    calculatorInstance.calculate(5);      ◁─┤ Will fail with an error because
                                               it's trying to assign four variables
                                               from a three-item tuple
```

It's also possible to set various properties of a `struct` from a tuple. For example, given this `struct`

```
struct Factors {
    uint alpha;
    uint beta;
}
```

it's possible to set its properties as follows:

```
var factors = Factors({alpha:0, beta:0});   │ Destructures the tuple result into the
(factors.alpha, factors.beta, ) =           │ properties of a Factors struct object. (Note
    calculatorInstance.calculate(5);    ◁───┤ that, as in the previous example, the _ok flag
                                            │ that calculate() returns has been ignored.)
```

5.3.8   Events

An event allows a contract to notify another contract or a contract client, such as a Dapp user interface, that something of interest has occurred. You declare events like you do in C# and Java and publish them with the `emit` keyword, as you can see in the following code extract from `SimpleCoin`:

```
pragma solidity ^0.4.16;
contract SimpleCoin {
    mapping (address => uint256) public coinBalance;
    //...
    event Transfer(address indexed from,          │ Defines the
        address indexed to, uint256 value);   ◁───┘ Transfer event
    //...

    function transfer(address _to, uint256 _amount) public {
        //...
        coinBalance[msg.sender] -= _amount;
        coinBalance[_to] += _amount;                    │ Publishes the Transfer
        emit Transfer(msg.sender, _to, _amount);  ◁─────┘ event with emit
    }
    //...
}
```

Events in Ethereum haven't only a real-time notification purpose, but also a long-term logging purpose. Events are logged on the transaction log of the blockchain, and you can retrieve them later for analysis. To allow quick retrieval, events are indexed against a key that you can define when you declare the event. The key can be composite and contain up to three of its input parameters, as you can see in the definition of Transfer shown previously:

```
event Transfer(address indexed from, address indexed to, uint256 value);
```

In chapter 6, you'll see how to listen and react to Solidity events from client JavaScript code. In chapter 13, you'll learn more about how events get logged on the blockchain and how you can reply to them and retrieve them.

5.3.9 Conditional statements

Solidity supports all classic conditional statements available in C-like and Java-like languages:

- if ... else
- while
- do ... while
- for

Loops support both continue and break statements.

You've completed the first part of your tour of Solidity. If you want to learn more about the syntax I've introduced in this chapter, I encourage you to consult the official documentation at https://solidity.readthedocs.io/en/develop/. In the next section, you'll apply what you've learned in this chapter to improve SimpleCoin. The Solidity tour will then continue in the next chapter, where you'll start writing code in an object-oriented way and learn about other advanced features of the language.

> **WARNING** Although you might think that because transactions are executed sequentially within the EVM, concurrency issues might not come up within a contract, this isn't entirely true. A contract might invoke a function on an external contract, and this might lead to concurrency issues, especially if the external contract calls back the caller, as you'll see in chapter 14 on security.

5.4 Time to improve and refactor SimpleCoin

In this section, you'll extend SimpleCoin's functionality as follows:

- You'll let the owner of an account authorize an allowance to another account.
- You'll restrict certain operations, such as minting coins or freezing accounts, only to the contract owner.

Before making any changes, open Remix and enter the latest version of the Simple-Coin code from chapter 4, as shown in the following listing, into the editor.

Listing 5.7   Latest version of `SimpleCoin` from chapter 4

```solidity
pragma solidity ^0.4.0;

contract SimpleCoin {
  mapping (address => uint256) public coinBalance;

  event Transfer(address indexed from, address indexed to, uint256 value);

  constructor(uint256 _initialSupply) public {
    coinBalance[msg.sender] = _initialSupply;
  }

  function transfer(address _to, uint256 _amount) public {
    require(coinBalance[msg.sender] > _amount);
    require(coinBalance[_to] + _amount >= coinBalance[_to] );
    coinBalance[msg.sender] -= _amount;
    coinBalance[_to] += _amount;
    emit Transfer(msg.sender, _to, _amount);
  }
}
```

Now you can try letting the owner of an account authorize an allowance that another account can use. This means that if account A has 10,000 coins, its owner can authorize account B to transfer a certain amount of coins (say up to a total of 200 in separate transfer operations) to other accounts.

5.4.1   *Implementing an allowance facility*

You can model a token allowance with a nested mapping:

```solidity
mapping (address => mapping (address => uint256)) public allowance;
```

This means that an account allows one or more accounts to manage a specified number of coins; for example:

```solidity
allowance[address1][address2] = 200;
allowance[address1][address3] = 150;
```

address2 can manage 200 coins of the address1 balance.

address3 can manage 150 coins of the address1 balance.

You can authorize an allowance by calling the following function:

```solidity
function authorize(address _authorizedAccount, uint256 _allowance)
    public returns (bool success) {
    allowance[msg.sender][_authorizedAccount] =
      _allowance;
    return true;
}
```

Allows authorizedAccount to manage a number of coins equal to _allowance

Once an account has been authorized an allowance, it can transfer a number of coins, up to the unused allowance, to another account, with the following function:

```
function transferFrom(address _from, address _to, uint256 _amount)
    public returns (bool success) {
    require(_to != 0x0);
    require(coinBalance[_from] > _amount);
    require(coinBalance[_to] +
        _amount >= coinBalance[_to] );
    require(_amount <=
        allowance[_from][msg.sender]);

    coinBalance[_from] -= _amount;
    coinBalance[_to] += _amount;
    allowance[_from][msg.sender] -= _amount;

    emit Transfer(_from, _to, _amount);

    return true;
}
```

Checks for overflow →

Checks unused allowance →

Prevents transfer to 0x0 address, which is a default address if not specified explicitly

Checks if the source account has enough coins

Debits source account

Increases recipient account

Decreases unused allowance

Raises Transfer event

The implementation of the allowance facility was relatively simple. Now you can see how to restrict some SimpleCoin functionality only to the contract owner.

5.4.2 *Restricting operations only to the contract owner*

The contract owner is the account from which the contract gets deployed. SimpleCoin already has an operation that's executed against the contract owner. As you'll remember, the constructor assigns the initial token supply to the contract owner, although this assignment is implicit:

```
constructor(uint256 _initialSupply) {
    coinBalance[msg.sender] = _initialSupply;
}
```

You can make the intention of the code more explicit by declaring the contract owner as address public owner; then you can change the constructor to

```
constructor(uint256 _initialSupply) public {
    owner = msg.sender;
    coinBalance[owner] = _initialSupply;
}
```

Initializes the contract owner with the address of the account deploying the contract

Assigns the initial token supply explicitly to the contract owner

MINTING COINS

After you've initialized the owner variable, you can restrict the execution of some functions to require that the contract owner invoke them. For example, you could extract the constructor code assigning the initial supply to the owner into a new, more general function:

```
function mint(address _recipient, uint256 _mintedAmount) public {
    require(msg.sender == owner);
    coinBalance[_recipient] += _mintedAmount;
    emit Transfer(owner, _recipient,
        _mintedAmount);
}
```

Assigns the minted amount to the recipient →

Restricts the invocation of this function only to the contract owner

Then you can change the constructor as follows:

```
constructor(uint256 _initialSupply) public {
    owner = msg.sender;
    mint(owner, _initialSupply);                    ◄─────┐  The initial supply is now
}                                                          │  generated through the
                                                           │  mint() function.
```

The `mint()` function now allows the owner to generate coins at will, not only at construction. The check performed on the first line of `mint()` makes sure only the owner can generate mint coins.

> **NOTE** When looking at the code of token modeling smart contracts, you'll often find that functions that generate new coins or tokens are named `mint()`, after the English verb that's associated with making conventional metallic coins as currency.

FREEZING ACCOUNTS

You might want to further extend the powers of the contract owner and grant them the exclusive ability to freeze accounts. You can model the set of accounts that have been frozen with the following mapping:

```
mapping (address => bool) public frozenAccount;
```

The ideal data structure probably would be a Python set (or a C# `Set` or a Java `HashSet`), which would allow you to store frozen addresses (the keys of the mapping above) and check them efficiently without having to store any associated value (for example, the Boolean flag in the previous mapping). But a mapping of an address to a Boolean can be considered a close approximation to a set of addresses.

You also can declare an event you can publish when freezing an account:

```
event FrozenAccount(address target, bool frozen);
```

The owner would then freeze an account with the following function:

```
function freezeAccount(address target, bool freeze) public{
    require(msg.sender == owner);                   ◄─────┐  Restricts the invocation
                                                           │  of this function only to
    frozenAccount[target] = freeze;                 ◄──────┤  the contract owner
                                                           │
    emit FrozenAccount(target, freeze);   ◄──┐             │  Adds the target account
}                                            │             │  to the set of frozen
                         Raises the event ───┘             │  accounts
```

> **NOTE** You can use the `freezeAccount()` function to freeze or unfreeze accounts depending on the value of the Boolean parameter.

You might have noticed that the check being performed on `msg.sender`, which restricts the caller of this function to only the owner, is exactly the same as what you have on `mint()`. Wouldn't it be nice to encapsulate this check in a reusable way? Hold on ... this is exactly the purpose of function modifiers!

CREATING THE ONLYOWNER MODIFIER

I know, I know! If you're among the readers who paid attention to the `onlyOwner` modifier I presented in listing 5.6, I bet you were wondering with frustration why I hadn't used it since the beginning of this section. Well, I wanted to show you the usefulness of modifiers the hard way. Now you can refactor the duplicated check of the message sender's address against the owner's address into the `onlyOwner` modifier:

```
modifier onlyOwner {
    if (msg.sender != owner) revert();    ◄─┐  Won't allow message callers
    _;                                       │  who aren't the contract owner
}                                            │  to call the modified function.
```

You can then simplify `mint()` and `freezeAccount()` as follows:

```
function mint(address _recipient, uint256  _mintedAmount)
    onlyOwner public {                               ◄─┐
    coinBalance[_recipient] += _mintedAmount;          │
    emit Transfer(owner, _recipient, _mintedAmount);   │  The onlyOwner
}                                                      │  modifier replaces
                                                       │  the previous check
function freezeAccount(address target, bool freeze)    │  on msg.sender.
    onlyOwner public {                               ◄─┘
    frozenAccount[target] = freeze;
    emit FrozenAccount(target, freeze);
}
```

You can see the improved `SimpleCoin` contract, including allowance setting and restricted coin minting and account freezing functionality, in the following listing.

Listing 5.8 Refactored version of `SimpleCoin` with extended functionality

```
pragma solidity ^0.4.24;
contract SimpleCoin {
  mapping (address => uint256) public coinBalance;
  mapping (address => mapping (address => uint256)) public allowance;
  mapping (address => bool) public frozenAccount;
  address public owner;

  event Transfer(address indexed from, address indexed to, uint256 value);
  event FrozenAccount(address target, bool frozen);

  modifier onlyOwner {
    if (msg.sender != owner) revert();
    _;
  }

  constructor(uint256 _initialSupply) public {
    owner = msg.sender;
```

```
        mint(owner, _initialSupply);
    }

    function transfer(address _to, uint256 _amount) public {
        require(_to != 0x0);
        require(coinBalance[msg.sender] > _amount);
        require(coinBalance[_to] + _amount >= coinBalance[_to] );
        coinBalance[msg.sender] -= _amount;
        coinBalance[_to] += _amount;

        emit Transfer(msg.sender, _to, _amount);
    }

    function authorize(address _authorizedAccount, uint256 _allowance)
        public returns (bool success) {
        allowance[msg.sender][_authorizedAccount] = _allowance;
        return true;
    }

    function transferFrom(address _from, address _to, uint256 _amount)
        public returns (bool success) {
        require(_to != 0x0);
        require(coinBalance[_from] > _amount);
        require(coinBalance[_to] + _amount >= coinBalance[_to] );
        require(_amount <= allowance[_from][msg.sender]);

        coinBalance[_from] -= _amount;
        coinBalance[_to] += _amount;
        allowance[_from][msg.sender] -= _amount;
        emit Transfer(_from, _to, _amount);
        return true;
    }

    function mint(address _recipient, uint256 _mintedAmount)
        onlyOwner public {

        coinBalance[_recipient] += _mintedAmount;
        emit Transfer(owner, _recipient, _mintedAmount);
    }

    function freezeAccount(address target, bool freeze)
        onlyOwner public {

        frozenAccount[target] = freeze;
        emit FrozenAccount(target, freeze);
    }
}
```

You've completed the implementation of the proposed improvements. Along the way, you've seen a function modifier in action. In the next chapter, which will focus on Solidity's more advanced object-oriented features, you'll further improve Simple-Coin's code.

Summary

- Various EVM languages have been developed, but Solidity is the most popular one.
- The structure of a Solidity smart contract is similar to the structure of an object-oriented class.
- Solidity has two main groups of types: value types, which include enums, primitive types (integer types, `bool`, `address`), and functions; and reference types, which include arrays, strings, structs, and mapping.
- You can store reference type objects in any memory or in storage.
- You always store state variables in storage, never in memory.
- Functions are the equivalent of object-oriented methods; they can accept several parameters and can return a single result or several results in a tuple.
- An unassigned variable is set with a default value depending on its type.
- You can destructure a tuple returned from a function into separate variables.
- You can define both state variables and functions with a specific accessibility level: private, internal, public, or external. (The latter only applies to functions.)

Writing more complex smart contracts

This chapter covers

- Building a crowdsale management Dapp showing how to structure complex contracts
- Extending the crowdsale management Dapp through single and multiple inheritance

The purpose of the previous chapter was to give you a foundation in Solidity, so I focused mainly on the basic syntax that the language offers. In the next two chapters, I'll introduce more advanced object-oriented (OO) features. I'll start with inheritance in chapter 6 and follow with abstract contracts and interfaces in chapter 7. These OO features allow you to reduce code duplication and make your contracts more composable.

The contract side of real-world Dapps is generally more complex than the single-contract Dapp you've seen so far with SimpleCoin. They often span many contracts interacting with each other, with each contract being a concrete instance of a potentially complex inheritance structure. In this chapter, I'll help you build Simple-Crowdsale, a basic crowdsale management Dapp. A crowdsale is the process through which investors fund a Dapp by buying tokens issued by the organization that's developing it. This sample application will give you an idea of how complex the smart contract layer of a realistic Dapp can be and how inheritance, abstract classes, and interfaces can help you model it appropriately.

I'll try to keep my presentation of inheritance and polymorphism as pragmatic as possible, so if you're among the readers who need a refresher on object-oriented programming, you'll still be able to follow easily. I'll start by building an application made of a simple contract, and I'll keep extending it throughout this chapter by introducing all the object features I've mentioned, bit by bit.

6.1   *Introducing SimpleCrowdsale, a crowdsale contract*

I bet you've heard the term crowdfunding, which is a way of funding a project or a cause through relatively small contribution amounts from a relatively large number of people. You might have even invested some funds toward the design of a new cool gadget at Kickstarter.com, Indiegogo.com, or Microventures.com. If so, depending on the amount of money you contributed and whether the project was successful, you might have been given an early version of the gadget, or you might have been given a considerable discount on the final official price of the product. This type of scheme is called *reward-based* crowdfunding.

Lately, a new crowdfunding scheme called *crowdsale* has emerged, mainly geared toward the funding of startup companies. Rather than being given a discounted product or service in recognition for your early contribution, you're offered some equity in the venture, generally in the form of a monetary token similar to SimpleCoin, whose value the organizers can set before the sale starts. Alternatively, the value can be determined dynamically during the campaign, depending on market factors such as initial token supply and actual demand. Often, the token or coin crowdsale is called an *initial coin offering (ICO)*, an expression that mirrors the more conventional initial public offering (IPO) of shares by companies that enter the stock market for the first time.

In this section, you'll build SimpleCrowdsale, a decentralized crowdsale management application that will teach you how to design Dapps based on multiple Solidity contracts and libraries. In a nutshell, the following list describes the minimum functionality a crowdsale contract generally provides, as illustrated in the diagram of the core crowdsale workflow in figure 6.1:

- It manages the funding that crowdsale investors provide during the funding stage, generally in the form of cryptocurrency. It also converts the cryptocurrency received into tokens and assigns them to the respective investors.
- If the crowdsale objectives, such as a minimum investment target or a time limit, have been met, it releases the tokens to the investors. The organization developing the Dapp keeps the Ether collected and will use it to fund project costs. A token bonus might be granted to the organizers, the development team, or other parties involved with the token sale. Releasing tokens means activating them so they can be used. *Investors can exchange tokens* through a token exchange for real cash as soon as the token has become profitable with respect to the initial investment. This process is similar to that of a company that goes

public and issues shares to investors in exchange for cash, which it will then use to fund its activities. Investors can subsequently trade their shares in a secondary market, and those shares can become more or less valuable depending on the success of the company.

- If the crowdsale is unsuccessful—the target investment isn't met, for example— the contract allows the investors to have their investments refunded.

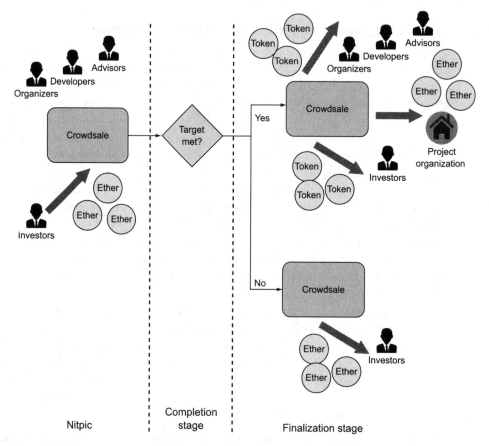

Figure 6.1   The core crowdsale workflow: 1) investors book crowdsale tokens by paying for them in cryptocurrency; 2) if the crowdsale has met the minimum funding target, tokens are released to the investors; a token bonus might be granted to the organizers, the development team, or other parties involved with the token sale; and the project organization keeps the Ether received and will use it to fund project costs; 3) if the crowdsale is unsuccessful, investors can be refunded.

Listing 6.1 gives you an idea of the functions a crowdsale Solidity contract would need to fulfill these requirements. (Don't enter the code in Remix yet!) In case you're wondering, `onlyOwner` is the same modifier I introduced earlier in 5.4.2 for `SimpleCoin`: only the contract owner is allowed to execute the `finalize()` function.

Listing 6.1   Core functionality a crowdsale contract provides

```
contract SimpleCrowdsale {
    function invest(address _beneficiary)
        public payable {}
    function finalize() onlyOwner public {}
    function refund() public {}
}
```

Allows an investor to book crowdsale tokens. (No parameter is necessary to specify the amount of Ether being invested because it's being sent through the msg.value property.)

Allows the crowdsale organizer, who is the contract owner, to release tokens to the investors, in case of successful completion, and grant a bonus to the development team, if applicable

Allows an investor to get a refund in case of unsuccessful completion

Let's build a basic implementation of this functionality, which we'll use as a starting point for a later discussion on advanced object-oriented features. I'm not expecting you to start entering the code into Remix until you reach 6.1.9, as I'll be refactoring the code progressively to explain concepts step-by-step. Then I'll recap everything in listing 6.5, which is fully executable. But if you want to give it a try as I go along, you're welcome to.

6.1.1   State variables

A crowdsale contract needs to maintain some configuration regarding the funding period during which investment contributions are accepted, the price of the token being sold, the minimum investment objective, and the address of the account accepting the investments. It also needs to keep a record of the contributions that investors submit. This data should be visible from the whole contract, so you should express it in the following state variables:

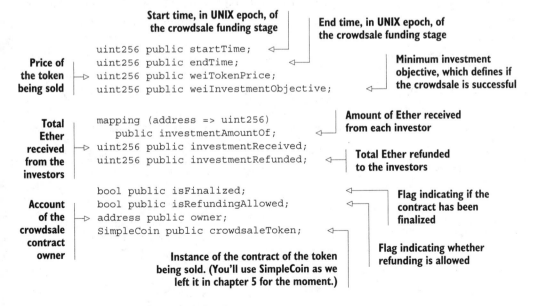

Start time, in UNIX epoch, of the crowdsale funding stage

End time, in UNIX epoch, of the crowdsale funding stage

Price of the token being sold

Minimum investment objective, which defines if the crowdsale is successful

```
uint256 public startTime;
uint256 public endTime;
uint256 public weiTokenPrice;
uint256 public weiInvestmentObjective;
```

Total Ether received from the investors

Amount of Ether received from each investor

```
mapping (address => uint256)
    public investmentAmountOf;
uint256 public investmentReceived;
uint256 public investmentRefunded;
```

Total Ether refunded to the investors

Account of the crowdsale contract owner

Flag indicating if the contract has been finalized

```
bool public isFinalized;
bool public isRefundingAllowed;
address public owner;
SimpleCoin public crowdsaleToken;
```

Instance of the contract of the token being sold. (You'll use SimpleCoin as we left it in chapter 5 for the moment.)

Flag indicating whether refunding is allowed

6.1.2 Constructor

The contract constructor should take all the input configurations I've described, validate them, and instantiate the contract of the token being sold. To make things easy, you'll use SimpleCoin, because you're already familiar with it. You shouldn't find anything surprising in the following code:

```
constructor(uint256 _startTime, uint256 _endTime,
    uint256 _weiTokenPrice, uint256 _etherInvestmentObjective) public
{
    require(_startTime >= now);
    require(_endTime >= _startTime);           Validates input
    require(_weiTokenPrice != 0);              configurations
    require(_etherInvestmentObjective != 0);

    startTime = _startTime;
    endTime = _endTime;                        Sets input
    weiTokenPrice = _weiTokenPrice;            configurations
    weiInvestmentObjective =                   into state
    _etherInvestmentObjective * 1000000000000000000;   variables

    crowdsaleToken = new SimpleCoin(0);        Instantiates the contract
    isFinalized = false;                       of the token being sold
    isRefundingAllowed = false;                in the crowdsale
    owner = msg.sender;            Sets the contract owner,
}                                  as seen in SimpleCoin
```

6.1.3 Implementing invest()

This is the most important function of the contract. Its purpose is to accept Ether funds from investors and convert them into crowdsale tokens. These tokens won't be released to their respective owners, though, until the crowdsale has completed successfully.

As you can see in the following implementation, you've declared the `invest()` function as `payable` and placed validation logic and token conversion logic in three internal functions. You've also declared a couple of events that these functions raise:

```
event LogInvestment(address indexed investor, uint256 value);
event LogTokenAssignment(address indexed investor, uint256 numTokens);

function invest() public payable {           Declares the invest() function
    require(isValidInvestment(msg.value));    as payable to accept Ether

    address investor = msg.sender;           Checks if the
    uint256 investment = msg.value;          investment is valid

    investmentAmountOf[investor] += investment;    Records the investment that
    investmentReceived += investment;              each investor contributes
                                                   and the total investment

    assignTokens(investor, investment);      Converts the Ether
    emit LogInvestment(investor, investment);    investment into
}                                            crowdsale tokens
```

Logs the investment event

Validates the investment

```
function isValidInvestment(uint256 _investment)
    internal view returns (bool) {
    bool nonZeroInvestment = _investment != 0;
    bool withinCrowdsalePeriod =
        now >= startTime && now <= endTime;


    return nonZeroInvestment && withinCrowdsalePeriod;
}
```

Checks that this is a meaningful investment

Checks that this is taking place during the crowdsale funding stage

```
function assignTokens(address _beneficiary,
    uint256 _investment) internal {

    uint256 _numberOfTokens =
        calculateNumberOfTokens(_investment);

    crowdsaleToken.mint(_beneficiary,
        _numberOfTokens);
}
```

Calculates the number of tokens corresponding to the investment

Generates the tokens in the investor account

```
function calculateNumberOfTokens(uint256 _investment)
    internal returns (uint256) {
    return _investment / weiTokenPrice;
}
```

Calculates the number of tokens

6.1.4 *Implementing finalize()*

The purpose of the finalize() function is to execute the closing actions of a crowdsale. If the crowdsale has met its minimum investment objective, the contract releases the tokens to the investors so they can be used. Additionally, a token bonus that depends on the total investment collected could be assigned and released to the development team. On the other hand, if the crowdsale is unsuccessful, it moves to a refunding state, and the investors are allowed to get their investments refunded to their accounts.

Before tokens are released to the investors, they should stay locked down, in an unusable state: token owners shouldn't be able to perform any operations on them, such as transferring them to other accounts. The contract should only release the initially locked tokens if the crowdsale is successful.

As you know, SimpleCoin operations (apart from minting(), which is restricted to the contract owner) aren't constrained in any way and don't depend on the contract owner unlocking any functionality. Consequently, SimpleCoin, as it stands, isn't suitable for a crowdsale. It seems you must create a modified version of SimpleCoin—say, ReleasableSimpleCoin—whose operations, such as transfer() and transferFrom(), aren't allowed to work unless the token has been released, as shown in the following listing.

Listing 6.2 ReleasableSimpleCoin, with locked transfer() and transferFrom()

```
contract ReleasableSimpleCoin {
    bool public released = false;
```

Flag determining whether the token is released

...   ◁───┤ **Same SimpleCoin code as before, omitted for brevity. (In case you're expecting inheritance..., it hasn't come yet.)**

```
function release() onlyOwner {          ◁───┐ New function to release the
    released = true;                          │ coin. (Only the contract
}                                             │ owner can call it.)

function transfer(address _to, uint256 _amount) public {
    require(_to != 0x0);
    require(coinBalance[msg.sender] > _amount);
    require(coinBalance[_to] + _amount >= coinBalance[_to] );

    if (released ) {
        coinBalance[msg.sender] -= _amount;
        coinBalance[_to] += _amount;
        emit Transfer(msg.sender, _to, _amount);

        return true;
    }
    revert();              ◁───┤ If the token hasn't
}                                │ been released, the
                                 │ state is reverted.

function transferFrom(address _from, address _to, uint256 _amount)
    public returns (bool success) {
    require(_to != 0x0);
    require(coinBalance[_from] > _amount);
    require(coinBalance[_to] + _amount >= coinBalance[_to] );
    require(_amount <= allowance[_from][msg.sender]);

    if (released ) {
        coinBalance[_from] -= _amount;
        coinBalance[_to] += _amount;
        allowance[_from][msg.sender] -= _amount;
        emit Transfer(_from, _to, _amount);

        return true;
    }
    revert();     ◁───┐
}                     │ If the token
                      │ hasn't been
                      │ released, the
...   ◁───────────────┘ state is reverted.

}
```

Now the transfer logic can be executed only if the token has been released.

6.1.5   *Small detour: Introducing inheritance*

The ReleasableSimpleCoin implementation in listing 6.2 works but has a major problem: it's duplicating most of SimpleCoin's code, with obvious maintenance disadvantages. If you decide to make a change in SimpleCoin, you must remember to replicate the same change in ReleasableSimpleCoin, which is time-consuming and error-prone. A way to avoid this is to *derive* ReleasableSimpleCoin from SimpleCoin through single inheritance and introduce the `isReleased` modifier, as shown in the following listing.

Listing 6.3 `ReleasableSimpleCoin` inherited from `SimpleCoin`

```solidity
pragma solidity ^0.4.18;
import "./Listing5_8_SimpleCoin.sol";
contract ReleasableSimpleCoin is SimpleCoin {
    bool public released = false;

    modifier isReleased() {
        if(!released) {
            revert();
        }

        _;
    }

    constructor(uint256 _initialSupply)
        SimpleCoin(_initialSupply) public {}

    function release() onlyOwner public {
        released = true;
    }

    function transfer(address _to, uint256 _amount)
        isReleased public {
        super.transfer(_to, _amount);
    }

    function transferFrom(address _from, address _to, uint256 _amount)
        isReleased public returns (bool) {
        super.transferFrom(_from, _to, _amount);
    }
}
```

- Directive to reference the file where SimpleCoin is defined (listing 5.8 downloadable from the book website)
- Makes ReleasableSimpleCoin inherited from SimpleCoin
- Flag determining whether the token is released
- *Modifier encapsulating check on released flag*
- Calls the base constructor to initialize the initialSupply state variable in SimpleCoin
- New function to release the coin. (Only the contract owner can call it.)
- *Overrides the original implementation. (Thanks to the isReleased modifier, this can be called successfully only if the token has been released.)*
- You call the original SimpleCoin implementation through super. The original implementation is now constrained by the isReleased modifier, though.

The `ReleasableSimpleCoin` contract has given you a concrete example of single inheritance in Solidity. Let's summarize the main Solidity keywords involved in inheritance:

- A contract is *derived* from another contract with the `is` keyword, as in

```
Contract ReleasableSimpleCoin is SimpleCoin
```

- The constructor of the derived contract must feed the *base constructor* all the necessary parameters, as shown here:

```
function ReleasableSimpleCoin(uint256 _initialSupply)
    SimpleCoin(_initialSupply)  {}
```

- A derived contract inherits all the public and internal functions from the parent contract. It's possible to *override* a function by reimplementing it in the child contract, as in

```
function transfer(address _to, uint256 _amount) isReleased public { ...
```

- An overridden function can *call the original implementation* from the base contract using the super keyword, as in

```
super.transfer(_to, _amount);
```

If you're not entirely familiar with object-oriented terminology, table 6.1 can help you understand it.

Table 6.1   Inheritance terminology

Definition	Explanation
To derive a contract	To inherit a contract—Acquire public and internal state variables and functions from the parent contract.
Derived contract	Inherited contract, subcontract, or child contract.
Base contract	Parent contract.
Overridden function	Function reimplemented in a derived contract—The overridden function is used instead of the parent one when the derived contract calls the function.

You can see the inheritance relationship between ReleasableSimpleCoin and Simple-Coin in the contract diagram in figure 6.2. I've used the same drawing convention used in UML class diagrams. Although you may be able to understand UML class

Token contract diagram

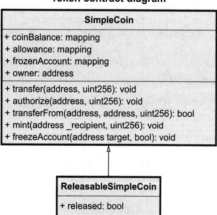

Figure 6.2   Contract diagram illustrating the token contract hierarchy: SimpleCoin is a base contract, and ReleasableSimpleCoin has been inherited from it.

diagrams intuitively, if you're not familiar with them and want to learn more, check out the related sidebar.

UML class diagrams

The Unified Modeling Language (UML) is a general-purpose modeling language that aims at standardizing the visualization of the design of a software system. It was developed in the 1990s by Grady Booch, Ivar Jacobson, and James Rumbaugh at Rational Software. It became an ISO standard in 2005.

UML covers a wide range of diagrams, including these categories:

- *Behavior diagrams*—Describe how a system works (how the components of the system interact with each other and with external agents)
- *Structure diagrams*—Describe the structure of the system at different levels (packages to be deployed, components within a package, and object-oriented classes within a component)

In this book, I'll only show you *contract diagrams*, which, given the similarity between the concepts of contract and class, are based on UML *class diagrams*, the lowest-level structure diagrams.

A contract diagram describes the content of a contract (state variables and functions) and the two main relationships between contracts:

- *Generalization*—A contract is inherited from a more general contract (its base or parent contract) or, as you'll learn later, from an interface.
- *Dependency*—One of the state variables is an instance of another contract.

I've annotated every section of text and every symbol in the sample contract diagram you see here, so you can refer back to it if you have any trouble understanding the contract diagrams that follow in the coming pages. I'll explain new symbols as I introduce them in the coming sections.

Contract diagram, adapted from the UML class diagram

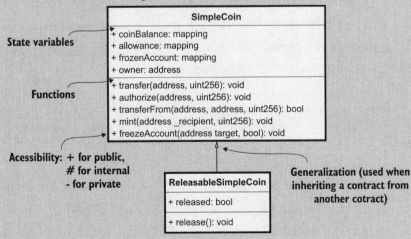

Contract diagram, with symbols and conventions adapted from the UML class diagram

> **(continued)**
> If you want to learn more about UML diagrams, I encourage you to look up the *UML Quick Reference Card*, at http://tnerual.eriogerg.free.fr/umlqrc.pdf, or this convenient *UML Cheatsheet*: http://mng.bz/jO5p. The best book on UML is The Unified Modeling Language User Guide, by Grady Booch, et al, published by Addison-Wesley.

6.1.6   *Implementing finalize(), take 2*

Now that you've implemented a token suitable for a crowdsale, you can go back to the state variables section and replace the definition of crowdsaleToken with

```
ReleasableSimpleCoin public crowdsaleToken;
```

and amend the token instantiation in the crowdsale constructor with

```
crowdsaleToken = new ReleasableSimpleCoin(0);
```

Now I can show you a possible implementation for the finalize() function:

```
function finalize() onlyOwner public {
    if (isFinalized) revert();

    bool isCrowdsaleComplete = now > endTime;
    bool investmentObjectiveMet =
        investmentReceived >= weiInvestmentObjective;

    if (isCrowdsaleComplete)
    {
        if (investmentObjectiveMet)
            crowdsaleToken.release();
        else
            isRefundingAllowed = true;

        isFinalized = true;
    }
}
```

Prevents calling finalize() on a finalized contract → `if (isFinalized) revert();`

Allows only the crowdsale contract owner to call finalize()

Conditions determining if a crowdsale has been successful

Releases crowdsale tokens so investors can use them

Allows investors to get refunded if the funding objective hasn't been met

As I mentioned earlier, onlyOwner is the same modifier I introduced in SimpleCoin at the end of chapter 5 to restrict the execution of some functions only to the contract owner:

```
modifier onlyOwner {
    if (msg.sender != owner) revert();
    _;
}
```

6.1.7   *Implementing refund()*

The last function you must implement to complete the first version of your crowdsale contract is refund(), which investors would call after an unsuccessful crowdsale:

```
event Refund(address investor, uint256 value);

function refund() public {
    if (!isRefundingAllowed) revert();          ←─  Only allows refunding if this
                                                     has been allowed at the
                                                     crowdsale finalization

    address investor = msg.sender;
    uint256 investment = investmentAmountOf[investor];     Only allows refunding if the
    if (investment == 0) revert();              ←─────────  investor has contributed a
    investmentAmountOf[investor] = 0;      ←─               meaningful amount
    investmentRefunded += investment;
    emit Refund(msg.sender, investment);       Keeps a record
                                               of all refunds

    if (!investor.send(investment)) revert();   ←─┐  Transfers Ether back to
}                                                 │  the investor and handles
                                                     possible transfer error
```

NOTE   I've decided to refund investors through send() rather than transfer(), only because transfer() has some quirks in Remix (at the time of writing) and might generate unwanted error messages that would slow down your learning experience. In a production environment, transfer() is recommended.

6.1.8   *Eliminating code duplication with inheritance*

As I noted, SimpleCoin and SimpleCrowdsale use the same onlyOwner modifier to restrict access to some operations to only the contract owner. The advantage is that you're using onlyOwner consistently across the two contracts. The downside is that you had to introduce the owner state variable and implement the onlyOwner modifier in both contracts. Wouldn't it be nice to place this modifier somewhere so you could then drop it into both SimpleCoin and SimpleCrowdsale without introducing code duplication? Fortunately, you can by encapsulating the ownership state and onlyOwner modifier into a separate contract, called Ownable, as shown in the following listing.

Listing 6.4   Ownable contract extracted from SimpleCrowdsale and SimpleCoin

```
pragma solidity ^0.4.18;
contract Ownable {                          Keeps the address of the contract
    address public owner;        ←─────     owner in a state variable

    constructor() public {             Assigns the contract
        owner = msg.sender;     ←─     owner at construction
    }

    modifier onlyOwner() {                 Checks if the function
        require(msg.sender == owner);  ←─  caller using this modifier
        _;                                 is the owner
    }
}
```

Now you can remove the owner state variable and the `onlyOwner()` modifier from both `SimpleCoin` and `SimpleCrowdsale` and inherit both contracts from `Ownable`, as shown in the contract diagram in figure 6.3 and in this code:

```
SimpleCoin is Ownable {
...
}

SimpleCrowdsale is Ownable {
...
}
```

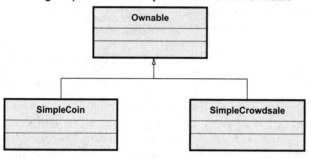

Deriving SimpleCoin and SimpleCrowdsale from Ownable

Figure 6.3   After moving ownership functionality into the `Ownable` contract, both `SimpleCoin` and `Simple-Crowdsale` can still use the `onlyOwner` modifier by inheriting it from `Ownable`.

You can see the refactored `SimpleCoin` contract inheriting from `Ownable` in appendix A. Congratulations! You've completed your first implementation of a crowdsale contract, which you can fully appreciate in the contract diagram in figure 6.4 and in listing 6.5.

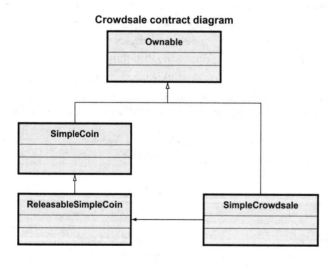

Crowdsale contract diagram

Figure 6.4   Crowdsale's contract diagram, including `Ownable` contract and token contract. Both `SimpleCrowdsale` and `SimpleCoin` are inherited from `Ownable`. `SimpleCrowdsale` has a `ReleasableSimpleCoin` state variable, so it depends on `ReleasableSimpleCoin`. (If you're unfamiliar with object-oriented class diagrams, the hollow-headed arrow means "inherited from," and the filled arrow means "depends on.")

NOTE   The arrow between `SimpleCrowdsale` and `ReleasableSimpleCoin` in figure 6.4 is a UML symbol that stands for *depends on*. I've included the arrow because the `SimpleCrowdsale` contract has a state variable of type `Releasable-SimpleCoin`, so it depends on `ReleasableSimpleCoin`.

Listing 6.5 Initial implementation of a crowdsale contract

```solidity
pragma solidity ^0.4.24;

import "./Listing6_3_ReleasableSimpleCoin.sol";
import "./Listing6_4_Ownable.sol";

contract SimpleCrowdsale is Ownable {
    uint256 public startTime;
    uint256 public endTime;
    uint256 public weiTokenPrice;
    uint256 public weiInvestmentObjective;

    mapping (address => uint256) public investmentAmountOf;
    uint256 public investmentReceived;
    uint256 public investmentRefunded;

    bool public isFinalized;
    bool public isRefundingAllowed;

    ReleasableSimpleCoin public crowdsaleToken;

    constructor(uint256 _startTime, uint256 _endTime,
      uint256 _weiTokenPrice,
      uint256 _weiInvestmentObjective)
      payable public
    {
        require(_startTime >= now);
        require(_endTime >= _startTime);
        require(_weiTokenPrice != 0);
        require(_weiInvestmentObjective != 0);

        startTime = _startTime;
        endTime = _endTime;
        weiTokenPrice = _weiTokenPrice;
        weiInvestmentObjective = _weiInvestmentObjective;

        crowdsaleToken = new ReleasableSimpleCoin(0);
        isFinalized = false;
    }

    event LogInvestment(address indexed investor, uint256 value);
    event LogTokenAssignment(address indexed investor, uint256 numTokens);
    event Refund(address investor, uint256 value);

    function invest() public payable {
        require(isValidInvestment(msg.value));

        address investor = msg.sender;
        uint256 investment = msg.value;
```

References Solidity code from other files or from other Remix code tabs

```
        investmentAmountOf[investor] += investment;
        investmentReceived += investment;

        assignTokens(investor, investment);
        emit LogInvestment(investor, investment);
    }

    function isValidInvestment(uint256 _investment)
        internal view returns (bool) {
        bool nonZeroInvestment = _investment != 0;
        bool withinCrowdsalePeriod = now >= startTime && now <= endTime;

        return nonZeroInvestment && withinCrowdsalePeriod;
    }

    function assignTokens(address _beneficiary,
        uint256 _investment) internal {

        uint256 _numberOfTokens = calculateNumberOfTokens(_investment);

        crowdsaleToken.mint(_beneficiary, _numberOfTokens);
    }

    function calculateNumberOfTokens(uint256 _investment)
        internal returns (uint256) {
        return _investment / weiTokenPrice;
    }

    function finalize() onlyOwner public {
        if (isFinalized) revert();

        bool isCrowdsaleComplete = now > endTime;
        bool investmentObjectiveMet =
investmentReceived >= weiInvestmentObjective;

        if (isCrowdsaleComplete)
        {
            if (investmentObjectiveMet)
                crowdsaleToken.release();
            else
                isRefundingAllowed = true;

            isFinalized = true;
        }
    }

    function refund() public {
        if (!isRefundingAllowed) revert();

        address investor = msg.sender;
        uint256 investment = investmentAmountOf[investor];
        if (investment == 0) revert();
        investmentAmountOf[investor] = 0;
        investmentRefunded += investment;
        emit Refund(msg.sender, investment);
```

```
        if (!investor.send(investment)) revert();
    }
}
```

6.1.9 *Running SimpleCrowdsale*

You've just started implementing `SimpleCrowdsale`, but if you want to see what you've built so far in action, copy listing 6.5 into a new Remix code tab (perhaps named Listing6_5_SimpleCrowdsale.sol). Make sure you've placed the dependent code specified in the import directives in related code tabs named appropriately:

- Listing5_8_SimpleCoin.sol (needed for Listing6_3_ReleasableSimpleCoin.sol)
- Listing6_3_ReleasableSimpleCoin.sol
- Listing6_4_Ownable.sol

(You can find these files in the code downloadable from the book website.)

DISABLING DATE CHECKS TEMPORARILY

Before instantiating `SimpleCrowdsale`, I recommend you pick version 0.4.24 in the Remix Compiler tab because this is the Solidity version I've used. I also suggest you temporarily disable checks on `startDate` and `endDate` to make your interaction with Remix easier. Modify this line in `isValidInvestment()`

```
bool withinCrowdsalePeriod = now >= startTime && now <= endTime;
```

to read

```
bool withinCrowdsalePeriod = true;
```

and this line in `finalize()`

```
bool isCrowdsaleComplete = now > endTime;
```

to read

```
bool isCrowdsaleComplete = true;
```

INSTANTIATING THE CONTRACT

Now you can feed `SimpleCrowdsale`'s constructor parameters in the text box next to the Deploy button. For example, I'll set a token price of 2,000,000,000,000,000 Wei and a funding objective of 15,000 Ether as follows:

```
2003526559, 2003526600, 2000000000000000, 15000
```

Because of your earlier modification, the 2003526559 and 2003526600 start and end dates will be ignored.

Now pick `SimpleCrowdsale` from the contract drop-down list and click Deploy. If `SimpleCrowdsale` doesn't appear, click the Compile tab and then Start to Compile. Take a note of which account is currently selected in the Account drop-down list at the top of the screen: this will be the contract owner of both `SimpleCrowdsale` and `ReleasableSimpleCoin`. `SimpleCrowdsale` will be activated, and a number of buttons corresponding to its state variables and functions will appear at the bottom of the screen.

INVESTING INTO THE CROWDSALE

You can simulate investors' activity by calling the `invest()` function as follows:

1 Click the SimpleCrowdsale drop-down in the Deployed Contracts bottom section generated after you clicked Deploy earlier.
2 Pick an Account from the drop-down list—perhaps the one starting with 0x147.
3 Enter an amount in the Value box at the top of the screen, specify the unit (100 Ether, for example), and click the invest button in the SimpleCrowdsale panel within the Deployed Contract bottom section. (You can see this button in figure 6.5.)
4 Check the total investment received by clicking investmentReceived.

Repeat these three steps with different accounts and investment amounts.

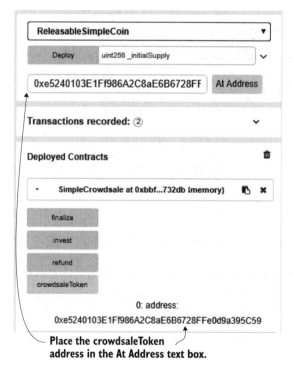

Place the crowdsaleToken address in the At Address text box.

Figure 6.5 Place in Releasable-SimpleCoin's At Address text box the address from `SimpleCrowdsale`'s `crowdsaleToken` state variable.

CHECKING THAT TOKENS HAVE BEEN ASSIGNED TO INVESTORS

Although investors at this point have received a number of tokens corresponding to the amount of Ether contributed, they aren't able to transfer them yet because the owner hasn't finalized the crowdsale. If you want to check that tokens have been assigned to each investor, you must activate the `ReleasableSimpleCoin` contract instance referenced in `SimpleCrowdsale`.

First of all, get its address by clicking crowdsaleToken. Copy this address and paste it in the textbox next to the Activate button (*not wrapped* with double quotes), as shown in figure 6.5 (but your address will be different):

Now click At Address, and a new panel showing `ReleasableSimpleCoin`'s functionality, mostly inherited from SimpleCoin, will appear at the bottom part of the screen, as shown in figure 6.6. You must click ReleasableSimpleCoin to expand the panel.

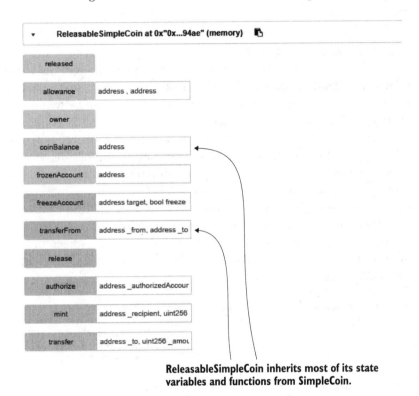

ReleasableSimpleCoin inherits most of its state variables and functions from SimpleCoin.

Figure 6.6 `ReleasableSimpleCoin`'s **state variables and functions**

You can now check the number of tokens assigned to each investor in the following way:

1 Pick the address from the Account drop-down corresponding to an investor you want to check, copy it by clicking the copy icon next to it, and paste it into the text box next to the coinBalance button. (Remember to wrap it with double quotes.)

2 Click coinBalance, and the expected number of tokens will appear next to it.

Repeat this for all accounts in the drop-down. In my case, I have the token breakdown shown in table 6.2.

Table 6.2   Number of tokens assigned to each investor

Investor account	Number of tokens
0xca35b7d915458ef540ade6068dfe2f44e8fa733c	10,100,000
0x14723a09acff6d2a60dcdf7aa4aff308fddc160c	150,000
0x4b0897b0513fdc7c541b6d9d7e929c4e5364d2db	653,500
0x583031d1113ad414f02576bd6afabfb302140225	284,000
0xdd870fa1b7c4700f2bd7f44238821c26f7392148	56,000

CHECKING THAT TOKENS ARE STILL LOCKED

As I explained, tokens that get assigned to investors during the crowdsale are unusable until it's been finalized successfully. This means an investor won't be able to transfer tokens to another account. Let's check that this is the case by trying to transfer some tokens from one account to another.

Pick an account from the Account drop-down, copy its address, and paste it into the transfer text box (wrapped, as usual, with double quotes). This will be the destination account for the token transfer. Then pick a different account from the Account drop-down. This will be the source of the token transfer.

Click Transfer. Now check the number of tokens associated with the source and destination account again, as you did earlier. You'll notice they haven't changed. Because the value of `released` is still `false` (the crowdsale hasn't been finalized yet), the transfer won't take place (but no error will be thrown), as you can see in the code extract from `transfer()`:

```
function transfer(address _to, uint256 _amount) public {
    ...

    if (released) {                                ⬅——— The value of released is still
        coinBalance[msg.sender] -= _amount;              false, so the token transfer
        coinBalance[_to] += _amount;                     isn't executed.
        emit Transfer(msg.sender, _to, _amount);
    }
}
```

FINALIZING A SUCCESSFUL CROWDSALE

If you want to test a successful crowdsale, make sure the amount of investment is above the investment objective (15,000 Ether in my example, equivalent to 15,000,000,000,000,000,000,000 Wei). Bear in mind, the amount shown next to the `investmentReceived` button is expressed in Wei. You can reach it quickly by making a few large Ether investments. Once the investment received is higher than the funding objective, select the `SimpleCrowdsale` contract owner account (the account you used to instantiate `SimpleCrowdsale`) and click Finalize.

Verify the crowdsale has been finalized by clicking isFinalized. The value displayed should be `true`. Verify `ReleasableSimpleCoin` has been released by clicking Released. The value displayed again should be `true`.

Now you can try to make a token transfer, as you did earlier. This time, though, the transfer will work because the value of `released` is now `true` and the transfer logic can get executed. You can verify that the number of tokens associated with the source and destination accounts have changed accordingly. In my case, I moved three coins from the account starting with 0x1472 to the account starting with 0x4b089. You can see their amended balances in table 6.3.

Table 6.3 Amended `ReleasableSimpleCoin` token balance after a token transfer

Investor account	Number of tokens
0xca35b7d915458ef540ade6068dfe2f44e8fa733c	10,100,000
0x14723a09acff6d2a60dcdf7aa4aff308fddc160c	149,997
0x4b0897b0513fdc7c541b6d9d7e929c4e5364d2db	653,503
0x583031d1113ad414f02576bd6afabfb302140225	284,000
0xdd870fa1b7c4700f2bd7f44238821c26f7392148	56,000

FINALIZING AN UNSUCCESSFUL CROWDSALE

If you're up for it, you can also test the scenario of an unsuccessful crowdsale. I recommend you restart from scratch and go through all the steps you took earlier up to the point you contribute Ether to the crowdsale through the `invest()` function from various investor accounts. This time, though, don't reach the funding objective.

Now, when you call `finalize()` by clicking the related button, `fundingObjectiveMet` is `false`. Consequently, the `isRefundingAllowed` gets enabled, as you can see in this extract from the `finalize()` code:

```
if (isCrowdsaleComplete)
{
    if (investmentObjectiveMet)
        crowdsaleToken.release();
    else
        isRefundingAllowed = true;

    isFinalized = true;
}
```

You can double-check this is the case by clicking isRefundingAllowed. With that enabled, you'll be able to successfully call the `refund()` function, as you'll see next. But before doing so, as an exercise I invite you to test that tokens haven't been released and it isn't possible to transfer them from one account to another, as you saw earlier.

GETTING A REFUND

Following unsuccessful finalization, investors are allowed to get refunded. Pick an address from the Account drop-down, check the amount of Ether associated with it (shown next to the address), and click Refund. You'll see that the Ether value next to the account address will increase because it has been transferred from the crowdsale contract back to the investor.

In the next few sections, you'll improve the functionality of the crowdsale contract by taking advantage of Solidity object-oriented features, such as single inheritance, which you've already used in the `ReleasableSimpleCoin` contract, multiple inheritance, and abstract classes.

6.2   *Extending functionality with inheritance*

The current crowdsale implementation assumes the price of the token being bought by the investors is fixed throughout the crowdsale, from start to end. A way to incentivize and reward early investors is to provide tranche-based pricing.

6.2.1   *Implementing a new token pricing contract with inheritance*

A *tranche* is a certain amount of total investment received. A different token price applies to each tranche, as shown in figure 6.7, so that early investors are attracted with a lower initial price. As the sale progresses, the token price rises when moving from one tranche to the next and eventually becomes constant after the minimum funding target has been met.

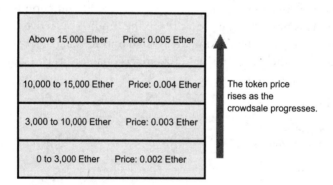

Figure 6.7   Tranche-based token pricing. The total investment up to the minimum funding objective is divided into several tranches, each with a different token price. The token price rises as the total investment received moves from one tranche to the next.

In the example shown in figure 6.7, the minimum funding target has been set at 15,000 Ether, and the organizers have decided to create four tranches, as defined in table 6.4.

Table 6.4   Token-based pricing: example of different prices at different points in the funding process

Total investment received (in Ether)	Token price (in Ether)
Above 15,000	0.005
From 10,000 to 15,000	0.004
From 3,000 to 10,000	0.003
From 0 to 3,000	0.002

TRANCHE-BASED TOKEN PRICING LOGIC

Now that you understand the principle of tranche-based pricing, let's see how you can implement it in Solidity. If you look back at listing 6.5, you'll notice that the only function that's directly accessing the token price is

```
function calculateNumberOfTokens(uint256 _investment)
    internal returns (uint256) {
    return _investment / weiTokenPrice;       ⊲─┤ weiTokenPrice is fixed because it
}                                                 isn't modified during the crowdsale.
```

You'll also notice that the value of weiTokenPrice is never modified from within the crowdsale contract, so you can consider it fixed throughout the whole crowdsale.

Here's a small challenge: How would you modify the implementation of calculate-NumberOfTokens() so the pricing becomes tranche-based according to the tranches defined in table 6.4? Here are some hints you could consider before attempting a solution:

- You could configure the tranches with a struct type, such as

```
struct Tranche {
    uint256 weiHighLimit;      ⊲─┘ Higher funding limit
    uint256 weiTokenPrice;          of the tranche
}                               ⊲─┐ Token price associated
                                    with the tranche
```

- You could store the entire tranche structure in a state variable defined with the following mapping

```
mapping(uint256 => Tranche) public trancheStructure;
```

and initialize the state variable in the contract constructor as follows

```
trancheStructure[0] = Tranche(3000 ether, 0.002 ether);
trancheStructure[1] = Tranche(10000 ether, 0.003 ether);
trancheStructure[2] = Tranche(15000 ether, 0.004 ether);
trancheStructure[3] = Tranche(1000000000 ether, 0.005 ether);
```

with the tranche limits and token price defined in Ether.

- You could maintain the current active tranche in a state variable

```
uint256 currentTrancheLevel;
```

and you'd initialize this state variable in the constructor as follows:

```
currentTrancheLevel = 0;
```

- You could update `currentTrancheLevel` and `weiTokenPrice` within `calculate-NumberOfTokens()`.

I strongly encourage you to give tranche-based pricing a try! Finished? You can compare your modified `calculateNumberOfTokens()` with that in the following listing.

Listing 6.6   `calculateNumberOfTokens()` based on tranche-based pricing

```
function calculateNumberOfTokens(uint256 investment)
    internal returns (uint256) {
    updateCurrentTrancheAndPrice();                    ◁    The only change to
    return investment / weiTokenPrice;                      calculateNumberOfTokens()
}

function updateCurrentTrancheAndPrice()            ◁    Updates the current
    internal {                                           tranche and, consequently,
    uint256 i = currentTrancheLevel;                     the current token price

    while(trancheStructure[i].weiHighLimit
        < investmentReceived)
        ++i;                            ◁    Tests tranches to identify where
                                             investmentReceived falls

    currentTrancheLevel = i;

    weiTokenPrice =                          Updates weiTokenPrice with the
        trancheStructure[currentTrancheLevel]    value from the current tranche-
            .weiTokenPrice;             ◁       based pricing crowdsale contract
}
```

As you can see in listing 6.6, only one extra function is necessary to calculate the token price based on a tranche basis. The rest of the code stays unaltered. I'm sure you might be wondering where you should place the amended `calculateNumberOf-Tokens()` and new `updateCurrentTrancheAndPrice()` functions. The simple answer is in a new crowdsale contract called `TranchePricingCrowdsale`, because you might still want to use the flat token pricing in other crowdsales. The next question is should I copy `SimpleCrowdsale`'s code, paste it into `TranchePricingCrowdsale`, and apply in it the modifications from listing 6.6? The answer is no, you shouldn't! As I explained when you created `ReleasableSimpleCoin` based on SimpleCoin, you'll be *inheriting* `TranchePricingCrowdsale` from `SimpleCrowdsale`, as shown in the following listing.

Listing 6.7 `TranchePricingCrowdsale` **derived from** `SimpleCrowdsale`

```solidity
pragma solidity ^0.4.24;

import "./Listing6_5_SimpleCrowdsale.sol";

contract TranchePricingCrowdsale
    is SimpleCrowdsale {          ◁─── TranchePricingCrowdsale is
                                       inherited from SimpleCrowdsale.

    struct Tranche {
      uint256 weiHighLimit;
      uint256 weiTokenPrice;
    }                                  Configuration of
                                       tranche structure
    mapping(uint256 => Tranche)
      public trancheStructure;    ◁──┘
    uint256 public currentTrancheLevel;  ◁───  Current tranche level with respect
                                               to the investment received so far

    constructor(uint256 _startTime, uint256 _endTime,
       uint256 _etherInvestmentObjective)
       SimpleCrowdsale(_startTime, _endTime,
       1, _etherInvestmentObjective)    ◁───  Calling constructor on base
    payable public                            contractor to complete the
    {                                         contract initialization
       trancheStructure[0] = Tranche(3000 ether,
          0.002 ether);
       trancheStructure[1] = Tranche(10000 ether,
          0.003 ether);
       trancheStructure[2] = Tranche(15000 ether,
          0.004 ether);
       trancheStructure[3] = Tranche(1000000000 ether,
          0.005 ether);
       currentTrancheLevel = 0;
    }

    function calculateNumberOfTokens(
       uint256 investment)        ◁───  Overrides the original
       internal returns (uint256) {      calculateNumberOfTokens()
       updateCurrentTrancheAndPrice();   implementation present in
       return investment / weiTokenPrice;  SimpleCrowdsale
    }
                                       New function to update
    function updateCurrentTrancheAndPrice()  ◁───  the token price based on
       internal {                            the current tranche
       uint256 i = currentTrancheLevel;

       while(trancheStructure[i].weiHighLimit < investmentReceived)
          ++i;

       currentTrancheLevel = i;

       weiTokenPrice = trancheStructure[currentTrancheLevel].weiTokenPrice;
    }
}
```

Initialization of tranche structure. (I've hardcoded this for simplicity, but it could be fed through constructor parameters.)

By inheriting `TranchePricingCrowdsale` from `SimpleCrowdsale`, I've shown you another example of single inheritance. I'll give you a quick summary of the inheritance features of Solidity you can appreciate in `TranchePricingCrowdsale`. This is almost a repeat of what you've already seen in `ReleasableSimpleCoin`, and hopefully it will help you consolidate the concepts:

- `TranchePricingCrowdsale` is *inherited* from `SimpleCrowdsale` with the is keyword:

```
contract TranchePricingCrowdsale is SimpleCrowdsale
```

- You've added *additional state variables* `trancheStructure` and `currentTranche-Level` to the inherited contract to handle tranche-specific functionality.
- `TranchePricingCrowdsale`'s constructor sets tranche-related state but also feeds the *base* `SimpleCrowdsale` constructor with the required parameters:

```
TranchePricingCrowdsale(uint256 _startTime, uint256 _endTime,
        uint256 _weiTokenPrice, uint256 _etherInvestmentObjective)
        SimpleCrowdsale(_startTime, _endTime,
            _weiTokenPrice, _etherInvestmentObjective)
    payable public
    {
        trancheStructure[0] = Tranche(3000 ether, 0.002 ether);
        …
```

- You've *overridden* `calculateNumberOfTokens()` in `TranchePricingCrowdsale` by providing a new implementation. Contrary to other languages, no special keywords are necessary to override a function in Solidity.

You can see the inheritance relationship between `TranchePricingCrowdsale` and `SimpleCrowdsale` in the contract diagram in figure 6.8.

I invite you to copy `TranchePricingCrowdsale`'s code from listing 6.7 into a new code tab of Remix and instantiate this contract. Then you can check how the token price rises when the tranche thresholds are hit.

You might have noticed I've used the expression single inheritance a few times. The reason I've done so is because Solidity also supports *multiple inheritance*. We'll explore this in the next section.

6.2.2 Composing functionality with multiple inheritance

Solidity is a young language that's still in the early stages of its development. Its syntax is continuously improving, and consequently best practice recommendations change frequently. Even the most experienced Solidity developers, who might have a length of experience that would make them barely junior developers in more established languages, have to continuously keep up with learning the latest techniques and recommendations, especially around security.

Realistically, once a contract has been deployed into the public production Ethereum network, it's unlikely to be modified on a regular basis. But a security flaw might

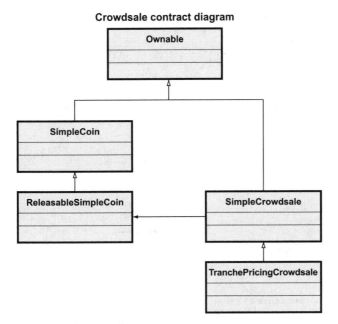

Crowdsale contract diagram

Figure 6.8 Contract diagram illustrating the crowdsale contract hierarchy, with the latest addition of `TranchePricing-Crowdsale`**, derived from** `SimpleCrowdsale`

be discovered, either because its developers weren't aware of a recent recommendation on safer syntax or because someone finds the flaw at the community, node client, or language level.

Given that the possibility of things going wrong is real and the consequent risk of Ether being lost or stolen isn't negligible, it has become common practice to include various forms of panic buttons in contracts. These range from a pause or halt function, which freezes the state and functionality of the contract until the contract owner decides to switch it on again, to a complete self-destruct function, which transfers the Ether stored in the contract to a safe account before making the contract permanently unusable.

MAKING A TOKEN CONTRACT PAUSABLE

Enough talking! The following listing shows how to add pausing functionality to `ReleasableSimpleCoin`, assuming you don't want to add it to `SimpleCoin` as well.

Listing 6.8 Adding pausable functionality to `ReleasableSimpleCoin`

```
pragma solidity ^0.4.24;
import "./Listing5_8_SimpleCoin.sol";
contract ReleasableSimpleCoin is SimpleCoin {
    ...                 ⟵───────  Same code as before
```

```
bool public paused = false;                          Flag holding the
                                                     paused state

modifier whenNotPaused() {
    require(!paused);
    _;
}

modifier whenPaused() {
    require(paused);
    _;
}

function pause() onlyOwner
    whenNotPaused public {
    paused = true;                                   Modifiers
}                                                    holding the
                                                     paused state
function unpause()
    onlyOwner whenPaused public {
    paused = false;
}

...            Same code as before

function transfer(address _to, uint256 _amount)
    isReleased whenNotPaused public {
    super.transfer(_to, _amount);
}

function transferFrom(address _from, address _to, uint256 _amount)
    isReleased whenNotPaused
    public returns (bool) {
    super.transferFrom(_from, _to, _amount);
}
}
```

Guarantees a transfer can only take place when the token contract hasn't been paused

EXTRACTING PAUSABILITY FUNCTIONALITY

After making `ReleasableSimpleCoin` pausable, you might want to do the same with `SimpleCrowdsale`. You might be tempted to duplicate the pausing functionality code you've written into `SimpleCrowdsale`. A smarter way to make both `ReleasableSimple-Coin` and `SimpleCrowdsale` pausable—without introducing code duplication—is to extract the pausable functionality from `ReleasableSimpleCoin` into a separate contract (called `Pausable`, for example) and then inherit both `ReleasableSimpleCoin` and `SimpleCrowdsale` from `Pausable`.

You can see the new Pausable contract extracted from `ReleasableSimpleCoin` in the following listing.

Listing 6.9 Pausable contract extracted from `ReleasableSimpleCoin`

```
pragma solidity ^0.4.24;
import "./Listing6_4_Ownable.sol";
contract Pausable is Ownable {                      State variable holding
    bool public paused = false;                     paused state
```

```
modifier whenNotPaused() {          ◁──  Modifier
    require(!paused);                     allowing
    _;                                    function to run
}                                         depending on
                                          paused state
modifier whenPaused() {             ◁──
    require(paused);
    _;
}

function pause() onlyOwner
    whenNotPaused public {          ◁──
    paused = true;                       Functions
}                                         changing
                                          paused state
function unpause() onlyOwner
    whenPaused public {             ◁──
    paused = false;
}
}
```

COMPOSING BASE CONTRACTS WITH MULTIPLE INHERITANCE

Now you can reapply pausability to `ReleasableSimpleCoin` by inheriting `Releasable-SimpleCoin` from `Pausable`, which, by the way, I've inherited from `Ownable` so it can use the `onlyOwner` modifier. But, hold on, as you'll remember, you're already inheriting `ReleasableSimpleCoin` from `SimpleCoin`. Is that a problem? The answer is no. Solidity supports *multiple inheritance*, so you can inherit a contract from several contracts, as shown here:

```
contract ReleasableSimpleCoin          ReleasableSimpleCoin is
    is SimpleCoin, Pausable {     ◁──  inherited from SimpleCoin
    ...                                and Pausable.
}
```

Multiple inheritance can make your code composable because you can create more complex contracts by inheriting from multiple simpler contracts. On the other hand, you should try to compose your contracts so they have only minimal cross dependencies, to avoid circular reference issues.

> **NOTE** A circular reference happens when contract C is inherited from contract P, which in turn is inherited indirectly from contract C.

You can see the multiple inheritance relationships present in `ReleasableSimpleCoin` in figure 6.9.

MAKING A CROWDSALE CONTRACT PAUSABLE

After extracting the pausable functionality into a standalone contract, it's easy to apply it to other contracts. For example:

```
contract SimpleCrowdsale is Pausable {
    ...
}
```

Inheritance hierarchy of ReleasableSimpleCoin contract

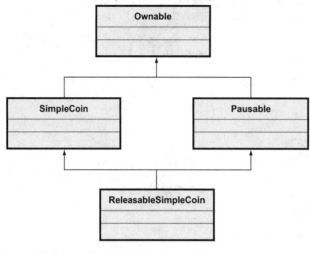

Figure 6.9   `Releasable-SimpleCoin` **is inherited both from** `SimpleCoin` **and** `Pausable`, **which is in turn inherited from** `Ownable`.

By inheriting `SimpleCrowdsale` from `Pausable`, you've also made `TranchePricing-Crowdsale` pausable. You can see the amended crowdsale contract structure in figure 6.10.

Crowdsale contract diagram including Pausable

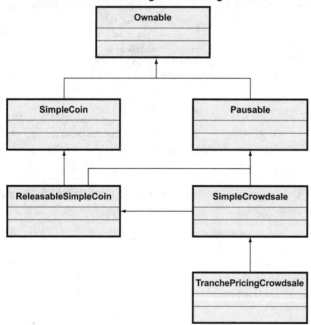

Figure 6.10   **Amended crowdsale contract structure including** `Pausable` **contract**

If you're not comfortable with the Pausable functionality, and you prefer, in case of emergency, to immediately transfer the Ether stored in the contract to a safe address and then destroy the contract so that malicious attackers can no longer manipulate it, you can encapsulate this functionality in a Destructible contract, as shown in the following listing.

Listing 6.10 A `Destructible` contract

```solidity
pragma solidity ^0.4.24;
import "./Listing6_4_Ownable.sol";
contract Destructible is Ownable {

    constructor() payable public { }

    function destroyAndSend(address _recipient) onlyOwner public {
        selfdestruct(_recipient);
    }
}
```

Destroys the contract after having transferred Ether to a safe specified account using the implicitly declared function selfdestruct() (as explained in 5.3.3)

You can now also make both ReleasableSimpleCoin and SimpleCrowdsale destructible by inheriting them from Destructible, as shown in figure 6.11 and the following snippet:

```solidity
contract ReleasableSimpleCoin is SimpleCoin,
    Pausable, Destructible {
    ...
}

contract SimpleCrowdsale is Pausable,
    Destructible {
    ...
}
```

ReleasableSimpleCoin and SimpleCrowdsale inheriting from Destructible

So far, you've learned how to take advantage of single and multiple inheritance to implement contracts with increasing functionality while avoiding code duplication. In the next chapter, you'll see how abstract classes and interfaces can help you further toward the maintainability of your contract code base.

Combined Crowdsale and SimpleCoin token contract diagram including Destructible

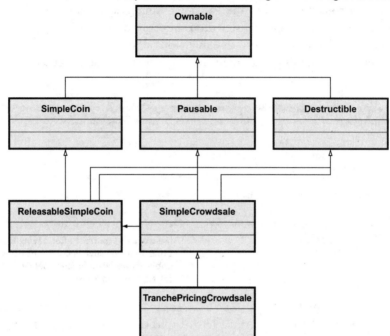

Figure 6.11 `ReleasableSimpleCoin` and `SimpleCrowdsale` are now also `Destructible`.

Summary

- The contract side of real-world Ethereum Dapps is generally made of many contracts that interact with each other.
- A crowdsale management application is an example of a multicontract Dapp.
- You can extend contract functionality while avoiding code duplication by using inheritance.
- Multiple inheritance allows you to compose a complex contract from several simpler contracts.

Generalizing functionality with abstract contracts and interfaces

7

This chapter covers
- Generalizing contracts by making them abstract
- Improving contract extensibility through interfaces
- A summary of Solidity object-oriented features
- Improving maintainability of utility code using libraries

The previous chapter introduced SimpleCrowdsale, which presented an example of a multicontract decentralized application, with a crowdsale management contract (SimpleCrowdsale) interacting with a token contract (ReleasableSimpleCoin).

You started to extend the functionality of SimpleCrowdsale by adding a new, more complex pricing strategy, and took advantage of contract inheritance to do so. You further extended the functionality by implementing pausability and destructibility as separate contracts and composing them into SimpleCrowdsale through multiple inheritance.

In this chapter, you'll keep extending SimpleCrowdsale's functionality by using other object-oriented features, such as abstract contracts and interfaces. I'll show you how an abstract contract can help you generalize a contract while avoiding code duplication. I'll also demonstrate how interfaces can add flexibility to the design of your contract so you can choose to plug in one of many possible implementations of a specific aspect of the contract functionality.

As with most languages, you achieve code reuse in Solidity by grouping and organizing functions you use often into shared libraries. I'll give you an idea of what Solidity libraries look like, and I'll explain how to call their functions.

You'll close this chapter by making further improvements to SimpleCoin using some of the object-oriented techniques you'll have learned in this chapter and the previous chapter. Specifically, I'll show you how to refactor SimpleCoin so it can comply with the Ethereum ERC20 token standard.

7.1 Making a contract abstract

At the moment, your crowdsale contracts can handle different pricing strategies. You derived TranchedSimpleCrowdsale from SimpleCrowdsale to provide specific (tranche-based) token pricing not available in the parent contract.

7.1.1 Implementing funding limit with inheritance

Let's imagine a client is interested in your crowdsale contracts, but they'd like a new feature: the ability to cap the crowdsale funding at a maximum total amount above which no further investments are accepted. A quick way to implement this would be to derive a new contract called CappedCrowdsale from SimpleCrowdsale, as shown in the following listing.

Listing 7.1 First implementation of `CappedCrowdsale`

```
pragma solidity ^0.4.24;
import "./Listing6_5_SimpleCrowdsale.0.5.sol";

contract CappedCrowdsale is SimpleCrowdsale {        State variable for
    uint256 fundingCap;                              configuring funding cap

    constructor(uint256 _startTime, uint256 _endTime,
        uint256 _weiTokenPrice, uint256 _etherInvestmentObjective,
        uint256 _fundingCap)
        SimpleCrowdsale(_startTime, _endTime,          Configures the rest of the
        _weiTokenPrice, _etherInvestmentObjective)     state variables through
        payable public                                 the base constructor
    {
        require(_fundingCap > 0);
        fundingCap = _fundingCap;
    }
                                                     Overrides
    function isValidInvestment(uint256 _investment)  isValidInvestment()
        internal view returns (bool) {
        bool nonZeroInvestment = _investment != 0;
        bool withinCrowdsalePeriod =                  Copies validations from
            now >= startTime && now <= endTime;       SimpleCrowdsale.isValidInvestment()

        bool isInvestmentBelowCap = investmentReceived +   Checks that the cap limit
            _investment < fundingCap;                      hasn't been breached
```

```
    return nonZeroInvestment && withinCrowdsalePeriod
        && isInvestmentBelowCap;
    }
}
```

ISSUES WITH THE CURRENT IMPLEMENTATION

This implementation might feel simple and satisfactory at first, but at closer look it has a couple of issues:

- The implementation of isValidInvestment() has been partially copied from SimpleCrowdsale.isValidInvestment(), creating some code duplication.
- The current implementation of CappedCrowdsale is inheriting the default token pricing code from SimpleCrowdsale, so you can't use it as it stands for a capped crowdsale with tranche-based token pricing (because TranchePricing-Crowdsale is a child of SimpleCrowdsale).

REMOVING DUPLICATION WITH A TEMPLATE METHOD

Let's try to tackle these issues one by one. First, you can avoid the partial code duplication within isValidInvestment() by reimplementing SimpleCrowdsale.isValid-Investment() as

```
contract SimpleCrowdsale is Ownable {
    ...
    function isValidInvestment(uint256 _investment)
        internal view returns (bool) {
        bool nonZeroInvestment = _investment != 0;          ◄─── Previous checks on
        bool withinCrowdsalePeriod = now >= startTime            investment validity
            && now <= endTime;

        return nonZeroInvestment && withinCrowdsalePeriod
            && isFullInvestmentWithinLimit(
            _investment);                      ◄─── Generic check against full
    }                                                investment received so far

    function isFullInvestmentWithinLimit(uint256 _investment)
        internal view returns (bool) {
        return true;    ◄─── The default implementation doesn't perform
    }                         any check at all; overridden implementations in
    ...                       inherited classes will do, as you'll see later.
}
```

Following this change, CappedCrowdsale no longer needs to override isValid-Investment(), but only isFullInvestmentWithinLimit(), as shown in the following listing.

Listing 7.2   Refactored `CappedCrowdsale`

```
pragma solidity ^0.4.18;
import "./Listing7_A_SimpleCrowdsale_forCapped.sol";   ◄─── References a modified
                                                            version of SimpleCrowdsale
                                                            implementing isFull-
contract CappedCrowdsale is SimpleCrowdsale {               InvestmentWithinLimit
    uint256 fundingCap;
```

```
    function CappedCrowdsale(uint256 _startTime, uint256 _endTime,
    uint256 _weiTokenPrice, uint256 _etherInvestmentObjective,
    uint256 _fundingCap) SimpleCrowdsale(_startTime, _endTime,
    _weiTokenPrice, _etherInvestmentObjective)
    payable public
    {
        require(_fundingCap > 0);
        fundingCap = _fundingCap;
    }

    function isFullInvestmentWithinLimit(uint256 _investment)
        internal view returns (bool) {
        bool check = investmentReceived + _investment
            < fundingCap;
        return check;
    }
}
```

This is the check that was being performed previously in the overridden isValidInvestment() function.

The isValidInvestment() function has now become a *template method*: it's a high-level function that dictates high-level steps whose logic is delegated to lower level functions, such as isFullInvestmentWithinLimit(), which you override with specific implementations in each derived contract.

> **NOTE**   A template method is a classic design pattern that appeared in the so-called *Gang of Four* book: *Design Patterns: Elements of Reusable Object-Oriented Software*, published by Addison-Wesley.

LIMITATIONS OF THE CURRENT FUNDING LIMIT STRATEGY IMPLEMENTATION

As I hinted previously, the current functionality to check the cap limit isn't composable as it stands. If you wanted to cap funding on a crowdsale with tranche-based token pricing, you'd have to implement the CappedTranchePricingCrowdsale contract, as shown in the next listing.

Listing 7.3   Capped funding and tranche-based pricing

```
pragma solidity ^0.4.24;
import "./Listing7_B_TranchePricingCrowdsale_forCapped.sol";

contract CappedTranchePricingCrowdsale is TranchePricingCrowdsale {
    uint256 fundingCap;

    constructor(uint256 _startTime, uint256 _endTime,
        uint256 _etherInvestmentObjective,
        uint256 _fundingCap)
        TranchePricingCrowdsale(_startTime, _endTime,
        _etherInvestmentObjective)
        payable public
    {
        require(_fundingCap > 0);
        fundingCap = _fundingCap;
    }
```

The same state variable introduced in CappedCrowdsale

```
function isFullInvestmentWithinLimit(uint256 _investment)
   internal view returns (bool) {
   bool check = investmentReceived + _investment
      < fundingCap;
   return check;
}
}
```

The same implementation written for CappedCrowdsale

As you can see, I've copied the code entirely from CappedCrowdsale. This is far from an ideal solution from a maintenance point of view.

Aside from duplication, the current crowdsale contract hierarchy shows another subtler issue: as you can see in figure 7.1, the hierarchy is asymmetrical, and not all contract names tell explicitly what token pricing strategy or funding limit strategy they're employing. For example, CappedCrowdsale, whose name doesn't make any reference to any token pricing strategy, inherits from SimpleCrowdsale, which implements fixed token pricing. A more precise name for this contract probably would be CappedFixedPricingCrowdsale. Equally, TranchePricingCrowdsale, whose name doesn't make any reference to any funding strategy, also inherits from SimpleCrowdsale, which implements an unlimited funding strategy. A more precise name for this contract probably would be UncappedTranchePricingCrowdsale.

Crowdsale contract hierarchy, including contracts with funding capping

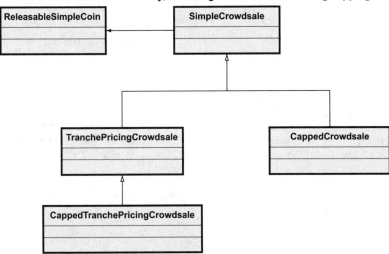

Figure 7.1   A UML contract diagram showing asymmetry in the crowdsale contract hierarchy and ambiguity regarding token pricing strategy or funding limit strategy in the name of some contracts. For clarity's sake, I've omitted ownable, pausable, and destructible base contracts.

7.1.2   *Generalizing funding limit strategy with an abstract contract*

Now I'll show you a better solution for implementing `CappedCrowdsale` and `CappedTranchePricingCrowdsale` based on the concept of abstract classes. I'll also show you how abstract classes can make the crowdsale contract hierarchy you saw in figure 7.1 symmetric and more explicit. This involves first encapsulating the funding limit strategy functionality into a completely separate contract, which I'll sketch for the moment as

```
contract FundingLimitStrategy{
    function isFullInvestmentWithinLimit(uint256 _investment,
        uint256 _fullInvestmentReceived)
        public view returns (bool);
}
```

> This is the function that performs the check on the funding cap, although it's not yet implemented at this stage.

You can imagine this is a base contract for all possible funding limit strategies. Here are two possible funding limit strategies:

- *CappedFundingStrategy*—Crowdsale with funding capped by `fundingCap` limit, as seen earlier in the `CappedTranchePricingCrowdsale` contract
- *UnlimitedFundingStrategy*—Crowdsale with unlimited (or uncapped) funding

You can derive the implementation for a capped crowdsale from `FundingLimitStrategy` as follows:

```
contract CappedFundingStrategy is FundingLimitStrategy {
    uint256 fundingCap;                              // Funding cap limit

    constructor(uint256 _fundingCap) public {
        require(_fundingCap > 0);
        fundingCap = _fundingCap;
    }

    function isFullInvestmentWithinLimit(
        uint256 _investment,
        uint256 _fullInvestmentReceived)
        public view returns (bool) {

        bool check = _fullInvestmentReceived + _investment < fundingCap;
        return check;
    }
}
```

> This is the same implementation you saw earlier in CappedTranche-PricingCrowdsale.

The implementation for an unlimited funding strategy is

```
contract UnlimitedFundingStrategy is FundingLimitStrategy {
    function isFullInvestmentWithinLimit(
        uint256 _investment,
        uint256 _fullInvestmentReceived)
        public view returns (bool) {
        return true;
    }
}
```

> No check is performed because the funding is unlimited.

Obviously, you can derive other funding limit strategies from `FundingLimitStrategy`. For example, you could implement a strategy with a dynamic funding limit, readjusted depending on various factors that might change during the crowdsale.

`FundingLimitStrategy` is considered an *abstract contract* because you've declared its `isFullInvestmentWithinLimit()` function but haven't implemented it. On the other hand, `CappedFundingStrategy` and `UnlimitedFundingStrategy` are considered *concrete contracts* because all of their functions have been implemented.

> **DEFINITION** A contract is considered *abstract* if it contains at least one declared but unimplemented function. An abstract contract is used as a base class for other contracts, but it can't be instantiated. A contract whose functions have all been implemented is considered a *concrete* contract.

The UML contract diagram in figure 7.2 shows the inheritance hierarchy of funding limit strategy contracts.

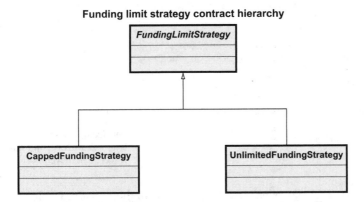

Figure 7.2 Funding limit strategy contract hierarchy, including an abstract base contract and two concrete child contracts

> **NOTE** You might have noticed that the name of *FundingLimitStrategy* in figure 7.2 is in italic. This is the UML convention for writing the name of abstract classes.

7.1.3 *Improving the token pricing strategy with an abstract contract*

You can apply the approach you took to make the funding limit base strategy contract abstract to tidy up the crowdsale contract hierarchy and make the token pricing strategy used by each contract more explicit, as shown in figure 7.3.

This is the main change taking place in `SimpleCrowdsale`:

```
contract SimpleCrowdsale {
    function calculateNumberOfTokens(uint256 investment)
        internal returns (uint256) ;        ⟵
}
```

This function has become abstract and has made SimpleCrowdsale abstract.

Refactoring of SimpleCrowdsale contract

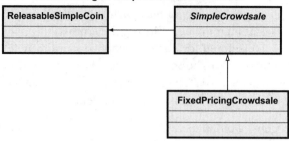

Figure 7.3 Making the crowdsale contract hierarchy symmetrical and more explicit. `SimpleCrowdsale` **has been made abstract by pushing the implementation of fixed token pricing down to a new** `FixedPricingCrowdsale` **contract.**

The fixed token pricing strategy previously in `SimpleCrowdsale` has been pushed down to the new `FixedPricingCrowdsale` contract:

```
contract FixedPricingCrowdsale is SimpleCrowdsale {

    constructor(uint256 _startTime, uint256 _endTime,
        uint256 _weiTokenPrice, uint256 _etherInvestmentObjective,
        uint256 _fundingCap)
        SimpleCrowdsale(_startTime, _endTime,
        _weiTokenPrice, _etherInvestmentObjective)
        payable public {
    }

    function calculateNumberOfTokens(uint256 investment)
        internal returns (uint256) {
        return investment / weiTokenPrice;            ◁─┤ This formula was in
    }                                                    SimpleCrowdsale, and now
}                                                        it has been moved here.
```

Meanwhile, `TranchePricingCrowdsale` is unaltered from the previous implementation.

7.1.4 *Reimplementing capped crowdsales with no duplication*

After having encapsulated the crowdsale funding limit strategy in the `FundingLimit-Strategy` contract hierarchy, and having slightly refactored the crowdsale contract hierarchy, you can attempt to reimplement `CappedCrowdsale` and `CappedTranche-PricingCrowdsale`, this time avoiding duplication.

First, you have to add the funding limit strategy to `SimpleCrowdsale` as a state variable: `fundingLimitStrategy`. You can instantiate a specific funding limit strategy in the constructor through a new function called `createFundingLimitStrategy()`, which here is declared as abstract and you must implement in the inherited contracts. Then you can use `fundingLimitStrategy` in the `isValidInvestment()` function:

```
contract SimpleCrowdsale is Ownable {
    //...

    FundingLimitStrategy internal            ┐ State variable holding the
        fundingLimitStrategy;            ◁───┘ funding limit strategy
```

```
//...
constructor(...) public {
    ...
    fundingLimitStrategy =
        createFundingLimitStrategy();
}

//...

function createFundingLimitStrategy()
    internal returns (FundingLimitStrategy);

function isValidInvestment(uint256 _investment)
    internal view returns (bool) {
    bool nonZeroInvestment = _investment != 0;
    bool withinCrowdsalePeriod = now >= startTime && now <= endTime;

    return nonZeroInvestment && withinCrowdsalePeriod
        && fundingLimitStrategy.
            isFullInvestmentWithinLimit(
              _investment,
              investmentReceived);
}

//...
}
```

A specific funding limit strategy is instantiated through createFundingLimitStrategy(), which is declared here as abstract.

Instantiates a specific FundingLimitStrategy. It's abstract, and you must implement it in inherited contracts.

The check against the funding limit is performed through the appropriate FundingLimitStrategy contract.

It's now possible to implement the four concrete crowdsale contracts that result from combining the token pricing strategy and the funding limit strategy in different ways, as shown in the amended crowdsale contract hierarchy in figure 7.4:

- UnlimitedFixedPricingCrowdsale—Derived from FixedPricingCrowdsale, with UnlimitedFundingStrategy instance
- CappedFixedPricingCrowdsale—Derived from FixedPricingCrowdsale, with CappedFundingStrategy instance
- UnlimitedTranchePricingCrowdsale—Derived from TranchePricingCrowdsale, with UnlimitedFundingStrategy instance
- CappedTranchePricingCrowdsale—Derived from TranchePricingCrowdsale, with CappedFundingStrategy instance

NOTE The two intermediate FixedPricingCrowdsale and TranchePricing-Crowdsale contracts have become abstract because they don't implement createFundingLimitStrategy().

The implementation of these four concrete contracts, which you can appreciate in listing 7.4, is succinct. These contracts derive from the abstract crowdsale contract with the relevant token pricing strategy (either FixedPricingCrowdsale or Tranche-PricingCrowdsale) and implement createFundingLimitStrategy() by returning a specific funding limit strategy. All the work is then delegated to the abstract contracts they derive from.

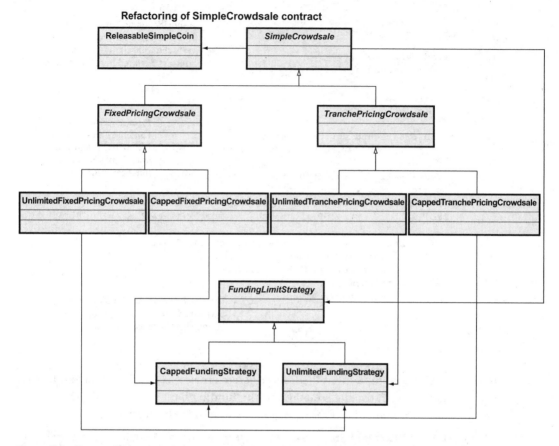

Figure 7.4   Reorganized crowdsale contract hierarchy, with two layers of abstract contracts at the top and a bottom layer of concrete contracts encapsulating all combinations of the contract pricing and funding limit options. The FundingLimitStrategy **contract hierarchy now encapsulates the checks on the funding limit in an efficient way that avoids code duplication.**

Listing 7.4   Crowdsale contracts combining different pricing and funding limit options

```
pragma solidity ^0.4.24;
import "./Listing7_C_FundingStrategies.sol";
import "./Listing7_E_PricingStrategies.sol";


contract UnlimitedFixedPricingCrowdsale is FixedPricingCrowdsale {

    constructor(uint256 _startTime, uint256 _endTime,
    uint256 _weiTokenPrice, uint256 _etherInvestmentObjective)
    FixedPricingCrowdsale(_startTime, _endTime,
    _weiTokenPrice, _etherInvestmentObjective)
    payable public  {
    }
```

⟵ **Only feeds the parent contract**

```
function createFundingLimitStrategy()
    internal returns (FundingLimitStrategy) {

    return new UnlimitedFundingStrategy();
}
}

contract CappedFixedPricingCrowdsale is FixedPricingCrowdsale {

    constructor(uint256 _startTime, uint256 _endTime,
    uint256 _weiTokenPrice, uint256 _etherInvestmentObjective)
    FixedPricingCrowdsale(_startTime, _endTime,
    _weiTokenPrice, _etherInvestmentObjective)
    payable public {
    }

    function createFundingLimitStrategy()
        internal returns (FundingLimitStrategy) {

        return new CappedFundingStrategy(10000);
    }
}

contract UnlimitedTranchePricingCrowdsale is TranchePricingCrowdsale {

    constructor(uint256 _startTime, uint256 _endTime,
    uint256 _etherInvestmentObjective)
    TranchePricingCrowdsale(_startTime, _endTime,
    _etherInvestmentObjective)
    payable public {
    }

    function createFundingLimitStrategy()
        internal returns (FundingLimitStrategy) {

        return new UnlimitedFundingStrategy();
    }
}

contract CappedTranchePricingCrowdsale is TranchePricingCrowdsale {

    constructor(uint256 _startTime, uint256 _endTime,
    uint256 _etherInvestmentObjective)
    TranchePricingCrowdsale(_startTime, _endTime,
    _etherInvestmentObjective)
    payable public {
    }

    function createFundingLimitStrategy()
        internal returns (FundingLimitStrategy) {

        return new CappedFundingStrategy(10000);
    }
}
```

Only feeds the parent contract

The only function implemented; overrides the abstract one in SimpleCrowdsale and provides a specific funding limit strategy

7.2   *Allowing multiple contract implementations with interfaces*

Before we leave `SimpleCrowdsale`, I'd like to show you one last object-oriented feature: interfaces. If you're familiar with other OO languages, you'll understand immediately how interfaces work in Solidity. If not, I'll explain them through an example, so you should still be able to pick up the concept quickly.

7.2.1   *Setting functional requirements with interfaces*

Imagine the client who asked you to customize the crowdsale with the capped funding strategy now wants another change. They're happy about your crowdsale contract, but they want to support other tokens, not necessarily your `ReleasableSimpleCoin`. You think this is a fair request that will also provide flexibility to new clients. After analyzing your current code, you realize your crowdsale contracts have only minimal interaction with `ReleasableSimpleCoin`. The only references to it are in `SimpleCrowdsale`, the base contract of the hierarchy, as highlighted here:

```
contract SimpleCrowdsale is Ownable {
    ...

    ReleasableSimpleCoin public          Defines crowdsaleToken
        crowdsaleToken;              ◁──  as a state variable
    ...

    function SimpleCrowdsale(uint256 _startTime, uint256 _endTime,
    uint256 _weiTokenPrice, uint256 _etherInvestmentObjective)
    payable public
    {
        ...
        crowdsaleToken =                     Initializes crowdsaleToken
            new ReleasableSimpleCoin(0);  ◁─  in the SimpleCrowdsale
    }                                        constructor


    function assignTokens(address _beneficiary,
        uint256 _investment) internal {

        uint256 _numberOfTokens = calculateNumberOfTokens(_investment);

        crowdsaleToken.mint(_beneficiary,
        _numberOfTokens);             ◁─┐  Mints tokens bought
    }                                    from the investor
    ...                                  into their account

    function finalize() onlyOwner public {
        ...

        if (isCrowdsaleComplete)
        {
```

```
        if (investmentObjectiveMet)
            crowdsaleToken.release();          ◁┐  Releases (unlocks) the token
        else                                      │  contract so investors can
            isRefundingAllowed = true;            │  transfer their tokens

        isFinalized = true;
    }
}


    ...

}
```

From your point of view, as the crowdsale contract developer, you only care that the token used in the crowdsale supports the following two functions:

```
mint(address _beneficiary, uint256 _numberOfTokens);
```

```
release();
```

Obviously, to be useful to the investor, the token contract should also support at least the following function:

```
function transfer(address _to, uint256 _amount);
```

The syntax construct that defines the minimum set of functions the token contract should support is called an *interface*. The token interface that SimpleCrowdsale would reference would look like this:

```
interface ReleasableToken {
    function mint(address _beneficiary, uint256 _numberOfTokens) external;
    function release() external;
    function transfer(address _to, uint256 _amount) external;
}
```

7.2.2 *Referencing a contract through an interface*

You can define a contract that implements this interface by inheriting from it. Here's an example:

```
contract ReleasableSimpleCoin is ReleasableToken {  ◁┐  ReleasableSimpleCoin already
    ...                                                 │  implements ReleasableToken
}                                                       │  as it stands.
```

You also can create other implementations:

```
contract ReleasableComplexCoin is ReleasableToken {
    ...
}
```

Figure 7.5 shows the relationship between an interface and its implementations. As you can see, you can represent in two ways how a concrete contract implements an interface.

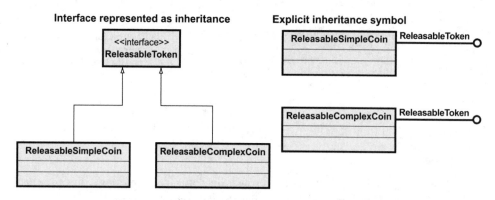

Figure 7.5 **Relationships between an interface and its concrete implementations. You can represent this relationship in two ways. The first one resembles inheritance, with the interface being the parent of its implementations. The second one uses an explicit interface symbol that's useful if you don't want to show all the interface implementations.**

Now you can modify `SimpleCrowdsale` so that it references the `ReleasableToken` interface rather than a concrete token contract. You should also instantiate the token contract in an overridden internal function rather than directly in the constructor, as you can see in the following listing.

Listing 7.5 `SimpleCrowdsale` **referencing** `ReleasableToken`

```
contract SimpleCrowdsale is Ownable {
    ...
    ReleasableToken  public crowdsaleToken;        ◁──   Now the crowdsale contract can
    ...                                                   be any token implementing
                                                          ReleasableToken.

    constructor(uint256 _startTime, uint256 _endTime,
        uint256 _weiTokenPrice, uint256 _etherInvestmentObjective)
        payable public {
        ...
        crowdsaleToken = createToken();        ◁──   Instantiates the token
        ...                                           contract in a function
    }                                                 that can be overridden

    ...

    function createToken()                         The default implementation
        internal returns (ReleasableToken) {       that the SimpleCrowdsale
            return new ReleasableSimpleCoin(0);  ◁──   abstract contract offers
        }                                          still instantiates
                                                   ReleasableSimpleCoin.
    ...
}
```

NOTE You also could have declared `createToken()` as an abstract function within `SimpleCrowdsale`. This would have been the purest approach, but it would have forced you to implement createToken() in all concrete contracts (such as UnlimitedFixedPricingCrowdsale). The individual implementation of createToken() in each concrete contract would have been the same as in listing 7.5. This duplication might seem unnecessary, though, given that in most cases you'd want to reference ReleasableSimpleCoin anyway. There's no right or wrong design in this regard, and the solution you choose depends on how you want to balance requirements and technical tradeoffs.

So far, nothing seems to have changed. You start enjoying the benefit of referencing an interface rather than a concrete contract when you implement a crowdsale contract that needs a custom token. Imagine your client wants to use a different token contract, such as

```
contract ReleasableComplexCoin is ReleasableToken {
...
}
```

You can easily implement a new crowdsale contract that supports this token by overriding the createToken() function:

```
contract UnlimitedFixedPricingCrowdsaleWithComplexCoin
    is UnlimitedFixedPricingCrowdsale {

    constructor(uint256 _startTime,
    uint256 _endTime,
    uint256 _weiTokenPrice, uint256 _etherInvestmentObjective)
    UnlimitedFixedPricingCrowdsale(_startTime, _endTime,
    _weiTokenPrice, _etherInvestmentObjective)
    payable public  {
    }

    function createToken()
        internal returns (ReleasableToken) {          ◁── To support a different token
            return new ReleasableComplexCoin();           contract, you need to
        }                                                  override this function.
}
```

You can see UnlimitedFixedPricingCrowdsaleWithComplexCoin's contract diagram in figure 7.6.

As you can see, an interface is a useful construct that increases the flexibility of one element or aspect of your contract (for example, the specific token used in your crowdsale). By referencing an interface rather than a concrete contract (Releasable-Token rather than ReleasableSimpleCoin in our example), your main contract (SimpleCrowdsale) can work seamlessly with any implementation of the interface (ReleasableSimpleCoin or ReleasableComplexCoin, for example). As a result, you're free to change the behavior of one element of your main contract (in the case we've been reviewing, the behavior of the crowdsale token used) without requiring any changes to the contract itself. This ability to switch seamlessly between different

Refactoring of SimpleCrowdsale contract

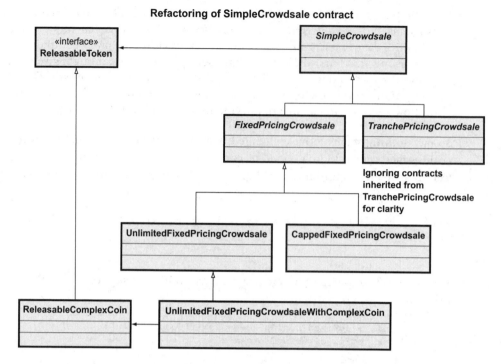

Figure 7.6 A contract diagram of UnlimitedFixedPricingCrowdsaleWithComplexCoin.
You can appreciate the relationships between the abstract SimpleCrowdsale **contract and the**
ReleasableToken **token interface and between the concrete** UnlimitedFixedPricing-
CrowdsaleWithComplexCoin **crowdsale contract and the concrete** ReleasableComplexCoin
token contract.

implementations of an interface is called *polymorphism*, and it's one of the main principles of object-oriented programming.

I'm sure you're wondering whether you could have achieved the same by making
ReleasableToken an abstract contract rather than an interface. You're right; it would
have worked equally well, but by doing so you'd introduce in your code base a contract you don't fully need yet. What you need at this stage is only the definition of the
minimum functionality that SimpleCrowdsale requires to interact with a token. That's
exactly the purpose of an interface.

Before leaving interfaces, let me quickly summarize how they work:

- An interface defines the set of functions that must be implemented; you must
  declare them with external visibility:

```
interface ReleasableToken {
    function mint(address _beneficiary, uint256 _numberOfTokens) external;
    function release() external;
    function transfer(address _to, uint256 _amount) external;
}
```

- A contract implements an interface by inheriting from it:

```
contract ReleasableSimpleCoin is ReleasableToken {
   . . .
}
```

- A contract must implement all the functions present in the interface it inherits from.

Congratulations! You've now completed a full implementation of a crowdsale contract hierarchy. This allows you to set up crowdsales with different token contracts, token pricing strategies, or funding limit strategies. The fruits of your hard work are shown in appendix B. I encourage you to take a break, browse through the code, and try to digest it slowly. You'll appreciate how all the pieces of the puzzle you've built in the last two chapters have come together. I'm sure that by looking at the entire code all the concepts you've learned will settle further into your head.

7.3 *Real-world crowdsale contracts*

Although `SimpleCrowdsale` is a good starting point, real-world crowdsale contracts can get much more complex because they offer much more functionality, such as the following:

- A prefunding stage, during which early investors provide initial funding, which gets converted into tokens, possibly at a special price, at the beginning of the public crowdsale
- More sophisticated token pricing strategies
- A funding limit based on the number of tokens purchased
- Finalization strategies, including the possibility of distributing additional tokens to the development team, the organizers, or the legal and advisory team
- Tokens with various characteristics

> **WARNING** In these two introductory chapters on Solidity, I haven't touched on security aspects you must be aware of before deploying a contract onto the public Ethereum network. I'll cover them in chapter 14.

The main objective of `SimpleCrowdsale` was to teach you inheritance, abstract classes, and interfaces in Solidity through a realistic use case, as well as to give you some technical details of how a crowdsale works. If you're interested in learning more about how to build a decentralized crowdsale management application, or you're curious to see how complex a real-world Dapp can be, I strongly encourage you to study the code of the TokenMarketNet ICO[1] GitHub repository, one of the best open source Ethereum crowdsale implementations, at https://github.com/TokenMarketNet/ico.

---

[1] Copyright © 2017 TokenMarket Ltd., Gibraltar, https://tokenmarket.net. Licensed under the Apache License, V2.0.

I encourage you to quickly review the contracts in this repository and compare them with the respective SimpleCrowdsale ones you saw earlier. You'll realize how complex a real-world Dapp can become both in size (number of contracts) and implementation.

A LITTLE CHALLENGE

As an exercise, I now leave you to try on your own to implement different finalization strategies, which you could encapsulate in yet another contract hierarchy with a base abstract contract, such as FinalizationStrategy. You could then create a new set of concrete contracts in which you inject such strategy at construction, as you've done when injecting the funding strategy.

7.4 Recap of Solidity's object-oriented features

If you're still alive after the hard work you've done so far in this chapter, I'm going to give you a break now. I'll summarize and generalize all you've learned through SimpleCrowdsale. In case you forget some details, you won't have to dig through the previous code listings and snippets to find the syntax associated with object-oriented features such as inheritance, abstract classes, and interfaces. Sit back and relax.

7.4.1 Inheritance

Solidity supports multiple inheritance, so a derived contract can inherit state variables and functions from one or more contracts, as shown here:

```
contract Parent1 {

    int256 public stateVar1;
    bool public stateVar2;

    function initialize() public {}
    function Parent1(int256 param1, bool param2) public {}

    function operation1(int256 opParam1) public returns (int256) {}

}

contract ParentA {

    int256 public stateVarA;
    int16 public stateVarB;

    function initialize() public {}
    function ParentA(int256 paramA, int16 paramB) public {}

    function operationA(bool opParamA) public {}
}

contract Child is Parent1, ParentA {

}
```

Child inherits the state variables stateVar1, stateVar2, stateVarA, and stateVarB, and the functions operation1() and operationA() from its parent contracts, Parent1 and ParentA

CALLING BASE CONSTRUCTORS

The constructor of a derived contract must call all the parent constructors (in the order you want them to be called):

```
function Child(int256 p1, bool p2, int256 pA, int16 pB)
    Parent1(p1, p2) ParentA(pA, pB) {
}
```

OVERRIDING FUNCTIONS

A derived contract can override any function inherited from its parent contracts by reimplementing it:

```
contract Child is Parent1, ParentA {
    ...
    function operationA(bool opParamA) public {      New implementation
                                                 ◁─  that replaces
    ...                                              ParentA.operationA()
    }
}
```

When a function is called on a contract, its most overridden implementation, at the bottom of the inheritance hierarchy, will get executed.

CALLING BASE FUNCTIONS

An overridden function can call a function located in a base contract, as follows:

```
contract Child is Parent1, ParentA {
    ...
    function operationA(bool opParamA) public {
        ParentA.operationA(opParamA);     ◁─  Calls
    }                                         ParentA.operationA()
}
```

In some cases, you might want to make sure all the base implementations of a function are called. In those cases, you can call all of them implicitly with the super keyword:

```
contract Child is Parent1, ParentA {
    ...

    function initialize() public {
        ...                               Calls Parent1.initialize()
        super.initialize();        ◁─     followed by
    }                                     ParentA.initialize()

    ...
}
```

7.4.2 Abstract contracts

A contract is considered *abstract*, rather than concrete, if at least one of its functions is abstract, which means it has been declared but not implemented, as is the case with operationA() in this contract:

```
contract AbstractContract {
    int256 public stateVar;

    constructor(int256 param1)  public {
        stateVar = param1;
    }

    function operation1(int256 opParam1, bool opParam2)
        returns (int256) {
        if (opParam2) return opParam1;
    }

    function operationA(int256 opParamA);
}
```

This is an abstract function, which makes AbstractContract abstract.

As in other statically typed languages, Solidity abstract contracts can't be instantiated; they can only be used as base contracts for other abstract or concrete contracts.

7.4.3   *Interfaces*

Interfaces in Solidity are similar to those offered in Java and C#. An interface defines the set of functions and events that must be implemented in their derived contracts, but it doesn't provide any implementation. All the functions declared on an interface are abstract, as shown here:

```
interface SampleInterface {
    function operation1(int256 param1, bool param2) external;
    function operationA(int16 paramA) external;
}
```

A contract derived from an interface must implement all of its functions, as shown here:

```
contract SampleContract is SampleInterface {
    function operation1(int256 param1, bool param2) {

    }

    function operationA(int16 paramA) {

    }
}
```

Implementation of operation1

Constructor definition

> **NOTE**   You can't define any variables, structs, or enums on an interface. Also, you can't derive an interface from other interfaces.

Although you can avoid code duplication by factoring a good class hierarchy where contracts at the bottom reuse function implementations located in their base classes, often common shareable logic isn't specific to the domain of a contract hierarchy and has a more generic purpose. For example, functions that manipulate low-level data structures, such as arrays, byte arrays, or strings, in a generic way might be useful in any contract. The naive way to import such functionality is to copy and paste the required functions from a function repository into the contracts that need them. But there's a much smarter way. Enter libraries.

7.4.4   *A word of caution*

I've presented in this chapter all of Solidity's object-oriented features, and I've shown you how real-world Dapps, such as TokenMarketNet, have been designed using advanced object-oriented principles. But remember that Solidity is meant to be used only to implement smart contracts and not rich general-purpose applications, so in most cases, you might not need a complex OO design after all. People fall into different schools of thought when it comes to designing smart contracts: whereas some are comfortable with taking advantage of Solidity's rich OO feature set, most Ethereum developers prioritize simplicity and security and are willing to sacrifice long-term maintainability to gain short-term predictability. I believe the latter approach is sensible, especially while you're still learning this new technology.

7.5   *Libraries*

A Solidity library is a shared function repository similar in purpose to a Java class package or a .NET class library. The code of a library looks like that of a C# or C++ static class, and it contains a collection of stateless functions. It can also include struct and enum definitions. You can get an idea of what a library looks like in listing 7.6, which shows SafeMath, a collection of functions to execute math operations that include safety checks around incorrect input or overflows. This library is part of OpenZeppelin,[2] an open source framework to build secure smart contracts in Solidity, which aims at standardizing common functionality required by most Solidity developers.

> **Listing 7.6   SafeMath library for performing checked math operations**

```
library SafeMath {
    //Taken from: https://github.com/OpenZeppelin/
    function mul(uint256 a, uint256 b)
        public pure returns (uint256) {
        if (a == 0) return 0;
        uint256 c = a * b;
        assert(c / a == b);
        return c;
    }

    function div(uint256 a, uint256 b)
        public pure returns (uint256) {
        uint256 c = a / b;
        return c;
    }
}
```

Uses the library keyword instead of the contract keyword

Checks on the input or on the result of the arithmetic operation

Functions in a library are defined exactly as in contracts.

---

[2] Copyright © 2016 Smart Contract Solutions, Inc., http://mng.bz/oNPv, under The MIT License (MIT).

```
function sub(uint256 a, uint256 b)
    public pure returns (uint256) {
    assert(b <= a);
    return a - b;
}

function add(uint256 a, uint256 b)
    public pure returns (uint256) {
    uint256 c = a + b;
    assert(c >= a);
    return c;
}
}
```

Checks on the input or on the result of the arithmetic operation

Functions in a library are defined exactly as in contracts.

A library has the following limitations, compared to a contract:

- It can't have state variables.
- It doesn't support inheritance.
- It can't receive Ether. (You can't decorate a function with the `payable` keyword and send Ether to it while invoking it.)

7.5.1 Library function invocation

A contract can reference a local copy of a library (located in the same `.sol` code file) directly by its name, as shown in listing 7.7. As you can see, you invoke library functions by prefixing them with the library name, like you invoke static functions in other languages. You also have to prefix library structs and enums with the library name.

Listing 7.7 How to call library functions

```
pragma solidity ^0.4.24;
import './Listing7_6_SafeMath.sol';

contract Calculator {
    function calculateTheta(uint256 a, uint256 b) public returns (uint256) {
        uint256 delta = SafeMath.sub(a, b);
        uint256 beta = SafeMath.add(delta,
            1000000);
        uint256 theta = SafeMath.mul(beta, b);

        uint256 result = SafeMath.div(theta, a);

        return result;
    }
}
```

SafeMath library functions are all prefixed with SafeMath.

7.5.2 Deployed libraries

True code reuse takes place when only one instance of the library is deployed on the network and all contracts accessing it reference it through its deployment address (conceptually the same as a contract address). Once deployed, the functions of a library are exposed with implicit *external* visibility to all the contracts referencing it. The usual way of calling a deployed library from a contract is to define a local abstract contract that matches the signature of the deployed library. Then you communicate with the library through this local abstract contract, which acts as a strongly typed proxy to the library, as shown in the following listing. The alternative would be to invoke the library functions directly through call(), but by doing so, you wouldn't guarantee type safety.

Listing 7.8 How to call library functions from a contract

```solidity
pragma solidity ^0.4.24;
contract SafeMathProxy {                      ◁──┐  This local abstract contract
    function mul(uint256 a, uint256 b)              emulates the functionality
        public pure returns (uint256);   ◁──       offered by the library.
    function div(uint256 a, uint256 b)           These are the
        public pure returns (uint256);   ◁──     same function
    function sub(uint256 a, uint256 b)           declarations
        public pure returns (uint256);   ◁──     present in the
    function add(uint256 a, uint256 b)           SafeMath library.
        public pure returns (uint256);   ◁──
}

contract Calculator {

    SafeMathProxy safeMath;
                                                       SafeMath library address
                                                       (copied from Remix, as
    constructor(address _libraryAddress) public  ◁──   show in figure 7.8)
    {
        require(_libraryAddress != 0x0);               References the SafeMath library
        safeMath = SafeMathProxy(_libraryAddress);  ◁── deployed at the specified address
    }                                                  through an implicit constructor
                                                       available for all contracts that
    function calculateTheta(uint256 a, uint256 b)      takes the contract address as
        public returns (uint256) {                     a parameter

        uint256 delta = safeMath.sub(a, b);      ┐
        uint256 beta = safeMath.add(delta,        │  Calls to the
            1000000);                             │  deployed
        uint256 theta = safeMath.mul(beta, b);    │  SafeMath
                                                  │  library
        uint256 result = safeMath.div(theta, a); ┘

        return result;
    }
}
```

Before trying this code, put the listing 7.6 code into a Remix code tab and instantiate the SafeMath library (by clicking Deploy, as for contracts). Copy the address by clicking the copy icon next to the contract instance panel, as shown in figure 7.7.

Now enter the code from listing 7.7 into a new Remix code tab. Then paste the SafeMath library address you copied earlier into the Calculator constructor text box next to the Deploy button, as show in figure 7.8. (Remember to wrap it with double quotes.)

**Click here to copy
the library address.**

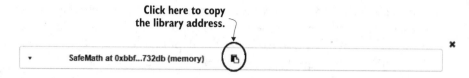

▼   SafeMath at 0xbbf...732db (memory)   🗐

Figure 7.7   Get the SafeMath library address from Remix by clicking the copy icon.

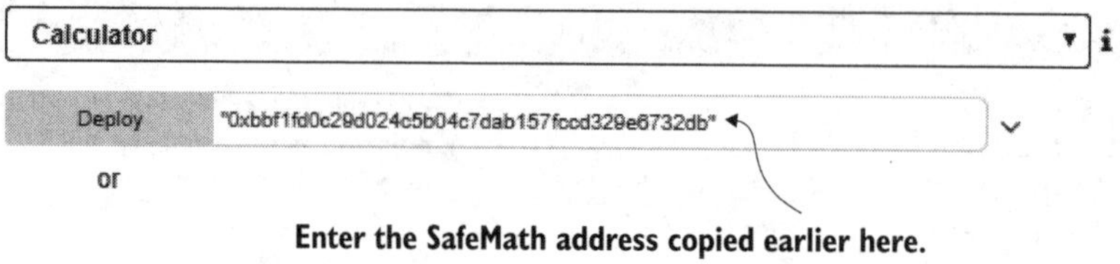

Calculator	▼ ⓘ

Deploy	"0xbbf1fd0c29d024c5b04c7dab157fccd329e6732db" ◄	⌄

or

Enter the SafeMath address copied earlier here.

Figure 7.8   Copy the SafeMath library address into the Calculator constructor text box.

Click Deploy, and the Calculator contract gets instantiated. Now you can call
calculateTheta() by entering a couple of values into its input parameters text box—
for example, 200, 33—and clicking calculateTheta.

After you click calculateTheta, various calls to remote SafeMath functions are performed through the safeMath proxy instance: sub(), add(), mul(), and div() are
executed in sequence and result is calculated. The output panel on the bottom left
of the screen shows that calculateTheta()'s function completed successfully. You can
then see the result by clicking the arrow next to the Debug button and checking the
Decoded Output field, as shown in figure 7.9.

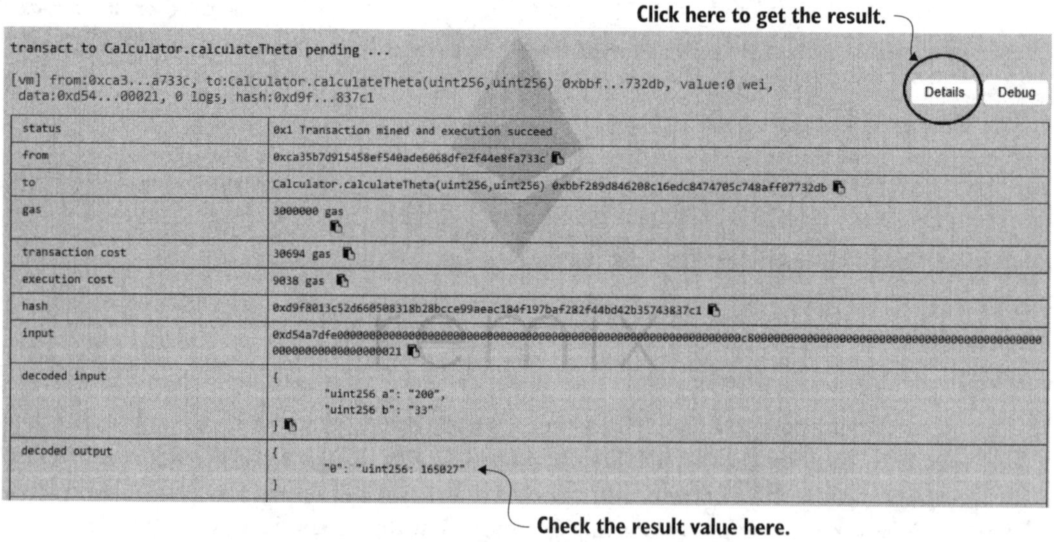

Click here to get the result.

transact to Calculator.calculateTheta pending ...

[vm] from:0xca3...a733c, to:Calculator.calculateTheta(uint256,uint256) 0xbbf...732db, value:0 wei,
data:0xd54...00021, 0 logs, hash:0xd9f...837c1   (Details) Debug

status	0x1 Transaction mined and execution succeed
from	0xca35b7d915458ef540ade6068dfe2f44e8fa733c 🗐
to	Calculator.calculateTheta(uint256,uint256) 0xbbf289d846208c16edc8474705c748aff07732db 🗐
gas	3000000 gas 🗐
transaction cost	30694 gas 🗐
execution cost	9038 gas 🗐
hash	0xd9f8013c52d660508318b28bcce99aeac184f197baf282f44bd42b35743837c1 🗐
input	0xd54a7dfe0000000000000000000000000000000000000000000000000000000000000000000000000000c800000000000000000000000000000000000000000000000000000000000000000000000021 🗐

decoded input	{
	    "uint256 a": "200",
	    "uint256 b": "33"
	} 🗐

decoded output	{
	    "0": "uint256: 165027" ◄
	}

Check the result value here.

**Figure 7.9   After the call to calculateTheta() completes, you can click Details and check the result in the
Decoded Output field.**

7.5.3   *Library function execution*

When a library function is called, its code is executed within the context of the calling contract. For example, if the code of a function library references msg, this isn't the message sent by the contract to the library, but the message received by the contract from its caller. Also, during a library function invocation, only the calling contract, not the library itself, accesses storage directly. This means library functions manipulate the value of any reference type variables with storage data locations passed to the functions. As mentioned earlier, libraries don't permanently hold any objects at all.

> **NOTE**   A library function is executed in the context of the calling contract because it's invoked through the DELEGATECALL opcode rather than the CALL opcode.

In the previous chapter, I introduced a small improvement to SimpleCoin by extracting the ownership functionality out to the Ownable contract. In this chapter, I'll present a new enhancement related to token standardization.

7.6   *Making SimpleCoin ERC20 compliant*

Creating a custom cryptocurrency or token contract has become such a common requirement for most decentralized applications that a standard token interface has been proposed. Such an interface would allow any contract (such as your Simple-Crowdsale contract) to interact with a token contract in a predictable way. The standard Ethereum token contract is called ERC20. The following listing shows the standard token functionality every ERC20-compliant token is expected to provide, expressed as an abstract contract.

Listing 7.9   ERC20 abstract contract, defining the Ethereum standard token

```
pragma solidity ^0.4.24;
contract ERC20 {
    uint256 public totalSupply;
    function balanceOf(address _owner)
        public view returns (uint256 balance);
    function transfer(address _to, uint256 _value)
        public returns (bool success);
    function transferFrom(address _from, address _to, uint256 _value)
        public returns (bool success);
    function approve(address _spender, uint256 _value)
        public returns (bool success);
    function allowance(address _owner, address _spender)
        public view returns (uint256 remaining);

    event Transfer(address indexed _from,
        address indexed _to, uint256 _value);
    event Approval(address indexed _owner,
        address indexed _spender, uint256 _value);
}
```

If you compare this with your latest implementation of SimpleCoin, shown in appendix A, which includes the modifications around contract ownership I introduced in chapter 5, you'll notice your token is almost ERC20-compliant. Table 7.1 summarizes the main differences between SimpleCoin and the ERC20 specification.

Table 7.1   Differences between the ERC20 specification and SimpleCoin

ERC20 specification	SimpleCoin equivalent
totalSupply	Not available
balanceOf()	coinBalance()
approve()	authorize()
allowance()	Not available (direct use of allowance state variable)
Approval	Not available

You can use table 7.1 to refactor SimpleCoin into a fully compliant ERC20 token. The following listing shows what such an implementation would look like, also taking into account the standard parameter names of functions and events.

Listing 7.10   SimpleCoin refactored to an ERC20 token

```solidity
pragma solidity ^0.4.24;

import "./Listing6_4_Ownable.sol";
import "./Listing7_9_ERC20.sol";

contract SimpleCoin is Ownable, ERC20 {

    mapping (address => uint256)
        internal coinBalance;                              ⊲─┐  These state variables have
    mapping (address => mapping                                 become internal. They're now
        (address => uint256)) internal allowances;   ⊲─┘  exposed externally through
    mapping (address => bool) public frozenAccount;          dedicated functions.

    event Transfer(address indexed from, address indexed to, uint256 value);
    event Approval(address indexed authorizer, address indexed authorized,
        uint256 value);                                   ⊲─┐
    event FrozenAccount(address target, bool frozen);         New event associated
                                                              with approving an
    constructor(uint256 _initialSupply) public {              allowance
        owner = msg.sender;

        mint(owner, _initialSupply);
    }
                                                          ┌─  Allows you to check
    function balanceOf(address _account)           ⊲─┘  coinBalance externally
        public view returns (uint256 balance) {
        return coinBalance[_account];
    }
```

```
function transfer(address _to, uint256 _amount) public returns (bool) {
    require(_to != 0x0);
    require(coinBalance[msg.sender] > _amount);
    require(coinBalance[_to] + _amount >= coinBalance[_to]);
    coinBalance[msg.sender] -= _amount;
    coinBalance[_to] += _amount;
    emit Transfer(msg.sender, _to, _amount);
    return true;
}

function approve(address _authorizedAccount, uint256 _allowance)
    public returns (bool success) {
    allowances[msg.sender][_authorizedAccount] = _allowance;
    emit Approval(msg.sender,
        _authorizedAccount, _allowance);        ⟵—  Raises an event when
    return true;                                      a balance is approved
}

function transferFrom(address _from, address _to, uint256 _amount)
    public returns (bool success) {
    require(_to != 0x0);
    require(coinBalance[_from] > _amount);
    require(coinBalance[_to] + _amount >= coinBalance[_to]);
    require(_amount <= allowances[_from][msg.sender]);
    coinBalance[_from] -= _amount;
    coinBalance[_to] += _amount;
    allowances[_from][msg.sender] -= _amount;
    emit Transfer(_from, _to, _amount);
    return true;
}

function allowance(address _authorizer,        | Allows you to check
    address _authorizedAccount)          ⟵—     allowances externally
    public view returns (uint256) {
    return allowances[_authorizer][_authorizedAccount];
}

function mint(address _recipient, uint256 _mintedAmount)
    onlyOwner public {

    coinBalance[_recipient] += _mintedAmount;
    emit Transfer(owner, _recipient, _mintedAmount);
}

function freezeAccount(address target, bool freeze)
    onlyOwner public {

    frozenAccount[target] = freeze;
    emit FrozenAccount(target, freeze);
}
}
```

Although the token constructor isn't part of the interface and consequently isn't included in the standard, ERC20 recommends initializing a token with the following useful information:

```
string public constant name = "Token Name";
string public constant symbol = "SYM";
uint8 public constant decimals = 18;
```

Number of decimal digits to consider in fractional token amounts

The ERC20 wiki (http://mng.bz/5NaD) also shows a recommended implementation. Although this is similar to SimpleCoin, I still encourage you to review it. I suggest you also have a look at the OpenZeppelin section on tokens at http://mng.bz/6jQ6.

Summary

- Abstract contracts generalize contract functionality and help minimize code duplication by providing default function implementations when appropriate.
- An interface provides the declaration of the minimum set of functions a contract should provide.
- You can seamlessly change the behavior of one element or aspect of a contract by modeling it with an interface. By doing so, you can instantiate a different implementation of the interface without having to alter the code of the contract using it.
- You can organize general purpose Solidity functions in libraries, which you can share across different contracts or applications.
- Creating a custom cryptocurrency or token contract is such a common requirement for most decentralized applications that a standard token interface called ERC20 has been proposed. Any decentralized application can use a token contract that follows the ERC20 standard in a predictable way.

Managing smart contracts with Web3.js

8

This chapter covers

- Deploying contracts and interacting with them through geth's console
- Simplifying console-based deployment with Node.js
- Deploying on a private network
- Deploying on a mock network

In chapter 4, you had a first taste of deploying a smart contract on the Ethereum network. You did so through the Ethereum wallet and through Remix (with MetaMask). It looked relatively easy, as it involved only a few clicks on a well-designed screen. On the other hand, the convenience and simplicity of the user interface hid from you the key steps that take place on the network when contract deployment is in progress. Did you ask yourself, for example, how the code you entered on the code editor (of the wallet or Remix) got compiled, packaged, and sent to the Ethereum network, and how it finally got installed on each node?

In the last three chapters, you learned in depth how to develop a smart contract with Solidity. It's time to learn the deployment process in depth as well. It's important knowledge to have if you want to truly understand how decentralized applications work under the hood, and if you want to be able to troubleshoot postdeployment issues you might experience.

In this chapter, you'll learn how to deploy and communicate with a smart contract through the geth console, using explicit Web3.js instructions. By doing so, you'll perform all the commands and operations the wallet UI did magically for you while deploying the contract or moving tokens between accounts. Not only will you deploy a contract the hard way on a public test network, but you'll go the extra mile and even set up a full private network and redeploy the contract on it. All of this will take much more effort than clicking a few buttons on the wallet UI, but you'll be rewarded by gaining a much deeper knowledge of how an Ethereum network and related blockchain are set up and configured, as well as firsthand insight into the deployment process and client-to-network interaction. Along the way, I'll also show you how to simplify the deployment process a little by running operations on Node.js.

Finally, after you've deployed a contract on a public test network and a private test network, you'll also learn how to deploy a contract on Ganache, a special client that emulates (or mocks) a full Ethereum network on a single host. This is a convenient environment for developing and system-testing your contracts without having to pay for the latency of operations that take place on a real network, such as waiting for transactions to be mined and added on a new block, especially through times of network instability.

Before leaving the chapter, we'll revisit SimpleCoin. This time, I'll take advantage of the fact that you'll have already learned how to deploy it on the network and communicate with it through Web3.js commands on the geth console. I'll be able to show you how to build a simple UI that uses the same Web3 commands, but from within an HTML page.

8.1   Revisiting deployment through geth's interactive console

When you installed geth, in chapter 3, you were pointing to MAINNET, the production Ethereum network. During development, I strongly advise you to point your tools, including your Ethereum client, to a test network instead, at least to avoid spending any real Ether directly or indirectly through accidental transactions or gas consumption. Various test networks are available at any given time, with a couple current examples being Ropsten and Rinkeby. Each test network is related to a slightly different version of the Ethereum platform, and you might find you have to upgrade geth to be able to run on a specific network. For the purposes of this chapter, I'll refer to a test network as TESTNET.

To point geth to TESTNET, you must shut down any instance running against MAINNET (if you have any) and restart geth from a new command shell with the --testnet option:

```
C:\Program Files\geth>geth --testnet
```

Geth will start synchronizing to the test network in exactly the same way it did when you started it in MAINNET.

> **NOTE** In case you want to experiment and point to the Rinkeby test network based on the Proof of Stake consensus algorithm, use the `--rinkeby` option instead of `--testnet` by typing `C:\Program Files\geth>geth --rinkeby`. The rest of the chapter assumes you're using `--testnet`.

Using bootnodes to connect to specific peers

Occasionally your geth client might take a long time to discover peers that can send you the blockchain blocks. In that case, try using the `--bootnodes` option, which will force geth to access the network by connecting to specific peers, rather than discovering all peers by itself. I've found these nodes to be up most of the time:

```
geth --testnet --bootnodes "enode://145a93c5b1151911f1a232e04dd1a76708
  dd12694f952b8a180ced40e8c4d25a908a292bed3521b98bdd843147116a52ddb645
  d34fa51ae7668c39b4d1070845@188.166.147.175:30303,enode://2609b7ee28b
  51f2f493374fee6a2ab12deaf886c5daec948f122bc83716aca27840253d191b9e63
  a6e7ec77643e69ae0d74182d6bb64fd30421d45aba82c13bd@13.84.180.240:3030
  3,enode://94c15d1b9e2fe7ce56e458b9a3b672ef11894ddedd0c6f247e0f1d3487
  f52b66208fb4aeb8179fce6e3a749ea93ed147c37976d67af557508d199d9594c35f
  09@188.166.147.175:30303" --verbosity=4
```

If you want to sync up your blockchain more quickly, you can also add these options:

```
--syncmode "fast" --cache=1024
```

From a separate command shell, you can now start an interactive console pointing to the test network exactly as you did when you were pointing to the main network:

```
C:\Program Files\geth>geth attach ipc:\\.\pipe\geth.ipc
```

(Note that since geth 1.8.0, you have to specify the IPC path.) When the console starts up, it shows environmental information about the network it's pointing to. As you can see in figure 8.1, `datadir` is pointing to `testnet`, which confirms you're now in TESTNET.

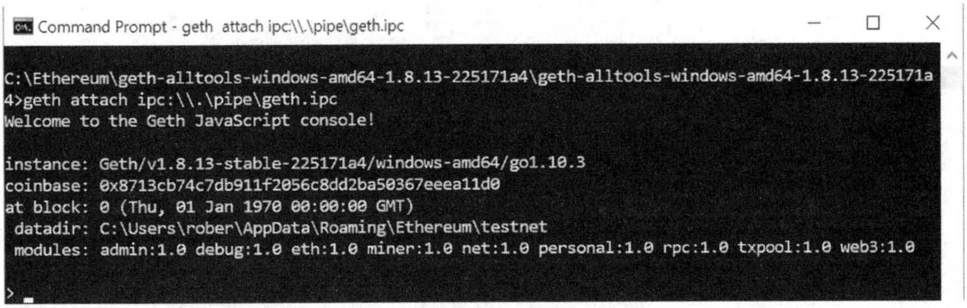

Figure 8.1 The geth interactive console showing it's connected to TESTNET

Deploying a contract through geth's console for the first time is slightly more involved than doing it with a few clicks on Ethereum's wallet. The wallet hides some of the steps that happen under the hood. By performing those steps explicitly, you'll learn how the contract build and deployment process works in detail. Also, once you've scripted the entire process, future redeployment will become much quicker and less error-prone.

8.1.1   *Contract build and deployment process*

The diagram in figure 8.2 shows all the main steps required to build and deploy the contract through the interactive console:

1 Compile the contract with the Solidity compiler.
2 Push the contract's *binary interface* (`abi`) and *bytecode* (`bin`) from the compiler to an output file.
3 Run a Web3.js command that creates a *contract factory* of the contract from its binary interface.
4 Run a Web3.js command that instantiates the contract by invoking the `new()` method of the contract factory and feeding it the bytecode.

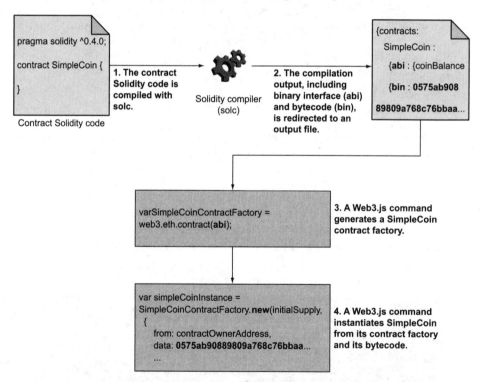

Figure 8.2   The contract build and deployment process: 1. the contract is compiled with the Solidity compiler; 2. the contract binary interface and bytecode are pushed to an output file; and 3. a JavaScript using Web3 is created. This does three things: a. creates a contract factory of the contract from its binary interface (ABI); b. instantiates the contract by invoking `new()` on the contract factory; and c. feeds the bytecode to it.

8.1.2 Deploying SimpleCoin through geth's console

Let's go through the steps from figure 8.2 in detail by redeploying SimpleCoin to the test network. Following the build and deployment diagram, you must first compile the contract using solc.

COMPILING A CONTRACT USING SOLC

You can download the solc compiler from this GitHub page: https://github.com/ethereum/solidity/releases. (I've downloaded solidity-windows.zip from the Version 0.4.24 section—please download an equivalent or later.) After downloading it, copy the executable into a folder; for example, C:\Ethereum\solidity-windows. (Feel free to name the folder after your OS.)

Create a new folder for your SimpleCoin code: C:\Ethereum\SimpleCoin. Then create a new text file called SimpleCoin.sol and, for simplicity, paste in it one of the early versions of the contract code you wrote, like the one shown in the following listing.

Listing 8.1 SimpleCoin.sol, containing an early version of SimpleCoin

```solidity
pragma solidity ^0.4.24;
contract SimpleCoin {
    mapping (address => uint256) public coinBalance;

    event Transfer(address indexed from, address indexed to, uint256 value);

    constructor(uint256 _initialSupply) public {
        coinBalance[msg.sender] = _initialSupply;
    }

    function transfer(address _to, uint256 _amount) public {
        require(coinBalance[msg.sender] > _amount);
        require(coinBalance[_to] + _amount >= coinBalance[_to] );
        coinBalance[msg.sender] -= _amount;
        coinBalance[_to] += _amount;
        emit Transfer(msg.sender, _to, _amount);
    }
}
```

Place this file in the SimpleCoin code folder you created. Then open a command-line shell and move to the SimpleCoin code folder. From there, invoke the compiler as follows:

```
C:\Ethereum\SimpleCoin>..\solidity-windows\solc.exe
➥ --bin -o bin --combined-json abi,bin SimpleCoin.sol
```

Table 8.1 explains the compiler options you've used.

Table 8.1　The solc compiler options used to compile `SimpleCoin`

Compiler option	Purpose
`--bin`	Produces the binary of the contract in hex format
`-o bin`	Creates the binary output in the bin folder
`--combined-json abi,bin`	Produces JSON output, including the ABI interface and the binary

The JSON output shown here will be redirected to the bin\combined.json file:

```
{"contracts":{"SimpleCoin.sol:SimpleCoin":{"abi":"[{\"constant\":false,\
"inputs\":[{\"name\":\"_to\",\"type\":\"address\"},{\"name\":\"_amount\",\
"type\":\"uint256\"}],\"name\":\"transfer\",\"outputs\":[],\"payable\
":false,\"type\":\"function\"},{\"constant\":true,\"inputs\":[{\"name\":\"\"
,\"type\":\"address\"}],\"name\":\"coinBalance\",\"outputs\":[{\"name\":\"\"
,\"type\":\"uint256\"}],\"payable\":false,\"type\":\"function\"},{\"inputs\"
:[{\"name\":\"_initialSupply\",\"type\":\"uint256\"}],\"payable\":false,\
"type\":\"constructor\"},{\"anonymous\":false,\"inputs\":[{\"indexed\":true
,\"name\":\"from\",\"type\":\"address\"},{\"indexed\":true,\"name\":\"to\",\
"type\":\"address\"},{\"indexed\":false,\"name\":\"value\",\"type\":\
"uint256\"}],\"name\":\"Transfer\",\"type\":\"event\"}]","bin":" 60806040523
480156100105760008 0fd5b5060405160208061039983398101806040528101908080519060 2
001909291905050508060008033733ffffffffffffffffffffffffffffffffffffffff1673fff f
ffffffffffffffffffffffffffffffffffffffffffffff168152602001908152602001600020819055505
0610313806100866000396000f3006080604052600436106100 4c576000357c0100000000000
00000000000000000000000000000000000000000000900463ffffffff168063a9059cbb146
10051578063fabde80c1461009e575b600080fd5b34801561005d57600080fd5b5061009c600
4803603810190808035 73fffffffffff...(shortened for brevity)"}}, "version"
:"0.4.24+commit.6ae8fb59.Windows.msvc" }
```

The JSON output includes two members:

- abi—This is the contract application binary interface (ABI). It shows the API that your contract exposes and that client applications that interact with the contract should use.
- bin—This is the contract bytecode in hex format. You'll need the contract's ABI and bytecode to deploy it.

DEPLOYING A CONTRACT THROUGH THE INTERACTIVE CONSOLE

Open geth's interactive console, which is pointing to TESTNET, and enter the code in listing 8.2. (Please make sure you use the code from the listing 8.2 file downloaded from the book website, as I've shortened it for brevity here.) You might have noticed that simpleCoinAbi has been assigned to the content of abi from combined.json, and data has been assigned to the content of bin, prefixed by 0x.

Listing 8.2　The geth interactive JavaScript instructions to deploy a contract

```
var initialSupply = 10000;          SimpleCoin
                                     constructor input

var simpleCoinAbi =
```

Contract ABI, copied from the abi member of the SimpleCoin.out compilation output file

```
[{"constant":false,"inputs":[{"name":"_to","type":"address"},{"name"
➡ :"_amount","type":"uint256"}],"name":"transfer","outputs":[],"payable":false
➡ ,"type":"function"},{"constant":true,"inputs":[{"name":"","type":"address"}]
➡ ,"name":"coinBalance","outputs":[{"name":"","type":"uint256"}],"payable"
➡ :false,"type":"function"},{"inputs":[{"name":"_initialSupply","type"
➡ :"uint256"}],"payable":false,"type":"constructor"},{"anonymous":false
➡ ,"inputs":[{"indexed":true,"name":"from","type":"address"},{"indexed":true
➡ ,"name":"to","type":"address"},{"indexed":false,"name":"value","type"
➡ :"uint256"}],"name":"Transfer","type":"event"}];    //abi interface from
➡ solc output
```

```
var SimpleCoinContractFactory =
    web3.eth.contract(simpleCoinAbi);
```
⟵ **Initializes contract factory with the contract ABI**

```
var simpleCoinInstance =
    SimpleCoinContractFactory.new(
    initialSupply,
    {
      from: web3.eth.accounts[0],
      data:
```
⟵ **Instantiates the contract**

⟵ **The contract bytecode, copied from the bin member of the SimpleCoin.out compilation output file**

```
'0x608060405234801561001057600080fd5b506040516020806103998339
➡ 810180604052810190808051906020019092919050505080600080373fffffffffffffffffff
➡ ffffffffffffffffffffffff1673fffffffffffffffffffffffffffffffffffffffff1681526020
➡ 0190815260200160002081905550506103138061008660003960f30060806040526004361
➡ 61004c576000357c01000000000000000000000000000000000000000000000000000000090
➡ 0463ffffffff168063a9059cbb14610051578063fabde80c1461009e575b600080fd5b348015
➡ 61005d57600080fd5b5061009c6004803603810190808035573fffffffff ...(shortened for
➡ brevity)',
```

```
    gas: '3000000'
  }, function (e, contract){
    console.log(e, contract);
    if (typeof contract.address !== 'undefined') {
        console.log('Contract mined! address: '
        + contract.address + ' transactionHash: '
        + contract.transactionHash);
    }
});
```
⟵ **Triggers registration of callback at completion of the deployment process**

After executing these instructions, you'll get the following error message:

```
Error: authentication needed: password or unlock undefined
```

To deploy the contract, you have to unlock the account it's being deployed through, web3.eth.accounts[0] (specified in the from property in listing 8.2). This will become the account owner.

If you don't remember what accounts[0] refers to, you can list on the interactive console the TESTNET accounts you created from the Ethereum wallet in the previous chapters. The first one in the results list is accounts[0], and it's named in the wallet as Main Account. This is what I got:

```
> web3.eth.accounts
["0xedde06bc0e45645e2f105972bdefc220ed37ae10",
➡  "0x4e6c30154768b6bc3da693b1b28c6bd14302b578",
```

```
    "0x70e36be8ab8f6cf66c0c953cf9c63ab63f3fef02",
    "0xc99048e9b98d3fcf8b5f0d5644794b562f9a2ea4",
    "0x47e3d3948f46144afa7df2c1aa67f6b1b1e35cf1",
    "0x70ff99d4bc8054b2e09269bcbfdddf8e1ae7d155"]
```

Enter the following command to unlock the account:

```
>personal.unlockAccount(
"0xedDE06bC0e45645e2f105972BDefC220ED37Ae10",
PASSWORD_OF_YOUR_ACCOUNT_0)
```

> ### Secure account unlocking
>
> The most secure way of unlocking an account is through a geth command in the operating system shell:
>
> ```
> geth --unlock <YOUR_ACCOUNT_ADDRESS> --password <YOUR_PASSWORD>
> ```
>
> This avoids potential security concerns due to the interactive console recording a history of all the operations that have taken place on it.

Try to re-execute the script in listing 8.2. This time, you won't get any error message. Wait for a few seconds, and the geth console will show a message similar to the following one:

```
Contract mined! address: 0x4291f37a727d32e5620a0a4ed61d27ffdad757af
    transactionHash: 0x2b7d2a015ca3397c1ec2b2d8e14b6c8ca7e3c06340d759a10d0e535
    843532fe6
```

Well done! You've deployed SimpleCoin on TESTNET through the geth interactive console. You can now examine the content of simpleCoinInstance:

```
> simpleCoinInstance
{
  abi: [{
      constant: false,
      inputs: [{...}, {...}],
      name: "transfer",
      outputs: [],
      payable: false,
      type: "function"
  }, {
      constant: true,
      inputs: [{...}],
      name: "coinBalance",
      outputs: [{...}],
      payable: false,
      type: "function"
  }, {
      inputs: [{...}],
      payable: false,
      type: "constructor"
```

```
}, {
    anonymous: false,
    inputs: [{...}, {...}, {...}],
    name: "Transfer",
    type: "event"
}],
address: "0x4291f37a727d32e5620a0a4ed61d27ffdad757af",
transactionHash: "0x2b7d2a015ca3397c1ec2b2d8e14b6c8ca7e3c06340d759a10d0e53
➡5843532fe6",
Transfer: function(),
allEvents: function(),
coinBalance: function(),
transfer: function()
}
```

An important property of the `simpleCoinInstance` object, which you'll reference later, is its blockchain address:

```
address: "0x4291f37a727d32e5620a0a4ed61d27ffdad757af"
```

For now, let's start interacting with `SimpleCoin` through `simpleCoinInstance`.

8.2 Interacting with SimpleCoin through geth's console

Once you've deployed `SimpleCoin` on TESTNET, you can perform the same operations you did manually through the wallet in chapter 4, section 4.2, but this time through the console.

8.2.1 Checking coin balances

First of all, check the balance of `accounts[0]` (or Main Account), which you used to deploy the contract, using the `coinBalance` getter property, as seen in the previous sections:

```
>simpleCoinInstance.coinBalance(eth.accounts[0])
10000
```

Then check the balance of all the other accounts in the same way. You'll get, as expected, the balances shown in table 8.2.

Table 8.2 Expected account balances

Account address	Account balance
0xedDE06bC0e45645e2f105972BDefC220ED37Ae10	10,000
0x4e6C30154768b6bc3Da693b1B28C6bd14302b578	0
0x70e36bE8AB8f6Cf66C0C953cF9c63aB63f3FeF02	0
0xc99048E9B98D3FcF8b5f0D5644794B562f9A2ea4	0

Try to check, as you did in the wallet, the balance of an invalid address, again obtained by modifying the last digit of the Main Account address:

```
>simpleCoinInstance.coinBalance(eth.accounts[0])
0
```

In this case, you won't get the validation error that the wallet returned—it doesn't allow you to enter invalid addresses—you'll get a zero balance. This is because the coin-Balance() getter doesn't perform any validation on the input address. (The wallet performs that validation instead.) It returns a valid balance for valid addresses contained in the coinBalance mapping, and the default int256 value (0) for anything else.

8.2.2 *Transferring coins*

The next operation you'll perform is a coin transfer. Try moving 150 coins from the Main Account to accounts[2] through SimpleCoin's transfer() function. To execute this, you also have to specify the maximum gas amount allowed for the operation:

```
> simpleCoinInstance.transfer(eth.accounts[2], 150,
    {from:eth.accounts[0],gas:200000});
```

When you attempt this operation, you'll get the following message:

```
Error: authentication needed: password or unlock
```

You must unlock the Main Account to digitally sign the transaction, as you did earlier (replace, as usual, your accounts[0] password):

```
>personal.unlockAccount(eth.accounts[0], 'PASSWORD_OF_ACCOUNT_0')
```

> **WARNING**   Although I'm showing you how to unlock an account through the geth console, this isn't entirely safe because the password is in clear text (it's not encrypted) and each operation is logged in the console history. See the "Secure account unlocking" sidebar earlier in this chapter for more information.

When you retry the transfer, the transaction will be successful, and you'll get the transaction hash. In my case, I got

```
"0xccd8211bde9ac8075a6d43fc51d705cf60db5c7f0a25769cf7c8cff94103af7e"
```

Recheck the balances of all of your accounts. You'll get, as expected, the balances shown in table 8.3.

Table 8.3   Expected new account balances

Account address	Account balance
0xedDE06bC0e45645e2f105972BDefC220ED37Ae10	9,850
0x4e6C30154768b6bc3Da693b1B28C6bd14302b578	0

Table 8.3 Expected new account balances *(continued)*

Account address	Account balance
0x70e36bE8AB8f6Cf66C0C953cF9c63aB63f3FeF02	150
0xc99048E9B98D3FcF8b5f0D5644794B562f9A2ea4	0

Now move 50 coins from accounts[2] to accounts[1] after unlocking accounts[2]:

```
>personal.unlockAccount(eth.accounts[2], PASSWORD_OF_ACCOUNTS[2])
>simpleCoinInstance.transfer(eth.accounts[1],
50, {from:eth.accounts[2],gas:200000});
```

After getting the transaction hash, you can recheck the balances. You'll get the balances shown in table 8.4.

Table 8.4 Expected account balances

Account address	Account balance
0xedDE06bC0e45645e2f105972BDefC220ED37Ae10	9,850
0x4e6C30154768b6bc3Da693b1B28C6bd14302b578	50
0x70e36bE8AB8f6Cf66C0C953cF9c63aB63f3FeF02	100
0xc99048E9B98D3FcF8b5f0D5644794B562f9A2ea4	0

Before we close this section, you'll learn how to reference a contract that has already been deployed, such as SimpleCoin. First you'll close the geth console and reattach it.

8.2.3 *Referencing a running contract*

Close the interactive geth console and reattach it from the operating system command-line shell:

```
C:\Program Files\geth>geth attach ipc:\\.\pipe\geth.ipc
```

As you'll remember from the end of section 8.1.2, when you deployed SimpleCoin on TESTNET from the geth console, the console returned the contract address:

```
0x4291f37a727d32e5620a0a4ed61d27ffdad757af
```

If you now want to interact with that deployed instance of SimpleCoin from the geth console, you must create a proxy to contract from its ABI and connect to the remote instance by feeding the address of the deployed contract to the at() method:

```
var remoteSimpleCoinAddress = "0x4291f37a727d32e5620a0a4ed61d27ffdad757af";
var simpleCoinAbi =
    [{"constant":false,"inputs":[{"name":"_to","type":"address"},
```

```
{"name":"_amount","type":"uint256"}],
"name":"transfer","outputs":[],"payable":false,"type":"function"},
{"constant":true,"inputs":[{"name":"","type":"address"}],
"name":"coinBalance","outputs":[{"name":"","type":"uint256"}],
"payable":false,"type":"function"},
{"inputs":[{"name":"_initialSupply","type":"uint256"}],
"payable":false,"type":"constructor"},{"anonymous":false,
"inputs":[{"indexed":true,"name":"from","type":"address"}],
{"indexed":true,"name":"to","type":"address"},
{"indexed":false,"name":"value","type":"uint256"}],          The abi interface from solc
"name":"Transfer","type":"event"}];                          SimpleCoin output
var SimpleCoinContractProxy =
    web3.eth.contract(simpleCoinAbi);            Creates a proxy to the
                                                 SimpleCoin contract
var simpleCoinInstance =
    SimpleCoinContractProxy.at(remoteSimpleCoinAddress);
```

**Connects to the instance of
SimpleCoin deployed earlier**

Connecting to a deployed contract from another contract is slightly different and is explained in the sidebar.

Referencing a deployed contract from another contract

In this chapter, we're focusing on the interaction between a Web3.js client (such as the geth console or, as you'll see later, the Node.js console or an HTML + JS web page) and a deployed Solidity contract. If you want to interact with a deployed Solidity contract from another Solidity contract, you'll use a technique similar to the one you saw in the previous chapter for connecting to a deployed library from a contract:

```
contract SimpleCoinProxy {
    function transfer(address _to, uint256 _amount) public;
}


contract MyContract {
    SimpleCoinProxy simpleCoinProxy;

    function MyContract(address _simpleCoinAddress)
    {
        require(_simpleCoinAddress != 0x0);
        simpleCoinProxy = SimpleCoinProxy(_simpleCoinAddress);
    }

    function transferSimpleCoin(address _to, uint256 _amount) {
        simpleCoinProxy.transfer(_to, _amount) ;
    }
}
```

In this case, you define a local proxy contract as an abstract contract mirroring the public interface of the remote contract. Then you instantiate the proxy by feeding the address of the deployed remote contract to its constructor.

To double-check that you're truly connected to the previously deployed SimpleCoin instance, recheck the value of the coinBalance property against all accounts, starting from:

```
>simpleCoinInstance.coinBalance(
"0xedde06bc0e45645e2f105972bdefc220ed37ae10")
```

You'll get the balances shown in table 8.5.

Table 8.5 Expected account balances

Account address	Account balance
0xedDE06bC0e45645e2f105972BDefC220ED37Ae10	9,850
0x4e6C30154768b6bc3Da693b1B28C6bd14302b578	50
0x70e36bE8AB8f6Cf66C0C953cF9c63aB63f3FeF02	100
0xc99048E9B98D3FcF8b5f0D5644794B562f9A2ea4	0

At this point, you can perform a new transfer operation; for example, move some coins from accounts[2] to accounts[3]. I leave it to you as an exercise.

In this chapter, you've learned how to deploy a contract on TESTNET from geth's interactive console. Deploying on MAINNET, the production Ethereum network, is identical to deploying on TESTNET, except for needing real Ether to run transactions (to fund the gas consumed) on MAINNET.

You might have found command-based deployment through geth's console inefficient and manually intensive: you had to compile the contract separately with the solc compiler, copy the ABI and bytecode manually from the compiler's output, and paste them into some Web3 instructions. It's possible to simplify deployment if you're willing to change the toolset and start using Node.js instead of the geth interactive console. This is what we'll explore in the next section.

8.3   *Simplifying command-based deployment with Node.js*

Node.js is a cross-platform runtime for developing server-side applications in JavaScript. If you're not familiar with Node.js, the sidebar tells a little more about it. You might be wondering why Node.js is relevant for Ethereum development. It's relevant because it can serve as an enhanced geth console that you can use to connect to the geth client and import many packages that will help improve and simplify your development efforts.

If you haven't already, I recommend you install the latest version of Node.js, if you can, or at least version 8.0 or higher. Once you've installed Node.js, it's a good idea to install the Web3 module through the node package manager (npm), so you can reference it from any JavaScript code you run on Node.js.

> **Node.js**
>
> Node.js is a server-side runtime environment for JavaScript. It's based on an event-driven architecture capable of handling asynchronous I/O. It includes a set of standard modules that are libraries of functions for networking (including TCP/IP, HTTP), binary data, file system I/O operations, data streams, and many others. You can create and distribute custom modules through the node package manager, also known as *npm*.
>
> The platform has two main objectives. The first is to allow JavaScript developers to write server-side applications using their favorite language. The second is to provide a server-side web scripting environment with increased scalability through asynchronous programming rather than explicit multithreading.
>
> You can download Node.js from https://nodejs.org/.

8.3.1   Installing Web3 and solc on Node.js

Before installing Web3, create a new folder, and initialize it for npm as follows:

```
C:\Ethereum>md SimpleCoinWithNode
C:\Ethereum>cd SimpleCoinWithNode
C:\Ethereum\SimpleCoinWithNode>npm init
```

You'll be asked to set up various properties of the package.json file that the initialization command (npm init) is going to create. Set the name as simple_coin and the version as 1.0.0 and leave all the other fields blank:

```
name: (SimpleCoinWithNode): simple_coin
Version: (1.0.0) 1.0.0
```

When asked to confirm whether the file being created is correct, type yes and press Enter:

```
Is this ok? (yes) yes
```

Then you can install Web3 (version 0.20.4, as I have done), as follows:

```
C:\Ethereum\SimpleCoinWithNode>npm install web3@0.20.4
```

You'll get output like this:

```
simple_coin@1.0.0 C:\Ethereum\SimpleCoinOnNodeJS
`-- web3@0.20.4
  +-- bignumber.js@2.0.7  (git+https://github.com/frozeman/bignumber.js
-nolookahead.git#57692b3ecfc98bbdd6b3a516cb2353652ea49934)
  +-- crypto-js@3.1.8
  `-- xmlhttprequest@1.8.0

npm WARN simple_coin@1.0.0 No description
npm WARN simple_coin@1.0.0 No repository field.
```

To test that Web3 is working as expected, you can try to retrieve a list of your TESTNET accounts through the Node.js console. Before doing so, you must have a geth instance running. You have to open a separate OS console, start geth on TESTNET, and expose RPC and various RPC interfaces:

```
C:\Program Files\geth>geth --testnet --rpc
--rpcapi="db,eth,net,web3,personal,web3"
```

Remember to also use the --bootnodes option from earlier if the geth console seems stale.

Now go back to the console you used to install the Web3 node package and start the interactive node console, as follows:

```
C:\Ethereum\SimpleCoinWithNode>node
```

You'll see a node console prompt:

```
>
```

Then you can retrieve your TESTNET account addresses, as follows:

```
>const Web3 = require('web3');
>web3 = new Web3(new Web3.providers.HttpProvider("http://localhost:8545"));
>web3.eth.getAccounts(console.log);
```

You'll get output like:

```
> null [ '0xedde06bc0e45645e2f105972bdefc220ed37ae10',
  '0x4e6c30154768b6bc3da693b1b28c6bd14302b578',
  '0x70e36be8ab8f6cf66c0c953cf9c63ab63f3fef02',
  '0xc99048e9b98d3fcf8b5f0d5644794b562f9a2ea4' ]
```

This confirms that Web3 is working as expected. Get out of the node console as follows (note the dot before exit):

```
>.exit
```

You should see the OS prompt:

```
 C:\Ethereum\SimpleCoinWithNode>
```

Then you can install the Solidity compiler solc (version 0.4.24, as I have done):

```
 C:\Ethereum\SimpleCoinWithNode>npm install solc@0.4.24
```

Now you're ready to create a deployment script to simplify the build and deployment process.

8.3.2   *Building and deploying interactively through the Node.js console*

The best way to create a build and deployment script is to try to compile and deploy a contract interactively on the Node.js shell and then place the sequence of commands you've proved to work in a file. You can later execute this file as a single task.

First of all, place SimpleCoin's code from listing 8.1 in the following file:

```
C:\Ethereum\SimpleCoinWithNode\SimpleCoin.sol
```

Now start the node console:

```
C:\Ethereum\SimpleCoinWithNode>node
```

Then you can reference the node JavaScript packages you'll be using, as follows:

```
>const fs = require('fs');          ◁──┐  File system package
>const solc = require('solc');      ◁───── Solidity compiler package
>const Web3 = require('web3');      ◁──┐  Web3 package
```

The following command creates an instance of the web3 object:

```
>const web3 = new Web3(
new Web3.providers.HttpProvider(
"http://localhost:8545"));
```

Set the initial SimpleCoin supply that will be fed to the SimpleCoin constructor:

```
>const initialSupply = 10000;
```

Then you can set account2 as the sender of the deployment transaction:

```
>const account2 = web3.eth.accounts[1];
>const sender = account2;
>const senderPassword = 'account2';
```

Load the source code of SimpleCoin and assign it to the source variable:

```
>const source = fs.readFileSync(
'c:/Ethereum/SimpleCoinWithNode/SimpleCoin.sol',
'utf8');
```

Then you can compile the contract and assign it to compiledContract:

```
>const compiledContract = solc.compile(source, 1);
```

Extract the ABI and bytecode from the compiled contract and assign them to two new variables (note that you must place '0x' before the bytecode):

```
>const abi = compiledContract.contracts[':SimpleCoin'].interface;
>const bytecode = '0x' +
compiledContract.contracts[':SimpleCoin'].bytecode;
```

Assign the gas estimate to a variable after having increased it, so you make sure the transaction runs to completion:

```
>const gasEstimate = web3.eth.estimateGas({ data: bytecode }) + 100000;
```

Now you can create a contract factory (or generator) initialized with `SimpleCoin`'s ABI:

```
>const SimpleCoinContractFactory = web3.eth.contract(JSON.parse(abi));
```

Before deploying the contract, unlock the account that will sign and send the deployment transaction:

```
>web3.personal.unlockAccount(sender, senderPassword);
```

You're now ready to deploy the contract and instantiate it in a single operation with the `new()` function, which also takes two callbacks: one called after successful deployment, the other one in case of errors:

```
>const simpleCoinInstance = SimpleCoinContractFactory.new(initialSupply, {
    from: sender,
    data: bytecode,
    gas: gasEstimate
  }, function (e, contract){
    console.log(e, contract);
    if (typeof contract.address !== 'undefined') {
        console.log('Contract mined! address: '
        + contract.address
        + ' transactionHash: '
        + contract.transactionHash);
    }
});
```

In the meantime, observe the geth console (not the Node.js console!). You should see output similar to this:

```
INFO [08-20|09:50:17] Imported new chain segment blocks=1
➥ txs=3  mgas=1.493 elapsed=6.016ms  mgasps=248.107  number=1521353 hash=
➥ acbacb...7212ed
INFO [08-20|09:50:18] Submitted contract creation fullhash=
➥ 0xb1a204653ba5f0cf5b2953eba15b3a55d3c73a358a1823f327f9cc02c4fc8a2e contract
➥ =0xa9d460c5aba794db20d005f54e8eefa80b76ff2e
INFO [08-20|09:50:26] Imported new chain segment blocks=1
➥ txs=0  mgas=0.000 elapsed=2.527ms  mgasps=0.000     number=1521354 hash
➥ =2e95c3...7f9f9b
```

Then, after a few seconds, in the Node.js console you should see something like this:

```
Contract mined! address: 0xa9d460c5aba794db20d005f54e8eefa80b76ff2e
➥ transactionHash: 0xb1a204653ba5f0cf5b2953eba15b3a55d3c73a358a1823f327f9cc0
➥ 2c4fc8a2e
```

Well done! Now that you've managed to deploy the SimpleCoin contract through the node console, you can automate all the steps you performed interactively.

8.3.3 *Creating a build and deployment script*

Copy all the commands you entered previously, collected in listing 8.3, into the following file:

```
C:\Ethereum\SimpleCoinWithNode\deploySimpleCoin.js
```

(Make sure you replace the password of your account 2 in the senderPassword assignment.)

Listing 8.3 SimpleCoin Node.js deployment script

```javascript
const fs = require('fs');
const solc = require('solc');
const Web3 = require('web3');
const web3 = new Web3(new
    Web3.providers.HttpProvider("http://localhost:8545"));

const account2 = web3.eth.accounts[1];
const sender = account2;
const senderPassword = 'PASSWORD OF ACCOUNT 2';
const initialSupply = 10000;

const source =
    fs.readFileSync('c:/Ethereum/SimpleCoinWithNode/SimpleCoin.sol',
    'utf8');
const compiledContract = solc.compile(source, 1);
const abi = compiledContract.contracts[':SimpleCoin'].interface;
const bytecode = '0x' + compiledContract.contracts[':SimpleCoin'].bytecode;
const gasEstimate = web3.eth.estimateGas({ data: bytecode }) + 100000;

const SimpleCoinContractFactory = web3.eth.contract(JSON.parse(abi));

web3.personal.unlockAccount(sender, senderPassword);

const simpleCoinInstance = SimpleCoinContractFactory.new(initialSupply, {
    from: sender,
    data: bytecode,
    gas: gasEstimate
}, function (e, contract){
    console.log(e, contract);
    if (typeof contract.address !== 'undefined') {
        console.log('Contract mined! address: ' + contract.address + '
    transactionHash: ' + contract.transactionHash);
    }
});
```

Now you can redeploy (and reinstantiate) SimpleCoin by running the script you've created from the OS command shell, as follows:

```
C:\Ethereum\SimpleCoinWithNode>node deploySimpleCoin.js
```

You should see the same output as before on both the geth and Node.js consoles:

```
Contract mined! address: 0x664e5f1df05e11bbf0c72c7c28419e1f8ed5821e
➥ transactionHash: 0x7191139eb5f164da7effbe9e5795fbd28fc212bfd629422da87dbebb
➥ eb13484c
```

You can adapt this script easily to compile other contracts, or multiple contracts, as required.

8.3.4 Interacting with a contract from Node.js

Once you've deployed the contract, you can interact with it through simpleCoin-Instance. For example, you can move some tokens from one account to another. Try to do this first interactively, so you can produce a script, as you did earlier.

First of all, reference the necessary JavaScript packages, as you did earlier:

```
>const fs = require('fs');
>const solc = require('solc');
>const Web3 = require('web3');
>const web3 = new Web3(new
    Web3.providers.HttpProvider("http://localhost:8545"));
```

Then also create a contract factory, as you did earlier:

```
const source = fs.readFileSync(
'c:/Ethereum/SimpleCoinWithNode/SimpleCoin.sol',
'utf8');
const compiledContract = solc.compile(source, 1);
const abi = compiledContract.contracts[':SimpleCoin'].interface;

const SimpleCoinContractFactory = web3.eth.contract(JSON.parse(abi));
```

Now assign the address of the SimpleCoin instance that you deployed interactively to an address variable:

```
const contractAddress =
'0xa9d460c5aba794db20d005f54e8eefa80b76ff2e';
//replace appropriately
```

Then you can connect to that SimpleCoin instance with the at() function:

```
const simpleCoinInstance = SimpleCoinContractFactory.at(contractAddress);
```

Now assign accounts[1] and accounts[2] to two variables:

```
>const account2 = web3.eth.accounts[1];
>const account3 = web3.eth.accounts[2];
```

Then do the same for the related balances:

```
>var account2Balance = simpleCoinInstance.coinBalance(account2);
>var account3Balance = simpleCoinInstance.coinBalance(account3);
```

You can display these balances as follows:

```
>console.log('BALANCES BEFORE transferring tokens');
>console.log('Account 2 balance: ' + account2Balance);
>console.log('Account 3 balance: ' + account3Balance);
```

Finally, unlock `account2` so you can sign and execute the transfer transaction from it:

```
>web3.personal.unlockAccount(account2, "account2");
```

Then you can execute the transfer transaction and assign its hash to a variable:

```
>var transactionHash = simpleCoinInstance.transfer(
account3, 20, {from:account2,gas:200000});
console.log(
'SUBMITTED transfer() transaction. Transaction hash: '
+ transactionHash);
```

Poll the status of the transaction until completion as follows:

```
>var transactionReceipt = null;
>while (transactionReceipt == null)
{
     transactionReceipt = web3.eth.getTransactionReceipt(transactionHash);
}
```

Then display information on the completed transaction:

```
>console.log('COMPLETED transfer() transaction. Transaction: ' +
transactionHash + 'has been consolidated on block: ' +
transactionReceipt.blockNumber);
```

You can now update the values of the account balance variables:

```
>account2Balance = simpleCoinInstance.coinBalance(account2);
>account3Balance = simpleCoinInstance.coinBalance(account3);
```

Finally, you can display the new balances after the transfer:

```
>console.log('BALANCES AFTER transferring tokens');
>console.log('Account 2 balance: ' + account2Balance);
>console.log('Account 3 balance: ' + account3Balance);
```

Having proven that the commands you've entered work correctly, you can move them into a file called transferTokens.js. The code appears in the following listing.

Listing 8.4   transferTokens.js script, which transfers coins between two accounts

```
const fs = require('fs');
const solc = require('solc');
const Web3 = require('web3');
const web3 = new Web3(new
     Web3.providers.HttpProvider("http://localhost:8545"));
```

```
const source = fs.readFileSync(
'c:/Ethereum/SimpleCoinWithNode/SimpleCoin.sol',
'utf8');
const compiledContract = solc.compile(source, 1);
const abi = compiledContract.contracts[':SimpleCoin'].interface;

const SimpleCoinContractFactory = web3.eth.contract(JSON.parse(abi));
const contractAddress =
'0xa9d460c5aba794db20d005f54e8eefa80b76ff2e';
//replace appropriately

const simpleCoinInstance = SimpleCoinContractFactory.at(contractAddress);

const account2 = web3.eth.accounts[1]; //account2
const account3 = web3.eth.accounts[2]; //account3

var account2Balance = simpleCoinInstance.coinBalance(account2);
var account3Balance = simpleCoinInstance.coinBalance(account3);

console.log('Account 2 balance: ' + account2Balance);
console.log('Account 3 balance: ' + account3Balance);

web3.personal.unlockAccount(account2, "PASSWORD OF ACCOUNT 2");

var transactionHash = simpleCoinInstance.transfer(
account3, 20, {from:account2,gas:200000});
console.log(
'SUBMITTED transfer() transaction. Transaction hash: '
+ transactionHash);

var transactionReceipt = null;
while (transactionReceipt == null)
{
    transactionReceipt = web3.eth.getTransactionReceipt(transactionHash);
}

console.log(
'COMPLETED transfer() transaction. Transaction: '
+ transactionHash + 'has been consolidated on block: ' +
    transactionReceipt.blockNumber);

account2Balance = simpleCoinInstance.coinBalance(account2);
account3Balance = simpleCoinInstance.coinBalance(account3);

console.log('BALANCES AFTER transferring tokens');
console.log('Account 2 balance: ' + account2Balance);
console.log('Account 3 balance: ' + account3Balance);
```

Run it as follows:

```
C:\Ethereum\SimpleCoinWithNode>node transferTokens.js
```

Before I close the topic of deployment, in the next section you'll learn how to deploy a contract on a private network. A private network is an Ethereum environment completely under your control.

8.4 *Deploying on a private network*

A private network can be useful if, during development, you don't want to deal with the delays involved in working with a public test network. For example, on the public test network, you generally have to wait a number of

- minutes to mine Ether through CPU mining
- minutes to resynchronize to the network, if you've disconnected and then reconnected after a few hours or days
- seconds for contract deployment or transactions confirmation

Occasionally, when you reconnect after a few days, TESTNET doesn't sync correctly due to major development or a fork that has happened in the meantime. In that case, you have to restart from scratch by deleting the whole blockchain stored on your node.

Another benefit of running against a private network is that you can efficiently test contracts whose logic depends on time-based expiration. Because contracts are isolated from external services, such as external clocks, you'll commonly emulate time with a number of blocks, under the assumption that it takes around 14 seconds to generate a new block.

Setting up a private network means starting up a custom blockchain, disconnected from the official Ethereum TESTNET or MAINNET blockchains. Before doing so, you should learn how geth manages the blockchain—how it records its history and what happens during synchronization.

8.4.1 *How geth accesses the blockchain*

When you start it up, geth looks at your Ethereum data folder before connecting to the network. As you know from chapter 3, when I presented the keystore, the Ethereum data folder is located in one of the following directories:

- Windows: C:\Users\username\%appdata%\Roaming\Ethereum\
- Linux: ~/.ethereum/
- Mac: ~/Library/Ethereum/

This folder contains the following folders:

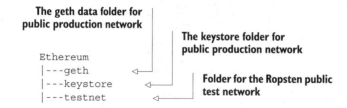

You already examined the content of the keystore back in chapter 3. Let's have a look at the content of each geth folder:

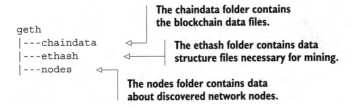

> **NOTE** As for the keystore, each geth folder is specific to a single network, so ethereum/geth and ethereum/testnet/geth contain completely different data. As a result, if you want to back up the blockchain and keystore for a specific environment, you need to take a copy of only the relevant geth and keystore folders.

8.4.2 Setting up a private test network

Now that you've learned where the public (test or main) blockchain is stored on your geth node, you'll be able to understand more easily the steps needed to set up a test network. We'll go through each of these steps in detail:

1. Create a custom genesis file.
2. Create a custom blockchain data folder.
3. Choose a name to identify your node.
4. Launch geth with a custom configuration to generate the genesis block.
5. Launch geth with a custom configuration to run a private network node.
6. Create the Etherbase account.
7. Start mining to get Ether on the Etherbase account.

CREATING A CUSTOM GENESIS FILE

A blockchain starts from a master or *genesis* block that has no parent and seeds the chain. All nodes in your private network will have to reference the same genesis block to agree with each other.

Create a new folder—for example, called C:\privatenetdev—and create within it a file called genesis.json. Then paste into it the following content:

```
{
    "config": {
        "chainId": 10101010,
        "homesteadBlock": 0,
        "eip155Block": 0,
        "eip158Block": 0
    },
```

Parameters to configure a specific Ethereum protocol version (Homestead, for example)

Protocol-specific parameters

Identifier of the network being created

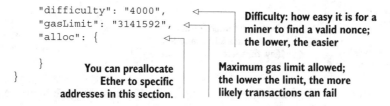

The most important settings are explained in table 8.6.

Table 8.6   Genesis file settings

Setting	Description
chainId	After you create this identifier, you can connect to the private network through it.
difficulty	A higher value increases the number of attempts a mining node needs to perform before finding a valid nonce so it can add a new block to the blockchain. To give you an idea, a value of 4000, for example, makes mining easy because it allows any miner to generate a new block roughly every five seconds. You'd have to increment the difficulty value exponentially if you wanted a node to be able to generate a new block only every few minutes or hours.
gasLimit	This is the maximum limit allowed for a transaction, regardless of the limit set on the transaction itself. The higher it is, the less likely it is that transactions will fail with the following error: "Error: exceeds block gas limit."

CREATING A CUSTOM BLOCKCHAIN DATA FOLDER

Create a folder in a different area with respect to the standard Ethereum data. An example would be C:\privatenet.

CHOOSING A NAME FOR THE TEST NODE

Assigning a name to the first node of your private network makes it easy to identify if you decide to add more nodes later on. For this example, try PrivateNetMaster.

LAUNCHING GETH WITH CUSTOM CONFIGURATION TO GENERATE THE GENESIS BLOCK

So far, you've always started geth with the default configuration. At most, you've specified whether to start it against testnet, with the --testnet option, or in console mode, by specifying the console or attach command.

To generate the custom genesis block of your private network, launch geth with the init command, as follows:

```
C:\program files\geth>geth --networkid 10101010
➥--identity "PrivateNetMaster" --rpc
➥--rpcapi="db,eth,net,web3,personal,web3"
➥--datadir "C:\privatenet" --port "30303" --nodiscover
➥--maxpeers 0 init C:\privatenetdev\genesis.json
```

Table 8.7 describes every option this geth launch command used. After launching geth, you should see output similar to that in the screenshot in figure 8.3.

Table 8.7 The options used to start geth against a private network

geth option	Description
`--networkid`	This identifies a specific Ethereum network. For example, TESTNET and MAINNET have their own `networkid` (default: 1, which is MAINNET).
`--identity`	This is useful to identify a specific node of the private network.
`--rpc`	This enables the JSON-RPC interface on the node (default: enabled).
`--rpcapi`	You enable the API over RPC (default: web3).
`--datadir`	The blockchain data folder
`--port`	The network listening port other peers of the same network use to connect to this node
`--nodiscover`	This disables discovery of the node by clients that are pointing to the same `networkid` and are referencing the same genesis block. You must add other nodes to this network manually.
`--maxpeers`	The maximum number of peers allowed from this node. By setting it to zero, you explicitly state you'll have only one node. If you need to add more network nodes, you must change this setting later.

Figure 8.3 The output from geth after generating the genesis block of your private network

LAUNCHING GETH WITH CUSTOM CONFIGURATION TO RUN A PRIVATE NETWORK NODE

Now that you've generated the genesis block, you can launch geth using the same parameters as before, except from the `init` command:

```
C:\program files\geth>geth --networkid 10101010
➥--identity "PrivateNetMaster" --rpc
➥--rpcapi="db,eth,net,web3,personal,web3"
➥--datadir "C:\privatenet" --port "30303"
➥--nodiscover --maxpeers 0
```

TIP You might have to close down any running geth instances pointing to MAINNET or TESTNET and/or any running wallet instance, depending on how you've configured port numbers.

If geth starts successfully, you should see a screen similar to the screenshot in figure 8.4. You'll notice the screen doesn't show any progress—no blocks are being generated. I'm sure you know why. It's because yours is the only node of the private network, and it's not mining!

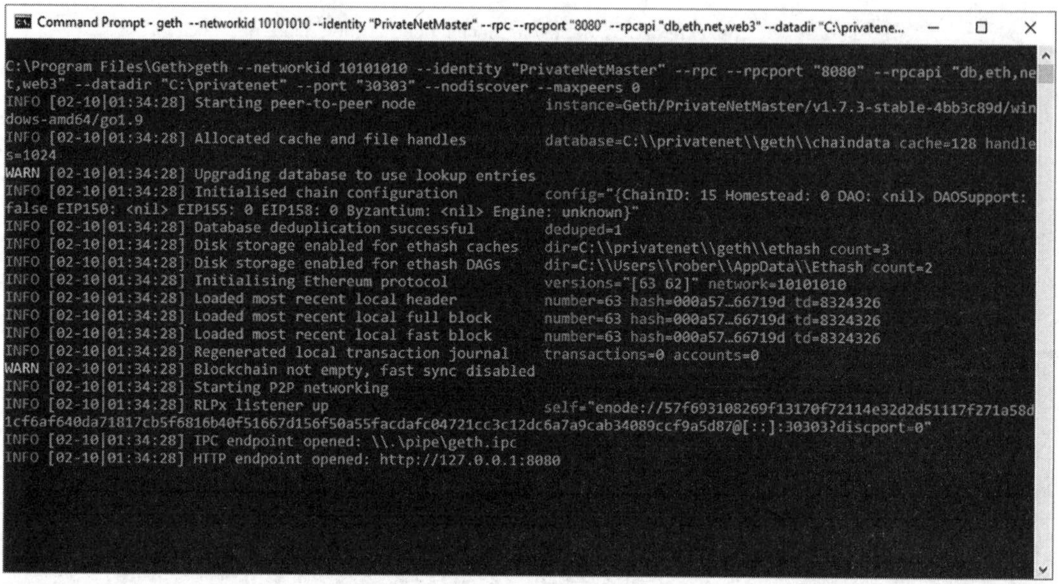

Figure 8.4   The output from geth after launching it against the private network you've created

You don't have any new accounts yet on your brand new blockchain. Before starting mining, you must create at least the Etherbase (or coinbase) account.

CREATING THE ETHERBASE ACCOUNT

Attach to the private network node by opening a new command-line console and then launching geth attach as usual. When the geth console opens, it will display the name and data directory of your private network, respectively, in the `instance` and `datadir` output, which confirms you're attached to the private network node:

```
C:\Program Files\Geth>geth attach ipc:\\.\pipe\geth.ipc
Welcome to the Geth JavaScript console!

instance: Geth/PrivateNetMaster/v1.7.3-stable-4bb3c89d/windows-amd64/go1.9
at block: 1 (Mon, 26 Jun 2017 09:31:42 BST)
 datadir: C:\privatenet
 modules: admin:1.0 debug:1.0 eth:1.0 miner:1.0 net:1.0 personal:1.0 rpc:1.0
➥ txpool:1.0 web3:1.0
```

You can now create an account as you saw in chapter 3, section 3.4.3 (entering your own password in place of the text "PASSWORD OF ETHERBASE ACCOUNT"):

```
>personal.newAccount("PASSWORD OF ETHERBASE ACCOUNT")
"0x3f9e54337cce348607b76200fc19f3f6e3e8e358"
```

You can set this account as an Etherbase account with the setEtherbase method of the miner object. Pass the address of the account you've created as an input:

```
>miner.setEtherbase("0x3f9e54337cce348607b76200fc19f3f6e3e8e358")
```

Before starting to mine, you can create additional accounts. For the moment, create one more account. You'll use it to interact with SimpleCoin on the private network (also here entering your own password instead of the text "PASSWORD OF ACCOUNT 2"):

```
>personal.newAccount("PASSWORD OF ACCOUNT 2")
"0x336a008e3a3b099bcd125cd54fc193070fe1d177"
```

START MINING TO GET ETHER ON THE ETHERBASE ACCOUNT

You can now start mining as you saw in the CPU mining section of chapter 3:

```
>miner.start()
```

Let the miner run for a few seconds and check the output from the main geth shell. You'll see the DAG gets generated (see chapter 3, section 3.3.4 to refresh your memory on the DAG, if needed), as shown in the screenshot in figure 8.5.

```
INFO [02-10|01:34:28] RLPx listener up                        self="enode://57f693108269f13170f72114e32d2d9
1cf6af640da71817cb5f6816b40f51667d156f50a55facdafc04721cc3c12dc6a7a9cab34089ccf9a5d87@[::]:30303?discport=0"
INFO [02-10|01:34:28] IPC endpoint opened: \\.\pipe\geth.ipc
INFO [02-10|01:34:28] HTTP endpoint opened: http://127.0.0.1:8080
INFO [02-10|02:26:16] Updated mining threads                  threads=0
INFO [02-10|02:26:16] Transaction pool price threshold updated price=18000000000
INFO [02-10|02:26:16] Starting mining operation
INFO [02-10|02:26:16] Commit new mining work                  number=64 txs=0 uncles=0 elapsed=1.002ms
INFO [02-10|02:26:18] Generating DAG in progress              epoch=0 percentage=0 elapsed=605.596ms
INFO [02-10|02:26:18] Generating DAG in progress              epoch=0 percentage=1 elapsed=1.228s
INFO [02-10|02:26:19] Generating DAG in progress              epoch=0 percentage=2 elapsed=1.892s
INFO [02-10|02:26:20] Generating DAG in progress              epoch=0 percentage=3 elapsed=2.535s
INFO [02-10|02:26:20] Generating DAG in progress              epoch=0 percentage=4 elapsed=3.146s
INFO [02-10|02:26:21] Generating DAG in progress              epoch=0 percentage=5 elapsed=3.868s
INFO [02-10|02:26:22] Generating DAG in progress              epoch=0 percentage=6 elapsed=4.535s
INFO [02-10|02:26:22] Generating DAG in progress              epoch=0 percentage=7 elapsed=5.122s
INFO [02-10|02:26:23] Generating DAG in progress              epoch=0 percentage=8 elapsed=5.740s
INFO [02-10|02:26:24] Generating DAG in progress              epoch=0 percentage=9 elapsed=6.351s
INFO [02-10|02:26:24] Generating DAG in progress              epoch=0 percentage=10 elapsed=6.959s
```

Figure 8.5   As soon as you launch mining for the first time, the DAG gets generated.

If you check the balance of the Etherbase account in the interactive shell, it will still be zero:

```
> eth.getBalance(eth.coinbase).toNumber();
0
```

After a few seconds you should see the first blocks being mined in the main geth shell, as shown in the screenshot in figure 8.6.

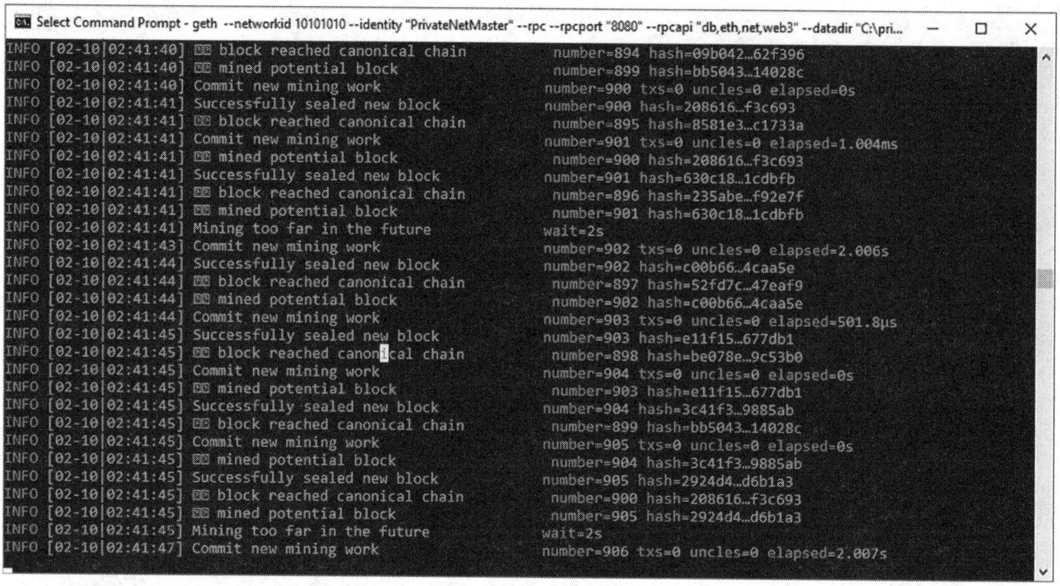

Figure 8.6   After the DAG has been generated and the first blocks get created

NOTE You might wonder where these initial blocks are coming from, as you haven't submitted any transactions yet. A miner will always try to create a block even if no transaction is available in its memory pool. Creating an empty block is perfectly legal and can happen in periods of low transaction activity. As you know, though, a miner is encouraged to include in a block as many transactions as possible through the collection of transaction fees, so empty blocks are rare in practice and tend to appear mainly in private networks.

The Etherbase balance will now show Ether (expressed in Wei)

```
>eth.getBalance(eth.coinbase).toNumber();
5000000000000000000
```

and you can stop the mining, if you want:

```
>miner.stop()
```

You've created your local private network. Now you can try to deploy SimpleCoin on it.

8.4.3   Deploying SimpleCoin on the private network

Working on a private network is identical to working on a public network, so you should be able to deploy the contract by yourself. But you should check to make sure everything goes as expected. Table 8.8 shows the accounts you have in the private network.

Table 8.8 Accounts in the private network

Account	Address
Main account	0x3f9e54337cce348607b76200fc19f3f6e3e8e358
Account 2	0x336a008e3a3b099bcd125cd54fc193070fe1d177

Make sure account 2 has some Ether, so you can deploy from it. You can get some from the Main account, which has acquired Ether through mining:

```
> personal.unlockAccount(eth.coinbase, "PASSWORD OF ETHERBASE ACCOUNT");
> eth.sendTransaction({from:eth.coinbase,
to:eth.accounts[1], value: web3.toWei(2.0, "ether")})
```

You can now deploy from account 2 by running the script you created in section 8.3.3 from the OS command shell, as follows:

```
C:\Ethereum\SimpleCoinWithNode>node deploySimpleCoin.js
```

Although you don't get any error messages, something seems to have gone wrong: the contract address appears as undefined. Remember, when you deployed on TESTNET, after a few seconds you got this output:

```
Contract mined! address: 0x4291f37a727d32e5620a0a4ed61d27ffdad757af
  transactionHash: 0x2b7d2a015ca3397c1ec2b2d8e14b6c8ca7e3c06340d759a10d0e5358
  43532fe6
```

But now you haven't received confirmation of the contract address. If you check on the output of the main geth shell, you'll see the screen hanging on

```
INFO [06-26|09:19:52] Submitted contract creation fullhash=
  0x2db88eadcd908f8c66294f2d427825e46bf820f089277f436ed5165f739efbbd
  contract=0xd144854e0d90e49726fab8e613115c217ee5262c
```

Think about what might be causing this problem. Yes, you're right: no mining is taking place! To complete the deployment transaction, this needs to get mined.

Go back to the geth interactive console and restart mining:

```
> miner.start()
```

(Remember, earlier you stopped mining through miner.stop().) The expected completion message will appear immediately:

```
Contract mined! address: 0xd144854e0d90e49726fab8e613115c217ee5262c
  transactionHash: 0x2db88eadcd908f8c66294f2d427825e46bf820f089277f436ed5165f
  739efbbd
```

If you now inspect `simpleCoinInstance`, it contains the contract address:

```
...

address: "0xd144854e0d90e49726fab8e613115c217ee5262c",
transactionHash:
"0x2db88eadcd908f8c66294f2d427825e46bf820f089277f436ed5165f739efbbd",
Transfer: function(),
allEvents: function(),
coinBalance: function(),
transfer: function()
}
```

Now that you've deployed the contract, if you want to save on electricity and keep your CPU cool, you can stop mining. Remember, though, that to interact with the contract, mining must be on; otherwise, transactions will never complete.

As an exercise, try to move some SimpleCoins from the Main Account to Account 2 while no mining is taking place, then check the coin balance of your two accounts. You'll prove that the transaction will get completed only when you switch mining back on.

8.5   *Making development more efficient by deploying on mock networks*

Although running a contract on a private network makes development relatively faster, especially if you configure the mining difficulty level appropriately, you still need to manage the private network correctly. For example, accounts you're using for development or testing must have some Ether, even if only test Ether, to make sure you can execute transactions to completion. Also, at least one node of the test network must perform some mining continuously.

One way to improve the efficiency of your development cycle is to deploy your contract on a mock network. A mock network, such as Ganache, runs in-memory, generally on the developer computer, and emulates or bypasses, where applicable, all infrastructural aspects of an Ethereum network, such as account management, transaction costs, mining, and connectivity. By deploying your contract on Ganache, you can focus only on the development and testing of the functionality of your contract, and by doing so you can speed up your development cycle considerably. But once the contract is working as expected from a functional point of view, you still need to retest it within a private network and ultimately, on the public test network, to make sure the contract is also sound from an infrastructural point of view.

8.5.1   *Installing and starting up Ganache*

It turns out that installing and setting up Ganache is easier than setting up a private network: Ganache is written in JavaScript, it uses `Ethereumjs` to emulate client behavior, and it's distributed as a Node.js package, which makes its installation easy.

Assuming you have an instance of Node.js (you must have at least version 6.9.1 at the time of writing), you can install Ganache with the Node.js console, as follows:

```
C:\Ethereum\SimpleCoinWithNode\>npm install -g ganache-cli@6.1.8
```

That's it! Now you should stop geth if it's running, and you can start Ganache from a new OS console:

```
c:\>ganache-cli
```

On start-up, Ganache will list the accounts it's going to support, as shown in the screenshot in figure 8.7.

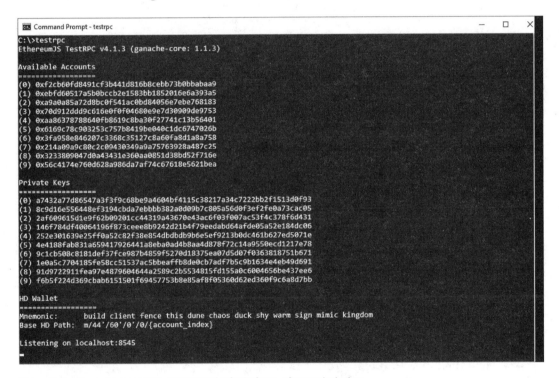

Figure 8.7   Ganache accounts and related private keys, shown at startup

8.5.2   *Deploying SimpleCoin on Ganache*

Because Ganache is emulating the Ethereum network, you can't use the geth console to deploy `SimpleCoin`'s contract on it. Your new console to the (mocked) Ethereum network is now the Node.js console.

Now you can deploy `SimpleCoin` exactly as you did when deploying on a public or private test network, as shown in the following listing, which has been adapted slightly for Ganache from listing 8.3.

Listing 8.5   Deploying SimpleCoinOnGanache.js

```
const fs = require('fs');
const solc = require('solc');
const Web3 = require('web3');
const web3 = new Web3(
new Web3.providers.HttpProvider("http://localhost:8545"));

const account2 = web3.eth.accounts[1];
const sender = account2;

const initialSupply = 10000;

const source = fs.readFileSync(
'c:/Ethereum/SimpleCoin/SimpleCoin.sol', 'utf8');
const compiledContract = solc.compile(source, 1);
const abi = compiledContract.contracts[':SimpleCoin'].interface;
const bytecode = '0x' + compiledContract.contracts[':SimpleCoin'].bytecode;
const gasEstimate = web3.eth.estimateGas({ data: bytecode }) + 100000;

const SimpleCoinContractFactory = web3.eth.contract(JSON.parse(abi));

const simpleCoinInstance = SimpleCoinContractFactory.new(initialSupply, {
    from: sender,
    data: bytecode,
    gas: gasEstimate
  }, function (e, contract){
    console.log(e, contract);
    if (typeof contract.address !== 'undefined') {
        console.log('Contract mined! address: '
        + contract.address
        + ' transactionHash: ' + contract.transactionHash);
    }
});
```

If you have a running geth instance, stop it. Make sure Ganache is running in a separate OS shell. Otherwise, start it again with

```
C:\>ganache-cli
```

Then run the deployment script in this way:

```
C:\Ethereum\SimpleCoinWithNode>node deployingSimpleCoinOnGanache.js
```

In the meantime, observe the OS shell running Ganache. You should see the following:

```
Listening on localhost:8545
eth_accounts
eth_estimateGas
eth_sendTransaction

  Transaction: 0x25a3ee4ef5f71e72ab1800a78782d42676aec61503eaab1ef8beaf
2e54993038
  Contract created: 0xdc6d598f56cf80201d95b4e9494e83bab8aa479e
```

```
Gas usage: 509317
Block Number: 1
Block Time: Wed Feb 21 2018 01:49:20 GMT+0000 (GMT Standard Time)
```

```
eth_newBlockFilter
eth_getFilterChanges
eth_getTransactionReceipt
eth_getCode
eth_uninstallFilter
```

Then you should see this in the Node.js console almost immediately:

```
Contract mined! address: 0xedaa9632746aa82b0f1f73185c38a437643116af
➥  transactionHash: 0xfa4d8a6e526d53ace153b2619c47f9e29359125dbf28e4d97d8f5af0
➥  cdd051d7
```

Can you spot the differences between deploying a contract on a public or private network and deploying it on Ganache? Yes, you're right:

- Deployment on Ganache was instantaneous, whereas deployment on a network was performed with some latency.
- You didn't need to unlock the account deploying the contract, contrary to what you did when deploying on a public or private network.

Here's an exercise for you before we continue. Try transferring coins between two accounts on Ganache, either interactively or through a script.

8.6 Smoother interaction with SimpleCoin through a web UI

So far, you've been interacting with deployed Ethereum smart contracts through various development tools, as shown in figure 8.8: manually through the Ethereum wallet and Remix (with the injected Web3 option) and through explicit Web3.js instructions from a geth console or a Node.js console. An end user can also interact with an Ethereum contract through Web3.js indirectly from a web UI. In this section, you'll build a web UI for SimpleCoin and, as a result, complete a minimal end-to-end decentralized application for the first time.

8.6.1 Building a minimalistic web UI for SimpleCoin

To keep things simple, you'll initially connect the web UI to an instance of Simple-Coin deployed on Ganache. If you've shut down Ganache, please start it up again and redeploy SimpleCoin on it, following the steps described in section 8.4.3.

Once SimpleCoin gets deployed, you should see, as before, a confirmation message similar to this:

```
Contract mined! address: 0xedaa9632746aa82b0f1f73185c38a437643116af
➥  transactionHash: 0xfa4d8a6e526d53ace153b2619c47f9e29359125dbf28e4d97d8f5af0
➥  cdd051d7
```

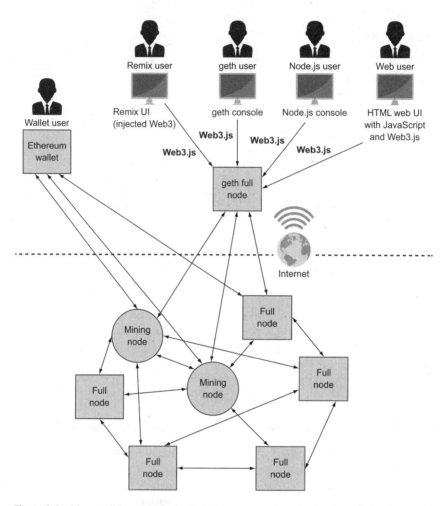

Figure 8.8 It's possible to interact with Ethereum smart contracts through development tools such as the Ethereum wallet and Remix. Alternatively, you can perform contract operations through explicit Web3.js instructions issued from the geth console or the Node.js console. You can execute the same Web3.js instructions implicitly from an HTML web UI.

NOTE Take a note of the contract address. You'll need to place it in the JavaScript code you'll be writing shortly.

You can build a minimalistic web UI with a small piece of HTML referencing a JavaScript script that handles coin transfers between accounts. In short, you need to implement two files:

- simplecoin.js
- simplecoin.html

SIMPLECOIN.JS

The JavaScript code required to handle the coin transfers between accounts, shown in listing 8.6, is similar to what you've already executed several times in this chapter—for example, what you saw earlier in listing 8.2. Make sure you replace the address of the contract in listing 8.6 with the one from the contract you deployed earlier on Ganache.

Listing 8.6 simplecoin.js

```
var web3 = new Web3(
new Web3.providers.HttpProvider("http://localhost:8545"));

var abi = "[{\"constant\":false,\"inputs\":[{\"name\":\"_to\",\"type\":\
"address\"},{\"name\":\"_amount\",\"type\":\"uint256\"}],\"name\":\
"transfer\",\"outputs\":[],\"payable\":false,\"type\":\"function\"},{\
"constant\":true,\"inputs\":[{\"name\":\"\",\"type\":\"address\"}],\"name\
":\"coinBalance\",\"outputs\":[{\"name\":\"\",\"type\":\"uint256\"}],\
"payable\":false,\"type\":\"function\"},{\"inputs\":[{\"name\":\
"_initialSupply\",\"type\":\"uint256\"}],\"payable\":false,\"type\":\
"constructor\"},{\"anonymous\":false,\"inputs\":[{\"indexed\":true,\"name\
":\"from\",\"type\":\"address\"},{\"indexed\":true,\"name\":\"to\",\"type\
":\"address\"},{\"indexed\":false,\"name\":\"value\",\"type\":\"uint256\
"}],\"name\":\"Transfer\",\"type\":\"event\"}]";
var SimpleCoinContractFactory = web3.eth.contract(JSON.parse(abi));
var simpleCoinContractInstance = SimpleCoinContractFactory.at(
'0xedaa9632746aa82b0f1f73185c38a437643116af');          ◁──   Replace this with the
var accounts = web3.eth.accounts;                                address of the SimpleCoin
                                                                 contract you just deployed
              Reports an    function refreshAccountsTable() {    on Ganache.
               updated          var innerHtml =
               account             "<tr><td>Account</td><td>Balance</td>";   ◁──   Builds the HTML
               balance                                                              account balance table
                                                                                    dynamically
                                for (var i = 0; i < accounts.length; i++) {   ◁──
                                    var account = accounts[i];                     All accounts are
                                    var balance =                                  iterated to build the
                                        simpleCoinContractInstance                 account balance HTML.
                                          .coinBalance(account);   ◁──
                                    innerHtml = innerHtml +                 Calls the coin
                                      "<tr><td>" +                         balance getter
                                      account + "</td><td>"
                                      + balance + "</td></tr>";
                                }

                                $("#accountsBalanceTable").html(innerHtml);
              }                                                 Gets the input from
                                                               the UI and feeds it to
              function transferCoins() {   ◁──                 the coin transfer
                  var sender = $("#from").val();               contract function
                  var recipient = $("#to").val();
                  var tokensToTransfer = $("#amount").val();
                  simpleCoinContractInstance.transfer(   ◁──   Invokes the coin
                      recipient,                                transfer contract
                      tokensToTransfer,                         function
```

```
                {from:sender,gas:200000},
                function(error, result){
                    if(!error)
                        refreshAccountsTable();         ◁─┐  The callback associated
                    else                                    with a successful
                        console.error(error);               transfer refreshes the
                }                                            account balance table.
            );
    }

    $( document ).ready(function() {     ◁─┐  Renders the account
        refreshAccountsTable();               balance table on
    });                                       opening the page
```

Create a folder on your machine, for example named C:\Ethereum\SimpleCoin-WebUI. Within this folder, create a file called simplecoin.js and copy into it the code from listing 8.6.

SIMPLECOIN.HTML

The HTML page required to collect the input and show the outcome of coin transfer operations is basic. It contains a few text boxes to gather the input and a button to trigger the transfer. Apart from the basic HTML, you need to reference the Web3.js and jQuery JavaScript libraries and the simplecoin.js script you just created. You can import Web3.js and jQuery locally with Bower (https://bower.io/), a package manager for building websites. Install Bower with npm as follows:

```
C:\Ethereum\SimpleCoinWebUI>npm install -g bower
```

Now import the Web3.js and JQuery libraries in the current directory:

```
C:\Ethereum\SimpleVotingWebUI>bower install web3#0.20.6
C:\Ethereum\SimpleVotingWebUI>bower install jquery
```

At this point, Bower will have downloaded Web3 and jQuery into respective directories within the bower_components folder:

```
bower_components
    |--web3
    |--jquery
```

You can now reference the JavaScript libraries as shown at the top of the following listing, which contains the entire HTML code you need.

> **Listing 8.7   simplecoin.html**

```
<html>
<head>
    <script src="bower_components/web3/dist/web3.min.js"></script>
    <script src="bower_components/jquery/dist/jquery.min.js"></script>
    <script src="./simplecoin.js"></script>
</head>
```

```
<body>
    <table>
       <tr><b>SimpleCoin</b></tr>
        <tr><table border="0" cellpadding="0" width="200"
    id='accountsBalanceTable'> </table></tr>
        <tr/>
        <tr/>
        <tr>Transfer coins</tr>
        <tr>
            <table border="0" cellpadding="0" width="200" id='transferCoins'>
                <tr>
                    <td>From:</td><td><input type="text" id="from" width="400"
    /></td>
                    <td>To:</td><td><input type="text" id="to" width="400"
    /></td>
                    <td>Amount:</td><td><input type="text" id="amount" /></td>
                    <td><button onclick="transferCoins()">Transfer</button></td>
                </tr>
            </table>
        </tr>
    </table>
</body>
</html>
```

Within the SimpleCoinWebUI folder, create a file called simplecoin.html. Copy into it the code from listing 8.7.

8.6.2 *Running the SimpleCoin web UI*

Open simplecoin.html with your browser. You'll see the screen shown in figure 8.9.

The screen shows the balance of all the accounts Ganache supports. As specified on the deployment script shown in listing 8.5, accounts[1], which is the contract owner, has 10,000 SimpleCoin tokens, and the other accounts have a nil balance.

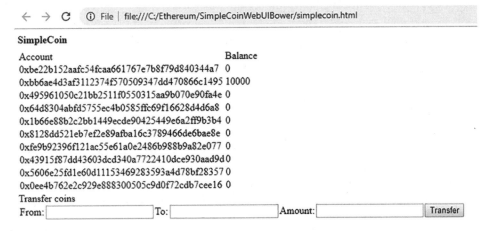

Figure 8.9 SimpleCoin web UI

Performing a transfer through the UI is simple. Specify the source and destination address, respectively, in the From and To text boxes and the number of tokens you want to transfer in the Amount text box. Then click the Transfer button. As an exercise, perform this transfer:

- From: 0xbb6ae4d3af3112374f570509347dd470866c1495
- To: 0x495961050c21bb2511f0550315aa9b070e90fa4e
- Amount: 150

After you click Transfer, the `transfer()` contract function is invoked and, if the operation completes successfully, the associated callback (mapped to the local `refresh-AccountsTable()` JavaScript function) updates the account balances table, as you can see in figure 8.10.

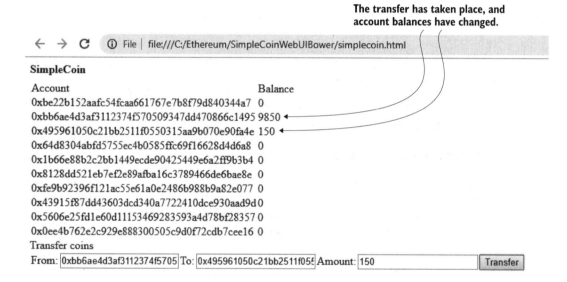

Figure 8.10   The balance of the source and destination accounts have changed following a successful coin transfer.

Summary

- Tools such as the Ethereum wallet and Remix allow you to deploy contracts and perform operations on them, but they hide the communication between the client and the Ethereum network.
- You can deploy contracts with explicit Web3.js instructions from geth's console.
- You also can execute contract operations through Web3.js instructions from geth's console.

- Because of the limitations of geth's console, deploying contracts and performing operations on them from it is a manually intensive and time-consuming process that isn't easy to automate.

- It's easier to compile and deploy contracts from Node.js, which also allows you to completely automate build and deployment Web3.js scripts.

- You can improve the development cycle by deploying contracts on a private Ethereum network completely under the control of the development team.

- You can further improve the development cycle by deploying contracts on a mock network, such as Ganache, which emulates accounts and bypasses high-latency operations such as mining.

- It's possible to execute contract operations from an HTML UI, through the same Web3.js instructions performed using a geth or Node.js console.

Part 3

Y ou can think of part 3 as the core of the book. After learning all the foundation content in the previous parts, you're ready to transition to real-world Ethereum. In chapter 9, you'll become familiar with the wider ecosystem, which includes, among other elements, the Ethereum Name Service (ENS); decentralized storage networks, such as IPFS and Swarm; and oracle and other development frameworks. Then you'll start to use professional development tools.

In chapter 10, you'll learn how to test smart contracts with the JavaScript Mocha framework, and in chapter 11, you'll improve the development cycle with the Truffle framework, which will allow you to easily compile, test, and deploy your contracts. Finally, in chapter 12, you'll put everything together by building an end-to-end voting Dapp from scratch.

After completing this part, you'll have achieved a major milestone: you'll understand how Ethereum works, inside and out, and will be aware of most of its ecosystem. If you're eager to build your own Dapp, though, I strongly encourage you to keep reading so you can learn the more advanced concepts in part 4.

The Ethereum ecosystem

9

This chapter covers

- A bird's-eye view of the full Ethereum ecosystem
- Decentralized address resolution with ENS
- Decentralized content storage on Swarm and IPFS
- External data access through oracles
- Dapp frameworks and IDEs

In previous chapters, you learned about the main components of the Ethereum platform and how to implement and deploy a decentralized application using simple tools such as the Remix IDE and the geth console. You then improved the efficiency of the development cycle by partially automating the deployment with Node.js. You made further efficiency improvements by deploying and running your smart contracts on a private network and, ultimately, on Ganache, where you progressively reduced and almost eliminated the impact of infrastructural aspects of the Ethereum platform on the run and test cycle.

The tool set you've used so far has been pretty basic, but it has helped you understand every step of the build and deployment process of a smart contract. You've also learned about every step of the lifecycle of a transaction, from its creation, through a Web3 call, to its propagation to the network, to its mining, and ultimately to its persistence on the blockchain. Although you might have found these tools helpful and effective for getting started quickly and for learning various concepts in detail, if you decide to develop Ethereum applications on a regular basis, you'd use a different tool set.

This chapter gives you an overview of the wider Ethereum ecosystem, both from a platform point of view and from a development tool set point of view. You'll learn about additional components of the Ethereum platform and alternative IDEs and frameworks that will allow you to develop and deploy Dapps with less effort. But before we start to explore the full Ethereum ecosystem, I'll recap the current view of the platform and the development tool set.

9.1   The core components

Figure 9.1 summarizes all you know so far about the Ethereum platform and the development toolset.

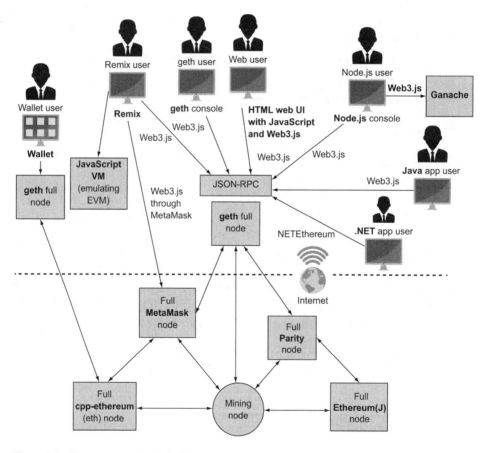

Figure 9.1   Core components of the Ethereum platform you've learned so far: geth, Ethereum wallet, MetaMask, Ganache, Remix, solc, and Web3.js

Although you've installed the Go Ethereum client (geth) and the Ethereum wallet, you're aware you could have installed alternative clients, such as cpp-ethereum (eth), Parity, Ethereum(J), or pyethapp. Most of these come with a related wallet. You also could have decided to connect to an external MetaMask node (in fact, an Infura node, as you'll see later) with MetaMask or to a mock node with Ganache.

You've developed your smart contracts in Solidity using Remix (Browser Solidity). When needed, you've moved the code to text files and compiled them with the solc compiler. In theory, you could have implemented smart contracts in other EVM languages, such as Serpent or LLL, but currently Solidity is widely regarded as the most reliable and secure language. Time will tell if Serpent makes a comeback or new alternatives such as Viper start to gather momentum.

You interacted with the network, including your deployed contracts, in Web3.js, initially through the interactive geth console. Then you moved to Node.js for better extensibility and automation.

Web3.js is a JavaScript-specific high-level API that wraps the low-level JSON-RPC API. Other high-level APIs are available that target other languages, such as web3.j (for Java), NETethereum (for .NET), and Ethereum.ruby (for ruby).

9.2 *A bird's-eye view of the full ecosystem*

Figure 9.2 provides a full view of the current Ethereum ecosystem, where you can see an additional set of development IDEs and frameworks, such as Truffle, aimed at improving the development experience. UI frameworks such as meteor and Angular aren't Ethereum-specific, but they're widely adopted to build modern Dapp UIs. Also, generic testing frameworks such as Mocha and Jasmine are becoming a common feature of Dapp development environments.

You can also see additional infrastructural elements:

- *Ethereum Name Service (ENS)*—This is a smart contract for the decentralized resolution of human-readable names, such as roberto.manning.eth, into Ethereum addresses, such as 0x829bd824b016326a401d083b33d092293333a830.

- *Swarm and IPFS*—These are two competing networks for decentralized storage of content that Ethereum blockchain transactions can then reference through hash IDs (or friendly names resolved into hashes by ENS). Swarm comes directly under the Ethereum umbrella and is Ethereum-aware; IPFS is a general technology-agnostic protocol that provides similar functionality.

- *Oracle frameworks*—These are smart contract frameworks (such as Oraclize) for accessing real-world data in a way that guarantees data authenticity and consistent processing of such data throughout the entire Ethereum network.

- *Whisper*—This is a network for decentralized messaging that provides Ethereum smart contracts with asynchronous peer-to-peer communication, with resilience and privacy as main features. The Whisper API allows contracts to send messages with various degrees of security and privacy, from plain text and fully traceable to encrypted and virtually untraceable (so-called *dark messages*).

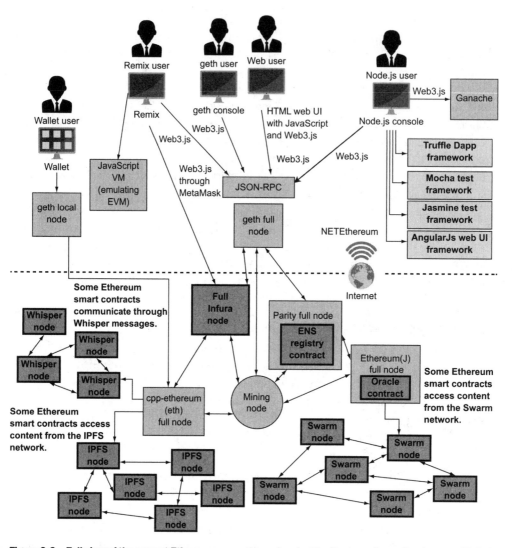

Figure 9.2   Full view of the current Ethereum ecosystem, showing the items we haven't yet covered in bold

- *Infura nodes*—This is a set of Ethereum nodes that are hosted by Infura, a service owned by ConsenSys (the company also behind Truffle). Infura provides clients as a cloud service, with built-in security and privacy features. As for conventional cloud providers, Infura allows startups and independent developers to build Ethereum applications professionally without having to buy physical servers. MetaMask connects to these nodes.

The next few sections will examine in detail ENS, Swarm, IPFS, and oracle frameworks.

Whisper falls in the realm of message-oriented protocols. This is an advanced topic, so I won't cover it further. But if you have experience in message-oriented applications and are eager to learn more, I encourage you to look at the Whisper documentation on the Ethereum wiki on GitHub (http://mng.bz/nQP4 and https://github.com/ethereum/wiki/wiki/Whisper).

From a conceptual point of view, Infura nodes work exactly like other full Ethereum nodes. Bear in mind, though, that Infura clients support a subset of the JSON-RPC standard, so you should check their technical documentation if you're interested in exploring them further.

Before closing this chapter, I'll briefly present the main development tools for building Dapps. When I move on to the next chapter, I'll focus on Truffle, the main smart contract development IDE, which I'll cover in detail through hands-on examples.

9.3   *Decentralized address resolution with ENS*

The Ethereum Name Service, also known as ENS, manages decentralized address resolution, offering a decentralized and secure way to reference resource addresses, such as account and contract addresses, through human-readable domain names. An Ethereum domain name is, as for internet domain names, a hierarchical dot-separated name. Each part of the domain name (delimited by dots) is called a label. Labels include the *root domain* at the right, for example eth, followed by the *domain name* at its immediate left, followed by child *subdomains*, moving further to the left, as illustrated in figure 9.3.

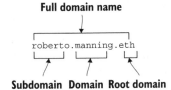

Full domain name

roberto.manning.eth

Subdomain Domain Root domain

Figure 9.3   The structure of an ENS name. You can see the root domain, eth, at the far right, followed by the domain name at its left, and nested child subdomains moving from right to left.

For example, you could send Ether to roberto.manning.eth (which is a subdomain of eth) rather than to 0xe6f8d18d692eeb02c3321bb9a33542903073ba92, or you could reference a contract with simplecoin.eth rather than with its original deployment address: 0x3bcfb560e66094ca39616c98a3b685098d2e7766, as illustrated in figure 9.4. ENS also allows you to reference other resources, such as Swarm and IPFS content hashes (which we'll meet later in the next section), through friendly names.

ENS is encapsulated as a smart contract, and because its logic and state are stored on the blockchain, and therefore decentralized across the Ethereum network, it's considered inherently more secure than a centralized service such as the internet Domain Name Service (DNS). Another advantage of ENS is that it's decentralized not only from an infrastructural point of view, but also from a governance point of view: domain names aren't managed by a central authority, but they can be registered directly by the interested parties through registrars. A registrar is a smart contract that manages a specific root domain, such as eth. Domains are assigned to the winners of

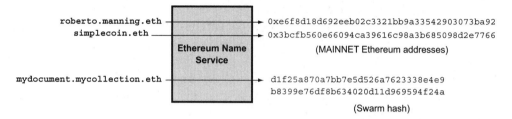

Figure 9.4   ENS resolves names into external (user) addresses, contract addresses, and Swarm content hashes. You can't tell from the domain name itself if it's mapped to an address or a Swarm hash. As you'll see later, a domain name must be mapped explicitly to a specific name resolver for either an address or a Swarm hash (or some other resource identifier).

open auctions executed on the related registrar contract, and they also become the owners of the child subdomains.

9.3.1   ENS design

The ENS system is structured as three main components:

- *Registrar*—This is a contract that manages domain ownership. You must claim a domain name through the registrar and associate it with one of your accounts before you can register specific full domain names associated with it. Specific registrars handle each root domain, such as .eth, which is the root domain for names associated with Ethereum mainnet addresses, or .swarm, which is the root domain for names associated with swarm content hashes. Note that you must perform the ownership of domain names pointing to TESTNET Ethereum addresses through a test registrar that manages the .test root domain. This is a separate registrar from the one managing the .eth root domain.

- *Resolvers*—These are smart contracts that implement a common ABI interface specified in Ethereum Improvement Proposal (EIP) 137, which you can consult here: http://eips.ethereum.org/EIPS/eip-137. A resolver translates a domain name into a resource identifier. Each resolver is specific to one resource type. For example, there's a resolver for Ethereum addresses (called public resolver), another resolver for IPFS content hashes, and so on.

- *Registry*—This is, in a nutshell, a map between domain (or subdomain) names and domain name resolvers.

The simple design of the ENS registry, shown in figure 9.5, makes it easily extensible, so you can reference custom resolvers implementing address translation rules of any complexity. Also, it can support a new resource type in the future without needing any modification and redeployment of the registry: a domain name for a new resource type will point to a new resolver. Figure 9.6 shows the domain name resolution process.

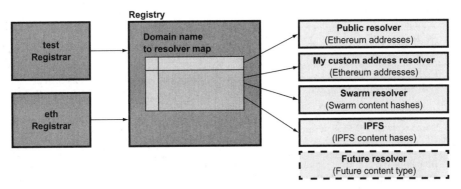

Figure 9.5   The ENS registry design. The ENS registry contract is a map between resource types and related domain resolver contracts. In the future, it can support a new resource type by pointing a domain name (associated with the new resource type) to a new resolver. Domain ownership is registered through a specific registrar.

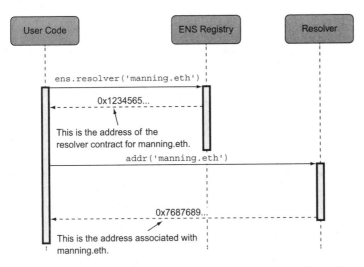

Figure 9.6   The domain name resolution process: 1. you query the Registry to identify the correct resolver; 2. you request the relevant resolver to translate the domain name into an address.

As you can see in figure 9.6, a domain name is resolved in a two-step process:

1 You query the Registry to identify the correct resolver associated with the domain name you want to resolve, and the Registry returns the contract address of the relevant resolver.
2 You request the relevant resolver to translate the domain name into a resource identifier, such as an Ethereum address or a Swarm hash.

Every mapping record stored on the registry contains the information shown in table 9.1.

Table 9.1   ENS registry mapping record

Field	Description	Example
Domain name	For performance and privacy reasons, a hash of the domain name, called Namehash, is used rather than the domain name itself. Read the sidebar if you want to know more about this.	0x98d934feea78b34… (Namehash of `Roberto.manning.eth`)
Domain owner	The address of the external (user) account or contract account owning the domain name	0xcEcEaA8edc0830C…
Domain name resolver	The address of the resolver contract able to resolve the domain name for the related resource type	0x455abc566… (public resolver address)
Time to live	This specifies how long the mapping record should be kept on the registry. It can be indefinite or a specified duration.	6778676878 (expiry date as UNIX epoch)

Namehash

For performance reasons and for the privacy of the domain owners, ENS works against a 32-byte hash of the domain name rather than its plain string representation. This hash is determined through a recursive algorithm called *Namehash*, which, if applied, for example, to `roberto.manning.eth`, works as follows:

1 Split the full domain name into labels, delimited by the dots; order them from the last to the first; and add an empty label as a first item:

```
labels = ['', 'eth', 'manning', 'roberto']
```

2 Pick the first item. Because it's empty, determine the associated namehash by setting it to 32 '0' bytes. The namehash corresponding to an increasing part of the full domain name is called *node*. So far, here's what you have:

```
node =
0x0000000000000000000000000000000000000000000000000000000000000000
```

3 Pick the second label (`'eth'`) and determine its associated label hash by applying the `keccak256` hashing function:

```
labelHash = keccak256('eth') =
0x4f5b812789fc606be1b3b16908db13fc7a9adf7ca72641f84d75b47069d3d7f0
```

4 Determine the node associated with the second label by hashing the concatenation of the previous node with the current label hash:

```
node = keccak256(node + labelhash) =
keccak256(
0x00000000000000000000000000000000000000000000000000000000000004f5
b81278
```
➥ `9fc606be1b3b16908db13fc7a9adf7ca72641f84d75b47069d3d7f0) =`
➥ `0x93cdeb708b7545dc668eb9280176169d1c33cfd8ed6f04690a0bcc88a93fc4ae`

5 Pick the third item (`'manning'`) and repeat steps 3 and 4.

6 Pick the fourth item (`'roberto'`) and repeat steps 3 and 4.

Finally, the namehash of `roberto.manning.eth` is

```
0x5fd962d5ca4599b3b64fe09ff7a630bc3c4032b3b33ecee2d79d4b8f5d6fc7a5
```

You can get an idea of the output taken by the Namehash algorithm to hash `roberto .manning.eth` in the table.

Namehash algorithm steps to hash `Roberto.manning.eth`

Step	Label	labelHash	keccak256 (node+labelHash)	Node
1	`' '`	N/A	N/A	0x000000000000...
2	`'eth'`	0x4f5b812789fc...	keccak256 (0x0000... 0x4f5b812789f...)	0x93cdeb708b7...
3	`'manning'`	0x4b2455c1404...	keccak256 (0x93cde... 4b2455c...)	0x03ae0f9c3e92...
4	`'roberto'`	0x6002ea314e6...	keccak256 (0x03e0... 6002ea3...)	0x5fd962d5ca4599b3b6

Here's a JavaScript implementation of the process from Nick Johnson's ENS utility library `ensutils.js` (see next section for more details), which you can run in the geth console or in the Node.js console:

```
function namehash(name) {
    var node =
'0x0000000000000000000000000000000000000000000000000000000000
    000000000000';
    if (name !== '') {
        var labels = name.split(".");
        for(var i = labels.length - 1; i >= 0; i--) {
            label = labels[i];
            labelHash = web3.sha3(label);
            node = web3.sha3(node + labelHash.slice(2),
            {encoding: 'hex'});
        }
    }
    return node.toString();
}
```

Node corresponding to empty label `' '`

Splits the full domain name into its constituent labels

Gets current label

Calculates label hash

Concatenates previous node with current label hash (removes '0x' from label hash) and calculates current node using hex encoding

Returns final node as a string

> **WARNING**   The web3.sha3() function creates a keccak256 hash. It doesn't follow the SHA-3 standard, as the name would suggest.

9.3.2   *Registering a domain name*

Enough theory! Let's see how to register a domain name on the ENS instance running on the Ropsten testnet from the geth console.

First of all, download the ENS JavaScript utility library from here: http://mng.bz/vN9r. Place this JavaScript file in a folder, for example, C:\ethereum\ens.

> **WARNING**   Although useful for learning ENS, the ENS JavaScript utility libraries ensutils.js and ensutils-testnet.js aren't meant to be used to build a production Dapp.

Now, from an OS shell, start up geth against TESTNET, as you've done several times before. (Remember to use the --bootnodes option if peer nodes aren't located quickly, as you did at the start of chapter 8.) Type the following:

```
C:\Program Files\geth>geth --testnet
```

Geth will start synchronizing, as expected. From a separate command shell, start an interactive console:

```
C:\Program Files\geth>geth attach ipc:\\.\pipe\geth.ipc
```

Then import the ENS utility library on the interactive geth console you've attached:

```
>loadScript('c:/ethereum/ens/ensutils-testnet.js');
```

Registering a domain on the TESTNET network means registering it on the .test root domain rather than on .eth, which is associated with MAINNET, the public production network. This means you must use the test registrar.

The domain name I'll be registering is roberto.manning.test. Pick a similar three-label domain name and adapt the instructions that I'm about to give you, accordingly.

CHECKING DOMAIN OWNERSHIP

First of all, I have to check if anyone else already owns the manning domain. If someone does, I won't be able to register my full domain name (roberto.manning.test); I'd have to ask the current owner to do it for me.

This is how you can check if the manning domain is free on the test registrar:

```
>var domainHash = web3.sha3('manning');
>
>var domainExpiryEpoch = testRegistrar.expiryTimes(domainHash)
.toNumber() * 1000;
>var domainExpiryDate = new Date(domainExpiryEpoch);
```

Check the value of domainExpiryDate (by entering it at the prompt). If it's earlier than today, the domain is free; otherwise, you must choose another domain and repeat the check.

> **NOTE** You might be wondering what happens in the unlikely event that ownership of 'manning' hasn't been registered yet but another name with the same web.sha3() hash has been registered. If this happens, you won't be able to register 'manning' because it would appear to the registrar as already taken.

REGISTERING DOMAIN OWNERSHIP

After checking that the account is free, you can claim it by registering it through the test registrar against one of your TESTNET accounts; for example, eth.accounts[0]. (Make sure accounts[0] has enough Ether to execute the transaction by checking, as usual: eth.getBalance(eth.accounts[0]); also, replace your accounts[0] password.) Enter the following:

```
>personal.unlockAccount(eth.accounts[0], 'PASSWORD_OF_YOUR_ACCOUNT_0');
>var tx1 = testRegistrar.register(domainHash,
eth.accounts[0], {from: eth.accounts[0]});
```

Check the value of tx1, and then check that the related transaction has been mined by going to Ropsten etherscan: https://ropsten.etherscan.io. Note that registering domain ownership on MAINNET is a more complex process. (See https://docs.ens .domains/en/latest/ for more details.)

REGISTERING THE DOMAIN NAME

Once the domain ownership transaction has been mined, it's time to set up the domain name mapping configuration you saw in table 9.1. You already set some of the configuration (the domain account owner) by registering the domain ownership through the registrar. Now you have to configure the resolver and the target address that the domain name will be mapped to.

You can map your domain name to the public resolver (which, as you know, maps a domain name to a given Ethereum address) through the ENS registry as follows:

```
>tx2 = ens.setResolver(namehash('manning.test'),
publicResolver.address, {from: eth.accounts[0]});
```

Check on Ropsten etherscan if tx2 has been mined, then configure the public resolver to point your domain name to the target address (for example, your test accounts[1]), as follows:

```
>publicResolver.setAddr(namehash('manning.test'),
eth.accounts[1], {from: eth.accounts[0]});
```

REGISTERING THE SUBDOMAIN

Registering the ownership of a subdomain is slightly different from registering the ownership of a domain, as you don't perform it through the registrar, but through the ENS registry. Assign the ownership of the subdomain `Roberto.manning` to `accounts[2]`, as follows:

```
>ens.setSubnodeOwner(namehash('manning.test'),
web3.sha3('roberto'), eth.accounts[2], {from: eth.accounts[0]});
```

> **WARNING** The account running the transaction must be the owner of the
> `'manning.test'` domain: `accounts[0]`.

Using `accounts[2]`, the owner of the `'roberto.manning.test'` subdomain, you can now map it to the public resolver as usual:

```
>ens.setResolver(namehash('roberto.manning.test'),
publicResolver.address, {from: eth.accounts[2]});
```

Finally, you can configure the public resolver to point your domain name to the target address (for example, your test `accounts[3]`), as follows:

```
>publicResolver.setAddr(namehash('manning.test'),
eth.accounts[3], {from: eth.accounts[2]});
```

9.3.3 *Resolving a domain name*

Resolving a domain name into an address is straightforward. Resolve `'manning.test'` first:

```
>var domainName = 'manning.test';
>var domainNamehash = namehash(domainName);
>var resolverAddress = ens.resolver(domainNamehash);
>resolverContract.at(resolverAddress).addr(namehash(domainNamehash));
```

You'll see

```
0x4e6c30154768b6bc3da693b1b28c6bd14302b578
```

and you can verify this is your `accounts[1]` address, as expected:

```
> eth.accounts[1]
```

This is a shortcut to resolve the domain name:

```
>getAddr(domainName);
0x4e6c30154768b6bc3da693b1b28c6bd14302b578
```

If you're interested in learning more about ENS—for example, to claim an .eth domain name in MAINNET through a commit-reveal bid—I encourage you to consult the official documentation written by Nick Johnson, the creator of ENS. You can find it at https://docs.ens.domains/en/latest/.

9.4 *Decentralized content storage*

A common use case for decentralized applications is to store a sequence of documents proving, for example, the provenance of goods traded through the applications. A typical example is diamonds, which traditionally are accompanied by paper certificates showing that they come from legitimate mines and traders. For more complex supply chains, such as in the field of international trade finance (https://en.wikipedia .org/wiki/Trade_finance), which involves multiple parties, such as a supplier, the bank of the supplier, a shipping company, an end client, and their bank, the paperwork might be more voluminous. Storing the equivalent electronic documentation directly on the blockchain would work but wouldn't be ideal for a couple of reasons:

- The electronic documentation would bloat transactions referencing it, which would be processed more slowly.
- Bigger transactions require more gas to process and are therefore more expensive.

An alternative solution would be to store the electronic documentation on an off-blockchain database and include in the transaction only a cryptographic hash of each of the documents, to prove their content. This solution isn't perfect, though, because the off-blockchain database would be a centralized resource not easily accessible by the Ethereum nodes. Even if the decentralized application could access the database where the documentation was stored, having this centralized repository would be contrary to the spirit of decentralized applications.

An ideal solution instead would be based on a decentralized storage repository. This is exactly what the Swarm platform, which is partially associated with Ethereum, aims to provide. Another valid alternative would be to use the existing IPFS distributed storage network. Let's explore these two options.

9.4.1 *Swarm overview*

Swarm is a content distribution platform whose main objective is to provide decentralized and redundant storage to Ethereum Dapps. It focuses specifically on holding and exposing smart contract data and code, as well as blockchain data.

Storage is decentralized in Swarm through a P2P network that makes it resistant to distributed denial of service (DDoS) attacks and censorship, and that provides fault tolerance and guarantees zero downtime because it has no single point of failure. The architecture of the P2P Swarm network, shown in figure 9.7, is similar to that of the Ethereum network: each node runs a Swarm client that manages local storage and communicates with its peer nodes through a common standard protocol called *bzz*. Currently, only one client implementation is available, written in the Go language, and it's included in the Geth & Tools package you can download from the Go Ethereum website. The main difference with the Ethereum network is that all Ethereum nodes have the same copy of the blockchain database, whereas each Swarm node contains a different set of data, also illustrated in figure 9.7.

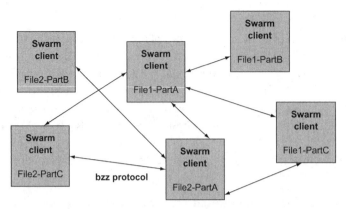

Figure 9.7   Architectural diagram of a Swarm network. The Swarm network, made of nodes each running a Swarm client, is similar to the Ethereum network, in which every node runs an Ethereum client. Contrary to Ethereum nodes, which all have the same copy of the blockchain data, each Swarm node contains a different set of data.

A Swarm node is linked to an Ethereum account known as a *swarm base account*. The (keccak 256-bit) hash of the address of the swarm base account determines the *swarm base address*, which is the address of a Swarm node within the Swarm network. A Swarm network is associated with a specific Ethereum network. For example, the main production Swarm network is associated with MAINNET, and a Swarm network is associated with the Ropsten Ethereum network. Because Swarm is part of the Ethereum technology stack, it makes full use of other components of the ecosystem, such as ENS.

When content is uploaded to Swarm, it's broken down into 4 KB *chunks* that get scattered throughout the Swarm network. The upload process is illustrated in figure 9.8.

It involves the following steps:

1 The caller uploads the content, typically a file, to the distributed preimage archive (DPA), which is the storage and retrieval gateway.

2 The DPA calls a component called *chunker.*

3 The chunker

   a chops the content up into 4 KB pieces called chunks

   b calculates cryptographic hashes of its chunks

4 The hashes of the chunks (or blocks) are placed in a chunks-index document.

5 If the chunks-index document is bigger than 4 KB, it's chopped up into chunks whose hashes are then placed into a further document. This process goes on until the chunks are organized into a tree structure with a root index document at the top, followed by a layer of index chunks in the middle and the content

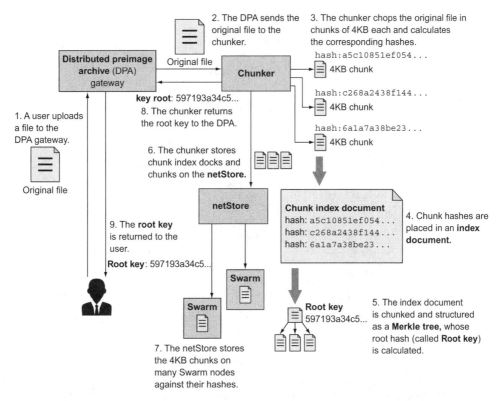

Figure 9.8 The Swarm upload process: 1. the caller uploads a file to the distributed preimage archive gateway; 2. the DPA sends the file to a chunker; 3. the chunker chops the file into 4 KB chunks and calculates a hash for each one; 4. the chunk hashes are placed in a chunk-index document; 5. the chunk-index document is chunked and reorganized in a Merkle tree structure, whose root hash is called root key; 6. the chunker stores each chunk onto the netStore against its hash; 7. the netStore distributes 4 KB chunks across the Swarm network; 8. the chunker returns the root key to the DPA; 9. finally, the DPA returns the root key to the caller.

chunks at the bottom, as illustrated in figure 9.9. This data structure is a Merkle tree, the same data structure a blockchain database uses to link its blocks.

6 The chunker stores each chunk on the netStore against its hash key.

7 The netStore is an implementation of a *distributed hash table* (DHT) across the Swarm network, so chunks are stored on many Swarm nodes. Because the key of this distributed hash table is a cryptographic hash key, which is a representation of the underlying content, this way of storing data is also known as *content addressable storage* (CAS).

8 The chunker returns the hash key of the root index document, known as *root key*, and hands it back to the DPA.

9 The DPA finally returns the root key to the caller. This will later be used to download the original file from Swarm.

Mekle tree of chunk indices and chunks

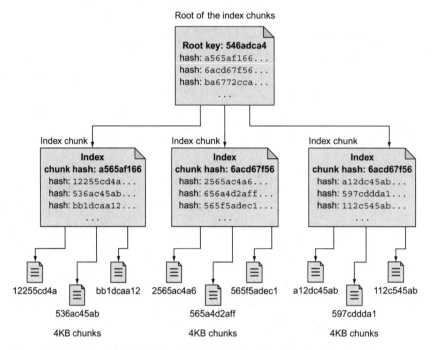

Figure 9.9 Chunk and chunk-index Merkle tree structure. The document at the top contains the hashes of chunks of the initial chunk-index document (containing the hashes of all 4 KB chunks). The intermediate layer is made of chunks of the initial chunk-index document. The layer at the bottom contains the 4 KB chunks of the original file.

The download process goes through a similar workflow, but in reverse order, as shown in figure 9.10:

1 A caller hands a root key to the DPA.

2 The DPA calls the chunker, and it supplies the root key.

3 The chunker retrieves the root chunk associated with the root key from the net-Store, then walks the tree until it has retrieved all the chunks from the Swarm network. While chunks are flowing from their netStore location (the specific Swarm node they're stored on) to the chunker, they get cached into each Swarm node they go through, so often if the same content is requested, subsequent downloads will be faster.

4 The chunker reconstructs the file from the chunks and returns it to the DPA.

5 The DPA returns the requested file to the caller.

From an operational point of view, the sustainability of the Swarm platform is based on monetary incentives aimed at encouraging and rewarding participants who provide the underlying storage resources. Storage is traded between participants who require it and those who provide it, so it tends to be allocated efficiently.

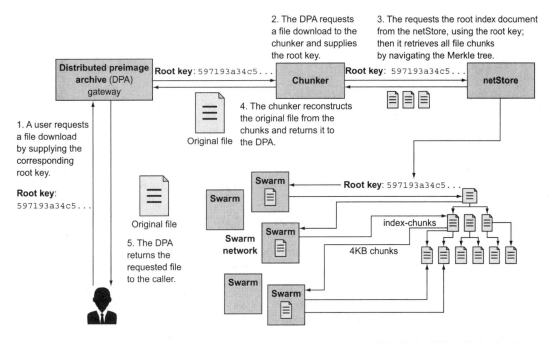

Figure 9.10   The Swarm download process: 1. a caller hands a root key to the DPA; 2. the DPA calls the chunker, and it supplies the root key; 3. the chunker retrieves the root chunk associated with the root key from the netStore, then walks the tree until it has retrieved all the chunks from the Swarm network; 4. the chunker reconstructs the file from the chunks and returns it to the DPA; 5. the DPA returns the requested file to the caller.

9.4.2   *Uploading and downloading content to and from Swarm*

In this section, I'll show you how to upload content to Swarm, get its root key, and then download it back from Swarm using the root key.

CONNECTING TO SWARM

The first step you have to take is to download the Swarm client, swarm.exe, from the Go Ethereum website. If you downloaded geth from the Geth & Tools archive (or installer) link, you should already have swarm.exe in the same folder you're running geth from. Otherwise, go back to the Go Ethereum website and download the Geth & Tools 1.8.12 package, which I believe is the latest archive still containing swarm.exe. Unzip it and copy swarm.exe into the same folder where you've placed geth.exe. In my case, I've placed it here: C:\Program Files\geth.

Now start up geth against TESTNET. (Remember to use the --bootnodes option if peer nodes aren't located quickly, as you did at the start of chapter 8.) Type the following:

```
C:\Program Files\geth>geth --testnet
```

Geth will start synchronizing, as expected. From a separate command shell, start an interactive console:

```
C:\Program Files\geth>geth attach ipc:\\.\pipe\geth.ipc
```

Then, from the interactive console, get the address of your testnet `accounts[1]`:

```
> eth.accounts[1]
"0x4e6c30154768b6bc3da693b1b28c6bd14302b578"
```

You'll run the Swarm client under this account by opening a new OS console and executing the following command from the folder where you placed the swarm executable (replacing your Ethereum testnet folder accordingly):

```
C:\Program Files\geth>swarm –datadir
➥ C:\Users\rober\AppData\Roaming\Ethereum\testnet
➥ --bzzaccount 0x4e6c30154768b6bc3da693b1b28c6bd14302b578
```

Table 9.2 explains the options I've used to start up the Swarm client.

Table 9.2 Options used to start up the Swarm client

Option	Purpose
--datadir	Specifies the `datadir` path related to the environment to use—in our case, TESTNET (Ropsten)
--bzzaccount	Specifies the Ethereum account to use—in our case, TESTNET `accounts[1]`

As you can see in figure 9.11, you'll be asked to unlock `accounts[1]` by providing its password. Enter the password, as requested, and the client will start up with output similar to that in the screenshot in figure 9.12.

```
Select Command Prompt - swarm  --bzzaccount 0x4e6c30154768b6bc3da693b1b28c6bd14302b578 --datadir C:\Users\rober\

C:\Program Files\Geth>swarm --bzzaccount 0x4e6c30154768b6bc3da693b1b28c6bd14302b578 --
ming\Ethereum\testnet
INFO [03-11|19:33:31] Maximum peer count                        ETH=25 LES=0 total=25
Unlocking swarm account 0x4e6C30154768b6bc3Da693b1B28C6bd14302b578 [1/3]
Passphrase:
```

Figure 9.11 Unlocking the Ethereum account you're using to start up the Swarm client

It might take a few minutes before your Swarm client synchronizes with a number of peers (by default up to a maximum of 25). Output similar to the following indicates capable peers have been found:

```
INFO [03-11|19:49:47] Peer faa9a1ae is capable (0/3)
INFO [03-11|19:49:47] found record <faa9a1aef3fb3b0792420a59f929907d86c0937d
➥ b9310d6835a46f44301faf05> in kaddb
INFO [03-11|19:49:47] syncronisation request sent with address: 00000000
➥ -00000000, index: 0-0, session started at: 0, last seen at: 0, latest
➥ key: 00000000
```

```
INFO [03-11|19:49:47] syncer started: address: -, index: 0-0, session
➥ started at: 933, last seen at: 0, latest key:
INFO [03-11|19:49:47] syncer[faa9a1ae]: syncing all history complete
INFO [03-11|19:49:50] Peer d3f2a5c8 is capable (0/3)
```

Figure 9.12 Swarm start-up output

UPLOADING CONTENT

Now that you're connected to the Swarm network, you can upload some sample text onto the network. Open a new OS console and submit this HTTP request to your Swarm client through curl:

```
C:\Users\rober>curl -H "Content-Type: text/plain"
➥ --data-binary "my sample text" http://localhost:8500/bzz:/
```

You'll immediately get a response showing the root key associated with the submitted content:

```
eab8083835dec1952eae934eef05dda96dadbcd5d0685251e8c9faab1d0a0f58
```

DOWNLOADING CONTENT

To get the content back from Swarm, you can now submit a new request that includes the root key you obtained:

```
C:\Users\rober>curl
➥ http://localhost:8500/bzz:/eab8083835dec1952eae934eef05dda96dadbcd5d068
➥ 5251e8c9faab1d0a0f58/
```

As expected, you'll get back the text you submitted earlier:

```
my sample text
```

The official documentation is an excellent resource to learn more about Swarm and to try out more advanced features: http://mng.bz/4OBv. But you also should be aware that the Swarm initiative has been criticized by some members of the decentralized web community for duplicating the effort of IPFS, a project with similar objectives but with a more general purpose. The following section explains IPFS and the reason for the controversy.

9.4.3   *IPFS overview*

IPFS stands for InterPlanetary File System and, as you might guess from its name, is a hypermedia distribution protocol whose objective is to support a decentralized way of storing and sharing files. With Swarm, storage is distributed over a P2P network, which you can consider a distributed file system. The IPFS way of storing files provides the same benefits as the Swarm network, such as zero downtime and resistance to DDoS attacks and censorship.

Files aren't stored in their entirety in a single network location; they're broken down into *blocks*, which are then transformed into IPFS objects and scattered across the network. An IPFS object is a simple structure containing two properties

```
{
     Data—Byte array containing data in binary form
     Links—Array of Link objects, which link to other IPFS objects
}
```

where a Link object has the following structure:

```
{
     Name—String representing the name of the link
     Hash—Hash of the linked IPFS object
     Size—Full size of linked IPFS document and all of its linked IPFS
➥ objects
}
```

Each IPFS object is referenced by its hash.

An example of the IPFS object associated with a small file that's decomposed into a single file block is shown in the following listing.

Listing 9.1   IPFS object associated with a file containing a single block

```
{
    "Links":[],                                          There are no links to other IPFS objects
    "Data":"\u0008\u0002\u0012\u0019        ◁——         because the file is made of a single block.
➥ This is some sample text.\u0018\u0019"  ◁——|         This is unstructured binary data contained
}                                                        in the file (up to a max of 256 KB).
```

An example of the IPFS object associated with a large file, bigger than 256 KB and broken down into multiple blocks, is shown in the following listing.

Listing 9.2   IPFS object of a file larger than 256 KB, split into various blocks

```
{
 "Links":[                    ◁————   This file has been split into multiple
   {                                  blocks of 256 KB, each corresponding
      "Name":"",                      to an item in the Links list.
      "Hash":
    "QmWXuN4UW2ZJ2fo5fj8xt7raMKvsihJJibUpwmtEhbHBci",   ◁———   Block hash
      "Size":262158            ◁┐
   },                           │   Block size
   {                            │   (256 KB)
      "Name":"",
      "Hash":"QmfHm32CQnagmHvNV5X715wxEEjgqADWpCeLPYvL9JNoMt",
      "Size":262158
   },
   . . .
   {
      "Name":"",
      "Hash":"QmXrgsJQGVxg7iH2tgQF8BV9dEhRrCVngc9tWg8VLFn7Es",
      "Size":13116
   }
 ],
  "Data":"\u0008\u0002\u0018��@ ��\u0010 ��\u0010 ��\u0010 ��\u0010 �f"
}
```

Block name → (pointing to "Name":"" and "Hash":)

Each block referenced in the Links array is represented by a document like that shown in listing 9.1. The workflow followed by an IPFS client for uploading a file on IPFS is illustrated in figure 9.13.

Let's follow the steps of the upload workflow in detail:

1 A user uploads a file to an IPFS node.
2 The IPFS node breaks the file down into blocks of a certain size (typically 256 KB).
3 An IPFS object is created for each file block. This looks like the one shown in listing 9.1. A cryptographic hash is calculated for each IPFS object and associated with it.
4 An IPFS object is created for the file. This contains links to IPFS objects associated with all the file blocks and looks like the IPFS object shown in listing 9.2. A cryptographic hash is calculated for this IPFS object.
5 Each block is stored at a different network location, and an index holding a map between block hashes and corresponding network locations is maintained on each node. You might have realized content is referenced by its own cryptographic hash key, as in the case of the Swarm platform, so you can also consider IPFS to be content addressable storage (CAS).

Given that content is referenced by its hash, this design is focused on managing efficiently immutable files. For example, only one copy of a document has to exist in the

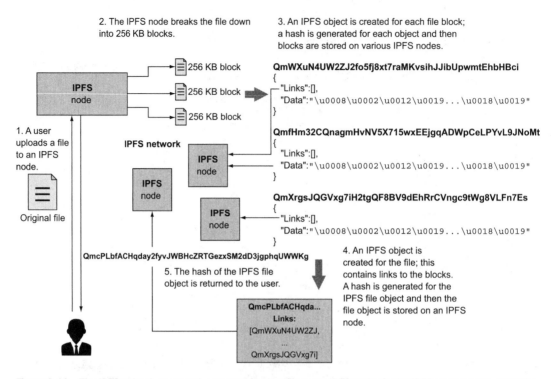

Figure 9.13   The IPFS upload process: 1. a user uploads a file to an IPFS node; 2. the IPFS node breaks down the file into 256 KB blocks; 3. an IPFS object is created for each file block; 4. an IPFS object is created for the file, and it contains links to IPFS objects associated with all the file blocks; 5. each block is stored at a different network location, and an index holding a map between block hashes and corresponding network locations is maintained on each node.

network because its hash must point only to one network location, so duplication is eliminated.

But IPFS is also capable of managing mutable documents by tracking their changes through versioning. When a file changes, only its amended blocks need to be hashed, stored on the network, and indexed, and the unaffected blocks will be reused. The workflow of the download process is shown in figure 9.14.

Here are the steps of the workflow in detail:

1   A user queries IPFS for a file associated with a certain IPFS file object hash key.
2   The IPFS client retrieves the network location of the IPFS file object associated with the provided hash key by looking it up on the local IPFS index, and then it requests the file object from the corresponding IPFS node.
3   The requested node returns the IPFS file object.
4   The IPFS client scans each link on the Links property of the IPFS file object. For each link, it retrieves the network location associated with the IPFS object

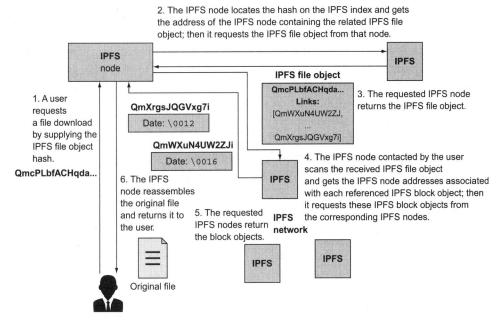

Figure 9.14 **The IPFS file download process: 1. IPFS is queried for a file associated with a certain IPFS file object hash key; 2. the IPFS client requests the file object from the corresponding IPFS node; 3. the requested node returns the IPFS file object; 4. the IPFS client scans each link on the Links property of the IPFS file object; 5. each requested IPFS node returns the corresponding IPFS block object; 6. the original file is recomposed on the IPFS node serving the request, and it's returned to the caller.**

   key from the local index and then uses the network location to retrieve the corresponding IPFS block object.

5 Each requested IPFS node returns the corresponding IPFS block object.

6 The original file is recomposed on the IPFS node serving the request, and it's returned to the caller.

Contrary to Swarm, IPFS gives no direct incentives to its P2P participants for contributing to the network's file storage resources, and it relies on FileCoin, a separate but related initiative based on the Bitcoin blockchain, to reward active participants.

   If you want to learn more about IPFS, download the client and give it a go at https://ipfs.io/docs/getting-started/. I recommend you also have a look at the Git book *The Decentralized Web Primer*, which has various tutorials on how to install an IPFS client and how to interact with the network and examine IPFS objects through common operations such as uploading and then downloading a file: http://mng.bz/ QQxQ. (Click the green Read button to access the content.)

9.4.4   *Swarm vs. IPFS*

At this point, do you think Swarm is duplicating the effort of IPFS, as some members of the decentralized web have argued? Now that you know about both decentralized content management infrastructures, you can probably judge for yourself whether the Swarm initiative has been worthwhile. Table 9.3, which summarizes the main features of both platforms, might help you answer the question.

Table 9.3   Comparison of Swarm vs. IPFS

Feature	Swarm	IPFS
Storage architecture	Decentralized	Decentralized
Network architecture	P2P	P2P
Content Accessible Storage	Yes	Yes
Block/chunk size	4 KB	256 KB
Native integration with Ethereum	Yes	No
Incentive strategy	Built-in	External (through FileCoin)

Fans of the Swarm platform argue that its smaller chunk size, which allows much lower transmission latency, and its deeper integration with Ethereum are by themselves two key reasons for the existence of Swarm. You can find further analysis of the difference between Swarm and IPFS online on various forums, such as Ethereum stack exchange: http://mng.bz/Xg0p.

9.5   *Accessing external data through oracles*

Conventional web applications consume a variety of external services, typically by performing REST API calls or invoking legacy web services. You might be surprised to hear that this isn't possible in the Dapp world. By design, Ethereum contracts can't access external sources. This is to avoid two main set of issues:

- *Trust issues*—Participants might be wary about the authenticity of the data and its potential manipulation before making it into the blockchain.
- *Technical issues*—The data provider might struggle to serve thousands of simultaneous requests coming from the Ethereum network, therefore compromising the block creation and validation process.

How do you get external data into your smart contract so you can work around the restrictions that the Ethereum infrastructure imposes and be confident about the data's authenticity? You do it through oracles. An *oracle* is, in short, a bridge between the blockchain network and the outside world. It takes care of fetching the queried data from external data providers, and then it returns it to the requesting contract together with a *proof of authenticity*. Having the process arranged that way, you can see an oracle as a middleman that merely plays a facilitating role. Although it's a point of centralization, the requesting contract doesn't need to trust the oracle because the oracle can't modify the data it's returning without invalidating it against the proof of authenticity (which the end user can verify). Figure 9.15 shows the main components that are part of a typical oracle-based data-feeding solution:

- *A contract*—This executes a query to retrieve some data.
- *An oracle*—This connects the contract to the relevant data provider by resolving the query and fetching the data from the data provider.
- *A set of data sources*—These might include REST APIs, legacy web services, online random generators, or online calculators, for example.
- *TLSNotary*—This service generates cryptographic proofs of online data.
- *IPFS store*—This is where data returned together gets stored with proof of authenticity for later off-blockchain verification, if needed.

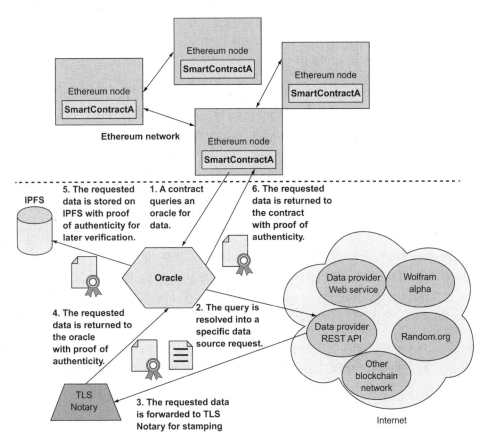

Figure 9.15   An oracle is a bridge between the blockchain network and the outside world. It takes care of fetching the requested data from external data providers and returns it to the requesting contract with a proof of authenticity.

9.5.1   *Feeding oracles*

You can use two main strategies for feeding an oracle so consumers can trust its data:

1   *Independent participants can feed an oracle.* In this case, the oracle aggregates the original data coming from the different participants through a consensus model, and then it feeds the data to the consumer.
2   *A single data provider can feed an oracle.* In this case, the oracle supplies the consumer a copy of the original data, accompanied with a proof of authenticity of that data.

ORACLE FED BY INDEPENDENT PARTICIPANTS

When independent participants feed an oracle, the approved data set is generated on a consensus basis, for example by averaging numeric values or selecting the most frequent non-numeric values. This way of feeding data, which happens in a decentralized fashion and is subject to a consensus, seems to naturally fit the spirit of decentralized applications. But it has various drawbacks:

- A high number of feeders might be necessary to generate a reliable data set.
- The oracle provider relies on feeders constantly keeping up with new data requests.
- All the data feeders might expect to get paid regardless of the quality of their data. This might prove expensive for the oracle provider.

ORACLE FED BY THE PROVIDER FROM A SINGLE DATA SOURCE

When a single source feeds an oracle, it demonstrates that the exposed data is genuine and untampered with by returning it to a client together with a proof of authenticity document. Services such as TLSNotary can generate the document, and it's based on various technologies, such as auditable virtual machines and trusted execution environments.

Oraclize offers one of the most popular frameworks for feeding smart contracts from a single source. This solution has two main advantages with respect to oracles fed by multiple participants:

1   Dapp developers and users don't need to trust Oraclize, as they can verify the truthfulness of the data independently against the proof of authenticity, both on-chain from within contract code and off-chain through web verification tools.
2   Data providers don't need to implement new ways of distributing data, on top of their current web services or web APIs, to feed decentralized applications.

Enough talking! I'll now show you how to build your first oracle consumer contract.

9.5.2   *Building a data-aware contract with Oraclize*

If you want to hook a contract into Oraclize, you have to

- import a Solidity file named oraclizeAPI.sol, available from the Oraclize GitHub repository
- inherit your contract from a base contract called usingOraclize

Your contract, as illustrated in the sample oracle shown in listing 9.3 (which comes from the Oraclize documentation), should contain

- one or more *state variables* holding the latest value of a copy of the external data being requested; in this example, ETHXBT (the Ether to Bitcoin exchange rate)
- an update() function that an end user can invoke to refresh the local copy of the external data through a request to Oraclize
- a callback function named __callback, which is invoked from the result transaction that Oraclize produces

Listing 9.3   Contract providing ETHXBT rate from the Kraken exchange through Oraclize

```
pragma solidity ^0.4.0;
import "github.com/oraclize/ethereum-api/         Imports the Oraclize client code
➥ oraclizeAPI.sol";                              from their GitHub repository


contract KrakenPriceTicker is usingOraclize {     Inherits from the base
                                                  contract usingOraclize

    string public ETHXBT;
                                                  Event logging whether
    event newOraclizeQuery(string description);   the data query has been
    event newKrakenPriceTicker(string price);     sent to Oraclize

                                                  Event logging whether Oraclize
                                                  has returned the requested data
    function KrakenPriceTicker() {
        oraclize_setProof(proofType_TLSNotary     Contract constructor
            | proofStorage_IPFS);
        update();                                 Specifies that the data requested should be
    }                                             accompanied by TLSNotary proof and that
                                                  the proof should get stored on IPFS
    function __callback(bytes32 myid,
        string result, bytes proof) {             Callback invoked by Oraclize
        if (msg.sender != oraclize_cbAddress()) throw;   when returning the requested
        ETHXBT = result;                          data to the contract
        newKrakenPriceTicker(ETHXBT);
        update();                                 Logs the requested data that
    }                                             Oraclize has returned

    function update() payable {                   Triggers the update of
        if (oraclize.getPrice("URL") > this.balance) {   ETHXBT, which can be
                                                  invoked by an end
                                                  user or internally, as
                                                  mentioned previously
```

State variable holding the external data: exchange rate for Ether to Bitcoin from Kraken

Sets the ETHXBT state variable when the contract is created

Updates the ETHXBT state with the value that Oraclize returned

Checks if the contract has enough Ether to fund the data request to Oraclize

Triggers a new update so that the contract keeps refreshing ETHXBT continuously

```
                newOraclizeQuery("Oraclize query was NOT sent,
    please add some ETH to cover for the query fee");
        } else {
                newOraclizeQuery("Oraclize query was sent,
    standing by for the answer..");
                oraclize_query(60, "URL",
        "json(https://api.kraken.com/0/public/Ticker?pair=ETHXBT).result.XETHXXB
        T.c.0");
        }
    }

}
```

Data request
query to Oraclize

ORACLIZE DATA REQUEST

Look closely at the data request to the Oraclize engine within the update method:

```
oraclize_query(60, "URL",
    "json(https://api.kraken.com/0/public/Ticker?pair=ETHXBT)
.result.XETHXXBT.c.0");
```

The data request is performed by calling the oraclize_query() function, inherited from the usingOraclize base contract, with a set of parameters, as shown in figure 9.16:

- *Request delay*—Number of seconds that should be waited before retrieving the data (can also be an absolute timestamp in the future)
- *Data source type*—Oraclize supports various data sources types, but we'll focus mainly on the following:
  - *URL*—Website or HTTP API endpoint
  - *IPFS*—Identifier of an IPFS file (content hash)
- *Query*—This is a single parameter or an array of parameters whose values depend on the data source type. For example, for requests of type URL, if you supply only one parameter (the URL of the data source), the call is assumed to be an HTTP GET request. If you supply two parameters, the second is assumed to be the body of an HTTP POST request. For a request of type IPFS, the only parameter that you should supply is the IPFS content hash.

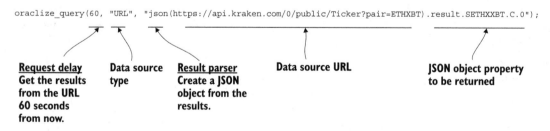

Figure 9.16 oraclize_query() **parameters**

As you can see in figure 9.16, results are extracted from the query through a result parser, which depends on the nature of the data source being called. Table 9.4 summarizes the supported parsers.

Table 9.4   Oraclize query result parsers

Parser type	Parser identifier	Description
JSON parser	`json`	Converts results to a JSON object, which you can extract specific properties from
XML parser	`xml`	Typically parses legacy web service results
HTML parser	`html`	Useful for HTML scraping
Binary helper	`binary`	Can extract items from binary results with `slice(offset, length)`

RESULTS CALLBACK FUNCTION

Now that you've learned how to perform a data request, we'll look at how the Oraclize engine responds with the results. As you saw in figure 9.15, when processing a request, the Oraclize engine grabs the results from the relevant data source, and then it creates a result transaction, which it sends back to the Ethereum network. This transaction is also known as an *Oraclize callback transaction*, because during its execution, it calls back the oracle contract performing the request on its __callback function:

```
function __callback(bytes32 myid, string result, bytes proof) {
    if (msg.sender != oraclize_cbAddress()) throw;
    ETHXBT = result;
    newKrakenPriceTicker(ETHXBT);
    update();
}
```

When you call the __callback function from the result transaction, the value of the ETHXBT state variable is updated. You can then use it in the rest of the code.

9.5.3   Running the data-aware contract

If you want to run the data-aware contract from listing 9.3, you need the Oraclize Remix plugin, which directly references the oraclizeAPI.sol file, including using the Oraclize contract from GitHub: http://mng.bz/y1ry.

A dialog box will appear, warning that "Remix is going to load the extension "Oraclize" located at https://remix-plugin.oraclize.it. Are you sure to load this external extension?" Click OK.

I encourage you to try out the KrakenPriceTicker.sol, which you can find already set up within the Gist menu on the left side of the screen (Gist > KrakenPriceTicker). Before running it

- check and make sure the compiler version is set to 0.4.24+commit.e67f0147 in the Solidity Version panel (on the Settings tab)
- check and make sure the Environment is set to JavaScript VM (on the Run tab)

After having done so, do the following:

1   Open the Run tab and click Deploy.
2   Click the KrakenPriceTicker drop-down in the bottom Deployed Contracts panel.
3   Click Update. (If you want to emulate the behavior of a contract call, you could also set the Value field at the top of the screen, for example to 20 Finney, but within Remix, this isn't necessary.) At this point, the value of ETHXBT gets updated.
4   Click the ETHXBT button to check the value of the exchange rate.

9.6   Dapp frameworks and IDEs

Four categories of tools can improve the Dapp development cycle:

- Development IDEs
- Development frameworks
- Testing frameworks
- Web UI frameworks

9.6.1   Development IDEs

Development IDEs and development frameworks are tools that help you speed up the development cycle. Although IDEs and development frameworks offer similar functionality, the former are slightly more focused on code editing and compilation, whereas the latter offer powerful deployment capabilities.

For a few months, Ethereum Studio appeared to be the de facto IDE for developing Ethereum Dapps, because it provided good code editing capabilities coupled with Web3 integration and smooth contract deployment functionality. But then ether.camp, the company behind it, stopped supporting it. As a result, developers are advised to instead use generic code editing tools, such as Sublime, Atom, Visual Studio Code, Vi, and Emacs, configured with the related Solidity plugin.

9.6.2   Development frameworks

The objective of Ethereum development frameworks is to streamline the development cycle and allow developers to focus on writing code rather than spending most of their time compiling it, redeploying it, and retesting it manually.

Various third-party smart contract frameworks have appeared since the launch of the Ethereum platform:

- Truffle
- Populus
- Dapp (formerly known as Dapple)
- Embark

TRUFFLE

Truffle is probably the most advanced Ethereum development framework, and it focuses mainly on simplifying the building, testing, packaging, and deployment of Solidity contracts. It's distributed as a Node.js package and provides a REPL console.

Truffle's key selling point is migration—the way this framework manages the scripting and configuration of contract deployment. This is the framework you'll use in the next few chapters.

POPULUS

Populus is functionally similar to Truffle in that it's designed to simplify the compile-test-deploy cycle by working on smart contract projects organized with a specific folder structure. It provides configuration management that allows you to progress smoothly throughout development from an in-memory blockchain such as Ganache, to a private internal network, and finally to a public one. The peculiarity of Populus with respect to other frameworks is that it allows a developer to script unit tests or deployment instructions in python.

EMBARK

Embark aims to be a platform-agnostic Dapp framework to simplify the development and deployment of any decentralized application. This framework simplifies the management of multicontract Dapps, and you can configure it to automatically deploy a contract when a code change is detected. It allows decentralized storage through the IPFS protocol (and Swarm) and decentralized messaging through the Whisper protocol.

DAPP

The Dapp framework is geared mainly toward the Linux world and is distributed through the Nix Package manager. The emphasis of this framework is on contract packaging under the Ethereum Smart Contract Packaging Specification (https://github .com/ethereum/EIPs/issues/190) and contract code storage decentralization through the IPFS protocol, which we examined in section 9.4. Dapp also provides a unit testing facility through ethrun and ds-test.

Deciding which development framework to adopt might be difficult, as all of them offer similar compile-test-deploy functionality, although delivered in slightly different ways. It might sound obvious, but the best way to determine which one suits your needs best is to try out all of them.

Given the bias of the Ethereum platform toward JavaScript, it's natural that several generic JavaScript frameworks have become a common feature of the Ethereum ecosystem. Let's see why you should consider including JavaScript testing and UI frameworks in your development environment.

9.6.3   *Testing frameworks*

Using a generic JavaScript testing framework, as opposed to the unit testing function-ality that a main development framework (such as Truffle or embark) offers, provides

- more advanced unit testing capabilities, for example, support for async calls, exit status values for continuous integration systems, timeout handling, meta-generation of test cases, and more extensibility around the use of `assert` libraries
- better system testing automation: you can automate tests involving end-to-end interaction through a private or public test network, and they can handle time-outs, retries, and other use cases around communication with the contract

The two most popular JavaScript unit testing frameworks used for developing decen-tralized applications are Mocha and Jasmine, and you'll be using Mocha in the next few chapters. Let's now move on to the web UI frameworks.

9.6.4   *Web UI frameworks*

Although the UI is an important element of a Dapp, because it connects the end user with the backend smart contracts, the Ethereum platform doesn't yet fully support any technology to develop the presentation layer of an Ethereum application. Because you can include and reference web3.js on the JavaScript of a plain html5 web page, it's natural to think that an easy way of exposing a Dapp is through web pages.

Given the abundance of excellent JavaScript UI frameworks, it's hard to recom-mend any one framework in particular. But it's worth mentioning that frameworks such as Meteor, Angular, Vue, and, more recently, React are getting increasing trac-tion in the Ethereum community. As far as we're concerned, we'll stick to minimalistic solutions based on plain HTML and JavaScript, but feel free to embellish the UI code with the framework of your choice.

Summary

- The previous chapters introduced a restricted view of the Ethereum ecosystem, limited to the following:
  - *Core infrastructural components*—The Go Ethereum (geth) client, the Ethe-reum wallet, MetaMask, and Ganache
  - *Core development tools*—Solidity (the EVM smart contract language), Remix (the online Solidity IDE), solc (the solidity compiler), JSON-RPC (the low-level Ethereum client API), Web3.js (a high-level Ethereum client API writ-ten in JavaScript), Node.js (not Ethereum-specific JavaScript runtime)
- The Ethereum ecosystem includes a wider set of infrastructural components, such as ENS (for decentralized name resolution to addresses), Swarm and IPFS (for decentralized content storage), Whisper (for decentralized messaging), oracles (for importing data from public web-based data providers), and Infura (for managed Ethereum nodes).

- The Ethereum Name Service, also known as ENS, offers a decentralized and secure way to reference resource addresses, such as account and contract addresses, through human-readable domain names. It has objectives similar to the internet DNS.
- Storing relatively big content on the blockchain isn't recommended because it's clumsy and expensive. A better solution is to use decentralized storage systems, such as Swarm and IPFS.
- Swarm is based on the Ethereum technology stack and is Ethereum network-aware, and it's often the preferred solution for storing content off-chain that can be referenced on the Ethereum blockchain through cryptographic hash-based identifiers.
- IPFS is a technology-agnostic protocol for content storage and offers a more widely known and tested solution, at the expense of inferior performance and looser Ethereum integration.
- Oracles, such as Oraclize, allow smart contracts to import data from outside the Ethereum network and accompany it with a proof of authenticity.
- The Ethereum ecosystem also includes a wider set of development tools, such as Truffle, the main smart contract framework; generic JavaScript testing frameworks, such as Mocha and Jasmine; and JavaScript web UI frameworks, such as Angular, ReactJS, and Meteor.

Unit testing contracts
with Mocha

This chapter covers

- Installing and setting up Mocha, a JavaScript unit testing framework
- Unit testing `SimpleCoin` with Mocha
- Writing tests performing negative checks, verifying expected exceptions are thrown
- Writing tests performing positive checks, verifying logic is executed successfully

In previous chapters, you learned how to develop an Ethereum Dapp by using simple tools that the platform offers. You were able, with some effort, to build an end-to-end Dapp, including a simple web UI and a smart contract layer (including libraries) and to deploy it to the public test network. You wrote Solidity and Web3.js code through Remix or even through plain text editors and launched simple deployment scripts manually, initially on the geth console and later on Node.js.

Although this way of developing a Dapp is acceptable while learning, it isn't efficient when you start to dedicate more time to developing decentralized applications, especially if you do it professionally. As you learned in the chapter dedicated to the Ethereum ecosystem, various third-party development tools are available to improve code editing to help you unit test your contracts and speed up the development cycle.

In this chapter, I'll present Mocha, a JavaScript unit testing framework that will allow you to easily automate unit tests for your contracts. In the next chapter, you'll learn how to set up Truffle, through which you'll automate build and deployment of your Dapps. Finally, you'll also incorporate Mocha tests within Truffle, making it your fully integrated development environment.

You'll learn Mocha by writing a unit test suite for SimpleCoin. Before you start, I'll show you briefly how to install the framework and set up the working directory.

10.1 Installing Mocha

Mocha is executed through Node.js, so you have to install it using npm. Because you'll be writing tests for various smart contracts, it's best to install it globally. (You might have to Run it as an Administrator, depending on your security configuration.) Here's how to install it:

```
c:\>npm install --global mocha
```

That's it! The next step is to prepare a working directory for your SimpleCoin tests.

10.2 Setting up SimpleCoin in Mocha

You should place tests against an Ethereum smart contract in a working directory configured for Node.js and set up with Ethereum packages such as Web3 and Ganache. Create a working directory for the SimpleCoin unit tests you're going to write. I've created mine as C:\Ethereum\mocha\SimpleCoin.

Now create a package.json configuration file for Node.js in this folder and set the test script to Mocha, as shown in the following listing.

> **Listing 10.1 package.json**

```
{
  "name": "simple_coin_tests",
  "version": "1.0.0",
  "description": "unit tests for simple coin",
  "scripts": {
    "test": "mocha"
  }
}
```

You can also create it interactively by opening an OS shell, moving to the working directory you've created, and running

```
C:\Ethereum\mocha\SimpleCoin>npm init
```

Once you have the directory and configuration file created, you can quickly try out how Mocha executes tests. Create a dummyTests.js file containing the example test shown in the following listing.

Listing 10.2   dummyTests.js

Imports the default
assert library
Names the test suite
Names the functionality
being tested

```
var assert = require('assert');     ←
describe('String', function() {       ←
  describe('#length()', function() {      ←
    it('the length of the string "Ethereum" should be 8',
      function() {        ←
      assert.equal(8, 'Ethereum'.length);   ←
    });                              Actual test
  });
});
```

Describes the
specific test

You can run this test file as follows:

```
C:\Ethereum\mocha\SimpleCoin>npm test dummyTests.js
```

And you'll get this output:

```
> simple_coin_tests@1.0.0 test C:\Ethereum\mocha\SimpleCoin
> mocha "dummyTests.js"

  String
    #length()
      √ the length of the string "Ethereum" should be 8

  1 passing (9ms)
```

As you may have noticed, the assert library referenced at the top of the test script is the default assert library that the framework provides. If you want, you can install and then reference any of the following assert frameworks:

- Should.js (https://shouldjs.github.io/)
- Expect.js (https://github.com/Automattic/expect.js/)
- Chai.js (www.chaijs.com/)
- Better-assert (https://github.com/tj/better-assert)
- Unexpected (https://github.com/unexpectedjs/unexpected)

The testing working directory is almost ready. Before you can use it for testing smart contracts, you must install the following node packages: solc, Web3, and Ganache. If you haven't installed them globally already, you can do so as follows:

```
C:\>npm install -g solc
C:\>npm install -g web3@0.20.0
C:\>npm install -g ganache-cli@6.1.8
```

Alternatively, you can install these packages only in the testing folder as follows:

```
C:\Ethereum\mocha\SimpleCoin>npm install solc
C:\Ethereum\mocha\SimpleCoin>npm install web3@0.20.0
C:\Ethereum\mocha\SimpleCoin>npm install ganache-cli@6.1.8
```

10.3 *Writing unit tests for SimpleCoin*

You're all set up to write some tests against `SimpleCoin`. Now I can show you how to unit test a solidity contract in Mocha. This isn't meant to be a tutorial on unit testing, though, and I'll assume you have basic knowledge of or experience in unit testing. If you don't know anything about unit testing but wish to learn more on the topic, I can recommend two excellent books that will give you a solid foundation: *Effective Unit Testing* by Lasse Koskela and *The Art of Unit Testing* by Michael Feathers and Robert C. Martin, both published by Manning.

You'll be creating tests against the functionality offered by the extended version of `SimpleCoin` you implemented back in chapter 5. I've repeated it in the next listing for your convenience, and you can place it in the following file: c:\Ethereum\mocha\ SimpleCoin\SimpleCoin.sol.

> **Listing 10.3 SimpleCoin.sol, latest code from chapter 5**

```solidity
pragma solidity ^0.4.24;
contract SimpleCoin {
    mapping (address => uint256) public coinBalance;
    mapping (address => mapping (address => uint256)) public allowance;
    mapping (address => bool) public frozenAccount;
    address public owner;

    event Transfer(address indexed from, address indexed to, uint256 value);
    event FrozenAccount(address target, bool frozen);

    modifier onlyOwner {
        require(msg.sender == owner);
        _;
    }

    constructor(uint256 _initialSupply) public {
        owner = msg.sender;
        mint(owner, _initialSupply);
    }

    function transfer(address _to, uint256 _amount) public {
        require(coinBalance[msg.sender] > _amount);
        require(coinBalance[_to] + _amount >= coinBalance[_to] );
        coinBalance[msg.sender] -= _amount;
        coinBalance[_to] += _amount;
        emit Transfer(msg.sender, _to, _amount);
    }

    function authorize(address _authorizedAccount, uint256 _allowance)
        public returns (bool success) {
        allowance[msg.sender][_authorizedAccount] = _allowance;
        return true;
    }

    function transferFrom(address _from, address _to, uint256 _amount)
        public returns (bool success) {
```

```
        require(_to != 0x0);
        require(coinBalance[_from] > _amount);
        require(coinBalance[_to] + _amount >= coinBalance[_to] );
        require(_amount <= allowance[_from][msg.sender]);
        coinBalance[_from] -= _amount;
        coinBalance[_to] += _amount;
        allowance[_from][msg.sender] -= _amount;
        emit Transfer(_from, _to, _amount);
        return true;
    }

    function mint(address _recipient, uint256 _mintedAmount)
        public onlyOwner {
        coinBalance[_recipient] += _mintedAmount;
        emit Transfer(owner, _recipient, _mintedAmount);
    }

    function freezeAccount(address target, bool freeze)
        public onlyOwner  {
        frozenAccount[target] = freeze;
        emit FrozenAccount(target, freeze);
    }
}
```

10.3.1 *The testing plan*

Unit testing a Solidity contract means verifying that all the public methods the contract exposes, including the contract constructor, behave as expected, with both valid and invalid input. First, I'll help you verify that the constructor initializes the contract as expected. You'll do so by correctly setting the contract owner value and the initial state according to the account used to execute the deployment transaction and the values fed to the constructor parameters.

Then I'll show you a set of tests for the typical negative and positive checks you want to perform against any contract function. By *positive* checks, I mean those verifying successful logic execution: a contract function invoked by an authorized user and fed with valid input within the constraints defined by all modifiers decorating the function and acceptable to the function logic executes successfully.

By *negative* checks I mean those verifying expected exceptions are thrown for an unauthorized caller or invalid input:

- A contract function that is restricted to certain callers through a modifier throws an expected exception if the caller isn't authorized to invoke it.
- A contract function that receives input that doesn't meet other constraints defined by additional modifiers or `require` conditions throws an expected exception.

Once you're familiar with these types of tests, you'll be able to write tests against any contract function. You can start by testing `SimpleCoin`'s constructor. While we look into that, I'll also give you a general idea of how to initialize and structure your tests.

10.3.2 *Unit testing the constructor*

As you know, testing a piece of code means executing the code under test and then verifying assumptions about what should have happened. You execute the code of the contract constructor only during its deployment, so your test must deploy SimpleCoin and then verify that the construction was executed correctly, specifically by checking the following:

- The contract owner is the same account as the sender of the deployment transaction.
- The token balance of the contract owner is the same as the initial supply amount being fed to the constructor.

Unit tests must generally run as quickly as possible, because you're likely to execute them many times through your development cycle. In the case of enterprise applications, the main source of latency comes from accessing environmental resources, such as the file system, databases, and network. The most common way of reducing or eliminating such latency is to emulate access to these resources with isolation (or mocking) frameworks, such as jMock and EasyMock for Java applications and Moq, NMock, and Rhino Mocks for .net applications.

When it comes to Ethereum Dapps, the main source of latency is transaction processing (including mining and block creation) and block propagation throughout the Ethereum network. As a result, it's natural to run contract unit tests against a mock network such as Ganache, which emulates the infrastructural aspects of the Ethereum platform without connecting to it.

This means your first test, against SimpleCoin's constructor, must deploy Simple-Coin on Ganache before performing the functional checks I've described (of contract ownership and the account balance of the owner). In fact, to ensure no interferences occur between tests, each test will redeploy SimpleCoin from scratch.

Deploying SimpleCoin onto Ganache... Hold on—you already did this in chapter 8! You can adapt listing 8.5 for unit testing. You can keep the script almost unchanged up to the instantiation of SimpleCoinContractFactory. The only modification is the path of SimpleCoin.sol, which is now c:\Ethereum\mocha\Simple-Coin. Here's the script:

```
const fs = require('fs');
const solc = require('solc');
const Web3 = require('web3');
const web3 = new Web3(
    new Web3.providers.HttpProvider("http://localhost:8545"));
var assert = require('assert');

const source = fs.readFileSync(
    'c:/Ethereum/mocha/SimpleCoin/SimpleCoin.sol',
    'utf8');
const compiledContract = solc.compile(source, 1);
const abi = compiledContract.contracts[':SimpleCoin'].interface;
```

The location of simplecoin.sol is now in c:/Ethereum/mocha/SimpleCoin.

```
const bytecode = '0x' + compiledContract.contracts[':SimpleCoin'].bytecode;
const gasEstimate = web3.eth.estimateGas({ data: bytecode }) + 100000;

const SimpleCoinContractFactory = web3.eth.contract(JSON.parse(abi));
```

Now that you've taken care of the infrastructural (nonfunctional) part of your first test, you can focus on the functional one. Bear in mind, though, that these initial lines of the script haven't deployed `SimpleCoin` yet; they've merely instantiated the contract factory.

Following the pattern in the mock test from listing 10.2, you can start to document the purpose of your first test through Mocha's `describe()` and `it()` statements:

```
describe('SimpleCoin', function() {          ←── Describes the entire testing
  describe('SimpleCoin constructor', function() {      suite you're creating
    it('Contract owner is sender', function(done) {   ←── Describes your first
    ...                                                     testing section, focused
    });                                 Describes your      on SimpleCoin's
  });                                    first test         constructor
});
```

It's time to write the core of your first test, which will, as I stated earlier, check that the contract owner is the same account as the sender of the deployment transaction. You can structure the test with an *AAA layout*, which includes the following three parts, as also illustrated in figure 10.1:

- *Arrange*—Sets up the input passed to the function under test and instantiates objects required for the testing
- *Act*—Calls the function under test
- *Assert*—Verifies the test assumptions

```
describe('SimpleCoin', function() {
  this.timeout(5000);
  describe('SimpleCoin constructor', function() {
    it('Contract owner is sender', function(done) {
        //arrange
        let sender = web3.eth.accounts[1];         Inputs to this test are the sender
        let initialSupply = 10000;                 of the deployment transaction
                                                   and the initial supply amount.
        //act
        let simpleCoinInstance =
            SimpleCoinContractFactory.new(initialSupply, {   ←── Triggers the
            from: sender, data: bytecode, gas: gasEstimate},      function under
            function (e, contract){                               test, SimpleCoin's
            if (typeof contract.address !== 'undefined') {        constructor,
                //assert                                          through contract
                assert.equal(contract.owner(), sender);           deployment
                done();      ←──
        }                          Signals to Mocha the
      });                          completion of the test
    });
  });
});
```

Following successful deployment, verifies the contract owner is the sender of the transaction

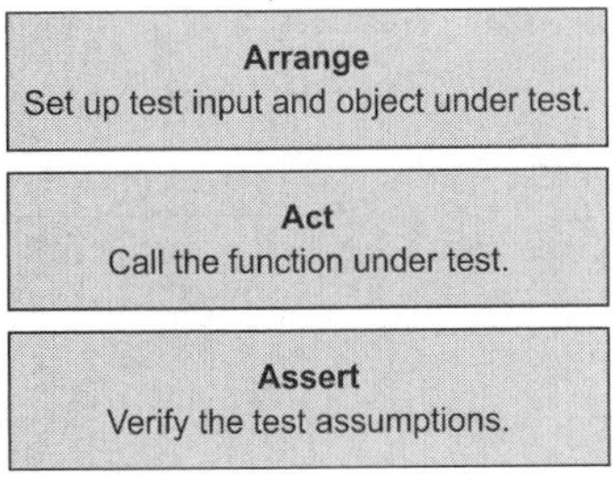

Figure 10.1   The typical AAA structure of a unit test: Arrange (set up test input and the object under test); Act (call the function under test); and Assert (verify the test expected outcome)

You're now ready to run your first unit test, which is shown in its entirety in the following listing. You can place this script in the following file: c:\Ethereum\mocha\SimpleCoin\SimpleCoinTests.js.

Listing 10.4   SimpleCoinTests.js

```javascript
const fs = require('fs');
const solc = require('solc');
const Web3 = require('web3');
const web3 = new Web3(
    new Web3.providers.HttpProvider("http://localhost:8545"));
var assert = require('assert');

const source = fs.readFileSync(
    'c:/Ethereum/mocha/SimpleCoin/SimpleCoin.sol', 'utf8');
const compiledContract = solc.compile(source, 1);
const abi = compiledContract.contracts[':SimpleCoin'].interface;
const bytecode = '0x' + compiledContract.contracts[':SimpleCoin'].bytecode;
const gasEstimate = web3.eth.estimateGas({ data: bytecode }) + 100000;

const SimpleCoinContractFactory = web3.eth.contract(JSON.parse(abi));

describe('SimpleCoin', function() {
  this.timeout(5000);
  describe('SimpleCoin constructor', function() {
    it('Contract owner is sender', function(done) {
        //arrange
        let sender = web3.eth.accounts[1];
        let initialSupply = 10000;

        //act
        let simpleCoinInstance = SimpleCoinContractFactory.new(initialSupply, {
            from: sender, data: bytecode, gas: gasEstimate},
            function (e, contract){
            if (typeof contract.address !== 'undefined') {
                    //assert
                    assert.equal(contract.owner(), sender);
                    done();
            }
        });
    });
  });
});
```

Before running the script, open a new console and start Ganache:

```
c:\>ganache-cli
```

Now go back to the console from which you executed the dummy test earlier and run your new test script:

```
C:\Ethereum\mocha\SimpleCoin>npm test SimpleCoinTests.js
```

You'll see output like what's shown in figure 10.2.

```
C:\Ethereum\mocha\SimpleCoin>npm test SimpleCoinTests.js

> simple_coin_tests@1.0.0 test C:\Ethereum\mocha\SimpleCoin
> mocha "SimpleCoinTests.js"



  SimpleCoin
    SimpleCoin constructor
      √ Contract owner is sender (505ms)


  1 passing (517ms)


C:\Ethereum\mocha\SimpleCoin>
```

Figure 10.2   Output of your first Mocha test, showing the name of the test suite, the name of the test section, and a description of your individual test. The test is passing!

The test is passing, which means the contract owner is indeed the sender of the deployment transaction. Good news! You can move on to the next test.

Before leaving the constructor, you should test whether the balance of the contract owner is equal to the initial supply fed with the initialSupply parameter. Add the following it() block within the describe() section associated with the SimpleCoin constructor:

```
it('Contract owner balance is equal to initialSupply', function(done) {
    //arrange
    let sender = web3.eth.accounts[1];
    let initialSupply = 10000;

    //act
    let simpleCoinInstance = SimpleCoinContractFactory.new(initialSupply, {
        from: sender, data: bytecode, gas: gasEstimate},
        function (e, contract){
            if (typeof contract.address !== 'undefined') {
                //assert
                assert.equal(
                    contract.coinBalance(contract.owner()),
```

```
        initialSupply);
        done();
    }
    });
});
```

> This is the only line differing from the previous test. It verifies whether the balance of the contract owner equals the initial supply.

NOTE You might be wondering why I didn't add the same assert line to the previous test. In general, it's good practice to keep each unit test focused on one specific thing. Given that this test has nothing to do with verifying contract ownership, I decided to create a completely separate test. As I mentioned earlier, you also should completely isolate every test from other tests to avoid cross-dependencies and side effects that might invalidate unrelated tests. That's why you should redeploy SimpleCoin at each test—by doing so, you can be confident that the test is truly isolated.

Now rerun the test script:

```
C:\Ethereum\mocha\SimpleCoin>npm test SimpleCoinTests.js
```

You can see from the output in figure 10.3 that both tests have passed. Also, if you look at the Ganache console, you can verify that while running this test session, SimpleCoin was indeed deployed twice—once for each test, as shown in figure 10.4.

```
C:\Ethereum\mocha\SimpleCoin>npm test SimpleCoinTests.js

> simple_coin_tests@1.0.0 test C:\Ethereum\mocha\SimpleCoin
> mocha "SimpleCoinTests.js"


  SimpleCoin
    SimpleCoin constructor
      √ Contract owner is sender (483ms)
      √ Contract owner balance is equal to initialSupply (718ms)


  2 passing (1s)

C:\Ethereum\mocha\SimpleCoin>
```

Figure 10.3 Amended test suite, including two constructor tests. Both have passed.

10.3.3 *Testing whether only authorized callers can invoke a function*

We'll now move to the set of tests you typically want to write against each contract function. If you look at listing 10.3, you'll notice both mint() and freezeAccount() restrict their execution to the contract owner through the onlyOwner modifier:

```
function mint(address _recipient, uint256  _mintedAmount)
    onlyOwner public {
        …
function freezeAccount(address target, bool freeze)
    onlyOwner public {
```

```
Transaction: 0x7517a9cdbc0610573032791918cfd0a0d2358365566318cd754808e69c39cd16
Contract created: 0x4e015656aac3b30be26ca6a224d1dbe69438bfd7
Gas usage: 509317
Block Number: 2
Block Time: Sun Apr 08 2018 18:05:17 GMT+0100 (GMT Summer Time)

eth_newBlockFilter
eth_getFilterChanges
eth_getTransactionReceipt
eth_getCode
eth_call
eth_uninstallFilter
eth_accounts
eth_sendTransaction

Transaction: 0xb9fbf9f3ae941ef70f969cfacc3a3ff66c8e13b104cff564b0dc026c805aea9c
Contract created: 0x6892fbaeef1a09fd666398b23d06ac6c44f187bb
Gas usage: 509317
Block Number: 3
Block Time: Sun Apr 08 2018 18:05:18 GMT+0100 (GMT Summer Time)

eth_newBlockFilter
eth_getFilterChanges
eth_getTransactionReceipt
eth_getCode
eth_call
eth_call
eth_uninstallFilter
```

Figure 10.4   Ganache output during test execution. `SimpleCoin` **is redeployed at each test execution.**

A test you should write for each of these functions is to verify that an exception is thrown if you try to call them from an account that isn't the contract owner. Here's how you write such a test for `mint()`:

```
describe('mint', function() {
    it('Cannot mint from non-owner account', function(done) {
        //arrange

        let sender = web3.eth.accounts[1];
        let initialSupply = 10000;

        let minter = web3.eth.accounts[2];
        let recipient = web3.eth.accounts[3];
        let mintedCoins = 3000;

        let simpleCoinInstance = simpleCoinContractFactory
            .new(initialSupply, {
                from: sender,
                data: bytecode,
                gas: gasEstimate},
            function (e, contract){
                if (typeof contract.address !== 'undefined') {
                    //act and assert
                    assert.throws(
                        ()=> {
                            contract.mint(recipient, mintedCoins,
                                {from:minter,
                                 gas:200000}));
```

Sender of the contract transaction (the contract owner)

The account calling mint() isn't the contract owner.

Verifies an exception is thrown when mint() is called, because the caller of mint() isn't the contract owner

```
                },
                /VM Exception while processing transaction/
            );
            done();
        }
    });
  });
});
```

As you can see, you verify that an exception is thrown when calling a function by wrapping it with the following assert statement:

```
assert.throws(
    () => contract.functionBeingTested(),
    /Expected exception/
);
```

You'll use this technique several times in upcoming sections.

10.3.4 *Testing if input constraints are met*

Even when the caller is authorized to invoke a function, they must feed it valid input. You should verify that if they don't do so, an exception is thrown for any breach to function modifiers or require conditions.

Recall that the transfer() function performs input validation through various require statements before executing the token transfer:

```
function transfer(address _to, uint256 _amount) public {
    require(_to != 0x0);
    require(coinBalance[msg.sender] > _amount);
    require(coinBalance[_to] + _amount >= coinBalance[_to] );
    coinBalance[msg.sender] -= _amount;
    coinBalance[_to] += _amount;
    Transfer(msg.sender, _to, _amount);
}
```

Ideally, you should write a test for each of the require statements. I'll show you how to write a test against the second require statement:

```
require(coinBalance[msg.sender] > _amount);
```

This constraint prevents the sender from sending more tokens than they own. If they try to do so, an exception is thrown. You can verify this is happening by using the same assert.throws statement you saw earlier:

```
describe('transfer', function() {
  it('Cannot transfer a number of tokens higher than that of tokens owned',
    function(done) {
    //arrange
    let sender = web3.eth.accounts[1];
```

```
        let initialSupply = 10000;
        let recipient = web3.eth.accounts[2];        Sets an amount to be
        let tokensToTransfer = 12000;            ◀── transferred that's higher
                                                      than the current balance
        let simpleCoinInstance =
          SimpleCoinContractFactory.new(initialSupply, {
            from: sender, data: bytecode, gas: gasEstimate},
            function (e, contract){
              if (typeof contract.address !== 'undefined') {
              //act and assert
Verifies that  ▷ assert.throws(
an exception       ()=>{
 is thrown           contract.transfer(recipient, tokensToTransfer, {
                       from:sender, gas:200000});
                   },
                   /VM Exception while processing transaction/   ◀── Expected
                 );                                                  exception
                 done();
               }
            });
         });
      });
```

The transfer() function has two other require statements. I encourage you to write similar tests for them.

10.3.5 *Testing invocation from an authorized account with valid input*

After you write tests performing negative checks so you're confident that no unauthorized accounts or accounts with invalid input can call the function, it's time to write a positive test proving the logic performs successfully when an authorized account invokes the function and feeds it with valid input. As an example, you could write a new test against the transfer() function dealing with a successful token transfer. In this case, you must verify that the sender account balance has decreased by the transferred amount, whereas the receiving account has increased by the same amount:

```
it('Successful transfer: final sender and recipient balances are correct',
  function(done) {
    //arrange
    let sender = web3.eth.accounts[1];
    let initialSupply = 10000;
    let recipient = web3.eth.accounts[2];        Sets amount to
    let tokensToTransfer = 200;              ◀──  be transferred

    let simpleCoinInstance =
      SimpleCoinContractFactory.new(initialSupply, {
        from: sender, data: bytecode, gas: gasEstimate},
        function (e, contract){
          if (typeof contract.address !== 'undefined') {
```

```
//act
contract.transfer(recipient, tokensToTransfer, {
  from:sender,gas:200000});
```

```
//assert
const expectedSenderBalance = 9800;       ⟵  Expected sender and recipient
const expectedRecipientBalance = 200;          balances after the transfer
```

```
let actualSenderBalance =
  contract.coinBalance(sender);       ⟵┐  Actual sender and
let actualRecipientBalance =              │  recipient balances
  contract.coinBalance(recipient);    ⟵┘  after the transfer
```

```
assert.equal(actualSenderBalance,
          expectedSenderBalance);      ⟵┐  Verifies actual sender
assert.equal(actualRecipientBalance,       │  and recipient balances
          expectedRecipientBalance);   ⟵┘  equal the expected ones
```

```
      done();
    }
  });
});
```

Add the two tests you've written against `transfer()` to the test script you started to write earlier against the constructor and rerun it:

```
C:\Ethereum\mocha\SimpleCoin>npm test SimpleCoinTests.js
```

As you can see in figure 10.5, the test output now shows two sections: one for the constructor tests and the other for the `transfer()` tests. All tests are passing.

```
C:\Ethereum\mocha\SimpleCoin>npm test SimpleCoinTests.js

> simple_coin_tests@1.0.0 test C:\Ethereum\mocha\SimpleCoin
> mocha "SimpleCoinTests.js"


  SimpleCoin
    SimpleCoin constructor
      √ Contract owner is sender (535ms)
      √ Contract owner balance is equal to initialSupply (704ms)
    transfer
      √ Cannot transfer a number of tokens higher than number of tokens owned (682ms)
      √ Succesful transfer: final sender and recipient balances are correct (1160ms)


  4 passing (3s)


C:\Ethereum\mocha\SimpleCoin>
```

Figure 10.5 Output of the amended test suite also including tests on the `transfer()` function. You can now see two sections: one for the constructor tests and the other for the `transfer()` tests. All tests are passing.

As an additional test to perform a positive check, you could write a test against the authorize() function, which has no modifiers and no input validation:

```
function authorize(address _authorizedAccount, uint256 _allowance)
    public returns (bool success) {
    allowance[msg.sender][_authorizedAccount] = _allowance;
    return true;
}
```

The most obvious test to write is therefore one that verifies that the allowance set is the expected one:

```
describe('authorize', function() {
  it('Successful authorization: the allowance of the authorized
      account is set correctly',
    function(done) {
      //arrange
      let sender = web3.eth.accounts[1];
      let initialSupply = 10000;
      let authorizer = web3.eth.accounts[2];
      let authorized = web3.eth.accounts[3];         Sets the allowance
      let allowance = 300;                           amount

      let simpleCoinInstance = SimpleCoinContractFactory.new(
        initialSupply, {
        from: sender, data: bytecode, gas: gasEstimate},
        function (e, contract){
          if (typeof contract.address !== 'undefined') {

              //act
            let result = contract.authorize(authorized, allowance, {
              from:authorizer,gas:200000});           Authorizes the
                                                       account to use the
            //assert                                   specified allowance
            assert.equal(contract.allowance(authorizer,
                  authorized), 300);          Verifies the allowance allocated
            done();                           to the authorized account is
              }                               the expected one
        });
    });
});
```

10.3.6 A little challenge

Now that we've covered all the typical tests, I invite you to refresh your memory on the transferFrom() function. That function allows an account to transfer an amount from another account within an allowance previously authorized by the account owner:

```
function transferFrom(address _from, address _to, uint256 _amount)
    public returns (bool success) {
    require(_to != 0x0);
    require(coinBalance[_from] > _amount);
    require(coinBalance[_to] + _amount >= coinBalance[_to] );
    require(_amount <= allowance[_from][msg.sender]);
```

```
    coinBalance[_from] -= _amount;
    coinBalance[_to] += _amount;
    allowance[_from][msg.sender] -= _amount;
    Transfer(_from, _to, _amount);
    return true;
}
```

Looking at its code, you might want to test at least these four scenarios:

- The authorized account can't transfer a number of tokens higher than that owned by the authorizer.
- An account can't transfer tokens from an account that hasn't authorized any allowance to any account.
- An account can't transfer tokens from an account that hasn't authorized it any allowance.
- An authorized account can transfer an amount within the allowance, the final balance of the authorizer has decreased by the amount transferred by the authorized account, and the balance of the recipient has increased by the same amount.

You might have noticed these tests are similar to ones you've already written, so I won't repeat myself here. But I encourage you to give these tests a shot and then compare your tests with mine, which you can find in listing C.1 in appendix C.

10.3.7 *The full testing suite*

You can see all tests, including the ones I've skipped, in listing C.1 of appendix C. You can also find them in the SimpleCoinTest.js file of the provided code. After adding all these tests to SimpleCoinTests.js, you can run the whole suite, as follows:

```
C:\Ethereum\mocha\SimpleCoin>npm test SimpleCoinTests.js
```

The output in figure 10.6 shows the tests nicely grouped in sections … and all passing.

This section has given you an idea of the typical tests you might want to write against a contract you're developing. You can find a summary in table 10.1.

Table 10.1 Purpose of the tests presented in this section

Function	Test	Purpose
Constructor	Contract owner is sender	Testing contract ownership
Constructor	Owner balance = supply	Testing correct state set from constructor parameters
Mint	Can't mint from nonowner account	Testing if an exception is raised when an unauthorized account invokes the function
Transfer	Can't transfer more tokens than owned	Testing if an exception is raised by invalid input breaching modifiers or `require` conditions
Transfer	Successful transfer	Testing contract state following successful transaction executed from valid account and with valid input

```
C:\Ethereum\mocha\SimpleCoin>npm test SimpleCoinTests.js

> simple_coin_tests@1.0.0 test C:\Ethereum\mocha\SimpleCoin
> mocha "SimpleCoinTests.js"


  SimpleCoin
    SimpleCoin constructor
      √ Contract owner is sender (519ms)
      √ Contract owner balance is equal to initialSupply (720ms)
    transfer
      √ Cannot transfer a number of tokens higher than number of tokens owned (739ms)
      √ Succesful transfer: final sender and recipient balances are correct (1172ms)
    authorize
      √ Successful authorization: the allowance of the authorized account is set correctly (1173ms)
    transferFrom
      √ Cannot transfer number of tokens higher than that owned by authorizer (1664ms)
      √ Cannot transfer tokens from an account that has not authorized any account (1807ms)
      √ Cannot transfer tokens by an account that has not been authorized (1931ms)
      √ Succesful transfer from authorizer to authorized: final source and destination balances are correct and allowanc
e is reduced as expected (2342ms)
    mint
      √ Cannot mint from no owner account (916ms)
      √ Succesful minting: the recipient has the correct balance (1012ms)
    freezeAccount
      √ Cannot freezing from no owner account (898ms)
      √ Succesful freezing: verify the account has been frozen (945ms)


  13 passing (16s)
```

Figure 10.6   Running the whole test suite. The output shows tests are grouped in sections ... and they're all passing.

The test suite I've presented covers the most obvious test cases, but it's by no means comprehensive. Like programming, unit testing is an art, not an exact science. You must always keep in mind the trade-off between coverage (Are all the functions of your contracts covered by tests? Are all logic branches covered by tests?) and accuracy (Are all boundary conditions of each function tested?) of your tests on one side and their cost (for implementation and maintenance) on the other side. Ideally, you might want to have maximum coverage and accuracy, but you might not have enough time and resources to implement and maintain all the necessary tests. In that case, you might want to focus on critical areas, especially on functionality for which Ether's at stake.

Summary

- You can write Ethereum contract unit tests relatively easily with Mocha, a generic JavaScript testing framework.
- You can install Mocha quickly with npm, the Node.js package manager.
- You can describe Mocha unit test packages and groups using describe() and individual tests using it().
- Your tests should cover negative checks, verifying expected exceptions are thrown in case the function is invoked from an unauthorized account or with invalid input.

- Your tests should cover positive checks, verifying the contract state has been successfully modified by the function logic when the function is called from an authorized account and with valid input.
- You also should write tests against the constructor to verify that the contract owner and the contract state are initialized correctly.

Improving the development cycle with Truffle

This chapter covers

- Installing Truffle, a smart-contract framework
- Setting up and compiling an Ethereum contract within Truffle
- Simplifying contract deployment through Truffle's migrations
- Simplifying contract unit testing with Truffle

In the previous chapter, you started to integrate unit testing into your development environment with Mocha. But you might have noticed that the unit test script didn't look ideal. It has a fairly complex setup, which includes explicit instructions on compiling SimpleCoin and creating a contract factory. Each test also includes an explicit deployment statement that references the contract factory. The main drawback is that all this infrastructural code distracts from the main objective of unit tests, which is to focus on functional aspects of a contract. Another disadvantage is that if you wanted to create a new test suite to cover a different contract, you'd have to duplicate all this infrastructural code.

Wouldn't it be nice if you had a way to simplify the deployment of a contract? This is the main objective of Truffle, an Ethereum contract development framework that focuses on streamlining deployment and consequently simplifying unit testing.

In this chapter, you'll set up Truffle, and then you'll use it to improve the compile -> deploy -> test cycle. The main focus will be on learning how to use the tool, so, to avoid getting distracted by contract-specific issues, you'll reuse our good old `Simple-Coin` contract yet again. If you're eager to implement something new, please bear with me: in the next chapter you'll develop a brand new Dapp from scratch using Truffle!

11.1 Setting up Truffle

You can install Truffle easily with Node.js npm, and then you can start to create a project. Install version 4.1.15, which is the one I have used, as follows:

```
C:>npm install -g truffle@4.1.15
```

> **WARNING** In order to run my code smoothly, don't install Truffle 5.0.0. My code is written against version 4.1.15, and is unlikely to work correctly under version 5.0.0.

11.2 Moving SimpleCoin under Truffle

You'll start with a minimal project, and then you'll integrate `SimpleCoin` in Truffle by walking through the entire development lifecycle, including the following steps:

- Setting up `SimpleCoin` in Truffle
- Compiling the contract
- Deploying the contract
- Unit testing the contract

11.2.1 Setting up SimpleCoin in Truffle

Create a working directory for the `SimpleCoin` Truffle project. I've created mine as follows:

```
C:\Ethereum\Truffle\SimpleCoin
```

Open an OS shell and move to this directory:

```
C:\>cd Ethereum\Truffle\SimpleCoin
```

Now you can initialize the Truffle project:

```
C:\Ethereum\Truffle\SimpleCoin>truffle init
```

Truffle will create the following directory structure and prepopulate it with some files:

```
/contracts
    Migrations.sol
/migrations
    1_initial_migration.js
/test
truffle.js
truffle-config.js
```

Table 11.1 provides a description of each directory.

Table 11.1 Truffle directory structure

Directory/filename	Description
/contracts	Directory for Solidity contract files you want to compile and deploy.
/contracts/Migrations.sol	Special contract that Truffle uses to deploy project contracts.
/migrations	JavaScript configuration files to perform *migrations* (more on this later).
/test	Truffle can automatically test both Solidity contract code and JavaScript application code through unit tests placed in this folder.
truffle.js	The Truffle project configuration file for Linux or macOS.
truffle-config.js	The Truffle project configuration file for Windows.

> **WARNING** If you're running Windows, keep truffle-config.js and remove truffle.js. If you're running on Linux or macOS, you can remove truffle-config.js and use truffle.js. In the rest of the chapter, I'll refer to truffle.js—you'll understand why shortly.

11.2.2 Compiling SimpleCoin

Copy the latest version of SimpleCoin from C:\Ethereum\mocha\SimpleCoin\SimpleCoin.sol to C:\Ethereum\Truffle\SimpleCoin\Contracts\SimpleCoin.sol. Downgrade the pragma solidity instruction of SimpleCoin.sol to 0.4.23 after copying the file, as the latest version of Truffle at the time of writing uses solc 0.4.23.

You perform contract deployment in Truffle through so-called *migrations*, as I'll explain shortly. You execute these through a Migrations contract, shown in the following listing, which was auto-generated in the contracts folder when you initialized the project with the truffle init command.

Listing 11.1 contracts/Migrations.sol

```
pragma solidity ^0.4.23;

contract Migrations {
  address public owner;
  uint public last_completed_migration;

  constructor() public {
    owner = msg.sender;
  }

  modifier restricted() {
    if (msg.sender == owner) _;
  }

  function setCompleted(uint completed) public restricted {
    last_completed_migration = completed;
  }
```

```
    function upgrade(address new_address) public restricted {
      Migrations upgraded = Migrations(new_address);
      upgraded.setCompleted(last_completed_migration);
    }
}
```

You can now kick the compilation

```
C:\Ethereum\Truffle\SimpleCoin>truffle compile
```

and you'll see output similar to this:

```
Compiling .\contracts\SimpleCoin.sol...
Writing artifacts to .\build\contracts
```

After a successful compilation, Truffle has created a new directory relative to the project folder, /build/contracts. The folder contains compilation artifacts, described in table 11.2, that you'll use during the deployment stage.

Table 11.2 Compilation artifacts

Artifact	Purpose
Migrations.json	ABI interface and bytecode of Migrations.sol
SimpleCoin.json	ABI interface and bytecode of SimpleCoin.sol

11.2.3 *Troubles with Truffle*

If you've started having issues at this point, it might be because you're working in Windows or have a compiler versioning problem. You'll need a solution so you can complete the work in this chapter. This two-part section provides some advice to help you solve such problems.

TRUFFLE ON WINDOWS

If you're working in Windows, you might experience issues when running any Truffle command. Specifically, if you're running Truffle compile in a Windows command shell, you might get the cryptic Microsoft JScript runtime error shown in figure 11.1.

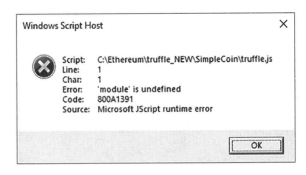

Figure 11.1   Error generated when running a Truffle command in Windows

The error occurs because Windows can't distinguish correctly between the Truffle.cmd command file in the npm folder (typically in C:\Users\YOURNAME\AppData\Roaming\npm) and the truffle.js file in your Truffle project folder. You have four options for solving this issue:

- Use a configuration file named truffle-config.js instead of truffle.js, as mentioned in the earlier setup section. Remove truffle.js from your Truffle project folder.
- If for any reason you want to use a configuration file named truffle.js rather than truffle-config.js, use Git Bash rather than the standard command shell.
- Call truffle.cmd explicitly, for example, `truffle.cmd compile`.
- Go to the directory where truffle.cmd is and copy it locally with another name, for example, truff.cmd. Then run `truff compile` instead of Truffle compile. If you decide to use this workaround, keep typing *truff* rather than Truffle for the rest of the chapter.

TROUBLESHOOTING TRUFFLE COMPILE ERRORS
If you get compilation errors, it might be because you're running an old version of the compiler or because Truffle is referencing an old version of the compiler, even if you've upgraded it recently. Specifically, after executing the `truffle compile` command, you might get some compilation error messages due to new constructor syntax introduced in solc 0.4.22. You have two options for fixing the issue. The best approach is to uninstall Truffle and reinstall it globally by entering

```
C:\Ethereum\Truffle\SimpleCoin>npm uninstall truffle -g
```

followed by

```
C:\Ethereum\Truffle\SimpleCoin>npm install truffle@4.1.15 -g
```

Now if you re-execute `truffle compile`, you should get at most some warnings associated, possibly, with the `Migrations` contract (in the contracts\Migrations.sol file). It might still be implemented under an old constructor convention, depending on the version of Truffle you're running. If you're running Truffle 4.1.15 or later, you shouldn't have any issues; the Migrations.sol file should have been autogenerated like in listing 11.1. If you're running an older version and want to get rid of the warnings, replace

```
constructor() public {
  owner = msg.sender;
}
```

with

```
function Migrations() public {
  owner = msg.sender;
}
```

If you recompile, you should no longer get any warnings:

```
C:\Ethereum\truffle\SimpleCoin>truffle compile
Compiling .\contracts\Migrations.sol...
Writing artifacts to .\build\contracts
```

The second way to fix compilation issues, which I'd leave as a last resort, is to reinstall solc, but only into the project folder:

```
C:\Ethereum\Truffle\SimpleCoin>npm install solc@0.4.24
```

11.2.4 Deploying SimpleCoin onto a mock network client through migrations

A migration is a deployment script. As seen before, migration scripts are in the migrations directory. Replace the content of 2_deploy_contracts.js with the script shown in the following listing.

> **Listing 11.2   2_deploy_contracts.js: `SimpleCoin`'s migration script**

artifacts.require is similar to Node.js require, and you have to initialize it with the name of a contract (not a contract filename).

You have to set the module.exports property to a function that accepts a deployer object, which is the component performing deployment tasks.

```
var SimpleCoin = artifacts.require("SimpleCoin")    ◁

module.exports = function(deployer) {    ◁
    deployer.deploy(SimpleCoin, 10000);    ◁
};
```

SimpleCoin gets deployed with an initial supply of 10,000 tokens.

During the first migration execution, you also have to deploy the `Migrations` contract. This contract gets deployed through its own migration script, shown in the following listing and contained in this file: C\Ethereum\Truffle\SimpleCoin\migrations\1_initial_migration.js.

> **Listing 11.3   1_initial_migration.js: `Migrations`' migration script**

```
var Migrations = artifacts.require("Migrations")

module.exports = function(deployer) {
    deployer.deploy(Migrations);
};
```

Once you've placed the migration scripts in the migrations directory, open a separate OS shell and move to the project folder:

```
C:\>cd Ethereum\Truffle\SimpleCoin
```

You'll be deploying `SimpleCoin` onto Ganache, the mock Ethereum client you already saw in chapters 8 and 10. Ganache is part of the Truffle framework. If you haven't already installed it, you can do so through npm, as usual:

```
C:\Ethereum\truffle\SimpleCoin>npm install -g ganache-cli@6.1.8
```

Then, after the installation is complete, start it up:

```
C:\>cd Ethereum\Truffle\SimpleCoin>ganache-cli
```

Make sure truffle.js (or truffle-config.js on Windows) is configured to point to Truffle Develop, as shown in the following listing, as opposed to pointing to a public test network. Amend its content as shown in the following listing.

Listing 11.4 truffle.js (or truffle-config.js): Truffle pointing to Test Develop

```
module.exports = {
  networks: {
    development: {
      host: "localhost",
      port: 8545,
      network_id: "*" // Match any network id
    }
  }
};
```

Deploying from a specific account

By default, your contracts will be deployed under Truffle from accounts[0], which is the default transaction sender. If you want the deployment transaction to be submitted from another account, you must specify the full address in the truffle.js file in the from property, as shown here:

```
module.exports = {
  networks: {
    development: {
      host: "localhost",
      port: 8545,
      from: "0xf17f52151ebef6c7334fad080c5704d77216b732",      ◁── This is Ganache's accounts[1], as shown on Ganache's startup screen.
      network_id: "*" // Match any network id
    }
  }
};
```

Go back to the previous console and run

```
C\Ethereum\Truffle\SimpleCoin>truffle migrate
```

Then you'll get output like this:

```
Using network 'development'.

Running migration: 1_initial_migration.js
  Deploying Migrations...
  ... 0x5823254426b34ec4220be899669e562d4691a72fa68fa1956a8eb87f9f431982
  Migrations: 0x8cdaf0cd259887258bc13a92c0a6da92698644c0
```

```
Saving successful migration to network...
   ... 0xd7bc86d31bee32fa3988f1c1eabce403a1b5d570340a3a9cdba53a472ee8c956
Saving artifacts...
Running migration: 2_deploy_contracts.js
  Deploying SimpleCoin...
   ... 0x21c4120f9f231ea5563c2a988de55440139ba087651d3d292f06ae65434580f7
   SimpleCoin: 0x345ca3e014aaf5dca488057592ee47305d9b3e10
Saving successful migration to network...
   ... 0xf36163615f41ef7ed8f4a8f192149a0bf633fe1a2398ce001bf44c43dc7bdda0
Saving artifacts...
```

This shows that `SimpleCoin` has been deployed successfully on Ganache's mock network. If you prefer to run the mock network client and Truffle commands from within the same OS shell, you can use a separate console called Truffle Develop. Have a look at the sidebar if you want to learn more. For the rest of the book, you'll keep using two separate consoles: one to run Ganache and the other to launch Truffle commands.

Executing Truffle commands from Truffle Develop's console

You can start Truffle Develop from the Truffle project folder, as follows:

```
C\Ethereum\Truffle\SimpleCoin>truffle develop
```

This will start a mock network client similar to Ganache (and TestRPC), but on port 9545, which means, if you have Ganache running, you don't need to shut it down.

Truffle Develop startup screen

(continued)

But if you want to use Truffle Develop, you need to change the truffle.js configuration to point to port 9545:

```
module.exports = {
  networks: {
    development: {
      host: "localhost",
      port: 9545,
      network_id: "*" // Match any network id
    }
  }
};
```

Now you'll be able to run Truffle commands, such as `migrate`, directly from the Truffle Develop console:

```
Truffle(develop)>migrate
```

You'll see exactly the same output as before.

11.2.5 *Deploying SimpleCoin onto a public test or production network*

Although in this chapter you'll be deploying contracts only on Ganache (or TestRPC), at some point you might want to deploy on the public test network or production network. If so, you must modify your truffle.js (or truffle-config.js) file and include configurations for a test network and a live network, as follows:

```
module.exports = {
  networks: {
    development: {
      host: "localhost",
      port: 8545,
      network_id: "*"
    },
    live: {
      host: "localhost",
      port: 80,
      network_id: 1,
    },
    ropsten: {
      host: "localhost",
      port: 80,
      network_id: 3,
    }
}};
```

This configuration assumes you're running a local geth node (the host is pointing to localhost), and the default Web 3 provider will be instantiated by Truffle as

```
new Web3.providers.HttpProvider("http://<host>:<port>")
```

But if you decide to use a different provider, for instance an HDWalletProvider pointing to a Ropsten Infura network, you must configure it explicitly with the provider property:

```
networks: {
  ...
  ropsten: {
    provider: new HDWalletProvider(mnemonic, "https://ropsten.infura.io/"),
    network_id: '3',
  },
  ...
```

Also, bear in mind, when deploying on a public network, you might want to specify other settings, such as the gas limit, the gas price, and the account the contract should be deployed through. If so, you can add relevant configuration properties as described in table 11.3, but I invite you to consult the official documentation before proceeding further: http://mng.bz/mmgy.

Table 11.3   The truffle.js configuration properties

Property	Purpose
`gas:`	Gas limit (default = 4712388)
`gasPrice:`	Gas price (default = 100,000,000,000 wei)
`from:`	Sender address of the deployment transaction (and contract owner)
`provider:`	The default is web3, as explained previously.

Once you've configured truffle.js (or truffle-config.js) appropriately, you can kick a deployment to the Ropsten network as follows:

```
C:\Ethereum\Truffle\SimpleCoin>truffle migrate --network ropsten
```

And, as you might have guessed, you'd deploy to MAINNET as follows:

```
C:\Ethereum\Truffle\SimpleCoin>truffle migrate --network live
```

11.2.6 *Testing SimpleCoin*

Truffle supports *clean-room testing*, which means that if a contract has been deployed on Ganache, its state will get reinitialized at the beginning of each test file being processed. If the contract has been deployed on a public network, the migrations will get re-executed at the start of each test file being processed, effectively redeploying the contract from scratch before the execution of the tests. In general, during development it's preferable to run unit tests against Test Develop, as they run up to 90% faster. It's advisable to run the tests on a private network, and ultimately on a public network, in later stages of the development cycle to make sure you've tested application aspects of communicating with a real network.

It's possible to write two different classes of tests with Truffle:

- *Solidity tests*—Test the contract logic from test contracts
- *JavaScript tests*—Test the contract from external Web3.js calls, which go through the same infrastructure as real calls

You must place all test scripts, whether written in Solidity or JavaScript, in the test directory of the Truffle project. We'll focus almost entirely on JavaScript tests, as Solidity tests are meant to test contract-to-contract interaction, which is a more advanced topic outside the scope of this book. But I'll give you some of the basics of working with Solidity tests.

11.2.7 Writing Solidity tests

You implement Solidity tests through custom test contracts whose code you have to place in .sol files within the project test directory. Solidity tests must be able to run against

- the assertion library that Truffle provides
- any other assertion library
- Ganache (or TestRPC)
- any Ethereum client (not only geth) and type of network (both private and public)

You structure a Solidity test contract the way TestSimpleCoin.sol does, as shown in listing 11.5. You must follow these guidelines and conventions:

- You must import an assertion library to check for equality, inequality, and emptiness. The default assertion library that Truffle provides is Truffle/Assert.sol.
- You must import the Truffle/DeployedAddresses.sol library so the test runner can access the addresses of contracts deployed through migrations. The DeployedAddresses library is recompiled each time the test contract is run, to guarantee clean-room testing.
- You must import the contract under test.
- The name of a test contract must start with Test (uppercase T) so the test runner can identify it easily.
- The name of a test function must start with test (lowercase t).
- A test function must return a Boolean value. Generally, this is returned through an assertion function such as `Assert.equal()`.

Listing 11.5 TestSimpleCoin.sol test contract

```
pragma solidity ^0.4.2;

import "Truffle/Assert.sol";              ◁──── Imports assert library
import "Truffle/DeployedAddresses.sol";   ◁──── Imports DeployedAddresses contract
import "../contracts/SimpleCoin.sol";     ◁──── Imports contract being tested: SimpleCoin
```

```
contract TestSimpleCoin {          ◀——— Testing contract

  function testInitialBalanceUsingDeployedContract() public {
    SimpleCoin simpleCoin = SimpleCoin(
      DeployedAddresses.SimpleCoin());    ◀─┐ SimpleCoin instance at
                                            │ the deployed address
    uint expected = 10000;

    Assert.equal(simpleCoin.coinBalance(tx.origin), expected,
      "Owner should have 10000 SimpleCoin initially");    ◀─┐ Verifies test
  }                                                         │ assumptions
}
```

First, place TestSimpleCoin.sol in the test folder and make sure Test Develop (or TestRPC) is still running. (If it's not running, restart it in a separate console.) You can then run Solidity tests by executing this command:

```
C:\Ethereum\Truffle\SimpleCoin>truffle test
```

You'll get output similar to this:

```
Using network 'development'.

Compiling .\contracts\SimpleCoin.sol...
Compiling .\test\TestSimpleCoin.sol...
Compiling Truffle/Assert.sol...
Compiling Truffle/DeployedAddresses.sol...

  TestSimpleCoin
    √ testInitialBalanceUsingDeployedContract (48ms)


  1 passing (530ms)
```

> **WARNING** Depending on the version of your solc compiler, you might get some warnings, especially around code raising events.

As I mentioned earlier, contract-to-contract testing is an advanced topic outside of the scope of this book, so I won't cover Solidity tests further. The next section will be dedicated entirely to JavaScript tests under Truffle.

11.2.8 Writing JavaScript tests

Do you remember the effort you put into writing tests in Mocha? It wasn't wasted: Truffle supports Mocha JavaScript testing, but with deeper integration with Ethereum. This means you

- won't have to decorate your test files with require statements for Ethereum libraries such as web3.js
- will be able to reference contracts that have been deployed through migrations, without having to compile them and deploy them manually

- will be able to reference accounts implicitly, without having to hardcode Ethereum addresses
- will be able to run the tests from within Truffle and integrate them within any continuous integration jobs that Truffle coordinates

To run in Truffle the JavaScript tests you wrote earlier in Mocha, you'll have to make minor changes, especially if you want to ensure they're executed in clean-room mode:

- Replace describe() calls with contract() calls, which ensures all contracts get redeployed onto the Ethereum client and tests are run with a *clean* contract state.
- Reference solidity contracts with artifacts.require(), as you did earlier when writing the migration scripts.
- Replace the callback section within the asynchronous deployment call you had on Mocha tests with a promise chain, where the first promise in the chain is a promise of a deployed contract, and the subsequent promises are chained through then() statements.

I'll demonstrate here how to rewrite some of the tests, so you can get a better idea of what the guidelines I've given mean. I'll start from the first test against SimpleCoin's constructor. For convenience, I've repeated the code from the original test you wrote in Mocha in the following listing, so you don't have to flip pages back and forth.

Listing 11.6 Original Mocha test on the constructor, verifying contract ownership

```
var assert = require('assert');

const source = fs.readFileSync('c:/Ethereum/mocha/SimpleCoin/SimpleCoin.sol',
    'utf8');
const compiledContract = solc.compile(source, 1);
const abi = compiledContract.contracts[':SimpleCoin'].interface;
const bytecode = '0x' + compiledContract.contracts[':SimpleCoin'].bytecode;
const gasEstimate = web3.eth.estimateGas({ data: bytecode }) + 100000;

const SimpleCoinContractFactory = web3.eth.contract(JSON.parse(abi));

describe('SimpleCoin', function() {
  this.timeout(5000);
  describe('SimpleCoin constructor', function() {
    it('Contract owner is sender', function(done) {
        //arrange
        let sender = web3.eth.accounts[1];
        let initialSupply = 10000;

        //act
        let simpleCoinInstance = SimpleCoinContractFactory.new(initialSupply,
    {
            from: sender, data: bytecode, gas: gasEstimate},
            function (e, contract){
            if (typeof contract.address !== 'undefined') {
                //assert
                assert.equal(contract.owner(), sender);
```

```
            done();
        }
        });
    });
});
});
```

Now create a file called testSimpleCoin.js and place it in the test directory. Fill it with the code shown in the following listing.

Listing 11.7 Truffle constructor test verifying contract ownership

```
const SimpleCoin = artifacts.require(        References SimpleCoin,
    "./SimpleCoin.sol");                     the code under test

contract('SimpleCoin', function(accounts) {   Name of the test suite
    contract('SimpleCoin.Constructor',
        function(accounts) {                  Name of the test section
        it("Contract owner is sender",
            function() {                      Gets a promise of a SimpleCoin contract instance
            return SimpleCoin.deployed()      deployed through the migration you set up earlier
            .then(function(instance) {
                return instance.owner();      Chains the promise of a SimpleCoin
            })                                instance to a new function
            .then(function(contractOwner) {
                assert.equal(contractOwner.valueOf(),   Chains the promise
                accounts[0],                            of the owner of the
                "accounts[0] wasn't the contract owner"); SimpleCoin instance
            });                                          to a new function
        });
    });
});
```

Description of the single test
Gets a promise of the owner of the SimpleCoin instance
Error message to display in case of test failure
The final function executed in the promise chain performs the test assertion.

NOTE As I mentioned in the deployment section, by default, contracts are deployed under Truffle from accounts[0]. That's why in the test you're comparing the address of the contract owner, contractOwner.valueOf(), with accounts[0].

You've surely noticed a few differences between Mocha and Truffle tests, such as those listed in table 11.4.

Table 11.4 Differences between Mocha and Truffle tests

Mocha tests	Truffle tests
Mocha's test script starts with a relatively long setup, during which we go through all the necessary low-level steps required for deploying SimpleCoin.	Truffle's test has hardly any setup at all and immediately references a deployed instance of SimpleCoin (through the migration framework).
Mocha's test execution is based on a callback associated with the deployment of a SimpleCoin instance.	Truffle's test execution is based on a chain of promises starting with a promise of a deployed SimpleCoin instance.

Table 11.4   Differences between Mocha and Truffle tests *(continued)*

Mocha tests	Truffle tests
Once you get ahold of a `SimpleCoin` instance (or a promise of it), Mocha's test code seems shorter and to the point.	After getting a `SimpleCoin` instance, Truffle's code goes through various steps to get ahold of the contract owner for subsequently comparing it with the expected one.

In summary, thanks to Truffle's migration framework, tests don't need much setup to access an instance of `SimpleCoin`. On the other hand, after referencing a `SimpleCoin` instance, Mocha's test seems less verbose than Truffle's.

Let's run the test! When you re-execute the Truffle test command, both Solidity and JavaScript tests will be run, and you'll get output similar to this:

```
C:\Ethereum\Truffle\SimpleCoin>Truffle test
Using network 'development'.

Compiling .\contracts\SimpleCoin.sol...
Compiling .\test\TestSimpleCoin.sol...
Compiling Truffle/Assert.sol...
Compiling Truffle/DeployedAddresses.sol...

  TestSimpleCoin
    √ testInitialBalanceUsingDeployedContract (49ms)

  Contract: SimpleCoin
    Contract: SimpleCoin.Constructor
      √ Contract owner is sender

  2 passing (1s)
```

You can rewrite the constructor test that verifies the owner balance is the initial supply. Add the following `it()` block in testSimpleCoin.js:

```
it("Contract owner balance is equal to initialSupply", function() {
    return SimpleCoin.deployed()
    .then(function(instance) {
        return instance.coinBalance(accounts[0]);
    }).then(function(contractOwnerBalance) {
        assert.equal(contractOwnerBalance.valueOf(),
            10000,
            "the contract owner balance is not equal to the full supply of
➥ 10000");
    });
});
```

NOTE As you might remember, `SimpleCoin`'s migration script (named 2_deploy_contracts.js and shown in listing 11.2) sets the initial supply to 10,000. That's why the contract owner balance is being compared to 10,000.

Rerun the tests:

```
C:\Ethereum\Truffle\SimpleCoin>Truffle test

  TestSimpleCoin
    √ testInitialBalanceUsingDeployedContract (49ms)

  Contract: SimpleCoin
    Contract: SimpleCoin.Constructor
      √ Contract owner is sender
      √ Contract owner balance is equal to initialSupply

  3 passing (1s)
```

IMPROVING JAVASCRIPT TESTS WITH AWAIT/ASYNC

In the file named testSimpleCoin_ALL_sync.js provided on the book website, you can find a full Truffle test suite equivalent to the test suite you wrote earlier in Mocha. I encourage you to go through the tests in detail and compare the related tests.

You'll come to the conclusion that the ideal structure for a test is a sort of chimera combining the easy setup of Truffle tests and the simple and direct code within Mocha's callbacks. There is indeed a way to achieve this chimera, and it's through JavaScript's async/await syntax.

> **NOTE** JavaScript's async/await syntax allows you to perform asynchronous processing through syntax that resembles that of synchronous programming—much simpler than that of typical asynchronous programming techniques such as callbacks or promise chains. If you're interested in learning more about JavaScript asynchronous coding, I recommend *Secrets of the JavaScript Ninja* by John Resig, et al, published by Manning.

> **WARNING** To take advantage of async/await, you must be running on Node.js version 8.0 or higher. I also advise you to install Truffle version 4.0 or higher.

Here's how the first constructor test, which verifies contract ownership, looks using async/await:

```
const SimpleCoin = artifacts.require("./SimpleCoin.sol");

contract('SimpleCoin', function(accounts) {
  contract('SimpleCoin.Constructor', function(accounts) {
    it("Contract owner is sender", async function() {

      let simpleCoinInstance =
        await SimpleCoin.deployed();          ⟵┘ Gets the deployed
                                                  instance of SimpleCoin
      let contractOwner =
        await simpleCoinInstance.owner();       ⟵┘ Gets the contract owner

      assert.equal(contractOwner.valueOf(),               Verifies the
        accounts[0],                                       contract owner is
        "accounts[0] wasn't the contract owner");  ⟵┘     what you expect
```

```
            });
        });
    });
```

As you can see, by replacing the promise chain of the initial test version with statements based on async/await, the code looks as simple as a plain synchronous implementation would look. You've achieved exactly what you were looking for:

- Minimal (zero) SimpleCoin contract setup
- Simple test implementation

Place this test in a new file—for example, called testSimpleCoin_asyncawait.js. Put it in the test folder and run it as usual (removing testSimpleCoin.js and TestSimpleCoin.sol from the test folder before doing so, so they don't get executed):

```
C:\Ethereum\Truffle\SimpleCoin>truffle test
```

You will get this output:

```
Using network 'development'.

  Contract: SimpleCoin
    Contract: SimpleCoin.Constructor
      √ Contract owner is sender


  1 passing (53ms)
```

I challenge you to convert the second constructor test, which verifies the owner balance is the initial supply, from the earlier version based on a promise chain to async/await statements. Look away and write your implementation before comparing your solution with mine!

Have you finished? Does your test look similar to this?

```
it("Contract owner balance is equal to initialSupply", async function() {
    let simpleCoinInstance = await SimpleCoin.deployed();
    let contractOwnerBalance =
        await simpleCoinInstance.coinBalance(accounts[0]);

    assert.equal(contractOwnerBalance.valueOf(),
        10000,
        "the contract owner balance is not equal to the full supply of
➥ 10000");
});
```

If you're still unconvinced of the benefits of moving from tests based on promise chains to tests based on async/await, I'll show you a more dramatic comparison. Here's the chain-promise-based version of a test on a successful transfer() operation:

```
contract('SimpleCoin.transfer', function(accounts) {
  it("Succesful transfer: final sender and recipient balances are correct",
    function() {
```

```
//arrange
let sender = web3.eth.accounts[0];
let recipient = web3.eth.accounts[1];
let tokensToTransfer = 200;

const expectedSenderBalance = 9800;
const expectedRecipientBalance = 200;

//act
return SimpleCoin.deployed()        ←—— Gets a promise of a deployed
then(function(instance) {                 SimpleCoin instance
    simpleCoin = instance;
       return simpleCoin.transfer(recipient,
            tokensToTransfer, {from: sender});    ←—— Gets a promise of the
}).then(function() {                                    SimpleCoin instance
       return simpleCoin.coinBalance(sender);          after performing the
}).then(function(balance) {                             transfer operation
       sender_ending_balance = balance.toNumber();     you're testing
       return simpleCoin.coinBalance(recipient);   ←—— Assigns the sender
}).then(function(balance) {                              balance to a variable
       recipient_ending_balance = balance.toNumber();  ←—— Assigns the recipient
                                                             balance to a variable
    //assert
    assert.equal(sender_ending_balance,
        expectedSenderBalance,
            "Amount wasn't correctly taken from the sender");
    assert.equal(recipient_ending_balance,
        expectedRecipientBalance,
            "Amount wasn't correctly sent to the receiver");
    });
  });
});
```

Gets a promise of the sender balance

Gets a promise of the recipient balance

As you can see, having to reference balances through promises before assigning them to variables makes the test rather convoluted. Here's the equivalent async/await version of this test:

```
contract('SimpleCoin.transfer', function(accounts) {
  it("Succesful transfer: final sender and recipient balances are correct",
➥ async function() {
    //arrange
    let sender = web3.eth.accounts[0];
    let recipient = web3.eth.accounts[1];
    let tokensToTransfer = 200;

    const expectedSenderBalance = 9800;
    const expectedRecipientBalance = 200;

    let simpleCoinInstance = await SimpleCoin.deployed();

    //act
    await simpleCoinInstance.transfer(recipient,
        tokensToTransfer, {from: sender});
    let sender_ending_balance =
        await simpleCoinInstance.coinBalance(sender);
```

```
    let recipient_ending_balance =
        await simpleCoinInstance.coinBalance(recipient);

    //assert
    assert.equal(sender_ending_balance.valueOf(),
        expectedSenderBalance,
        "Amount wasn't correctly taken from the sender");
    assert.equal(recipient_ending_balance.valueOf(),
        expectedRecipientBalance,
        "Amount wasn't correctly sent to the receiver");

    });
});
```

Isn't this clearer? I'm so confident you can understand this version of the test without any explanation that I decided I didn't need to annotate the code at all. If you have Node.js 8 (or higher) installed, you should definitely consider writing your tests with async/await rather than promise chains. I encourage you to try and convert all the chain-promise-based Truffle tests you find in the testSimpleCoin_ALL_sync.js file to equivalent async/await ones.

Summary

- When writing a Mocha test, you must typically provide fairly complicated initialization code at the top of your script to deploy your contract through various steps, including solc compilation. Your test is placed in the callback associated with the contract deployment call.
- Truffle is a contract development environment that simplifies contract compilation, deployment, and testing.
- Truffle performs contract deployment through migrations, based on simple configuration.
- When writing a Truffle test, you don't need to provide any initialization code for contract compilation and deployment, but you must write tests with asynchronous code based on a promise chain, which might not be as readable as equivalent Mocha tests.
- A way to make Truffle tests much more readable is to write them using async/await. But to do so, you must upgrade to Node.js 8 or higher.

Putting it all together:
Building a complete
voting Dapp

12

This chapter covers

- Designing and implementing a voting contract showcasing most Solidity features, such as modifiers and events
- Integrating the voting contract in Truffle, for integrated compilation, testing, and deployment
- Implementing an asynchronous web UI seamlessly connected to the contract through the truffle-contract JavaScript library
- Deploying onto the public test network from Truffle

In the previous chapter, you started to enjoy the benefits of using Truffle to improve the development lifecycle:

- Contract compilation became as easy as executing a simple `truffle compile` command. You didn't have to instruct the solc compiler explicitly to push its output to specific files to be reused later for deployment.

- Contract deployment became much easier than you were used to, thanks to Truffle's migrations functionality based on minimalistic configuration. Truffle did all the hard work of packaging the compilation output and feeding the contract ABI and bytecode to the deployment transaction behind the curtains. No more manual copying and pasting of long text!
- Also, testing became much simpler than when you performed it through Mocha. You didn't need complicated initialization to deploy the contract at each test, and you could keep testing logic by writing asynchronous JavaScript based on async/await.

I decided to introduce Truffle through `SimpleCoin` to focus exclusively on the functionality of the tool and avoid being distracted by the presentation of new concepts a new contract would have introduced. Also, by having you rewrite in Truffle the same `SimpleCoin` unit tests you had written in Mocha, I could compare more explicitly the advantages and disadvantages of one framework versus the other.

In this chapter, we'll go one step further. Now that you're relatively familiar with Truffle, I believe you're ready to take advantage of this framework to build an entirely new Dapp from scratch, including a smart contract, some unit tests, and a web UI. We'll start gently: I'll give you some background on what functionality the voting contract should provide, and I'll help you design and implement it. After you've completed the contract, I'll guide you through the usual steps of deploying it within the development environment and unit testing it. Then I'll show how you can simplify the web UI of an Ethereum Dapp by importing the ABI from a file generated during Truffle compilation—no more copying and pasting ABI and addresses here either!

This chapter is long, but I hope to keep you engaged until the end, especially if you're eager to learn more. After completing this chapter, you'll know most of the tool set you need to develop a Dapp from start to end. Now it's time to start!

12.1 Defining the requirements of a voting Dapp

A voting Dapp can be simple or complex, depending on the requirements of the elections you wish to support. Voting can be on a small number of preselected proposals (or candidates), or on a potentially large number of proposals suggested dynamically by the voters themselves. The electorate can be made up of a small number of individuals, all known to the organization coordinating the elections, or it can include all the residents of a certain administrative area or of an entire country. In the latter case, a registration process might be necessary to run the election process efficiently and transparently. The outcome might be decided by simple majority: the proposal that gets more votes wins. Or it might require a qualified majority (or quorum): a proposal is passed only if it gets a minimum predefined percentage of votes. The ballot can be secret or open. The vote can be delegated to other individuals or kept exclusively direct. This is only a subset of the options and variants a voting process can include. With technology, the voting process can become even more sophisticated. For example, a vote could be split by the voter into fractions, such that each is assigned to a different proposal, or it could be split similarly, but with each fraction delegated to a different individual.

You might be ambitious and try to design an ultrageneric application that could cater to all possibilities. For our purposes, and to keep the length of this chapter reasonable, I'll constraint the voting application to a limited set of requirements:

- You'll write the Voting Dapp within a small organization. Voters, all of whom the organization knows, are white-listed through their Ethereum address, can submit new proposals during a proposal registration session, and can vote on the proposals during the voting session.
- The vote isn't secret; every voter is able to see other people's votes.
- The winner is determined by simple majority; the proposal that gets more votes wins.

As you might remember from chapter 1, even such a simple voting Dapp has a major advantage over a centralized one: a Dapp decentralizes vote processing and storing and consequently makes tampering much less likely than if voting was running through a centralized application.

Figure 12.1 shows the workflow of the entire voting process. Let's walk quickly through it:

1 The voting administrator registers a *white list* of voters identified by their Ethereum addresses.
2 The voting administrator starts the proposal registration session.
3 Registered voters are entitled to register their proposals while the registration session is active.
4 The voting administrator ends the proposal registration session.
5 The voting administrator starts the voting session.
6 Registered voters cast their votes for their favorite proposals.
7 The voting administrator ends the voting session.
8 The voting administrator tallies the votes.
9 Anyone can check the final details of the winning proposal.

If you're eager to develop a more generic voting Dapp, at the end of the chapter I'll give you a few pointers to help you step into cutting-edge e-voting territory. For now, though, we'll stick with the constraints I outlined.

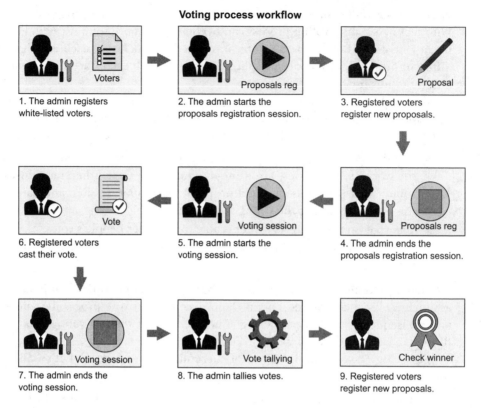

Figure 12.1   The workflow of the voting process. Some steps are performed by the administrator, other steps by voters.

12.2   *The development plan*

Before you start to get your hands dirty, I'll give you an idea of all the steps you'll be going through to build your voting Dapp. You can get a more visual idea of the development cycle in figure 12.2, but here's a list of the steps:

1 Create a new Truffle project.
2 Design and implement SimpleVoting, the voting contract, according to the initial requirements.
3 Compile and deploy SimpleVoting on Ganache.
4 Write and execute unit tests for SimpleVoting.
5 Create a web UI that connects to the voting contract by reading the ABI and contract address from Truffle's output.
6 Run the voting workflow through the web UI.
7 Deploy the Dapp onto a public test network.

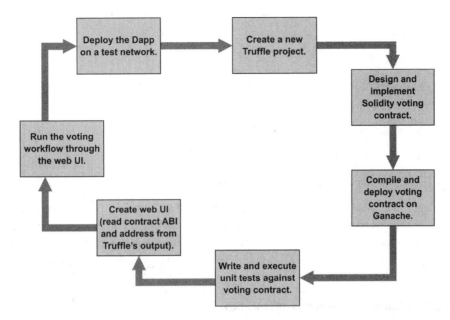

Figure 12.2   The Dapp development plan, including all the steps, from creation of a Truffle project to final deployment onto a public test network

12.3   *Starting the Truffle project*

Enough talking—it's time to get started! Create a new directory within your Ethereum project folder—C:\Ethereum\truffle\SimpleVoting—then open an OS shell and initialize a Truffle project:

```
C:\Ethereum\truffle\SimpleVoting>truffle init
```

As usual, you should get output like that shown in the screenshot in figure 12.3.

```
C:\Ethereum\truffle\SimpleVoting>truffle init
Downloading...
Unpacking...
Setting up...
Unbox successful. Sweet!

Commands:

  Compile:        truffle compile
  Migrate:        truffle migrate
  Test contracts: truffle test

C:\Ethereum\truffle\SimpleVoting>_
```

Figure 12.3   Truffle project initialization

If you're working on Windows, remember to delete truffle.js; otherwise, delete truffle-config.js. Initially, you'll be deploying on Ganache, as you did in the previous chapter, so make sure truffle.js (or truffle-config.js) is configured as follows:

```
module.exports = {
  networks: {
    development: {
      host: "localhost",
      port: 8545,
      network_id: "*" // Match any network id
    }
  }
};
```

Now you're ready to create the voting contract!

12.4   Implementing the voting contract

I believe you could attempt to implement the contract by yourself, based on the requirements outlined earlier. Why don't you give it a go and then come back here later?

Are you already back? Read on. Arguably, the most important entities involved in an election are the proposal, the voter, and the voting workflow. Let's look at how to model them.

12.4.1   *Modeling proposal, voter, and workflow*

A registered voter creates a proposal and adds it dynamically to the list of existing proposals during a proposal registration session. The `Proposal` type should expose a (`string`) description that its author provides and the (`uint`) number of votes cast against it. You don't want to capture the author because they might want to remain anonymous:

```
struct Proposal {
    string description;
    uint voteCount;
}
```

What data would you like to capture about a voter? How about whether the voter has been registered (only white-listed accounts will be allowed to vote), whether they've already voted (to prevent double voting), and, if they've voted, which proposal they've voted for? Try this:

```
struct Voter {
    bool isRegistered;
    bool hasVoted;
    uint votedProposalId;
}
```

You can easily represent the voting workflow I described earlier in this section with the following enumeration:

```
enum WorkflowStatus {
    RegisteringVoters,
    ProposalsRegistrationStarted,
    ProposalsRegistrationEnded,
    VotingSessionStarted,
```

```
        VotingSessionEnded,
        VotesTallied
    }
```

12.4.2 Contract state

As for most contracts, you're interested in assigning a management role to the Ethereum address that submits the contract deployment transaction. This will become (at construction) the voting administrator:

```
address public administrator;
```

Two main processes take place from the start of the election: the proposal registration session, during which any registered voter is entitled to submit a proposal, and the voting session, which starts immediately afterwards. The voting administrator is responsible for starting and ending each session, presumably on the basis of an agreed start and end time. You'll capture the status of the voting workflow with this state variable:

```
WorkflowStatus public workflowStatus;
```

Obviously, the most important state of the contract has to do with voters and proposals:

1 A Voter mapping associates the voter address, which is their identifier, with the voter object:

```
mapping(address => Voter) public voters;
```

2 A Proposal array captures the registered proposals

```
Proposal[] public proposals;
```

The proposal ID's array index implicitly represents it.

Once votes have been tallied, you want to capture the ID of the winning proposal:

```
uint private winningProposalId;
```

This state variable shouldn't be exposed directly to the Dapp users because its value should be revealed only after votes have been tallied, through getter functions.

12.4.3 Function modifiers

You need the state variables you've defined to determine the identity of a function caller and the status of the voting workflow. As you know, you can create function modifiers to check the conditions under which a function should be called. You could create a function modifier to check if the caller is the voting administrator

```
modifier onlyAdministrator() {
    require(msg.sender == administrator,
      "the caller of this function must be the administrator");
    _;
}
```

or they're a registered voter:

```
modifier onlyRegisteredVoter() {
    require(voters[msg.sender].isRegistered,
      "the caller of this function must be a registered voter");
    _;
  }
```

You could create other function modifiers to verify whether voters are being registered

```
modifier onlyDuringVotersRegistration() {
    require(workflowStatus == WorkflowStatus.RegisteringVoters,
      "this function can be called only before proposals registration has
 started");
    _;
  }
```

or whether the proposals registration session is active:

```
modifier onlyDuringProposalsRegistration() {
    require(workflowStatus == WorkflowStatus.ProposalsRegistrationStarted,
      "this function can be called only during proposals registration");
    _;
}
```

Similarly, you can implement modifiers to verify whether the proposals registration has ended (onlyAfterProposalsRegistration), whether the voting session is active (onlyDuringVotingSession) or has ended (onlyAfterVotingSession), or whether vote tallying has already taken place (onlyAfterVotesTallied). You'll find all of these modifiers useful for simplifying the logic of the functions you'll implement shortly.

12.4.4 Events

Because blockchain operations take a few seconds to complete from the moment they're triggered, it's useful from a user point of view to get notified as soon as their execution has taken place. Therefore, at the end of each action, the voting contract will publish an event that alters the state of the contract. This will also happen at every workflow status change so that clients, such as a UI, can update their screens accordingly. The contract will publish these events:

```
event VoterRegisteredEvent (address voterAddress);
event ProposalsRegistrationStartedEvent ();
event ProposalsRegistrationEndedEvent ();
event ProposalRegisteredEvent(uint proposalId);
event VotingSessionStartedEvent ();
event VotingSessionEndedEvent ();
event VotedEvent (address voter, uint proposalId);
event VotesTalliedEvent ();

event WorkflowStatusChangeEvent (
    WorkflowStatus previousStatus,
    WorkflowStatus newStatus
);
```

12.4.5 *Constructor*

At contract construction, you should identify the sender of the contract transaction and make them the voting administrator. You should also set the initial workflow status:

```
constructor() public {
    administrator = msg.sender;
    workflowStatus = WorkflowStatus.RegisteringVoters;
}
```

12.4.6 *Functions*

If you look back at the workflow of the voting process in figure 12.1, you'll see that the voting administrator is responsible for registering voters:

```
function registerVoter(address _voterAddress)
    public onlyAdministrator onlyDuringVotersRegistration {

    require(!voters[_voterAddress].isRegistered,
      "the voter is already registered");

    voters[_voterAddress].isRegistered = true;
    voters[_voterAddress].hasVoted = false;
    voters[_voterAddress].votedProposalId = 0;

    emit VoterRegisteredEvent(_voterAddress);
}
```

The voting administrator is also responsible for starting and ending the proposal registration session (and, similarly, starting and ending the voting session):

```
function startProposalsRegistration()
    public onlyAdministrator onlyDuringVotersRegistration {
    workflowStatus = WorkflowStatus.ProposalsRegistrationStarted;

    emit ProposalsRegistrationStartedEvent();
    emit WorkflowStatusChangeEvent(
        WorkflowStatus.RegisteringVoters, workflowStatus);
}

function endProposalsRegistration()
    public onlyAdministrator onlyDuringProposalsRegistration {
    workflowStatus = WorkflowStatus.ProposalsRegistrationEnded;

    emit ProposalsRegistrationEndedEvent();
    emit WorkflowStatusChangeEvent(
        WorkflowStatus.ProposalsRegistrationStarted, workflowStatus);
}
```

As you can see, function modifiers you defined earlier have simplified the code so much that it has been reduced to only one line and the publishing of a couple of events.

While the proposal registration session is active, registered voters submit proposals with this function:

```
function registerProposal(string proposalDescription)
    public onlyRegisteredVoter
       onlyDuringProposalsRegistration {          ◄─────┐  Checks if the caller is a registered
    proposals.push(Proposal({               ◄────────┐ │  user and whether the proposal
        description: proposalDescription,            │ │  registration session is active
        voteCount: 0                                 │ │
    }));                                             │ │  Creates the proposal and adds it
                                                     │ │  to the proposals array
    emit ProposalRegisteredEvent(proposals.length - 1);
}
```

Also in this case, function modifiers perform the hard work of checking whether the caller is a registered voter and whether the proposal registration session is active. The logic of the function itself is minimal: it creates a new proposal with the provided description and adds it to the proposals array.

Once the voting session has been started, a registered voter can cast their vote with this function:

```
function vote(uint proposalId)                      Checks that the caller is a
    onlyRegisteredVoter                             registered voter and the
    onlyDuringVotingSession public {    ◄───┐      voting session is open
    require(!voters[msg.sender].hasVoted,
      "the caller has already voted");

    voters[msg.sender].hasVoted = true;            Flags that the
    voters[msg.sender].votedProposalId = proposalId;   caller has voted and
                                                       records their vote

    proposals[proposalId].voteCount += 1;  ◄───┐ Assigns the vote to the chosen proposal.
                                                 (Note that Ethereum has no concurrency
    emit VotedEvent(msg.sender, proposalId);     issue because transactions are processed
}                                                sequentially on the miner's EVM when a
                                                 new block is being created.)
```

Checks that the caller hasn't voted yet

After the administrator has ended the voting session, they can tally the vote with the following function, which finds the ID of the winning proposal and assigns it to the corresponding state variable you defined earlier:

```
function tallyVotes()
    onlyAdministrator                    Verifies the administrator has called the
    onlyAfterVotingSession               function only after the voting session has
    onlyBeforeVotesTallied public {  ◄── ended and it hasn't already been called
    uint winningVoteCount = 0;
    uint winningProposalIndex = 0;
                                                   Iterates over the proposals
                                                   to find the one with the
    for (uint i = 0; i < proposals.length; i++) {  ◄── higher vote count
        if (proposals[i].voteCount > winningVoteCount) {
            winningVoteCount = proposals[i].voteCount;
            winningProposalIndex = i;
        }                                      Assigns the array index of
    }                                          the winning proposal to the
                                               corresponding state variable
    winningProposalId = winningProposalIndex;  ◄──┐
    workflowStatus = WorkflowStatus.VotesTallied;  ◄── Flags votes that
                                                       have been tallied
```

Records the array index of the winning proposal so far

```
    emit VotesTalliedEvent();
    emit WorkflowStatusChangeEvent(
        WorkflowStatus.VotingSessionEnded, workflowStatus); ◁
}
```

It's convenient to create a set of views—read-only functions that return a slice of the current contract state—for consumption by UI and other clients. For example, during and after the proposal registration session, it would be possible to check the number of proposals and their descriptions with these read-only functions:

```
function getProposalsNumber() public view
    returns (uint) {
        return proposals.length;
}

function getProposalDescription(uint index) public view
    returns (string) {
        return proposals[index].description;
}
```

After votes have been tallied, it would be possible to retrieve the final results (winning proposal ID, description, and vote count) through the following functions:

```
function getWinningProposalId() onlyAfterVotesTallied
    public view
        returns (uint) {
        return winningProposalId;
}

function getWinningProposalDescription() onlyAfterVotesTallied
    public view
        returns (string) {
        return proposals[winningProposalId].description;
}

function getWinningProposalVoteCounts() onlyAfterVotesTallied
    public view
        returns (uint) {
        return proposals[winningProposalId].voteCount;
}
```

Anyone should be entitled to check the winning proposal, not only the administrator or voters, so no modifiers should be present.

It's also convenient to write other functions to check the identity of the caller. For example, you could write a function that checks whether an address is a registered voter

```
function isRegisteredVoter(address _voterAddress) public view
    returns (bool) {
    return voters[_voterAddress].isRegistered;
}
```

or the administrator:

```
function isAdministrator(address _address) public view
    returns (bool){
    return _address == administrator;
}
```

And a view of the current voting workflow status could also be useful:

```
function getWorkflowStatus() public view
    returns (WorkflowStatus) {
    return workflowStatus;
}
```

12.4.7 The full voting contract

You can see the full contract in listing D.1 in appendix D. I encourage you to enter it in Remix and play with it before placing it under Truffle.

12.5 Compiling and deploying SimpleVoting

Place the code in listing D.1 (from the book website) in a file named SimpleVoting.sol in the following folder: C:\Ethereum\truffle\SimpleVoting\contracts. Now, go to the migrations folder: C:\Ethereum\truffle\SimpleVoting\migrations. Create a new file called 2_deploy_contracts.js and place in it the contents of the following listing, which I've adapted from the migration configuration you wrote earlier for SimpleCoin.

> **Listing 12.1   2_deploy_contracts.js: migration configuration for SimpleVoting**

```
var SimpleVoting = artifacts.require("SimpleVoting");

module.exports = function(deployer) {
  deployer.deploy(SimpleVoting);
};
```

You can now kick the compilation

```
C:\Ethereum\Truffle\SimpleVoting>truffle compile
```

and you'll see output similar to this:

```
Compiling .\contracts\SimpleVoting.sol...
Writing artifacts to .\build\contracts
```

> **NOTE**   If you're experiencing compilation issues, have a look at chapter 11, section 11.2.3, "Troubleshooting truffle compile errors."

After a successful compilation, start up Ganache in a new OS console:

```
C:\Ethereum\truffle\SimpleVoting>ganache-cli
```

Then go back to the OS console you were using to execute Truffle commands and perform a migration:

```
C:\Ethereum\truffle\SimpleVoting>truffle migrate
```

You'll see the following output:

```
Using network 'development'.

Running migration: 1_initial_migration.js
  Deploying Migrations...
  ... 0xf3ab00eef045a34e2208f6f4dfa218950f7d1a0d30f3f32982febdff55db6a92
  Migrations: 0x2f90a477697c9a0144acf862ab7dd98372dd7b33
Saving successful migration to network...
  ... 0x7af1903172cab2baac3c05f7ff721c8c54aa0f9f34ad64c3a26495bb591c36c9
Saving artifacts...
Running migration: 2_deploy_contracts.js
  Deploying SimpleVoting...
  ... 0x37ecb76d6cd6051c5d122df53db0063d1336e5b3298150b50d62e8ae845e9bbb
  SimpleVoting: 0xaf18e4e373b90709cc08a231ce24015a0da4f8cc
Saving successful migration to network...
  ... 0x19ac99d629c4053bf699c34c83c47288666afe6fa8994b90438d0e78ec204c96
Saving artifacts...
```

12.6 *Writing unit tests*

By now, you should know how to write unit tests in Truffle. Bear in mind, though, that SimpleVoting's workflow is more complex than SimpleCoin's, as described in section 12.1. For example, actions such as registering a proposal or voting can happen only after the administrator has opened the related session, so you should aim some of your tests at verifying that these constraints are being respected. Table 12.1 shows a small sample of what your tests should cover.

Table 12.1 Sample of unit tests you should cover against SimpleVoting

Test case
Only the administrator can register voters.
You aren't allowed to register the same voter twice.
Only the administrator can start the proposal registration session.
Only the administrator can end the proposal registration session, after starting it.
Only a registered voter can submit a proposal.
A registered voter can submit a proposal only after the administrator has started the proposal registration session.
A registered voter can't vote before the voting session has started.

Each of these test cases generally requires that you write at least a *negative test* that proves an exception is thrown if the underlying conditions aren't met, and a *positive test* that verifies the functionality works as expected when all constraints have been met. As an example, if you want to test that "Only the administrator can end the proposal registration session, after starting it," you should write these tests (with the code shown in listing 12.2):

- A negative test that verifies an exception is thrown if a voter other than the administrator tries to end the proposal registration session
- A negative test that verifies the administrator isn't allowed to end the proposal registration session if it hasn't started yet
- A positive test that verifies the administrator can successfully end the proposal registration session after it has started

Listing 12.2   testSimpleVoting.js: testing ending the proposal registration session

```
const SimpleVoting = artifacts.require("./SimpleVoting.sol");

contract('SimpleVoting', function(accounts) {
  contract('SimpleVoting.endProposalRegistration -
    onlyAdministrator modifier ',
    function(accounts) {
    it("The voting administrator should be able to end the proposal
 registration session only after it has started",
        async function() {                          ⟵——— First negative test
        //arrange
        let simpleVotingInstance = await SimpleVoting.deployed();
        let votingAdministrator = await simpleVotingInstance.administrator();

        let nonVotingAdministrator = web3.eth.accounts[1];

        try {
            //act
            await simpleVotingInstance.endProposalsRegistration(
              {from: nonVotingAdministrator});
            assert.isTrue(false);           ⟵——┐  If this line is reached, it means
        }                                         no exception has been thrown,
        catch(e) {                                and the test should fail.
            //assert
            assert.isTrue(votingAdministrator != nonVotingAdministrator);
            assert.equal(e, "Error: VM Exception while processing
 transaction: revert - the caller of this function
 must be the administrator");     ⟵——┐  The test passes if the
        }                                    expected exception
    });                                      has been thrown.
  });

  contract('SimpleVoting.endProposalRegistration -
    onlyDuringProposalsRegistration modifier',
    function(accounts) {
    it("An account that is not the voting administrator must not be able
 to end the proposal registration session",
        async function() {           ⟵——┐
        //arrange                         Second negative test
```

```
let simpleVotingInstance = await SimpleVoting.deployed();
let votingAdministrator = await simpleVotingInstance.administrator();


try {
  //act
    await simpleVotingInstance.endProposalsRegistration(
      {from: votingAdministrator});
    assert.isTrue(false);
}
catch(e) {
    //assert
    assert.equal(e, "Error: VM Exception while processing
transaction: revert - this function can be called only
during proposals registration");
    }
  });
});
```

If this line is reached, it means no exception has been thrown, and the test should fail.

The test passes if the expected exception has been thrown.

```
contract('SimpleVoting.endProposalRegistration - successful',
    function(accounts) {
    it("An account that is not the voting administrator must
not be able to end the proposal registration session",
      async function() {
      //arrange
      let simpleVotingInstance = await SimpleVoting.deployed();
      let votingAdministrator = await simpleVotingInstance.administrator();


      await simpleVotingInstance.startProposalsRegistration(
        {from: votingAdministrator});
      let workflowStatus = await simpleVotingInstance.getWorkflowStatus();
      let expectedWorkflowStatus = 1;


      assert.equal(workflowStatus.valueOf(), expectedWorkflowStatus,
        "The current workflow status does not correspond
to proposal registration session started");


      //act
      await simpleVotingInstance.endProposalsRegistration(
        {from: votingAdministrator});
      let newWorkflowStatus = await simpleVotingInstance
        .getWorkflowStatus();
      let newExpectedWorkflowStatus = 2;


      //assert
      assert.equal(newWorkflowStatus.valueOf(), newExpectedWorkflowStatus,
        "The current workflow status does not correspond
          to proposal registration session ended");
      });
    });
});
```

Positive test, verifying successful outcome

The test passes if the workflow status changes to the expected value.

If you want to run these unit tests, copy the code from listing 12.2 into a file called test-SimpleVoting.js in the test folder: C:\Ethereum\truffle\SimpleVoting\test. (I recommend you use the file from the book website.) Then you can execute them as usual

```
C:\Ethereum\truffle\SimpleVoting>truffle test
```

and you'll see familiar-looking output, as shown in the screenshot in figure 12.4.

```
C:\Ethereum\truffle\SimpleVoting>truffle test
Using network 'development'.


  Contract: SimpleVoting
    Contract: SimpleVoting.endProposalRegistration - onlyAdministrator modifier
      √ The voting administrator should be able to end the proposal registration session only after it has started

    Contract: SimpleVoting.endProposalRegistration - onlyDuringProposalsRegistration modifier
      √ An account that is not the voting administrator must not be able to end the proposal registration session (47ms)
    Contract: SimpleVoting.endProposalRegistration - successful
      √ An account that is not the voting administrator must not be able to end the proposal registration session

  3 passing (660ms)
```

Figure 12.4 Output of `SimpleVoting` unit tests on ending the proposal registration session

12.7 Creating a web UI

The voting website needs two web pages: one for the voting admin, and one for the voters. You'll create the website by going through these steps:

1 Prepare the dependencies, such as required JavaScript libraries and the smart-contract ABI json file.
2 Set up a web server so you can read local JSON files from your web page.
3 Write the admin page HTML.
4 Write the admin page JavaScript.
5 Write the voter page HTML.
6 Write the voter page JavaScript.
7 Run the admin and voter web pages.

12.7.1 Preparing the UI dependencies

First of all, open a new OS command shell and create a new directory for the voting web UI, say: C:\Ethereum\SimpleVotingWebUI. In case you didn't install Bower globally back in chapter 8, install it locally in this directory:

```
C:\Ethereum\SimpleVotingWebUI>npm install bower
```

Now import the Web3.js and JQuery libraries into the current directory, as you did in chapter 8. This time, you'll also install truffle-contract, a library that allows you to import the ABI and contract address seamlessly from the output of `truffle compile`:

```
C:\Ethereum\SimpleVotingWebUI>bower install web3#0.20.6

C:\Ethereum\SimpleVotingWebUI>bower install jquery

C:\Ethereum\SimpleVotingWebUI>bower install truffle-contract
```

As you know, Bower will download these libraries into respective directories within the bower_components folder:

```
bower_components
    |-- web3
    |-- jquery
    |-- truffle-contract
```

Now you'll be able to reference these local copies of Web3.js, jQuery, and truffle-contract from your JavaScript code.

To call the SimpleVoting contract from the web UI, you need to reference its ABI. Truffle generates this during contract compilation in a file called SimpleVoting.json, which is located in this folder: C:\Ethereum\truffle\SimpleVoting\build\contracts. Create a folder called contracts within your web UI directory: C:\Ethereum\SimpleVoting-WebUI\contracts. Now copy SimpleVoting.json into it.

You might remember that when you created SimpleCoin's web UI, you copied the ABI manually into the page JavaScript:

```
var abi = "[{\"constant\":false,\"inputs\":[{\"name\":\"_to…
var SimpleCoinFactory = web3.eth.contract(JSON.parse(abi));
var simpleCoinInstance = SimpleCoinFactory.at('0x773dc5fc8fc3e...');
```

Now you're trying to improve the process of building a web UI, and ideally you'd like to import the contract ABI directly from SimpleVoting.json. But web browsers don't allow you to read JSON files from your hard drive, so the following JavaScript will fail to execute when loaded directly from your hard drive:

```
window.onload = function() {
    $.getJSON("./contracts/SimpleVoting.json", function(json) {
        SimpleVoting = TruffleContract( json );
    ...
```

This same JavaScript will work as expected, though, if it's served to the browser through a web server. Bear in mind, Dapp web UIs are served through conventional web servers, so you must set one up to prepare for a realistic deployment.

> **WARNING** If you make modifications to your contract (for example, you add a new function), after recompiling it (with truffle compile) and remigrating it (with truffle migrate), you have to copy SimpleVoting.json again from Truffle's build\contracts folder to your web project contracts folder. If you shut down Ganache, when you restart it, the deployed instance of SimpleVoting won't be present, so it's best to force a new clean migration with truffle migrate --reset and then copy the SimpleVoting.json file across to your web project.

12.7.2   *Setting up a minimalistic web server with Node.js*

You can easily set up a simple web server, handling only static pages including plain HTML and JavaScript, using Connect and ServerStatic, two Node.js packages, as described in the Stack Overflow article "Using Node.js as a simple web server" (http://mng.bz/oNR2).

First of all, install them into your web UI directory:

```
C:\Ethereum\SimpleVotingWebUI>npm install connect serve-static
```

Then, create a file called webserver.js with this code in it:

```
var connect = require('connect');
var serveStatic = require('serve-static');
connect().use(serveStatic(__dirname)).listen(8080, function(){
    console.log('Web server running on 8080...');
});
```

Finally, start up the website:

```
C:\Ethereum\SimpleVotingWebUI>node webserver.js
```

You should see an initialization message:

```
Server running on 8080...
```

You'll now be able to browse any HTML page located in the SimpleVotingWebUI folder through an HTTP connection to localhost on port 8080. For example, create a dummy page called test.html with this markup:

```
<html>
<table><tr><td><b>test</b></td></tr></table>
</html>
```

Then access it through your browser: http://localhost:8080/test.html.

Now that you've set up a web server, you're ready to create the SimpleVoting website. You'll start from the admin page.

12.7.3   *Writing the admin page HTML*

The admin web page should authenticate the user through an Ethereum address. Only the voting administrator address will be allowed to use the page.

NOTE   When running against Ganache, any password will be valid. But when you move to a public test network, only the valid password associated with the administrator public address will be accepted to execute the contract functionality.

The voting administrator will use this page to

- register voters
- start and end the proposal registration session

- start and end the voting session
- tally the votes

You can get an idea of the layout of this page from figure 12.5.

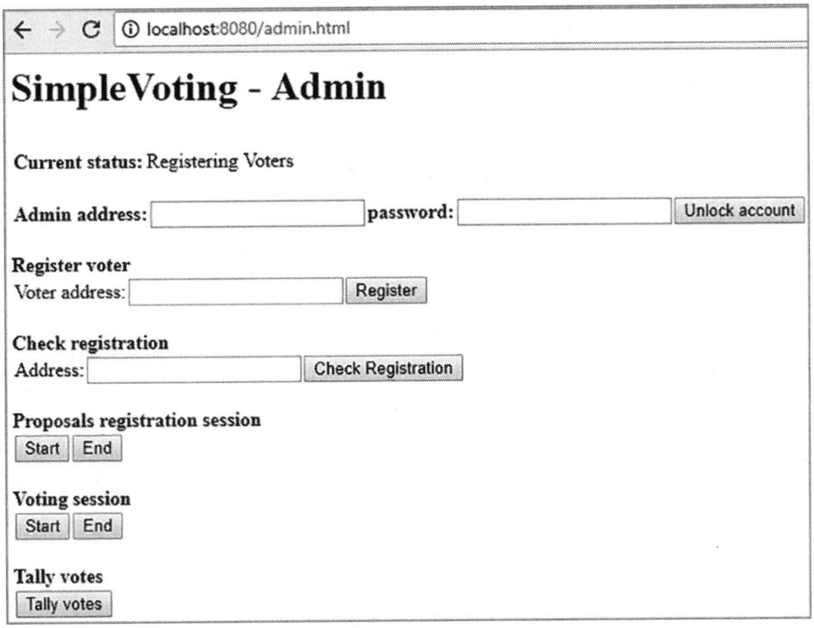

Figure 12.5   The admin web page. The voting administrator will use this page to register voters, start and end the proposal registration session, start and end the voting session, and tally the votes

Although you can look at the entire HTML of this web page on the book website, and I invite you to download and experiment with it (SimpleVotingWebUI folder), I'll highlight the most frequently recurring elements that you'll find across both admin and voter pages:

- JavaScript include files
- Table row showing current voting workflow status
- Administrator address and password fields
- Input fields, such as address for voter registration
- Buttons triggering smart contract function calls
- Feedback message cells, to show error messages that the JavaScript validating the input produces or the contract returns

JAVASCRIPT INCLUDES

These are the JavaScript files that the admin.html page references:

```
<head>
    <script src="bower_components/web3/dist/web3.min.js"></script>
    <script src="bower_components/jquery/dist/jquery.min.js"></script>
    <script src="bower_components/truffle-contract/dist/truffle-
    contract.js"></script>
    <script src="./simplevoting.js"></script>
</head>
```

As you can see, the admin page references Web3.js, jQuery, and truffle-contract through their respective Bower download folders. For simplicity, and to avoid code duplication, I've decided to place all the JavaScript needed by the admin and voter web pages in a single file called simplevoting.js. I'll present it to you in the next section.

TEXT DISPLAYING CURRENT WORKFLOW STATUS

At the top of the page, a row displays the current status of the voting workflow; for example, "Registering Voters" or "Proposal Registration Session Open:"

```
<table border="0" cellpadding="0" id='currentStatus'>
    <tr>
            <td><b>Current status:</b></td>
                        <td id='currentWorkflowStatusMessage'></td>
            <td></td>
            <td></td>
    </tr>
</table>
```

This is useful from two points of view:

- It reminds the user which processing step they're in, so it prevents them from attempting incorrect operations.
- From a technical point of view, the workflow description is retrieved from the voting contract at page load, so correct rendering confirms the contract is running as expected.

ADMINISTRATOR ADDRESS AND PASSWORD FIELDS

The page captures the administrator address and password through input fields:

```
<table border="0" cellpadding="0" id='user'>
    <tr>
        <td><b>Admin address:</b></td>
        <td><input type="text" id="adminAddress" width="400" /></td>
        <td><b>password:</b></td>
        <td><input type="text" id="adminPassword" width="400" /></td>
        <td><button onclick="unlockAdmin()">Unlock account</button></td>
        <td id='adminMessage'></td>
    </tr>
</table>
```

This input is needed to

- unlock the administrator account by clicking Unlock Account (If the password is correct, the specified account will be unlocked, and the user will be able to perform operations on this page for three minutes, before the account gets locked again.)
- authenticate the account as the administrator so the user is allowed to access the web page functionality
- attach the address as the sender of the contract function calls associated with this web page, which are all restricted to the administrator account, so they can get authorized

NOTE When connecting to Ganache, it isn't necessary to unlock the administrator account to perform operations on the web page, but when you connect to the test network, you'll have to do so.

OTHER INPUT FIELDS

Input fields also capture input specific to the functionality provided by the page, such as the registration of voters; for example, the field for the voter address:

```
<td>Voter address:</td>
<td><input type="text" id="voterAddress" width="400" /></td>
```

BUTTONS TRIGGERING SMART CONTRACT FUNCTION CALL

Some buttons, such as the one associated with the voter registration, trigger a Java-Script function (in this case `registerVoter()`), which gathers the associated input (in this case the voter address) and includes it in the contract call together with the administrator address:

```
<td><button onclick="registerVoter()">Register</button></td>
```

Other buttons, such as the one that starts the voting session, trigger a JavaScript function (`startVotingSession()`) that doesn't take any input apart from the administrator address before creating and submitting the related contract call:

```
<table border="0" cellpadding="0" id='proposalsRegistration'>
    <tr>
        <td><button
    onclick="startProposalsRegistration()">Start</button></td>
        <td><button onclick="endProposalsRegistration()">End</button></td>
        <td id='proposalsRegistrationMessage'></td>
    </tr>
</table>
```

FEEDBACK MESSAGE CELLS

Next to most buttons is a cell to show error or success messages that the JavaScript validating the input or the contract call return:

```
<td id='voterRegistrationMessage'></td>
```

As I mentioned previously, you can find the full HTML of the admin.html page on the book website. I encourage you to examine the code before running it.

12.7.4   *Writing the admin page JavaScript*

Before starting this section, I'd like to make it clear I'll be presenting JavaScript code based on asynchronous calls for two reasons:

- It's best practice to write asynchronous JavaScript in web applications.
- If you want to use Web3 providers recommended from a security point of view, such as Mist or MetaMask, they only support asynchronous calls to an Ethereum contract.

> **NOTE**   I believe that even if you aren't familiar with asynchronous JavaScript, you should be able to follow this section. But if you're struggling, I've also implemented a synchronous version of the code I'll be presenting, which you can find on the book website.

I'll present only the JavaScript around the registration of a voter address by the administrator. This is an interesting use case because it requires common functionality needed by most administrator operations, such as JavaScript code that

- connects to the contract on page load
- displays the voting workflow status on page load
- unlocks the administrator account
- validates user input; for example, checking whether the administrator address is valid or whether the operation the administrator is attempting is compatible with the current workflow status
- executes a contract transaction
- handles contract events

Once you've understood this use case, you should be able to implement the rest of the administrator functionality by yourself. I encourage you to do so and then compare your code with mine from the book website. Let's go step by step.

CONNECTING TO THE VOTING CONTRACT

The JavaScript code connecting the web page to the voting contract is similar to the code you wrote for connecting to SimpleCoin back in chapter 8. But, thanks to truffle-contract

- The contract ABI is read directly from SimpleVoting.json, a file that truffle compile generates, with no need of hardcoding.
- The contract address isn't hardcoded anymore, and it's also read from Simple-Voting.json, specifically from its networks dictionary; a new network entry is added every time ganache is restarted, whereas the contract address is updated when executing truffle migrate:

```
"networks": {
    "1526138147842": {        "events": {},
        "links": {},
        "address": "0xaf18e4e373b90709cc08a231ce24015a0da4f8cc",
        "transactionHash":
            "0x37ecb76d6cd6051c5d122df53db0063d1336e5b3298150b50d62e8ae845e9bbb"
    },
    ...
    "1526683622193": {
        "events": {},
        "links": {},
        "address":
            "0xdaef7d6211bc0c0639178f442c68f468494b7ea2",
        "transactionHash":
            "0xea66f69e35ccc77845405dbc183fc0c3ce831cd977f74c5152d6f97a55ebd8af"
    }
}
```

Network entry generated at Ganache restart → (points to "1526683622193")

Contract address updated when migrating (deploying) the contract → (points to "address": "0xdaef7d6211bc0c0639178f442c68f468494b7ea2")

Here's how the code looks:

```
var SimpleVoting;

window.onload = function() {
    $.getJSON("./contracts/SimpleVoting.json",
        function(json) {
        SimpleVoting = TruffleContract( json );

        SimpleVoting.setProvider(
            new Web3.providers.HttpProvider(
                "http://localhost:8545"));
```

Variable to store a reference to the deployed voting contract instance → (points to `var SimpleVoting;`)

References SimpleVoting through truffle-contract, which imports the contract ABI from SimpleVoting.json → (points to `TruffleContract( json );`)

Reads SimpleVoting.json → (points to `function(json) {`)

Sets up Web3 to point to the local Ethereum client (currently Ganache) → (points to `"http://localhost:8545"));`)

As I mentioned earlier in section 12.7.1, the jQuery instruction to read SimpleVoting.json will fail if you try to browse on the admin.html page directly from disk, but it will work if you browse through the website you created earlier on:

```
http//localhost:8080/admin.html
```

DISPLAYING THE VOTING WORKFLOW STATUS

The voting workflow status ("Registering Voters," "Proposals Registration Started," and so on) is displayed at page load and refreshed at each status change with this JavaScript function:

```
function refreshWorkflowStatus()
{
    SimpleVoting.deployed()
    .then(instance => instance.getWorkflowStatus())
    .then(workflowStatus => {
      var workflowStatusDescription;

      switch(workflowStatus.toString())
      {
        case '0':
          workflowStatusDescription = "Registering Voters";
          break;
```

References the deployed contract → (points to `SimpleVoting.deployed()`)

Gets the workflow status ID from the contract → (points to `instance.getWorkflowStatus()`)

Determines the related status description → (points to `switch(workflowStatus.toString())`)

```
        case '1':
          workflowStatusDescription = "Proposals Registration Started";
          break;
        ...
        default:
            workflowStatusDescription = "Unknown Status";
    }
```

```
    $("#currentWorkflowStatusMessage").html(
      workflowStatusDescription);
      });
}
```
> Binds the status description
> to the HTML table cell where
> it should be displayed

As you know, because the contract function getWorkflowStatus() is a read-only view, its invocation is considered a plain call and doesn't generate a blockchain transaction. As a result, you don't need to specify the caller and set other transaction details, such as the gas limit.

You'll call the workflow status function in two places. The first one is at the end of the code block setting the SimpleVoting reference to the instance of the voting contract, which happens at page load:

```
$.getJSON("./contracts/SimpleVoting.json", function(json) { ...



    ...
    refreshWorkflowStatus();
});
```

The other one is in the event handler associated with the WorkflowStatusEvent event that the voting contract publishes at every status change. We'll examine that later.

UNLOCKING THE ADMINISTRATOR ACCOUNT

As you might remember, to invoke any contract function that alters contract state and consequently generates a blockchain transaction, you need to unlock the account of the caller (who becomes the transaction sender). Before performing any state-changing operation on this web page, such as registering a voter or starting the voting session by clicking on the corresponding button, you need to unlock the administrator account. This unlocking takes place through the following function:

```
function unlockAdmin()
{
    var adminAddress = $("#adminAddress").val();
    var adminPassword = $("#adminPassword").val();

    var result = web3.personal.unlockAccount(
      adminAddress, adminPassword, 180);
    if (result)
          $("#adminMessage").html('The account has been unlocked');
    else
          $("#adminMessage").html('The account has NOT been unlocked');
}
```
> Unlocks the account
> for three minutes

As you might recall, I've registered the execution of this function to the click event of the Unlock Account button:

```
<td><button onclick="unlockAdmin()">Unlock account</button></td>
```

As a result, you must click this button before performing any state-changing operation. But if you prefer, you can get rid of the button and call this function just before any contract call that generates a transaction. For example, you could place it just before the contract call `instance.registerVoter()` within your JavaScript `register-Voter()` function:

```
function registerVoter()
{
...
unlockAdmin(adminAddress, adminPassword);
SimpleVoting.deployed()
.then(instance => instance.registerVoter(voterToRegister, ...
```

VALIDATING USER INPUT

As for centralized applications, it's good practice to validate user input before passing it to an external function call, to avoid having bad input generate an exception. To implement that, the first few lines of your `registerVoter()` JavaScript function are dedicated to capturing user input from the HTML and checking it:

```
function registerVoter() {

    $("#voterRegistrationMessage").html('');

    var adminAddress =
        $("#adminAddress").val();          ◁──┐ Gets admin and voter
    var voterToRegister =                      │ addresses from the HTML
        $("#voterAddress").val();          ◁──┘

    SimpleVoting.deployed()
    .then(instance => instance.isAdministrator(
        adminAddress))                     ◁──┐ Checks if the specified
    .then(isAdministrator => {                 │ address belongs to the
        if (isAdministrator)                   │ administrator
        {
            return SimpleVoting.deployed()
            .then(instance =>
                instance.isRegisteredVoter(
                    voterToRegister))      ◁──┐ Checks if the specified
            .then(isRegisteredVoter => {       │ address belongs to a
                if (isRegisteredVoter)         │ registered voter
                    $("#voterRegistrationMessage")
                    .html(
                    'The voter is already registered');  ◁──┐ Shows validation
                else                                         │ error message
                {
                    ...
                }
            });
```

```
        }
        else
        {
            $("#voterRegistrationMessage")
                .html(
                'The given address does not correspond
                    to the administrator');            ◁──┐  Shows validation
        }                                                 │  error message
    });
}
```

As you can see, you can call some contract read-only view functions to validate the input you're going to then submit to a transaction-generating function. You might also want to validate if the JavaScript `registerVoter()` function is being called during the correct workflow step (voter registration) to avoid contract-side exceptions you'll receive if you attempt to register a voter when the proposal registration session has already started; for example:

```
return SimpleVoting.deployed()
        .then(instance => instance.getWorkflowStatus())
        .then(workflowStatus => {
            if (workflowStatus > 0)
                $("#voterRegistrationMessage")
                .html('Voters registration has already ended');
            else
        {
        ...
```

You've performed substantial validation. Now you can call the contract `register-Voter()` with more confidence that it won't throw an exception.

> **NOTE** You might wonder whether a user might be able to hack the Dapp if they can modify the JavaScript and bypass the validation. This would be pointless. The purpose of JavaScript input validation isn't to provide a layer of security but to avoid unnecessary transaction costs the user will incur when their transaction is reverted by contract-side validation code. For example, trying to register a voter from a nonadministrator account by bypassing the JavaScript performing the `isAdministrator()` check will end in an exception being thrown by the contract-side `onlyAdministrator` function modifier.

CALLING A TRANSACTION GENERATING CONTRACT FUNCTION

While you're here, I'll tell you more about JavaScript code around the execution of a contract transaction such as `instance.registerVoter()`. As you know, when calling a function that alters contract state, you're generating a blockchain transaction. In this case, you must supply

- the transaction sender
- transaction details, such as at least the gas limit
- a callback to handle errors in case of unsuccessful completion, or results in case of successful completion

You can see all these details in the `registerVoter()` call:

Calls registerVoter function

```
SimpleVoting.deployed()        ◁─┘  References deployed contract
.then(instance => instance.registerVoter(
    voterToRegister,
        {from:adminAddress, gas:200000}))  ◁─  Specifies transaction sender and gas limit. (Generally you set it to the lowest amount that allows transaction completion consistently, and you can find the value during testing.)
.catch(e => $("#voterRegistrationMessage")
    .html(e));      ◁─┐  Handles errors from the contract call
```

HANDLING CONTRACT EVENTS

Before leaving this section on the JavaScript of the admin page, I'd like to show you how to handle workflow status change events that the contract publishes. This would allow you to, for example, update the current workflow status description at the top of the page and show registration confirmations for each voter that the administrator adds.

First of all, you must declare a variable to reference the contract `WorkflowStatus-ChangeEvent` event type:

```
var workflowStatusChangeEvent;
```

You instantiate this variable at page load, after having set the reference to the contract:

```
window.onload = function() {
    $.getJSON("./contracts/SimpleVoting.json", function(json) {
    ...
    SimpleVoting.deployed()
    .then(instance => instance
        .WorkflowStatusChangeEvent())      ◁─  References contract WorkflowStatusChangeEvent event
    .then(workflowStatusChangeEventSubscription => {
            workflowStatusChangeEvent =
                workflowStatusChangeEventSubscription;

        workflowStatusChangeEvent
            .watch(function(error, result){      ◁─  Registers handler with the contract event
            if (!error)
                refreshWorkflowStatus();      ◁─┐  When the event is handled, invoke client-side function to refresh UI
            else
                console.log(error);
        });
    });
    ...
```

As you can see, every time the workflow status changes, the function refreshing its description is invoked. The contract event that notifies a voter registration confirmation, `VoterRegisteredEvent()`, is handled in exactly the same way, with the only difference being that the UI is refreshed inline and not through a client-side function:

```
SimpleVoting.deployed()
.then(instance => instance.VoterRegisteredEvent())
.then(voterRegisteredEventSubscription => {
```

```
        voterRegisteredEvent = voterRegisteredEventSubscription;

        voterRegisteredEvent.watch(function(error, result) {
        if (!error)
            $("#voterRegistrationMessage")
            .html('Voter successfully
                registered');          <───┐  Refreshes
        else                                │  voterRegistrationMessage
            console.log(error);             │  label
        });
    });
```

12.7.5 *Writing the voter page HTML*

The voter page, which you can see in figure 12.6, shares many elements in common with the admin page. As I said earlier, the main purpose of the voter page is to register proposals and to vote on them. It's worthwhile to highlight the proposal table, which is updated dynamically every time a new proposal is added by a voter:

```
<tr><table border="0" cellpadding="0" width="600" id='proposalsTable'>
    </table></tr>
```

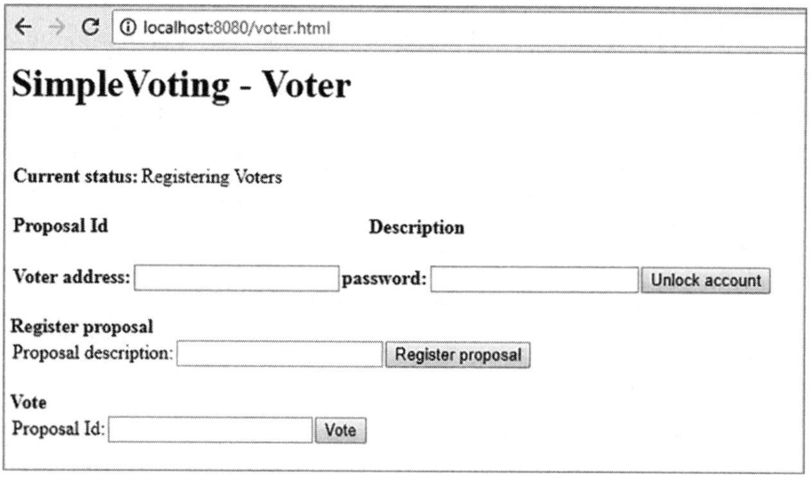

Figure 12.6   Screenshot of the voter page

12.7.6 *Writing the voter page JavaScript*

Let's see how the proposal table update takes place. If you have a look at the register-Proposal() function in simplevoting.js, you'll notice many similarities to register-Voter() that we examined earlier. The main difference is that the event handler associated with the event that the contract fires upon proposal registration, Proposal-RegisteredEvent(), doesn't only confirm that the registration has taken place by refreshing the related HTML label. In addition, it calls a function that generates a dynamic HTML table listing of all the proposals added so far:

```
...
proposalRegisteredEvent.watch(function(error, result) {
    if (!error)
    {
        $("#proposalRegistrationMessage")
            .html('The proposal has been
                registered successfully');
        loadProposalsTable();
    }
    else
        console.log(error);
});
```

Refreshes proposal registration confirmation label

Refreshes table listing all proposals registered so far

Here's how the proposals table is refreshed dynamically:

```
function loadProposalsTable() {
    SimpleVoting.deployed()
    .then(instance => instance.getProposalsNumber())
    .then(proposalsNumber => {

        var innerHtml = "<tr><td><b>Proposal
    ID</b></td><td><b>Description</b></td></tr>";

        j = 0;
        for (var i = 0; i < proposalsNumber; i++) {
            getProposalDescription(i)
            .then(description => {
                innerHtml = innerHtml + "<tr><td>" + (j++) +
                    "</td><td>" + description + "</td></tr>";
                $("#proposalsTable").html(innerHtml);
            });
        }
    });
}


function getProposalDescription(proposalId)
{
    return SimpleVoting.deployed()
        .then(instance => instance.getProposalDescription(proposalId));
}
```

12.7.7 Running the admin and voter web pages

Now that you understand the code for both web pages, it's time to run them. I'll guide you through the entire voting workflow so you'll see how the application works from start to end.

PRELIMINARIES

Before starting, make sure Ganache is running in a console. I suggest you start it with an instruction to redirect the output to a log file, which will come in handy later:

```
C:\Ethereum\truffle\SimpleVoting>ganache-cli > c:\temp\ganache.log
```

Because you've restarted Ganache, you must redeploy `SimpleVoting` (in a separate console):

```
C:\Ethereum\truffle\SimpleVoting>truffle migrate --reset
```

Next, recopy SimpleVoting.json from Truffle's build\contracts folder to the website's contracts folder. Now you can restart the website (in a separate console):

```
C:\Ethereum\SimpleVotingWebUI>node webserver.js
Server running on 8080...
```

REGISTERING VOTERS

Browse the admin webpage

```
http://localhost:8080/admin.html
```

and you'll see the screen I showed you earlier in figure 12.5. You might have noticed that the initial current status is "Registering Voters," as expected, as you can see in figure 12.7.

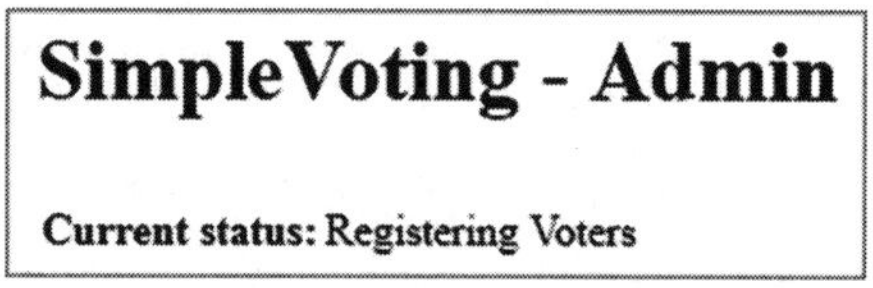

SimpleVoting - Admin

Current status: Registering Voters

Figure 12.7   The initial workflow status shown on the admin web page at startup

Unless your truffle.js is configured to run the migrations from a specific account, they'll be executed against `accounts[0]`, which, as you know, will become the voting administrator. Because you're deploying on Ganache, look at the `ganache.log` file you're redirecting the output to:

```
Ganache CLI v6.1.0 (ganache-core: 2.1.0)

Available Accounts
==================
(0) 0xda53708da879dced568439272eb9a7fab05bd14a
(1) 0xf0d14c6f6a185aaaa74010d510b975ca4caa1cad
(2) 0x5d6449a4313a5d2dbf7ec326cb8ad204c97413ae
...
```

Copy the address corresponding to account (0) into the Admin Address text box and, because you're running against Ganache, leave the password field empty, as shown in figure 12.8. You can then register the voters' addresses.

Admin address: `0xda53708da879dced56843` password: `                    `   Unlock account

Figure 12.8   Copying the administrator's account into the corresponding text box

Because shortly you'll be running some voter functionality, I suggest you register (1), (2), (3), ... from Ganache's startup screen as voters. When registering account (1), you enter the corresponding address in the Voter Address text box, as shown in figure 12.9.

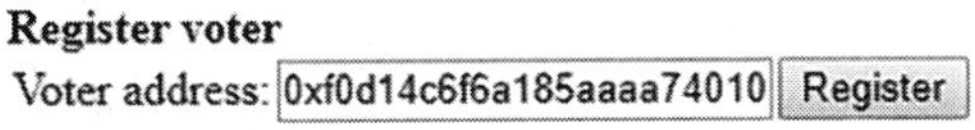

Register voter

Voter address: `0xf0d14c6f6a185aaaa74010` Register   **Figure 12.9 Entering the voter address**

Before submitting the voter registration transaction, you must unlock the admin account, so click Unlock Account. You'll get a confirmation that the account has been unlocked. Then click Register. If everything has gone well, you should get a confirmation message next to the Register button; otherwise, you'll get an error message.

Register a few voters using the other account addresses from Ganache's log file. If you do so within the next three minutes, you don't need to unlock the administrator account again before registering the accounts.

> **NOTE** As I said earlier, when running on Ganache, you don't need to enter any administrator password, and you don't even need to unlock the corresponding account, as accounts are all indefinitely unlocked. But it's best to get used to the account unlock operation for a smoother transition to the public test network later.

If you want to verify that these accounts are indeed registered, you can use the Check Registration verification area. For example, to verify that account (1) is a registered voter, enter the corresponding address in the Address text box and click Check Registration. You should see a confirmation message like the one shown in figure 12.10.

Check registration

Address: `0xf0d14c6f6a185aaaa74010` Check Registration This is a registered voter

Figure 12.10 Checking whether an account has been registered as a voter

Before we move to the next workflow step, I suggest you see what happens if you try to

- register a voter by specifying in the admin address text box a different account; for example, account (4)
- perform an operation that shouldn't happen at this stage; for example, you click the Tally votes button

You should receive corresponding error messages.

STARTING THE PROPOSAL REGISTRATION SESSION

Once you've registered a few voters, you can start the proposal registration session by clicking Start in the related area of the screen. This will call the JavaScript startProposalsRegistration() function, which in turn will call the start-ProposalsRegistration() contract function. The contract function will raise the WorkflowStatusChangeEvent event, which the client-side JavaScript refreshWorkflow-Status() function that's in charge of refreshing the workflow status label to "Proposals Registration Started" will handle, as you can see in figure 12.11.

SimpleVoting - Admin

Current status: Proposals registration Started

Figure 12.11   After you start the proposals registration session, the Current Status label will be refreshed with the corresponding status description.

REGISTERING PROPOSALS

At this point, voters are allowed to register proposals. Open the voter web page in a separate browser tab: http://localhost:8080/voter.html.

You'll see a screen similar to the one shown in figure 12.6, with a small difference: the current status will be "Proposals Registration Started" as on the Admin page. This confirms the page is connected correctly to the voting contract.

Now register a proposal under Ganache's account (1), who is a valid registered user. Enter the corresponding address in the Voter Address text box, and leave the password blank, as you did for the administrator. Then enter a proposal description, for example, "Proposal Zero." If you want, before clicking Register, you can check what happens if you submit a vote at this stage (say against proposal ID = 0). You should get an error message.

Now click Register. You'll get a confirmation message next to the button. You'll also see at the top of the screen the proposal you've entered together with the related ID, returned from the contract, as shown in figure 12.12.

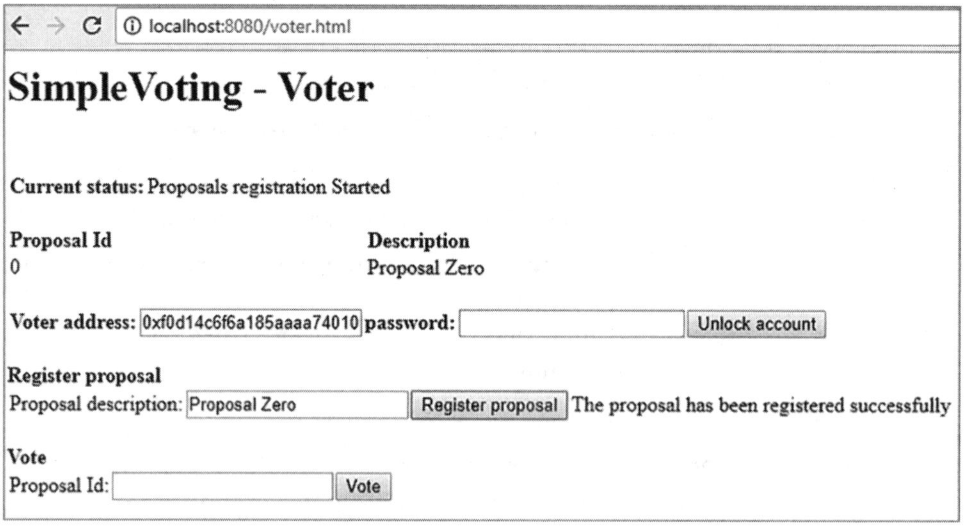

← → C	ⓘ localhost:8080/voter.html

SimpleVoting - Voter

Current status: Proposals registration Started

Proposal Id	**Description**
0	Proposal Zero

Voter address: `0xf0d14c6f6a185aaaa74010` password: `[            ]` `Unlock account`

Register proposal
Proposal description: `Proposal Zero` `Register proposal` The proposal has been registered successfully

Vote
Proposal Id: `[          ]` `Vote`

Figure 12.12   Registering a new proposal

Keep registering more proposals, using all the accounts you've registered as voters. If you want, you can register more than one proposal against the same account, as you didn't set any constraints on this. You can also check what happens if you try to register a proposal against the administrator account or against some account that you didn't register as a user.

ENDING THE PROPOSAL REGISTRATION SESSION

After registering a few proposals, you can end the proposal registration session. Go back to the admin page and, if the administrator account address is still in the related text box, click End in the Proposal Registration Session area. You should get a confirmation message next to the button and the new workflow status in the Current Status area, as shown in figure 12.13.

SimpleVoting - Admin

Current status: Proposals registration Ended

Figure 12.13   Ending the proposal registration session

As usual, you can try to attempt actions that aren't supposed to take place at this stage. For example, try ending the voting session.

STARTING THE VOTING SESSION

Time to start the voting session! Click Start corresponding to the voting session, and the Current Status description at the top of the screen will change accordingly to "Voting Session Started."

VOTING

Go back to the voter's screen. You'll see that the status at the top of the screen has also changed to "Voting Session Started." This confirms that it has been refreshed by the `WorkflowStatusChangeEvent` event that the contract published at the end of the `startVotingSession()` function and the voter's page JavaScript handled. At this point, you're allowed to vote.

Enter the address of one of the voter accounts in the Voter Address text box, and then put one of the Proposal IDs you see at the top of the screen in the Proposal ID text box. Then click Vote. You'll see a confirmation message next to the Vote button. If you try to vote again, you'll see an exception from the voting contract that's preventing you from voting twice. Continue by casting various votes from the accounts you registered earlier.

ENDING THE VOTING SESSION

After you've voted from various registered accounts, you can end the voting session the same way you started it: go back to the admin page, move the mouse in the Voting Registration area, and click End. As usual, you'll see a confirmation message and a change of state at the top of the screen. If you now try to go back to the voter page and cast a vote through a registered account that you didn't use, you'll be prevented from voting.

TALLYING THE VOTES

It's the moment of truth: time to tally the votes! On the admin page, click Tally Votes. Apart from the usual confirmation message and status description stage, you'll see a new table appearing at the bottom of the screen summarizing the vote results. The handler of the WorkflowStatusChangeEvent event has generated this table, with a specific check on the status ID corresponding to votes tallied.

If you flip back to the voter page, you'll see the same results table at the bottom of the screen, as you can verify in figure 12.14. The same table appears because both pages were listening to the same event.

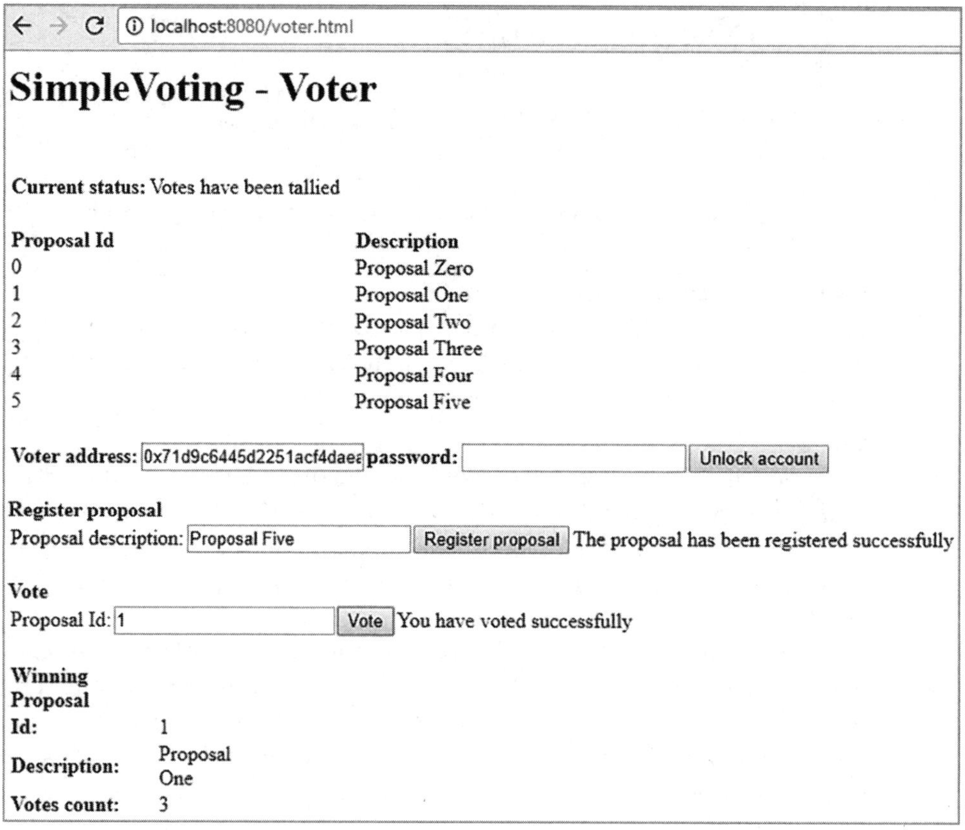

Figure 12.14   The voter page after the votes have been tallied

Congratulations! You've designed, implemented, tested, and run a full voting Dapp. You should consider this an important achievement. It's the first time (in the book) you've built a complete Dapp from scratch, covering all the layers from the smart contract to the web UI. You've come a long way from chapter 1, when you started to learn about new concepts, such as blockchain and Dapp, and experimented with a simple embryonic version of SimpleCoin. Now you should have a good understanding of smart contracts, how to write them in Solidity, how to communicate with them with Web3.js, and how to create a simple web UI to interact with them in an easier way. Before leaving the chapter, you'll deploy the Dapp into the public test network and check that everything is still working as expected.

12.7.8 *Deploying to the public network*

Here are the steps you must take to deploy SimpleVoting onto Ropsten, the public test network:

1 Stop Ganache.
2 Start geth, configured to point to Ropsten.
3 Configure Truffle to point to the Ropsten network and deploy from one of your Ropsten accounts.
4 Unlock the Ropsten account you'll use for deployment.
5 Perform a Truffle migration to Ropsten.
6 Check that the UI still works correctly.

STOPPING GANACHE

You should be able to do everything pretty much by yourself but, just in case, let me walk through these steps with you. Start with an easy one: press CTRL+C or close down the Ganache window.

STARTING GETH ON ROPSTEN

You've done this a couple of times already, but I'll save you some page flipping. You can see in the following code the full command to connect to Ropsten through some seed nodes, including the option to perform a fast synchronization, in case you haven't been connected to the test network for a while. Also, I've highlighted the last two parameters, which open geth's communication through RPC on port 8545 and allow cross-origin resource sharing (CORS) so that the JavaScript of your web page will be allowed to communicate directly with geth:

```
C:\Program Files\geth>geth --testnet --bootnodes
"enode://145a93c5b1151911f1a232e04dd1a76708dd12694f952b8a180ced40e8c4d25a908
a292bed3521b98bdd843147116a52ddb645d34fa51ae7668c39b4d1070845@188.166.147
.175:30303,enode://2609b7ee28b51f2f493374fee6a2ab12deaf886c5daec948f122bc837
16aca27840253d191b9e63a6e7ec77643e69ae0d74182d6bb64fd30421d45aba82c13bd@13
.84.180.240:30303,enode://94c15d1b9e2fe7ce56e458b9a3b672ef11894ddedd0c6f247e
0f1d3487f52b66208fb4aeb8179fce6e3a749ea93ed147c37976d67af557508d199d9594c35f
09@188.166.147.175:30303"
--verbosity=4 --syncmode "fast" --cache=1024 --rpc --rpcport 8545
--rpccorsdomain "http://localhost:8080" --rpcapi "eth,net,web3,personal"
```

> **NOTE** If your geth client doesn't seem to synchronize with the public test network, attach a console to geth and manually add the Ropsten peers specified on this GitHub page: http://mng.bz/6jAZ.

CONFIGURING TRUFFLE TO POINT TO ROPSTEN

In the previous chapter, I explained how to point Truffle to a test or live network. Modify your truffle.js (or truffle-config.js) file as follows:

```
module.exports = {
  networks: {
    development: {
      host: "localhost",
      port: 8545,
      network_id: "*" // Match any network id
    },
    ropsten: {
      host: "localhost",
      port: 8545,
      network_id: 3,
      from:
      "0x70e36be8ab8f6cf66c0c953cf9c63ab63f3fef02",
      gas: 4000000
    }
  }
};
```

Matches the port open on geth for RPC communication (as noted previously)

Replace this account with the Ropsten account you want to use to deploy.

This should be enough gas to deploy SimpleVoting.

Make sure the Ropsten account you choose to deploy SimpleVoting has some (test) Ether in it!

UNLOCKING THE ACCOUNT USED FOR DEPLOYMENT

To unlock the Ropsten account you've specified for deployment, start by opening a new console and attaching it to geth:

```
C:\Program Files\geth>geth attach ipc:\\.\pipe\geth.ipc
```

Once the geth JavaScript console has started, unlock the deployer address (for 300 seconds) as follows:

```
> web3.personal.unlockAccount("0x70e36be8ab8f6cf66c0c953cf9c63ab63f3fef02",
    "YOUR_PASSWORD", 300);
true
```

PERFORMING A TRUFFLE MIGRATION TO ROPSTEN

To perform a migration on a network other than the development one, you must provide it explicitly through the --network option (on a separate console):

```
C:\Ethereum\truffle\SimpleVoting>truffle migrate --network ropsten
```

> **WARNING** Make sure your geth client is fully synchronized with Ropsten before attempting this operation. You can check the latest Ropsten block against https://ropsten.etherscan.io/ and compare it with what you see on your client's console.

If your geth client is actively connected to Ropsten and you've configured everything correctly, you should see some output confirming that deployment has taken place:

```
Running migration: 1_initial_migration.js
  Deploying Migrations...
  ... 0x8ec9c0b3e1d996dcd2f6f8b0ca07f8ce5e5d15bd0cc2eea3142f351f53070499
  Migrations: 0xeaf67f4ce8a26aa432c106c2d59b7dbeaa3108d8
Saving successful migration to network...
  ... 0xadffddd1afe362a802fc6a80d9c60dc2e4a85f9e850ff3c252307ec9255988af
Saving artifacts...
Running migration: 2_deploy_contracts.js
  Deploying SimpleVoting...
  ... 0xbe1ca60296cc8fb94a6e97c74bf6c20547b2ed7705e8db84d51e17f38904fa09
  SimpleVoting: 0x3a437f22d092b6ae37d543dcb765de4366c00ecc
Saving successful migration to network...
  ... 0x37f90733539ba00f946ef18b456b5f7d6b362f93e639583d789acd36c033e5d2
Saving artifacts...
```

CHECKING THE UI STILL WORKS

If you look back at the first lines of simplevoting.js, the initialization looks at a web3 provider coming from `localhost:8545`. Geth is exposing to RPC the same port number that Ganache was previously exposing, so everything should still work, right? Let's find out! First of all, copy the new SimpleVoting.json from Truffle's build\contracts to the website contracts folder. Then try to browse on admin.html as you did previously. (Make sure the website is still running; otherwise, restart it with: `node webserver.js`.) Type the following:

```
http://localhost:8080/admin.html
```

Yes! The page loads correctly, and it shows the initial "Registering Voters" status as expected. You can now go through the whole workflow, from voters' registration to vote tallying, as you did when running on Ganache. Before doing so, make sure the TESTNET admin and voter accounts have enough Ether to perform the related operations.

> **NOTE** Bear in mind that when you perform operations on TESTNET, you must unlock the related account at each operation. Also, every time you perform an operation, from either the admin account or a voter account, you'll have to wait for the related transaction to be mined, so it will take longer (around 15 seconds) to receive confirmations.

> **WARNING** If your UI seems unresponsive and you don't get a confirmation that the operation you attempted completed, check potential errors on the console of your browser's development tools. For example, on Chrome, you can click F12 and then select Console from the top menu. If the issue is related to account unlocking, it might be due to changes in Web3 around this area. If that's the case, you can unlock the administrator or the voter account from an attached Geth console, as you've seen in previous chapters, rather than using the Unlock Account button.

12.8   *Food for thought*

I hope you've found this chapter useful for tying together all you learned in the previous chapters. At this point, you should feel confident you can start building your own Dapp, and you should be geared up to take on a new challenge. If you're eager to practice your newly acquired skills a little more before moving on to the next chapter on advanced topics in contract design and security, I've prepared for you a little plan you can use as a springboard for improving SimpleVoting. I have two sets of improvements in mind:

- Technical improvements
- Functional improvements

12.8.1 *Possible technical improvements*

I designed SimpleVoting with the main objective of presenting the full Ethereum Dapp development lifecycle in one shot, so I decided to keep it as simple as possible to focus mainly on the big picture. Also, I understand that not all readers have the same background and experience in web development and continuous integration, so I avoided introducing relatively advanced techniques in either of these areas. If you'd like to improve the web UI, there's room for improvement in various respects, including these two:

- Using a standard Web3 provider
- Automating build and deployment with a web build tool

USING A STANDARD WEB3 PROVIDER

Your application shouldn't be served through a plain web browser, but through a standard Web3 provider, such as Mist or MetaMask, that provides enhanced security. These providers require you to call contract functions asynchronously, though, so reimplementing your SimpleVoting.js using asynchronous features would also be beneficial for this reason. After you've reimplemented your JavaScript code accordingly, you can detect a standard provider by replacing this line

```
SimpleVoting.setProvider(
  new Web3.providers.HttpProvider(
  "http://localhost:8545"));
```

with this:

```
var web3Provider;
if(typeof web3 != 'undefined')          Uses standard provider
    web3Provider = new Web3(web3.currentProvider);   ◁──  (such as Metamask or
else                                                      Mist) if available
    web3Provider = new Web3(
      new Web3.providers.HttpProvider(      Instantiates default
      "http://localhost:8545"));    ◁──     provider if none is
                                            available
SimpleVoting.setProvider(web3Provider);
```

How do you supply a standard provider? First, remember to log in. Then, assuming you installed the MetaMask browser plugin, as explained in chapter 3, make my suggested code change at the top of SimpleVoting.js, and finally browse on the admin or voter page. By doing this, the Web3 provider will be set to MetaMask.

AUTOMATING BUILD AND DEPLOYMENT WITH A WEB BUILD TOOL

If you have experience in using web build tools, you might have found it a bit annoying to copy SimpleVoting.json from Truffle's build\contracts to the web project contracts folder every time you made a change. You might be wondering whether Truffle supports a build pipeline. It does, and, in fact, you can plug in your favorite build tool, such as Webpack or Grunt.

The Truffle documentation website also includes a Webpack Truffle Box (https://truffleframework.com/boxes/webpack), which is a template project developed with Webpack support. You can use it as a base to build your Webpack integration, or at least to understand how it works.

12.8.2 *Possible functional improvements*

The current voting application is intentionally limited from a functional point of view. After the admin registers the voters (one by one), voters can register (potentially many) proposals and then vote on one of them. The winning proposal is decided based on simple majority: the one that gets the most votes is chosen. Also, you're recording the proposal that each voter chooses, so there's no anonymity. Here are some ways you could enrich the voting Dapp functionality:

- Allow the admin to register voters in bulk.
- Allow a voter to delegate their vote to another registered voter.
- Decide the winning proposal with a qualified majority.
- Implement token-based voting.
- Implement anonymous voting.

REGISTERING VOTERS IN BULK

The admin could register voters in a single bulk registration, rather than one by one, saving on administrative time and transaction costs. You could implement this enhancement with a new function taking in an array of addresses.

DELEGATING VOTES

A voter could delegate their vote to another registered voter. Then the delegator wouldn't be able to vote, and the person delegated would cast as many votes as they've been delegated to cast by as many voters.

These are some hints on how to start the implementation:

- You could change the voter struct as follows:

```
Voter
{
    HasVoted: boolean,
    CanVote: Boolean,
```

```
    NumVotes: int
}
```

- You could add a new function so that the caller can delegate their vote to another registered voter. This would be similar to `SimpleCoin`'s `authorize` function to allocate an allowance to another account:

```
delegateVote(address delegatedVoter)
```

- The function's implementation should alter the state of both delegator (`CanVote = false`) and delegated (`NumVotes +=1`).
- To check easily whether a voter is still entitled to vote, you could implement a `canvote` modifier around the `CanVote` property.

DECIDING THE WINNING PROPOSAL WITH A QUALIFIED MAJORITY

You could introduce the concept of a qualified majority. To win, a proposal should reach a predefined quorum: a minimum percentage of the cast votes.

- You'd introduce a new variable defining the quorum, initialized in the constructor:

```
uint quorum
```

- You'd modify the `tallyVotes()` function so the winning proposal would set the winner only if the quorum was reached.

IMPLEMENTING TOKEN-BASED VOTING

The current voting Dapp allows a voter account to increment the vote count of one of the proposals. This creates strong coupling between the voter and the chosen proposal, which can be slightly softened through vote delegation. In addition, the delegated voter will assign the entire vote of the delegator to a single proposal.

An interesting concept that has appeared in the crypto space is that of token-based voting. It works like this:

- Each voter is assigned a voting coin or token, similar to our dear `SimpleCoin`.
- The voter then casts a vote by transferring the voting token to the proposal address.

Because a vote has to be "spent," this would prevent double voting. Things could get more sophisticated. A voter could, for example, do one of the following:

- Transfer the voting token entirely or partially to one or many other voters through a transfer operation similar to that you've seen in `SimpleCoin`. (You could look at this as fractional delegation of the original vote.)
- Vote for one or many proposals, by assigning them specific fractions of the initial token.

You could build a token-based voting Dapp by implementing a voting token (along the lines of `SimpleCoin`) and then integrating it into the voting contract in the same way you integrated the crowdsale token in the crowdsale contract.

ANONYMOUS VOTING

As you might remember, you're recording the proposal ID that each voter chooses in the `votedProposalId` property of the voter struct. If you think you could implement anonymous voting by not recording the proposal chosen by the voter and by incrementing its vote count, you're wrong. As you know, votes are cast through transactions, which are all recorded in the blockchain and can be inspected, so it would be easy to find out who voted for which proposal.

Anonymizing voting is possible, but it's complicated because there's no out-of-the-box functionality for anonymizing transactions. This is a complex topic based on advanced cryptographic concepts such as *zero-knowledge proof*, which you might have heard associated with popular cryptocurrencies such as Zcoin, Zcash, and Monero.

Some researchers at Newcastle University, UK, have implemented an Ethereum anonymous voting Dapp based on a protocol called Open Vote Network. They've made both their paper and their code publicly available on GitHub,[1] together with a video tutorial and many academic references on the topic. I recommend you review this material!

Summary

- The SimpleVoting Dapp smart contract shows an effective implementation of predefined requirements, based on events and modifiers.
- You can build a web UI based on truffle-contract, a JavaScript library that easily connects a web page to a contract that has been previously deployed using Truffle.
- The truffle-contract library reads the contract ABI and address from a JSON file generated during Truffle contract compilation.
- To read the contract ABI and address from a JSON file, you must render a web page through a web server. You can set up a minimal web server through Connect and ServerStatic, two Node.js packages.
- Once you've implemented a Dapp, unit tested it, deployed it, and run it successfully against Ganache, a mock Ethereum client, you can deploy it on a public test network.

---

[1] See "Open Vote Network" on GitHub at http://mng.bz/nQze for more information.

Part 4 is aimed at readers who are eager to build their own Dapp and are planning to deploy it onto MAINNET, the production Ethereum network. Chapter 13 covers important operational aspects, such as event logging and contract upgradeability. You'll go through different techniques that allow you to amend a deployed contract after discovering a bug or security vulnerability. Chapter 14 is entirely focused on security and describes common vulnerabilities and typical forms of smart contract attack. Chapter 15 is for all readers who want to keep learning about Ethereum and blockchain technology in general. It gives an overview of alternative Ethereum implementations aimed at enterprise use. It also briefly presents other blockchain and distributed ledger platforms. You'll have plenty of options to consider if you want to continue your journey beyond Ethereum.

13

Making a Dapp production ready

This chapter covers

- How to generate event logs
- How to upgrade your libraries after deploying them
- How to upgrade your contracts after deploying them

In the previous chapter, you built an end-to-end Dapp from scratch for the first time, using most of the knowledge you'd acquired throughout the book and most of the available Ethereum development tools. Although it was a good exercise that helped you to consolidate your Ethereum development skills, you might not be ready to deploy your first Dapp into the public production network. Before doing so, you might want to consider strengthening your Dapp so it can cope with real-world operational requirements, such as being able to generate, store (on the blockchain), and query (from the blockchain) event logs; upgrade your libraries after deploying them; and upgrade your contracts after deploying them.

I've already touched on some of these topics briefly, but in this chapter, I'll revisit them in more detail. I'll keep my usual pragmatic approach, and I'll walk you through examples and code. Designing an upgradeable library or contract, though, requires advanced techniques whose implementation touches Solidity syntax that's outside the scope of this book. But I still believe you should be aware of the concepts, which I'll try to explain by sketching some contract or sequence diagrams.

You might be surprised I haven't included security in the list. I consider it such an important topic that I'm dedicating the entire next chapter to it.

13.1   *Event logging*

Let's start with event logging. You already know how to declare and raise events on smart contracts. In the previous chapter, you saw how to handle contract events from a web UI.

For example, you refreshed the workflow status description at the top of both admin and voter pages every time you moved to a new step of the voting process. Also, you refreshed the proposals table at the top of the voter page every time a voter registered a new proposal. The entire workflow of the proposal registration, with related event handling, is illustrated in figure 13.1, which, if you remember, is similar to figure 1.8 from chapter 1. If you didn't fully get it in chapter 1, it should definitely click now.

If you've done any event-driven or reactive programming before, you might think there's nothing unusual about how contracts publish events and how a client subscribed to them, such as a web page, can handle them. But contracts differ in an important way: whereas in most languages, events are transient objects that disappear from the system after being handled, Ethereum events are logged permanently on the blockchain. As a result, you can also retrieve events that happened before starting up the UI client, if you want. Curious to see how? Keep reading!

13.1.1   *Retrieving past events*

You've already seen how to register listeners of contract events on your JavaScript with `eventFilter.watch`. For example, you wrote this code at the top of SimpleVoting.js (though I'm slightly simplifying it here) for registering a callback to a workflow status change event:

```
var workflowStatusChangeEvent =                        Sets an event filter
    contractInstance.WorkflowStatusChangeEvent();   ◁— listening to events of type
                                                       WorkflowStatusChangeEvent
workflowStatusChangeEvent
    .watch(function(error, result) {        ◁—  Registers a callback
    if (!error)                                 to the event filter
        refreshWorkflowStatus();
    else
        console.log(error);
});
```

The variable `workflowStatusChangeEvent` is known as an *event filter* because it defines the set of events to listen to—in our case, all events of type `WorkflowStatusChangeEvent`. As you'll see later, you can define the filter in a more restrictive way.

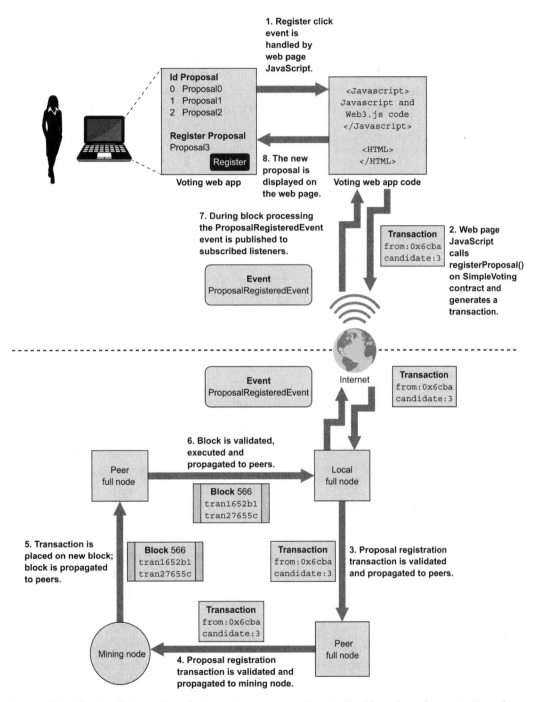

Figure 13.1 Event handling on the voter page. A new proposal is submitted from the web page to the voting contract. The contract then fires a `ProposalRegisteredEvent` event on registration completion. The event is propagated throughout the network until it reaches the node the web page is communicating with. Finally, the webpage handles the event, and a new item is added on the proposal table.

When you register a callback to an event filter through `eventFilter.watch`, you'll handle events that take place from the moment the web page is opened. If you want to access past events—for example, to verify that all the workflow status changes took place in the correct sequence—you can do so through `eventFilter.get`, which accepts a similar callback as `watch`. First of all, you must define the filter in a slightly different way, by specifying the starting block and final block of your event search:

```
var pastWorkflowStatusChangeEvent =
    contractInstance.WorkflowStatusChangeEvent(
        {},
        {fromBlock: 5000, toBlock: 'latest'});
```

Only gets the events from block 5000 onwards

Then you register the callback to the event filter with `get` rather than `watch`:

```
pastWorkflowStatusChangeEvent.get(
    function(error, logs) {
    if (!error)
        logs.forEach(log => console.log(log.args));
    else
      console.log(error);
});
```

Retrieves the past events

Displays the past event arguments to the console

If you want to retrieve *all* past events the contract has broadcast, not only the `WorkflowStatusChangeEvent` events, you can create the event filter using the `allEvents` function, as follows:

```
var allEventPastEvents = contractInstance.allEvents(
    {}, {fromBlock: 1000000, toBlock: 'latest'});
```

Filter on all event logs raised by the contract since block 1000000

Then you can register a callback on them through `get`, as before:

```
allEventPastEvents.get((error, logs) => {
  logs.forEach(log => console.log(log.args))
});
```

If you want to retrieve only a subset of past events—for example, only the proposals that a certain voter registered—you can perform the search more efficiently by indexing some of the parameters of the event in question. You'll see how in a moment.

13.1.2 *Event indexing*

When declaring an event on a contract, you can index up to three of its parameters. Event filters associated with these parameters will perform much better. For example, in the case of SimpleCoin, you might remember from section 3.5.1 that the `Transfer` event was defined as

```
event Transfer(address indexed from, address indexed to, uint256 value);
```

This allows you to efficiently filter transfer events against specific source and destination addresses when retrieving event logs:

```
var specificSourceAccountAddress =
    '0x8062a8850ef59dCd3469A83E04b4A40692a873Ba';
var transactionsFromSpecificAccount =
    simpleCoinInstance.Transferred(
    {from: specificSourceAccountAddress},
    {fromBlock: 5000, toBlock: 'latest'});
transactionsFromSpecificAccount.get((error, logs) => {
    logs.forEach(log => console.log(log.args));
});
```

In the case of `SimpleVoting`, you might remember that the `ProposalRegisteredEvent` event was defined as

```
event ProposalRegisteredEvent(uint proposalId);
```

As it stands, you can't use this event in a meaningful way as a log. How would you modify its definition so that you could query it to provide useful information? Think about it for a few seconds.... You could amend it like this:

```
event ProposalRegisteredEvent(
    address author, uint proposalId, string proposalDescription);
```

As an exercise, here's a question for you: How would you index this event to efficiently retrieve all the proposals that have been registered from a specific address? Take your time... Yes, you're right! Obviously, you'd index the author parameter as

```
event ProposalRegisteredEvent(
    address indexed author,
    uint proposalId, string proposalDescription);
```

Let's now move to a completely different topic, also important from an operational point of view: What do you do when something goes wrong in your contract? Is it possible to fix it and redeploy it as you would for a conventional software component, such as a library or a microservice? I'll discuss the answer to that question in the next few sections.

13.2 Designing an upgradeable library

When developing a new contract, some of your requirements might be similar to those of other contracts that other developers have already deployed on the blockchain. You saw in chapter 7 how you can place common functionality into libraries and reference it from various contracts, therefore avoiding wasted reimplementation effort and code duplication. For example, you practiced how to perform safe arithmetic operations with a copy of the OpenZeppelin SafeMath library. What you did, though, is still not ideal: your deployment of OpenZeppelin libraries may be only one of the many instances present on the blockchain. Other developers, like you, may have included a copy of such libraries in their solution and may have performed their own private deployment, as shown in figure 13.2.

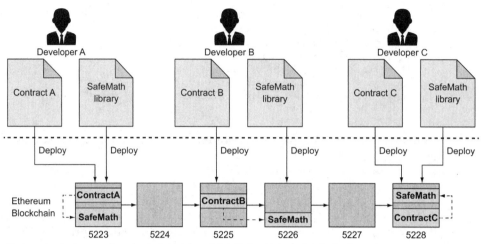

Each contract references its own private instance of SafeMath, which creates duplication and additional deployment cost for each developer.

Figure 13.2 Duplicated deployment of an OpenZeppelin library. Only one client contract uses each privately deployed instance.

You can imagine how many instances of OpenZeppelin libraries are out there on TESTNET and MAINNET! The drawbacks of this approach include the following:

- *Unnecessary costs*—Each separate deployment of the same library has to pay for its own deployment transaction gas fees.
- *Unnecessary bytecode duplication*—The same bytecode is associated on the blockchain with different deployment addresses (although nodes in fact deduplicate identical bytecode).
- *Uncoordinated maintenance*—If a problem in the library is detected, you can't fix it centrally; the owner of each contract instance has to patch it independently, with obvious consequences.

The most obvious solution to these issues is to have one official *golden instance* of the library on the blockchain and expect all its clients to reference it at that single address, as you saw briefly in chapter 7, section 7.5.2. This solution has one major drawback: once you've deployed a library, you can't patch it. If you find a problem, a new deployment is necessary, with the consequence that all its client contracts must also be repointed to the new library address and redeployed, as shown in figure 13.3. This is far from an ideal solution!

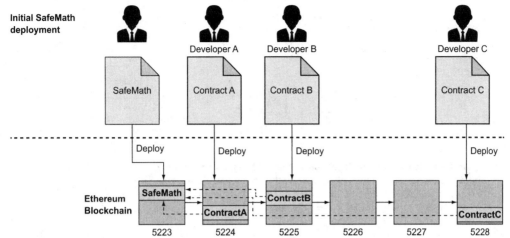

Initial SafeMath deployment

All contracts reference the same golden instance of SafeMath. This seems a good solution, until you find a bug in SafeMath.

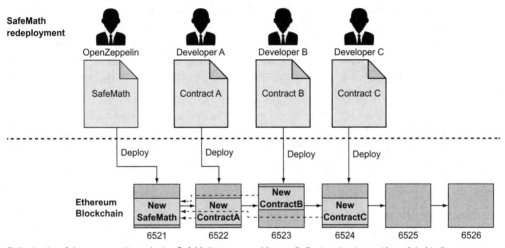

SafeMath redeployment

Following bug fixing, you need to redeploy SafeMath to a new address; all client contracts must be pointed to the new instance.

Figure 13.3 Fixing a shared library means redeploying it at a new address, which requires client contracts to be modified and redeployed.

An elegant solution that Manuel Araoz, CTO of Zeppelin, presented in an article on Medium[1] is to create a proxy to the library. His solution is a library proxy contract that acts as a layer of indirection between a client contract using the library and the library itself, as illustrated in figure 13.4.

---

[1] See "Proxy Libraries in Solidity," March 6, 2017, http://mng.bz/Xgd1.

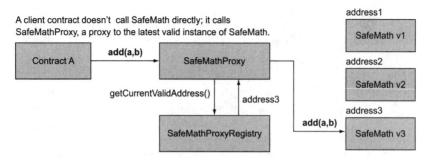

Figure 13.4　When you introduce a proxy to the library, client contracts no longer directly reference an instance of the library; they communicate with the proxy (or library dispatcher), which gets from another contract the latest valid address of the library and then forwards calls to the valid instance.

These are the components of the proxy library solution:

- A client contract references the address of a library proxy (or dispatcher) contract (SafeMathProxy) rather than directly referencing an instance of the library.
- The *library proxy* (SafeMathProxy) is a contract that retrieves the address of the latest valid deployed library instance from a library proxy registry contract (SafeMathProxyRegistry) and then forwards the call to the latest deployed library instance.
- The *library proxy registry contract* (SafeMathProxyRegistry) is a contract containing a list of addresses for different versions of the library. It also possibly contains a state variable holding the default address, which is typically the latest address that has been added to the list. The library owner updates the address list and the default address at each new deployment of the library.

When a client contract invokes a library function, it performs a corresponding delegatecall on the library proxy instead. This retrieves the correct library address for the client contract to use from the library proxy registry and then performs a delegatecall on the relevant instance of the library. From the point of view of the client contract, the whole call chain behaves exactly like a normal library function invocation.

> **NOTE** Library functions are implicitly invoked through the delegatecall EVM opcode, which executes in the context of the caller, as explained in section 3.2.5, and as I'll further explain in chapter 14 on security.

In summary, if you find that a library you'd like to use provides a proxy, use it rather than hardwiring to a specific deployed instance. You'll gain maintainability. The catch, though, is that you must trust the contract owner won't maliciously forward your calls to a new implementation of the library that has nothing to do with the original one.

If you find the idea of designing an upgradeable library interesting and want to learn further, I encourage you to review Araoz's Medium article, where you can find code samples.

> **WARNING** You should thoroughly understand the proxy library technique before you attempt to implement it; weak implementations have been found subject to malicious attacks. I recommend reading the Medium post "Malicious backdoors in Ethereum Proxies," by Patricio Palladino, to make sure you're aware of the weak spots: http://mng.bz/vNz1.

13.3 Designing an upgradeable contract

As you might have already guessed, contracts suffer from the same limitation as libraries: once you deploy a contract, you're stuck with it. If you discover a bug or security vulnerability after deployment, you can at most freeze it or destroy it—if you included this kind of panic button functionality. The best bet is to plan for the worst-case scenario beforehand and design your contract with built-in upgradeability.

As in the case of proxy libraries, although this solution makes the contract safer from your side, from the point of view of the users, you're introducing a layer of obfuscation. The most security-conscious users might not trust your good intentions and might fear the possibility that, all of a sudden, you could start redirecting client calls to a malicious contract.

I'll illustrate for you these two main techniques for making a contract upgradeable:

- Use the same proxy technique I've shown you for libraries
- Separate state and logic into two contracts, both inherited from an abstract `Upgradeable` contract

13.3.1 Connecting to the upgraded contract through a proxy

Imagine various contracts, among which `SimpleCrowdsale`, from chapters 6 and 7, would like to use your marvelous `SimpleCoin` contract. You decide to make `SimpleCoin` upgradeable through a `SimpleCoinProxy` contract to avoid headaches not only to you, but also to all of your clients. As you can see in figure 13.5, the solution is identical to what you saw for SafeMath.

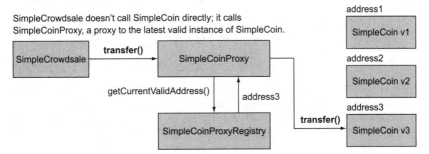

Figure 13.5 If you decide to make `SimpleCoin` upgradeable through `SimpleCoinProxy`, client contracts such as `SimpleCrowdsale` will call functions on `SimpleCoinProxy`, which will dispatch them to a specific deployed version of `SimpleCoin`, generally the latest one.

13.3.2   *Inheriting from an abstract Upgradeable contract*

Nick Johnson, the author of ENS, has taken a slightly different approach to making a contract upgradeable.[2] He has proposed to split the state (storage and Ether) and the logic of a contract into two separate contracts, both inherited from a common abstract contract called `Upgradeable`:

- A *dispatcher*—This would hold the state and would dispatch all the calls to a target contract through the Solidity `delegatecall()` function (which explicitly executes the EVM `delegatecall` opcode). Consequently, the function would execute in the context of the dispatcher. You'll see more about `delegatecall()` in chapter 14 on security.
- A *target contract*—You would delegate the entire functionality to this contract, which you could upgrade later on. This contract would also control the upgrade process.

With this design, illustrated in figure 13.6, when the target contract got upgraded, the dispatcher would still keep an unaltered state while it transferred all the calls to the latest version of the target contract.

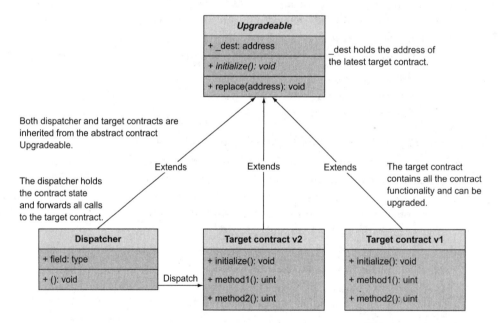

Figure 13.6   Upgradeability by splitting a contract into two contracts, both inherited from the same abstract `Upgradeable` contract: a dispatcher holding the state and a target contract holding the functionality. The dispatcher forwards all calls to the target contract. If an upgrade occurs, the dispatcher keeps holding the same unaltered state and forwards the calls to the latest version of the target.

---

[2] See "Mad blockchain science: A 100% upgradeable contract," Reddit+r/ethereum, May 24, 2016, http://mng.bz/y1Yo.

If you're eager to try out this approach, I encourage you to look at Nick's code at http://mng.bz/4OZD. If you're interested in learning more about solutions around library or contract upgradeability, I recommend the Medium article "Summary of Ethereum Upgradeable Smart Contract R&D," by Jack Tanner, based on his research across all the currently known techniques: http://mng.bz/QQmR.

> **WARNING** Designing an upgradeable contract using Nick's technique requires a thorough understanding of the inner workings of EVM and EVM assembly, which is outside the scope of this book. Also, using an upgradeable contract poses risks, as I explained earlier.

Summary

- Whereas in most languages events are transient objects that disappear from the system after being handled, Ethereum events are logged permanently on the blockchain.
- You can replay and query past events by registering a handler on the event filter with `get` rather than `watch`.
- You can improve the performance of past-event retrieval by indexing some of the event parameters when defining the event.
- You can make a library upgradeable by introducing a proxy to it. Client contracts no longer directly reference an instance of the library, but rather communicate with the proxy (or library dispatcher), which gets the latest valid address of the library from a registry contract and then forwards calls to the valid instance.
- You can make a contract upgradeable by using a proxy contract (as for libraries) or by separating state and logic into two contracts, both inherited from an abstract `Upgradeable` contract.
- Making a contract upgradeable makes it safer on one hand; for example, if you discover a problem after deployment, you can fix the contract and route the calls to the new amended version. But it might introduce security risks if you don't implement it correctly.
- Using an upgradeable library raises security concerns from the point of view of the contract user, who might worry about being routed to unintended functionality.

Security considerations

This chapter covers

- Understanding Solidity weak spots and risks associated with external calls
- Performing safe external calls
- Avoiding known security attacks
- General security guidelines

In the previous chapter, I gave you some advice on areas you should look at before deploying your Dapp on the production network. I believe security is such an important topic that it should be presented separately, so I've decided to dedicate this entire chapter to it.

I'll start by reminding you of some limitations in the Solidity language that, if you overlook them, can become security vulnerabilities. Among these limitations, I'll particularly focus on external calls and explain various risks you might face when executing them, but I'll also try to give you some tips for avoiding or minimizing such risks. Finally, I'll present classic attacks that might be launched against Ethereum Dapps so that you can avoid costly mistakes, especially when Ether is at stake.

14.1 Understanding general security weak spots

You should pay attention to certain limitations in the Solidity language because they're generally exploited as the first line of attack by malicious participants against unaware developers:

- *Data privacy*—If privacy is a requirement, you should store data in encrypted form rather than clear form.
- *Randomness*—Some Dapps, for example, betting games, occasionally need to randomize. You must ensure equal processing on all nodes without exposing the application to manipulation that takes advantage of the predictability of pseudo-random generators, and that can be tricky.
- *View functions*—You should be aware that functions defined as `view` might modify state variables, as mentioned in chapter 5, section 5.3.5.
- *Gas limits*—You should be careful when setting the gas limits of your transactions, whether they're low or high, because attackers might try to exploit them to their advantage.

Some of these vulnerabilities, such as those around randomness, might have more severe consequences, such as losing Ether. Other vulnerabilities, such as those around gas limits, have less severe consequences; for example, they can be exploited for denial of service attacks that can only cause temporary malfunctions. Whether they seem severe or not, you shouldn't underestimate *any* of these vulnerabilities.

14.1.1 Private information

As you already know, data stored on the blockchain is always public, regardless of the level of access of the contract state variables it has been stored against. For example, everybody can still see the value of a contract state variable declared as private.

If you need privacy, you need to implement a *hash commit–reveal* scheme like the one that the MAINNET ENS domain registration uses, as described in chapter 9, section 9.3.2. For example, to conceal a bid in an auction, the original value must not be submitted. Instead, the bid should be structured in two phases, as shown in figure 14.1:

1. *Hash commit*—You should initially *commit* the hash of the original value, and possibly of some unique data identifying the sender.
2. *Reveal*—You'll *reveal* the original value in a second stage, when the auction closes and the winner must be determined.

Auction based on a hash commit-reveal scheme

Commit phase

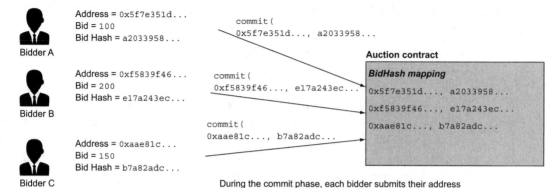

During the commit phase, each bidder submits their address
and the hash of a document containing the sender address,
the bid value and a secret.

Reveal phase

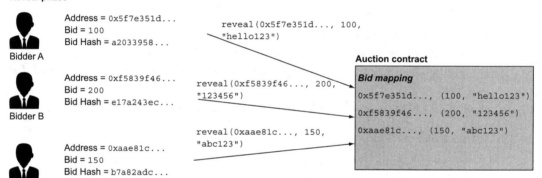

During the reveal phase, each bidder submits their address
and the original bid value together with the secret.

Determination of bid winner

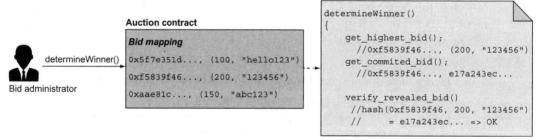

The winner is determined by finding the highest bid and then verifying its hash
matches the hash previously committed by its bidder.

**Figure 14.1   A hash commit–reveal scheme used for auction bid privacy. 1. During the *commit phase*, you commit
a hash of a document containing the sender address, the bid value, and a secret instead of the bid value in clear.
2. During the *reveal phase* you reveal the bid values together with their secrets. 3. The winner is determined by
finding the highest revealed bid. You then verify the results by calculating the hash from its sender address, bid
value, and password and comparing it against the previously submitted hash.**

14.1.2 Randomness

If you want the state of your decentralized application to depend on randomness, you'll face the same challenges associated with concealing private information that you saw in the previous section. The main concern is preventing miners from manipulating randomness to their advantage while also making sure the logic of your contract is executed exactly in the same way on all nodes.

Consequently, the way you should handle randomness in a Dapp should be similar to the commit–reveal scheme for private data. For example, as you can see in figure 14.2, in a decentralized roulette game the following should happen:

1 All players submit their bets (specific number, color, odd, or pair).
2 A random value provider is requested to supply a random number and, so as to keep the number secret until the last moment, the provider initially returns (commits) the number encoded using a one-way hash algorithm.
3 The completed transaction, including bets and the generated random number, is processed identically by all nodes, which will query the randomness provider for the original number associated with the hash. The provider reveals the original random number, and the winners are determined. If the randomness provider supplies a random number incompatible with the hash, the roulette spinning transaction fails.

14.1.3 Calling view functions

Defining a function as a `view` doesn't guarantee that nothing can modify the contract state while you're running it. The compiler doesn't perform such a check (but version 0.5.0 or higher of the Solidity compiler will perform this check), nor does the EVM. The compiler will only return a warning. For example, if you define the `authorize()` function of SimpleCoin as

```
function authorize(address _authorizedAccount, uint256 _allowance)
    public view returns (bool success) {
    allowance[msg.sender][_authorizedAccount] = _allowance;
    return true;
}
```

you'll get the following warning, because the state of the allowance mapping is being modified:

```
Warning: Function declared as view, but this expression (potentially)
    modifies the state...
```

If the contract state gets modified, a transaction is executed (rather than a simple call), and this consumes gas. An attacker might take advantage of the fact that the contract owner didn't foresee gas expenditure for this function and might cause consequences, ranging from a few transaction failures to sustained DoS attacks. To avoid

Roulette game based on a hash commit-reveal scheme

Commit phase

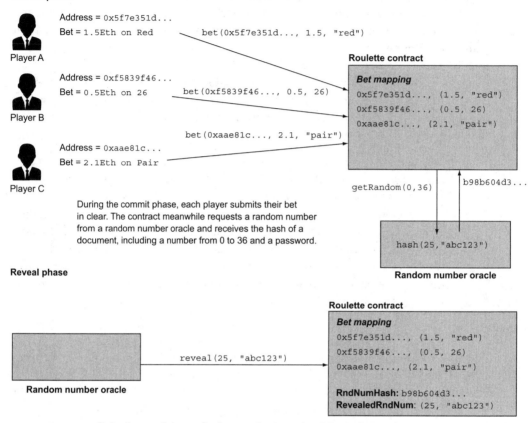

During the commit phase, each player submits their bet
in clear. The contract meanwhile requests a random number
from a random number oracle and receives the hash of a
document, including a number from 0 to 36 and a password.

Reveal phase

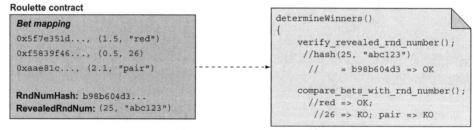

During the reveal phase, after the game has been closed, the random number
oracle reveals the random number in clear and the password.

Determination of game winners

During the reveal phase, after the game has been closed, the random number
oracle reveals the random number in clear and the password.

Roulette contract

Bet mapping
0x5f7e351d..., (1.5, "red")
0xf5839f46..., (0.5, 26)
0xaae81c..., (2.1, "pair")

RndNumHash: b98b604d3...
RevealedRndNum: (25, "abc123")

```
determineWinners()
{
    verify_revealed_rnd_number();
    //hash(25, "abc123")
    //     = b98b604d3 => OK

    compare_bets_with_rnd_number();
    //red => OK;
    //26 => KO; pair => KO
}
```

The random number that the oracle revealed is verified against the hash submitted
previously; if verification is succesful, bets are compared with the random number.

Figure 14.2   A hash commit–reveal scheme used for providing reproducible randomness. 1. All players submit their bets. 2. A randomness provider commits the hash of a generated random number, emulating a roulette spin. 3. A transaction, including bets and a random number hash, is processed. All nodes query the provider, which reveals the random number so that winners and losers can be determined.

this mistake, you should pay attention to compiler warnings and make sure you rectify the code accordingly.

14.1.4 Gas limits

As you know, to be processed successfully, a transaction must not exceed the block gas limit that the sender set. If a transaction fails because it hits the gas limit, the state of the contract is reverted, but the sender must pay transaction costs, and they don't get refunded.

The gas limit that the transaction sender sets can be favorable or detrimental to security, depending on how it's used. Here are the two extreme cases, as illustrated in figure 14.3:

- *High gas limit*—This makes it more likely that a transaction completes without running out of gas, and it's safer against attacks trying to fail the transaction by blowing the gas limit. On the other hand, a high gas limit allows a malicious attacker to manipulate the transaction more easily, because they can use more costly resources and computation to alter the expected course of the transaction.
- *Low gas limit*—This makes it more likely that a transaction can fail to complete because it runs out of gas, especially if something unexpected happens. Consequently, a transaction would be more exposed to attacks trying to fail it by blowing the gas limit. On the other hand, a low gas limit restricts how a malicious attacker can manipulate a transaction.

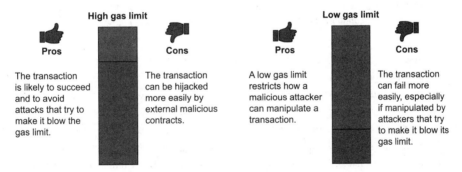

Figure 14.3 Pros and cons of high and low gas limits

In general, the best advice is to set the lowest possible gas limit that allows all genuine transactions to be completed against the expected logic. But it's hard to nail a reasonable gas estimate that's safe for both completion and security.

For example, if the logic executing a transaction includes loops, the transaction sender might decide to set a relatively high gas limit to cover the eventuality of a high number of loops. But it would be difficult to figure out in advance whether the gas limit would be hit, especially if the number of loops was determined dynamically and depended on state variables. If any of the state variables were subject to user input, an attacker could manipulate them so that the number of loops became very big, and the transaction would be more likely to run out of gas. Trying to bypass this problem by setting a very high gas limit defeats the purpose of the limit itself and isn't the right solution. In the next few sections, we'll explore correct solutions.

14.2   *Understanding risks associated with external calls*

Calls to external contracts introduce several potential threats to your application. This section will help you avoid or minimize them.

The first word of advice is to avoid calling external contracts if you can use alternative solutions. External calls transfer the flow of your logic to untrusted parties that might be malicious, even if only indirectly. For example, even if the external contract you're calling isn't malicious, its functions might in turn call a malicious contract, as shown in figure 14.4.

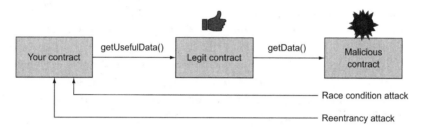

Figure 14.4   Your contract might get manipulated by an external malicious contract, even when you're confident the contract it directly interacts with is legit.

Because you lose direct control of the execution of your logic, you're exposed to attacks based on *race conditions* and *reentrancy*, which we'll examine later. Also, after the external call is complete, you must be careful about how to handle return values, especially in case of exceptions. But often, even if it might feel risky, you have no choice but to interact with external contracts, for example, at the beginning of a new project, when you want to make quick progress by taking advantage of tried and tested components. In that case, the safest approach is to learn about the related potential pitfalls and write your code to prevent them—read on!

14.2.1   *Understanding external call execution types*

You can perform external calls to invoke a function on an external contract or to send Ether to an external contract. It's also possible to invoke the execution of code while simultaneously transferring Ether. Table 14.1 summarizes the characteristics of each way of performing an external call.

> **WARNING**   Both send() and call() are becoming obsolete starting with version 0.5 of the Solidity compiler.

Table 14.1 Characteristics of each external call execution type

Call execution type	Purpose	External function called	Throws exception	Execution context	Message object	Gas limit
`externalContractAddress .send(etherAmount)`	Raw Ether transfer	Fallback	No	N/A	N/A	2,300
`externalContractAddress .transfer(etherAmount)`	Safe Ether transfer	Fallback	Yes	N/A	N/A	2,300
`externalContractAddress .call.(bytes4(sha3( "externalFunction()")))`	Raw function call in context of external contract	Specified function	No	External contract	Original msg.	Gas limit of orig. call
`externalContractAddress .callcode.(bytes4(sha3( "externalFunction()")))`	Raw function call in context of caller	Specified function	No	Calling contract	New msg. created by caller	Gas limit of orig. call
`externalContractAddress .delegatecall.(bytes4(sha3 ("externalFunction()")))`	Raw function call in context of caller	Specified function	No	Calling contract	Original msg.	Gas limit of orig. call
`ExternalContract(external ContractAddress) .externalFunction()`	Safe function call	Specified function	Yes	External contract	Original msg.	Gas limit of orig. call

When using `call()`, `callcode()`, and `delegatecall()`, you can transfer Ether simultaneously with the call invocation by specifying the Ether amount with the `value` keyword, as follows:

```
externalContractAddress.call.value(etherAmount)(
    bytes4(sha3("externalFunction()")
```

It's also possible to transfer Ether without calling any function, in this way:

```
externalContractAddress.call.value(etherAmount)()
```

This way of sending Ether has advantages and disadvantages: it allows the recipient to have a more complex fallback function, but for the same reason, it exposes the sender to malicious manipulation. As you can understand from table 14.1, various aspects of external calls might affect security when performing an external call:

- What external function can you call?
- Is an exception thrown if the external call fails?
- In which context is the external call executed?

- What's the message object received?
- What's the gas limit?

Let's examine them one by one.

14.2.2 *What external function can you call?*

It's possible to group call execution types into two sets: those only allowing you to transfer Ether and those allowing you to call any function.

PURE ETHER TRANSFER

The send() and transfer() calls can only call (implicitly) the fallback() function of the external contract, as shown here:

```
contract ExternalContract {
    ...
    function payable() { }          ◁─┐  This is the fallback function,
}                                      │  which send() calls implicitly,
                                       │  as explained in section 5.3.2.
contract A {
    ...
    function doSomething()
    {
        ...
        externalContractAddress.send(etherAmount);
    }
}
```

In general, a fallback function can contain logic of any complexity. But send() and transfer() impose a gas limit of 2,300 on the execution of the fallback function by transferring only a budget of 2,300 to the external function. This is such a low gas limit that, aside from transferring Ether, the fallback function can only perform a logging operation.

The low limit reassures the sender against potential *reentrancy* attacks (which I'll describe shortly). It does so because when the control flow is transferred to the fallback function, the external contract isn't able to perform any operations other than accepting the Ether transfer. On the other hand, this means you can't use send() and transfer() if you need to execute any substantial logic around the Ether payment. If you haven't fully understood this point yet, don't worry: it'll become clear when you learn about reentrancy attacks in the pages that follow.

INVOCATION OF CUSTOM FUNCTIONS

All other execution types can invoke custom external functions while transferring Ether to the external contract. The downside of such flexibility is that although you can associate logic of any complexity with an Ether transfer (thanks to a gas limit that can be as high as the sender wishes), the risk of a malicious manipulation of the external call, and consequently of diversion of Ether, is also higher.

As I explained earlier, it's possible to also purely transfer Ether without calling any function, as follows:

```
externalContractAddress.call.value(etherAmount)()
```

This way of sending Ether has the advantages and disadvantages associated with external calls through `call()`. The unrestricted gas limit on `call()` allows the recipient to have a more complex fallback function that can also access contract state, but for the same reason, it exposes the sender to potential malicious external manipulation.

> **TIP** The safest way to make an Ether transfer is to execute it through `send()` or `transfer()` and consequently to have it completely decoupled from any business logic.

14.2.3 *Is an exception thrown if the external call fails?*

From the point of view of the behavior when errors occur in external calls, you can divide call execution types into raw and safe. I'll discuss those types here and then move on to discuss the different contexts that you can execute calls in.

RAW CALLS

Most call execution types are considered *raw* because if the external function throws an exception, they return a Boolean `false` result but don't revert the contract state automatically. Consequently, if no action is taken after the unsuccessful call, the state of the calling contract may be incorrect, and any Ether you sent will be lost without having produced the expected economic benefit. Here are some examples of unhandled external calls:

```
externalContractAddress.send(etherAmount);

externalContractAddress.call.value(etherAmount)();

externalContractAddress.call.value(etherAmount)(
    bytes4(sha3("externalFunction()"));
```

If send() fails and isn't handled, etherAmount is lost; the 2,300 gas budget transferred to the external fallback function is lost.

If externalFunction fails, the etherAmount sent isn't returned and is lost; all the gas transferred to externalFunction is also lost.

If call() fails and isn't handled, etherAmount is lost; all the gas is transferred to the external fallback function and is lost.

Following the external call, you have two ways to revert the contract state if the call fails. You can use `require` or `revert()`.

The first way to manually revert the state if errors occur is to introduce `require()` conditions on some of the state variables. You must design the `require()` condition to fail if the external call fails, so the contract state gets reverted automatically, as shown in this snippet:

```
contract ExternalContract {
    ...
    function externalFunction payable (uint _input) {
    ...
```

Something wrong happens here, and externalFunction throws an exception.

```
        }
    }

    contract A {
        ...
        function doSomething ()
        {
            uint stateVariable;

            uint initialBalance = this.Balance;
            uint commission = 60;
            externalContractAddress.call.value(commission)(
                bytes4(sha3("externalFunction()")), 10);

            require(this.Balance == initialBalance - commission);
            require(stateVariable == expectedValue);
        }
    }
```

Two require () conditions are set against the Ether balance and the state of the contract. If any condition isn't met, both the Ether balance and the contract state are reverted.

An external function is called and following its failure, a Boolean false value is returned.

The second way is to perform explicit checks followed by a call to revert() if the checks are unsuccessful, as shown in this code:

```
contract ExternalContract {
    ...

    function externalFunction payable (uint _input) {
        ...
    }
}
contract A {
    uint stateVariable;

    ...
    function doSomething ()
    {
        uint initialBalance = this.Balance;
        uint commission = 60;

        if (!externalContractAddress.call.value(commission)(
            bytes4(sha3("externalFunction()")), 10))
            revert();
    }
    ...
```

Something wrong happens here, and externalFunction throws an exception.

SAFE CALLS

Two types of external calls are considered *safe* in that the failure of the external call propagates the exception to the calling code, and this reverts the contract state and Ether balance. The first type of safe call is

```
externalContractAddress.transfer(etherAmount);
```

If transfer() fails, the external failure triggers a local exception, which reverts the state and balance of the calling contract.

The second type of safe call is a high-level call to the external contract:

```
ExternalContract(externalContractAddress)
    .externalFunction();
```

If externalFunction fails, this triggers a local exception, which reverts the state and balance of the calling contract.

TIP Favor safe calls through `transfer()`, for transferring Ether, or through direct high-level custom contract functions, for executing logic. Avoid unsafe calls such as `send()` for sending Ether and `call()` for executing logic. If a safe call fails, the contract state will be reverted cleanly, whereas if an unsafe call fails, you're responsible for handling the error and reverting the state.

14.2.4 Which context is the external call executed in?

You can execute a call in the *context of the calling contract*, which means it affects (and uses) the state of the calling contract. You can also execute it in the *context of the external contract*, which means it affects (and uses) the state of the external contract.

EXECUTION IN THE CONTEXT OF THE EXTERNAL CONTRACT

If you scan through the values in the execution context column of table 14.1, you'll realize that most call execution types involve execution in the context of the external contract. The code in the following listing shows an external call taking place in the context of the external contract.

Listing 14.1 Example of execution in the context of an external contract

```
contract A {
    uint value;
    address  msgSender;          State variables
    address externalContractAddress = 0x5;

    function setValue(uint _value)
    {
        externalContractAddress.call.(            External call performed on
            bytes4(sha3("setValue()")), _value);   ExternalContract.setValue ()
    }
}

contract ExternalContract {

    uint value;                  State variables
    address msgSender;           defined on contract A

    function setValue(uint _value) {     Modifies ExternalContract.value
        value = _value;                   and sets it to _value
        msgSender = msg.sender;        Modifies ExternalContract.msgSender
    }                                    and sets it to the original msg.sender
}                                        sent to contract A
```

Through the example illustrated in figure 14.5, I'll show you how the state of `ContractA` and `ExternalContract` change following the external call implemented in listing 14.1.

Execution in the context of the external contract

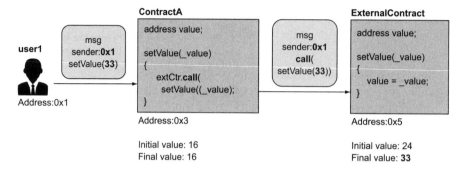

When an external function is invoked through **call()**, it's executed in the **context of the external contract** (ExternalContract), which means the function ExternalContract.setValue() modifies the state of ExternalContract.

Figure 14.5 Example illustrating execution in the context of an external contract

The addresses of the user and contract accounts used in the example are summarized in table 14.2.

Table 14.2 User and contract account addresses

Account	Address
user1	0x1
user2	0x2
ContractA	0x3
ContractB	0x4
ExternalContract	0x5

The initial state of the contracts before the external call takes place is summarized in table 14.3. The state of the contracts will change to that shown in table 14.4.

Table 14.3 Initial state of the contracts

	ContractA	ExternalContract
Value	16	24

Now imagine user1 performs the following call on ContractA; for example, from a web UI, through Web3.js, as you saw in chapter 12:

```
ContractA.setValue(33)
```

Table 14.4 State of the contracts and msg object following an external call

	ContractA	**ExternalContract**
Value	16	**33**
msg sender	0x1	**0x1**

In summary, the state of ContractA hasn't changed, whereas the state of External-Contract has been modified, as shown in table 14.4. The msg object that External-Contract handles is the original msg object that user1 generated while calling ContractA.

EXECUTION IN THE CONTEXT OF THE CALLING CONTRACT WITH DELEGATECALL

Execution through delegatecall takes place in context of the calling contract. The code in the following listing shows an external call taking place in the context of the external contract.

Listing 14.2 Example of delegatecall execution in the context of a calling contract

```
contract A {
    uint value;
    address msgSender;                State variables
    address externalContractAddress = 0x5;

    function setValue(uint _value)
    {
        externalContractAddress.delegatecall.(          External call performed on
            bytes4(sha3("setValue()")), _value);   ◁—   ExternalContract.setValue ()
    }
}


contract ExternalContract {

    uint value;               State variables defined
    address msgSender;        as in ContractA

    function setValue(uint _value) {       Modifies ContractA.value
        value = _value;               ◁—   and sets it to _value
        msgSender = msg.sender;   ◁—
    }                                  Modifies ContractA.msgSender and
}                                      sets it to the original msg.Sender
                                       sent to ContractA
```

As I did earlier, through the example illustrated in figure 14.6, I'll show you how the state of ContractA and ExternalContract change following the external call implemented in listing 14.2.

The initial state of the contracts before the external call takes place is summarized in table 14.5.

Execution in the context of the calling contract through delegatecall

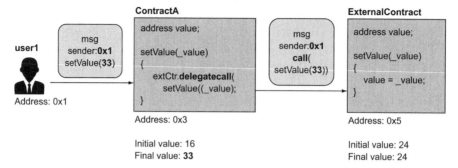

When an external function is invoked through **delegatecall**(), it's executed in the **context of the calling contract** (ContractA), which means the function ExternalContract.setValue() modifies the state of ContractA.

Figure 14.6   Example illustrating `delegatecall` **execution in the context of the calling contract**

Table 14.5   Initial state of the contracts

	ContractA	ExternalContract
Value	16	24

Now imagine user1 performs the following call on ContractA, for example, from a web UI:

```
ContractA.setValue(33)
```

In summary, the state of ContractA has been modified, whereas the state of External-Contract hasn't changed, as shown in table 14.6. The msg object that External-Contract handles is still the original msg object that user1 generated while calling ContractA.

Table 14.6   State of the contracts and msg **object following an external call through** delegatecall

	ContractA	ExternalContract
Value	33	24
msg sender	0x1	0x1

EXECUTION IN THE CONTEXT OF THE CALLING CONTRACT WITH CALLCODE

The last case to examine is when the implementation of `ContractA.setValue()` uses `callcode` rather than `delegatecall`, as shown here:

```
function setValue(uint _value)
{
    externalContractAddress.callcode.(bytes4(sha3("setValue()")), _value);
}
```

Assuming the same initial state as before, after user1's call, illustrated in figure 14.7, the state of the contracts will be that shown in table 14.7.

Execution in the context of the calling contract through callcode

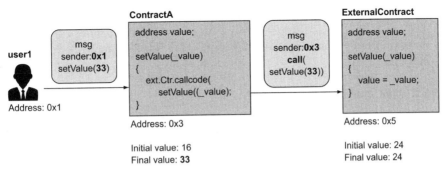

When an external function is invoked through **callcode()**, it's executed in the **context of the calling contract** (ContractA), which means the function ExternalContract.setValue() modifies the state of ContractA. callcode **doesn't propagate** to ExternalContract the original msg object from user1, as delegatecall does, but creates a new msg object whose sender is ContractA.

Figure 14.7 Example illustrating `callcode` execution in the context of the calling contract

Table 14.7 State of the contracts following an external call through `callcode`

	ContractA	ExternalContract
Value	33	24
`msg` sender	0x1	0x3

As you can see, an external function that `callcode` calls is still executed in the context of the caller, as when the call was performed through `delegatecall`. But `ContractA` generates a new `msg` object when the external call takes place, and the message sender is `ContractA`.

From a security point of view, execution in the context of the external contract is clearly safer than in the context of the calling contract. When execution takes place in the context of the calling contract, such as when calling external functions through `callcode` or `delegatecall`, the caller is allowing the external contract read/write access to its state variables. As you can imagine, it's safe to do so only in limited circumstances, mainly when the external contract is under your direct control (for example, you're the contract owner). You can find a summary of the context and the msg object used for each call type in table 14.8.

Table 14.8   Summary of execution context and msg object in each call type

Call type	Execution context	msg object
call	External contract	Original msg object
delegatecall	Caller contract	Original msg object
callcode	Caller contract	Caller contract-generated msg object

> **TIP**   If you need to use call(), favor calls through call(), in the context of the external contract rather than in the context of the calling contract. Bear in mind, though, that call() will become obsolete starting with version 0.5 of Solidity.

14.2.5   *What's the msg object received?*

In general, a message object is supposed to flow from its point of creation up to the last contract of an external-call chain, which might span several contracts. This is true when invoking external calls through all external call types, apart from callcode, which generates a new message instead, as you saw when comparing the external call execution under callcode and delegatecall. The delegatecall opcode was introduced as a bug fix for the unwanted message-creating behavior of callcode. Consequently, you should avoid using callcode if possible.

> **TIP**   Avoid callcode if possible and choose delegatecall instead.

14.2.6   *What's the gas limit?*

Apart from send() and transfer(), which impose a gas limit of 2,300 gas on the external call that's only sufficient to perform an Ether transfer and a log operation, all the other external call types transfer to the external call the full gas limit present in the original call. As I explained previously, both low and high gas limits have security implications, but when it comes to transferring Ether, a lower limit is preferable because it prevents external manipulation when Ether is at stake.

> **TIP**   Favor a lower gas limit over a higher gas limit.

14.3   *How to perform external calls more safely*

You should now have a better idea of the characteristics and tradeoffs associated with each external call type, and you might be able to choose the most appropriate one for your requirements. But even if you pick the correct call type, you might end up in trouble if you don't use it correctly. In this section, I'll show you some techniques for performing external calls safely. You'll see how even performing an Ether transfer through the apparently safe and inoffensive `transfer()` can end up in a costly mistake if you don't think through all the scenarios that could lead your call to fail.

14.3.1 *Implementing pull payments*

Imagine you've developed an auction Dapp and you've implemented an `Auction` contract like the one shown in the open source *Ethereum Smart Contract Best Practices* guide coordinated by ConsenSys,[1] which I've provided in the following listing. Have a good look at this listing, because I'll reference it a few times in this chapter.

> **Listing 14.3   Incorrect implementation of an `Auction` contract**

```
contract Auction {//INCORRECT CODE //DO NOT USE!//UNDER APACHE LICENSE 2.0
    // Copyright 2016 Smart Contract Best Practices Authors
    address highestBidder;
    uint highestBid;

    function bid() payable {                        Reverts the transaction if the
        require(msg.value >= highestBid);   ◁────── current bid isn't the highest one

        if (highestBidder != 0) {                   If the current bid is the
            highestBidder.transfer(highestBid);  ◁─ highest, refunds the
        }                                           previous highest bidder

        highestBidder = msg.sender;    │ Updates the details of the
        highestBid = msg.value;        │ highest bid and bidder
    }
}
```

What happens if one of the bidders has implemented a fallback, as shown in the following listing, and then they submit a bid higher than the highest one?

> **Listing 14.4   A malicious contract calling the `Auction` contract**

```
contract MaliciousBidder {
    address auctionContractAddress = 0x123;
    function submitBid() public {
        auctionContractAddress.call.value(
            100000000000)(bytes4(sha3("bid()")));
    }

    function payable() {           │ This contract will revert its state and
        revert ();            ◁──── throw an exception every time it
    }                              │ receives an Ether payment.
    ...
}
```

---

[1]   See "Recommendations for Smart Contract Security in Solidity," http://mng.bz/MxXD, licensed under Apache License, Version 2.0.

As soon as the `MaliciousBidder` contract submits the highest bid through `submitBid()`, `Auction.bid()` refunds the previous highest bidder then sets the address and value of the highest bid to those of the `MaliciousBidder`. So far, so good. What happens next?

A new bidder now makes the highest bid. `Auction.bid()` will consequently try to refund `MaliciousBidder`, but the following line of code fails, even if the new bidder has done nothing wrong and the logic of the `bid()` function seems correct:

```
highestBidder.transfer(highestBid);
```

This line fails because the current `highestBidder` is still the address of `Malicious-Bidder`, and its fallback, which `highestBidder.transfer()` calls, throws an exception. If you think about it, no new bidder will ever be able to pass this line, because a refund to `MaliciousBidder` will be attempted on every occasion. Also, the call to `highest-Bidder.transfer()` will keep failing before the address and value of a new highest bid can ever be updated, as illustrated in figure 14.8. That's why `MaliciousBidder` is . . . malicious!

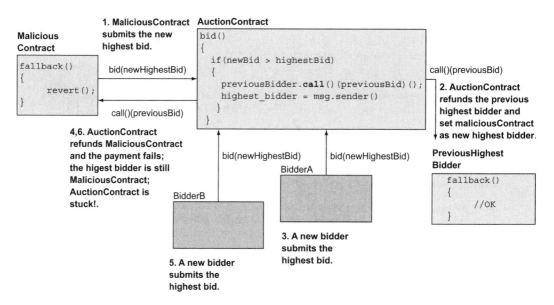

Figure 14.8 **After the malicious contract has become the highest bidder, the `Auction` contract becomes unusable because it will unsuccessfully try to refund the malicious contract at every new higher bid and will never be able to set the new highest bidder.**

What about replacing `transfer()` with `send()`? An exception will be thrown in the `bid()` function following a failure in `send()`. As a result, using `send()` instead of `transfer()` in the recommended way, as shown in the following line of code, doesn't solve the problem:

```
require(highestBidder.send(highestBid));
```

With your current `bid()` implementation, you don't even need a malicious external bidder contract to end up in trouble. Also, unintentional exceptions that are thrown by any external bidding contract that has a faulty `fallback()` can rock the boat. For example, a sloppy developer of a bidder contract, unaware of the gas limitations associated with `transfer()` (or `send()`) might have decided to implement a complex fallback function, such as the one shown in the code that follows, that accepts the refund and processes it by modifying its own contract state. That would consequently blow the `transfer()` 2,300 gas stipend and almost immediately throw a "ran out of gas" exception:

```
function () payable() {
    refunds +=  msg.value;    ⟵── As soon as the state variable refund is updated,
}                                  the function execution runs out of the 2,300 gas
                                   stipend imposed by transfer() and fails.
```

As you can see, the current implementation of `bid()` relies heavily on the assumption that you're dealing with honest and competent external contract developers. That might not always be the case.

A safer way to accept a bid is to separate the logic that updates the highest bidder from the execution of the refund to the previous highest bidder. The refund will no longer be pushed automatically to the previous highest bidder but should now be pulled with a separate request by them, as shown in the following listing. (This solution also comes from the ConsenSys guide I mentioned earlier.)

Listing 14.5 Correct implementation of an `Auction` contract

```
//UNDER APACHE LICENSE 2.0
//Copyright 2016 Smart Contract Best Practices Authors
//https://consensys.github.io/smart-contract-best-practices/
contract Auction {
    address highestBidder;
    uint highestBid;
    mapping(address => uint) refunds;

    function bid() payable external {                    Now this function only stores
        require(msg.value >= highestBid);                the amount to refund because
                                                         of a new higher bidder in the
        if (highestBidder != 0) {                        refund mapping. No Ether
            refunds[highestBidder] += highestBid;  ⟵──   transfer takes place.
        }
                                                    The update of the new highest bid and
        highestBidder = msg.sender;               ╱│ bidder will now succeed because bid()
        highestBid = msg.value;                   ╱│ no longer contains external operations
    }                                              │ that might get hijacked, such as the
                                                   │ previous transfer() call.
    function withdrawRefund() external {
        uint refund = refunds[msg.sender];          If this transfer fails—for example,
        refunds[msg.sender] = 0;                     when paying MaliciousBidder—the
        msg.sender.transfer(refund);     ⟵──         state of the Auction contract is now
        }                                            unaffected.
    }
}
```

Pull payments also come in handy in case the function that makes a payment performs a number of payments in a loop. An example would be a function that refunds all the accounts of the investors in an unsuccessful crowdsale, as shown in the following listing.

Listing 14.6 Incorrect implementation of a function making several payments

```
contract Crowdsale {
   address[] investors;
   mapping(address => uint) investments;

   function refundAllInvestors() payable onlyOwner external {
      //INCORRECT CODE //DO NOT USE!

      for (int i =0; i< investors.length; ++i) {
         investors[i].send(investments[investors[i]]);
      }
   }
}
```

If an attacker makes very small investments from a very high number of accounts, the number of items in the investors array might become so big that the for loop will run out of gas before completing, because each step of the loop has a fixed gas cost. This is a form of DoS attack exploiting gas limits. A safer implementation is to keep only the refund assignment in refundAllInvestors() and to move the Ether transfer operation into a separate pull payment function called withdrawalRefund(). This is similar to the one you saw earlier in the Auction contract, as you can see in the following listing.

Listing 14.7 Improved refundAllInvestors() implementation

```
contract Crowdsale {
   address[] investors;
   mapping(address => uint) investments;
   mapping(address => uint) refunds;

   function refundAllInvestors() payable onlyOwner external {

      for (int i =0; i< investors.length; ++i) {
         refunds[investors [i]] = investments[i];
         investments[investors[i]] = 0;
      }
   }

   function withdrawRefund() external {
      uint refund = refunds[msg.sender];
      refunds[msg.sender] = 0;
      msg.sender.transfer(refund);
   }
}
```

14.3.2 *Implementing a minimal fallback function*

Although pull payments are a good solution from the point of view of the contract that's transferring Ether out, now put yourself in the shoes of the bidder. If you're expecting Ether from an external contract, such as the `Auction` contract, don't assume the external contract is implementing safe pull-payment functionality, as shown in listing 14.7. Assume instead that the external contract has been implemented in a suboptimal way, as in listing 14.6, the initial implementation you looked at. In this case, if you want to make sure the refund operation executed with `transfer()` (or `send()`) succeeds, you must provide a minimal fallback function: empty or at most with a single log operation, as shown here:

```
function() public payable {}
```

14.3.3 *Beware of Ether coming to you through selfdestruct()*

Unfortunately, you can't make sure your contract doesn't receive Ether from unknown sources. You might think that having a fallback that always throws an exception or reverts the state of your contract when called, as shown here, should be sufficient to stop this undesired inflow of Ether:

```
function() public payable {revert();}
```

But I'm afraid there's a way to transfer Ether to any address that doesn't require any payable function on the receiving side—not even a fallback function. This can be achieved by calling

```
selfdestruct(recipientAddress);
```

The `selfdestruct()` function was introduced to provide a way to destroy a contract in case of emergency, and with the same operation, to transfer all the Ether associated with the contract account to a specified address. Typically, this would be executed when a critical bug was discovered or when a contract was being hacked.

Unfortunately, `selfdestruct()` also lends itself to misuse. If an external contract contains at least 1 Wei and self-destructs, targeting the address of your contract, there isn't much you can do. You might think receiving unwanted Ether wouldn't be a serious issue, but if the logic of your contract depends on checks and reconciliations performed on the Ether balance, for example, through `require()`, you might be in trouble.

14.4   *Avoiding known security attacks*

Now that we've reviewed Solidity's known security weak spots associated with external calls, it's time to analyze known attacks that have taken place exploiting such weaknesses. You can group attacks on Solidity contracts into three broad categories, depending on the high-level objective of the attacker. The objective can be to

- manipulate the outcome of an individual transaction
- favor one transaction over other transactions
- make a contract unusable

Table 14.9 summarizes manipulation techniques associated with each attack category. The next few sections will define and present in detail each attack technique included in the table.

Table 14.9   Security attacks, strategies, and techniques

Attack objective	Attack strategy	Attack technique
Individual transaction manipulation	Race condition	Reentrancy, cross-function race condition
Favoring one transaction over others	Front-running	Front-running
Making contract unusable	Denial of service	Fallback calling `revert()`, exploiting gas limits

> **WARNING**   This section only covers the most common attacks, mainly to give you an idea of how malicious participants can manipulate a contract. Also, new security attacks are continuously discovered, so you must learn about and constantly keep up to date with the latest security breaches by consulting the official Solidity documentation and the many other websites and blogs that cover the topic. I'll point you to some resources in section 14.5.

14.4.1   *Reentrancy*

Reentrancy attacks target functions containing an external call and exploit a race condition between simultaneous calls to this function caused by the possible time lag that takes place during the external call. The objective of the attack is generally to manipulate the state of the contract, often having to do with an Ether or custom cryptocurrency balance, by calling back the targeted function many times simultaneously while the attacker hijacks the execution of the external call. If we go back to the example of the auction Dapp I showed you earlier, an attacker could launch a reentrancy attack on an incorrect implementation of `withdrawRefund()` by requesting a refund many times in parallel while hijacking each refund call, as illustrated in figure 14.9.

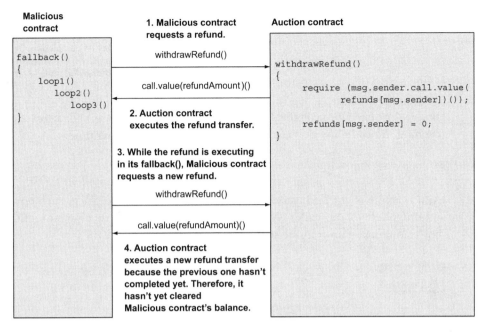

Figure 14.9 If you were to implement `Auction.withdrawRefund()` incorrectly, for example, by clearing the balance of the caller only after the Ether transfer has been completed, an attacker could attempt to call it many times in parallel while hijacking each call, by slowing down the execution of the receiving `fallback()` function. Various of these simultaneous Ether transfers are allowed and can complete successfully until one of them finally completes and the balance of the caller is cleared. Before this happens, many illegitimate refunds might take place.

The following code shows an incorrect implementation of `withdrawRefund()` (also from the ConsenSys guide) that will put your contract in danger:

```
function withdrawRefund() external { {//INCORRECT CODE //DO NOT USE!
    // UNDER APACHE LICENSE 2.0
    // Copyright 2016 Smart Contract Best Practices Authors
    uint refund = refunds[msg.sender];
    require (msg.sender.call.value(refund)());       ⟵  Calls to an external contract
    refunds[msg.sender] = 0;   ⟵                         fallback function, which might
}                              Executes only after the previous   take a relatively long time
                               external call is complete
```

As I mentioned, an attacker contract might call `withdrawRefund()` several times while hijacking each external call to the fallback function that enables the payment, as shown here:

```
contract ReentrancyAttacker {
    function() payable public () {
        uint maxUint = 2 ** 256 - 1;
        for (uint I = 0; i < maxUint; ++i)
        {
            for (uint j =0; j  < maxUint; ++j)
```

```
            {
                for   (uint k =0; k < maxUint; ++k)
                {
                    . . .
            }
    }
}
```

> The fallback contains only code to delay its completion. Before this completes, the attacker calls withdrawRefund() several times.

Such a slow execution of the Ether transfer would prevent `withdrawRefund()` from reaching the code line that clears the caller balance for a long time:

```
refunds[msg.sender] = 0;
```

Until this line is reached, various Ether transfers might take place, each equal to the amount owed to the caller. As a result, the caller could receive more Ether than they're owed, as shown in the sequence diagram in figure 14.10.

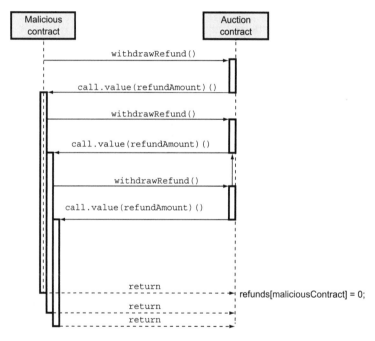

Figure 14.10   Sequence diagram of parallel invocations of an incorrect implementation of `withdrawRefund()` by an attacker

NOTE   The reason why I wanted to include in this chapter the auction Dapp from the ConsenSys guide, and particularly its incorrect implementation of the `withdrawRefund()` function, is that this code shows one of the vulnerabilities that contributed to the initial success of the DAO attack.

You can prevent this attack using a couple of methods:

- If you can, use `transfer()` or `send()` instead of `call.value()()`, so the attacker will have a gas limit of 2,300 and be prevented from implementing any transfer-delaying code in their `fallback()` function.
- Place the external call performing the Ether transfer as the last operation, so the Ether balance can be cleared before the call takes place rather than after, as shown in listing 14.8. If the attacker tried to call `withdrawRefund()` again, the value of `refunds[msg.sender]` would be zero, and consequently the refund would be set to zero. Therefore, the new Ether payment wouldn't have any effect.

Listing 14.8 Correct `withdrawRefund` implementation

```
function withdrawRefund() external {
    uint refund = refunds[msg.sender];
    refunds[msg.sender] = 0;
    require (msg.sender.call.value(refund)());    <──┐
}
```
Now the transfer takes place after the balance has been cleared, so subsequent calls to withdraw-Refund() have no effect.

14.4.2 *Cross-function race conditions*

You've learned that reentrancy attacks exploit a race condition between simultaneous calls to the same function. But an attacker can also exploit race conditions between simultaneous calls on separate functions that try to modify the same contract state—for example, the Ether balance of a specific account.

A cross-race condition also could happen on `SimpleCoin`. Recall `SimpleCoin`'s `transfer()` function:

```
function transfer(address _to, uint256 _amount) public {
    require(coinBalance[msg.sender] > _amount);
    require(coinBalance[_to] + _amount >= coinBalance[_to] );
    coinBalance[msg.sender] -= _amount;
    coinBalance[_to] += _amount;
    emit Transfer(msg.sender, _to, _amount);
}
```

Now, imagine you decided to provide a `withdrawFullBalance()` function, which closed the SimpleCoin account of the caller and sent them back the equivalent amount in Ether. If you implemented this function as follows, you'd expose the contract to a potential cross-function race condition:

```
function withdrawFullBalance() public {//INCORRECT CODE //DO NOT USE!
    uint amountToWithdraw = coinBalance[msg.sender] * exchangeRate;
    require(msg.sender.call.value(
        amountToWithdraw)());         <──┐
    coinBalance[msg.sender] = 0;
}
```
The attacker contract calls transfer() at this point of the execution of withdrawFullBalance().

A cross-function race condition attack works in a similar way to the reentrancy attack shown earlier. An attacker would first call `withdrawFullBalance()` and, while they were hijacking the external call from their fallback function, as shown in the following code, they'd call `transfer()` to move the full SimpleCoin balance to another address they own before the execution of `withdrawBalance()` cleared this balance. In this way, they'd both keep the full SimpleCoin balance and get the equivalent Ether amount:

```
contract RaceConditionAttacker {
    function() payable public () {
        uint maxUint = 2 ** 256 - 1;
        for (uint I = 0; i < maxUint; ++i)
        {
            for (uint j =0; j  < maxUint; ++j)
            {
                for    (uint k =0; k < maxUint; k++)
                {
                    . . .
            }
        }
    }
}
```

The solution is, as was the case for the reentrancy attack, to replace `call.value()()` with `send()` or `transfer()`. You would also need to make sure the external call that performs the balance withdrawal takes place in the last line of the function, after the caller balance has already been set to 0:

```
function withdrawFullBalance() public {
    uint amountToWithdraw = coinBalance[msg.sender];
    coinBalance[msg.sender] = 0;
    require(msg.sender.call.value(                The external call is now
        amountToWithdraw)());          ◁—        performed after the caller
}                                                balance has been cleared.
```

More complex cases of reentrancy involve call chains spanning several contracts. The general recommendation is always to place external calls or calls to functions containing external calls at the end of the function body.

14.4.3 *Front-running attacks*

The attacks based on race conditions you've seen so far try to manipulate the outcome of a transaction by altering its expected execution flow, generally by hijacking the part of the execution that takes place externally.

Other attack strategies work at a higher level and target decentralized applications for which the ordering of the execution of the transactions is important. Attackers try to influence the timing or ordering of transaction executions by favoring and prioritizing certain transactions over others. For example, a malicious miner might manipulate a decentralized stock market-making application by creating new buy order transactions when detecting in the memory pool many buy orders for a certain stock. The miner would then include only their own buy order transactions on the new block, so their transactions would get executed before any other similar order present in the memory pool, as illustrated in figure 14.11. If the miner's PoW was successful, their buy order would become official. Subsequently, the stock price would rise because of the many buy orders that have been submitted but not executed yet. This would generate an instant profit for the miner.

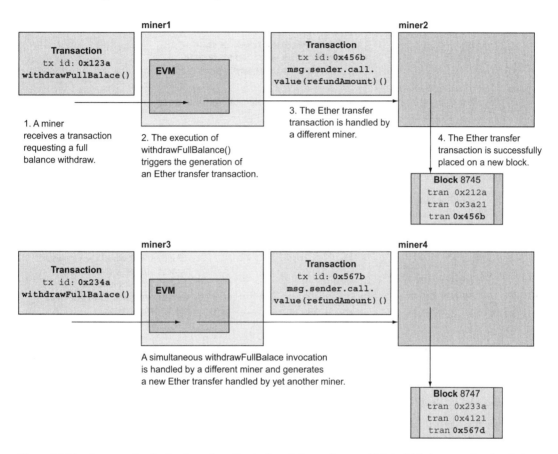

Figure 14.11   An example of a front-running attack. A malicious miner could detect big buy or sell orders being sent to a stock market-making Dapp and still in the memory pool. They could then decide to front run them by ignoring these big orders and including their own orders in the new block they would try to create, therefore making an unfair profit if the block got mined.

This manipulation is an example of *front running*, which is the practice of malicious stock brokers who place the execution of their own orders ahead of those of their clients. A way to avoid this attack is to design the order clearing logic on *batch execution* rather than individual execution, with an implementation similar to batch auctions. With this setup, the auction contract collects all bids and then determines the winner with a single operation. Another solution is to implement a commit–reveal scheme similar to that described earlier in this chapter to disguise order information.

14.4.4 *Denial of service based on revert() in fallback*

Some attacks aim to bring down a contract completely. These are known as denial of service (DoS) attacks.

As I've already shown you in the Auction contract, at the beginning of this chapter, an attacker could make a contract unusable by implementing the following fallback and then calling the targeted contract in such a way that it triggers an incoming payment:

```
function payable() {          This contract will revert its state
    revert();          ◁──    and throw an exception every time
}                             it receives an Ether payment.
```

If the targeted contract implements a function as shown here, it will become unusable as soon as it tries to send Ether to the attacker:

```
function bid() payable {//INCORRECT CODE//DO NOT USE!
    //UNDER APACHE LICENSE 2.0
    //Copyright 2016 Smart Contract Best Practices Authors

    require(msg.value >= highestBid);      ◁──  Checks if the current bid is higher
                                                than the current highest bid

    if (highestBidder != 0) {
        highestBidder.transfer(highestBid));   ◁──  The previous highest bidder is
    }                                                refunded, but when the previous
                                                     highest bidder is the malicious
    highestBidder = msg.sender;                      contract, the transfer fails, and a
    highestBid = msg.value;                          new higher bidder and bid value
}                                                    can no longer be set.
                      Sets new higher
                      bidder and bid values
```

As you already know, you can avoid this attack by implementing a pull payment facility rather than an automated push payment. (See section 14.3.1 for more details.)

14.4.5 *Denial of service based on gas limits*

In the section on pull payments, you saw the example of an incorrectly implemented function that refunds all the accounts of the investors in an unsuccessful crowdsale:

```
contract Crowdsale {
    address[] investors;
    mapping(address => uint) investments;

    function refundAllInvestors() payable onlyOwner external {
        //INCORRECT CODE //DO NOT USE!
        for (int i =0; i< investors.length; ++i) {
            investors[i].send(investments[investors[i]]);
        }
    }
}
```

I already warned you that this implementation lends itself to manipulation by an attacker who makes very small investments from a very high number of accounts. The high number of `for` loops required by the large investments array will damage the contract permanently, because any invocation of the function will blow the gas limit. This is a form of DoS attack exploiting gas limits. Refunds based on pull payment functionality also prevent this attack.

You've learned about the pitfalls associated with external calls and how to avoid the most common forms of attack. Now I'll close the chapter by sharing with you some security recommendations I've been collecting over time from various sources.

14.5 General security guidelines

The official Solidity documentation has an entire section dedicated to security considerations and recommendations,[2] which I invite you to consult before deploying your contract on public networks. Other excellent resources are available, such as the open source *Ethereum Smart Contract Best Practices* guide (http://mng.bz/dP4g), initiated and maintained by the Diligence (https://consensys.net/diligence/) division of ConsenSys, which focuses on security and aims at raising awareness around best practices in this field. This guide, which I've referenced in various places in this chapter, is widely considered to be the main reference on Ethereum security. I've decided to adopt its terminology to make sure you can look up concepts easily, if you decide you want to learn more about anything I've covered here.

In table 14.10, I've listed an additional set of useful free resources on Ethereum security that ConsenSys Diligence has created. Presentations and posts by Christian Reitwiessner,[3] the head of Solidity at Ethereum, are also a must-read.

Table 14.10 Ethereum security resources ConsenSys Diligence has distributed

Resource	Description
Secure smart contract philosophy[1]	Series of *Medium* articles written by ConsenSys Diligence on how to approach smart contract security
EIP 1470: SWC[2]	Standardized weakness classification for smart contracts, so tool vendors and security practitioners can classify weaknesses in a more consistent way
0x security audit report[3]	Full security audit of ConsenSys 0x smart contract system, carried out by ConsenSys Diligence. This gives a good idea of the weaknesses assessed during a thorough security audit.
Audit readiness guide[4]	Guidelines on how to prepare for a smart contract security audit

1. See "Building a Philosophy of Secure Smart Contracts," http://mng.bz/ed5G.
2. See these GitHub pages: https://github.com/ethereum/EIPs/issues/1469 and http://mng.bz/pgVR.
3. See http://mng.bz/O2Ej.
4. See Maurelian's "Preparing for a Smart Contract Code Audit," September 6, 2017, at http://mng.bz/YPqj.

---

[2] See "Security Considerations" at http://mng.bz/a7o9.
[3] See "Smart Contract Security," June 10,2016, http://mng.bz/GWxA, and "How to Write Safe Smart Contracts," November 10, 2015, http://mng.bz/zMx6.

I'll summarize in a short list the most important points all the resources I've mentioned tend to agree on. I reiterate, though, that it's important to constantly keep up to date with the latest security exploits and discovered vulnerabilities on sites such as http://hackingdistributed.com, https://cryptonews.com, or https://cryptoslate.com. Here's the list:

- *Favor a simple contract design.* The same design recommendations that generally apply to object-oriented classes are also valid for smart contracts. Aim for small contracts, focused on only one piece of functionality, with a small number of state variables and with short functions. This will help you avoid mistakes and will help fellow developers understand your code correctly.

- *Amend code that raises compiler warnings.* Understand any compiler warnings and amend your code accordingly. Aim to remove all the warnings you get, if possible, especially those related to deprecated functionality. Solidity syntax has been amended often because of security concerns, so take the advice from warnings seriously.

- *Call external contracts as late as possible.* As you've learned in the sections dedicated to reentrancy, you should avoid changing the state of your contract after returning from an external call. This call might get hijacked, and you might not be able to return from it safely. The recommended pattern to adopt is called *check–effects–interaction*, according to which you structure a function on the following ordered steps:
  - *Check*—Validate that the message sender is authorized, function input parameters are valid, Ether being transferred is available, and so on. You generally do this directly through `require` statements or indirectly through function modifiers.
  - *Effects*—Change the state of your contract based on the validated function input.
  - *Interaction*—Call external contracts or libraries using the new contract state.

- *Plan for disaster.* As you learned in the previous chapter, once a contract has been deployed, you can't modify it. If you discover a bug or, even worse, a security flaw, and Ether is at risk, you can't apply a hot-fix as you'd do on a conventional centralized application. You should plan for this eventuality beforehand and provide the contract owner with an emergency function, such as `freeze()` or `selfDestruct()`, as I mentioned in chapters 6 and 7 when presenting Simple-Crowdsale. Such functions can disable the contract temporarily, until you understand the defect, or even permanently. Some developers have taken a more proactive approach and have implemented auto-freezing (or fail-safe) functionality based on contract state pre- or postcondition checks on each contract function. If the condition isn't met, the contract moves into a fail-safe mode in which all or most of its functionality is disabled. Regardless of whether you decided to fit your contract with an interactive or automated emergency stop, ideally you should also plan for an upgrade strategy, as I discussed in chapter 13.

- *Use linters.* A linter is a static code analysis tool that aims at catching breaches against recommended style, efficient implementation, or known security vulnerabilities. The two most well-known Solidity linters are Solium (now Ethlint) (https://github.com/duaraghav8/Solium) and Solint (https://github.com/SilentCicero/solint). They both provide integration plugins for most common general code editors, such as Atom, Sublime, VS Code, and JetBrains IDEA. Apart from highlighting security vulnerabilities, these tools give feedback on coding style and best practices in general, so they can help you learn Solidity quickly.

- *Use security analysis frameworks.* If you want to go the extra mile, don't stop at linters. Instead, aim at integrating security analysis into your development cycle with frameworks such as the Mythril Platform,[4] which combines a variety of static and dynamic analyzers.

- *Follow the wisdom of the crowds.* If you're not sure about the safety of smart contracts you'd like to connect to, you could look up their ratings in Panvala,[5] a system that attempts to gather the level of security of smart contracts from their users.

- *Commission a formal security audit.* If your smart contract handles anything valuable, such as cryptocurrency or tokens, before going into production you should consider commissioning a formal security audit from one of the many consultancies that are starting to specialize in this area.

Summary

- Attackers generally exploit limitations in the Solidity language, the EVM, and the blockchain as the first line of attack against unaware developers, especially around data privacy, random numbers, integer overflows, and gas limits.

- If not well understood, external calls can expose a contract to manipulation by malicious participants. For example, some external calls throw exceptions, whereas others don't, or some execute in the context of the caller contract, and others in the context of the called contract. You must understand the risks of each type and handle returned value and contract state accordingly.

- Various techniques are available to perform safer external calls and reduce the chance of external manipulation. Examples include pull payment (rather than automated payment) functionality and Ether transfer based on `transfer()` and `send()`, which restrict the gas limit on an external fallback function.

- The minimum line of defense is to prepare at least against well-known attacks, such as reentrancy, front-running attacks, and denial of service (DoS) attacks.

- The official Solidity documentation and various online security guides, sites, and blogs provide up-to-date information on the latest attacks and guidelines for avoiding them.

---

[4] See Bernhard Mueller, "MythX Is Upping the Smart Contract Security Game," http://mng.bz/ 0WmE, for an introduction to Mythril.

[5] See "Introducing Panvala," http://mng.bz/K1Mg, for an introduction to Panvala.

15 *Conclusions*

This chapter covers
- The evolution of Ethereum
- Alternative Ethereum implementations
- Capabilities beyond the Ethereum blockchain

You've finally reached the end of this book. I'm sure you've learned a lot, and you should now feel equipped to continue the journey by yourself. Don't rest on your laurels, though. Both Ethereum and the landscape around it are constantly changing.

Before I say goodbye, I'd like to give you a heads-up on topics you should particularly keep an eye on if you're considering building your own Dapp. I'd also like to briefly present you with some alternative forks of mainstream Ethereum, in case you have needs the mainstream implementation can't fulfill. Finally, I'll give you a quick view of the current blockchain landscape, in case you want to explore alternative blockchain offerings.

Before I start, I'd like to be clear on one thing: this chapter is only meant to give you ideas for further learning, so I'm not aiming to cover any topic in depth. I'll only try to stimulate your mind and enthusiasm.

15.1 Evolution of Ethereum

As I've repeated various times throughout the book, Ethereum is continuously evolving, and at this stage many of its building blocks are still in flux, such as the EVM, the Solidity language, the Web3.js library, the consensus algorithm, and some elements of the ecosystem. I'll give you an idea of how these elements are likely to evolve, but I strongly recommend you keep updated through online resources.

15.1.1 Evolution of EVM

The current implementation of the EVM supports dynamic jumps (which means the address is supplied as an argument on the stack), but they make control-flow and data-flow analysis complicated and slow. Ethereum Improvement Proposal 615[1] aims at a partial redesign of the EVM (version 1.5) targeted at introducing subroutines (through static jumps and `return`) and disallowing dynamic jumps and other misuses of the stack. This would bring several benefits, including better compilation from Solidity, faster interpretation, improved optimization to native code, and better static analysis and formal verification tools. It would also allow better compilation from and to eWASM.

If you're wondering what eWASM is, WASM stands for WebAssembly (https://webassembly.org/), and it's a new binary instruction format that W3C is designing as an open standard. This standard specifies an instruction set, an intermediate source format (WAST), and a binary encoded format (WASM). Most mainstream JavaScript engines, including those behind Node.js, Chrome, Edge, and Firefox, will provide native support for WebAssembly. eWASM (https://github.com/ewasm) is a subset of WASM designed to support Ethereum smart contracts. The ultimate objective is, among other benefits, to provide a library and instructions to write Ethereum contracts in C and in Rust.

15.1.2 Evolution of Solidity

If you're among the MEAP readers of this book, you might have noticed Solidity has been changing frequently since you started playing with it. The developers of Solidity have often introduced new keywords and deprecated others. This continuous evolution is making Solidity a more robust language, especially from a security point of view. The biggest change that's taking place, and you should be aware of, is the deprecation of `send()` and `call()`, so I strongly encourage you to use `transfer()` instead.

15.1.3 Evolution of Web3.js

Although throughout the book I've been referencing Web3.js version 0.24 because it works reliably with all the current tools, you should try to move to version 1.0 as soon as you can. This is still in beta at the time of writing, but the candidate release is coming soon.

---

[1] See EIPs/eip-615.md on GitHub at http://mng.bz/9OMq.

15.1.4   *Evolution of the consensus algorithm*

MAINNET, the public production network, is still based on the Proof of Work (PoW) consensus algorithm. As you might recall, the PoW algorithm is designed so that many miners are competing to append a new block to the blockchain by simultaneously trying to solve a cryptographic puzzle. They keep re-hashing the proposed new block until they find a *nonce* that generates a correct hash (for example, a hash with many leading zeros). The hashing process is CPU-intensive and therefore energy-intensive. The simultaneous re-hashing of a new block performed trillions of times per second throughout the Ethereum network has been widely blamed for being energy-wasteful. Developers are experimenting with a couple of alternative consensus algorithms to overcome this issue, namely *Proof of Stake* (PoS) and *Proof of Authority* (PoA).

PROOF OF STAKE

The *Proof of Stake* algorithm[2] is designed so that only one miner has the right to append a new block during a certain time slot. A new block is consequently processed only once every few seconds throughout the network, rather than trillions of times per second, which eliminates the problem of electricity consumption. As you can imagine, the term "miner" no longer applies under this algorithm: candidates for appending blocks are called *validators* instead, as shown in figure 15.1.

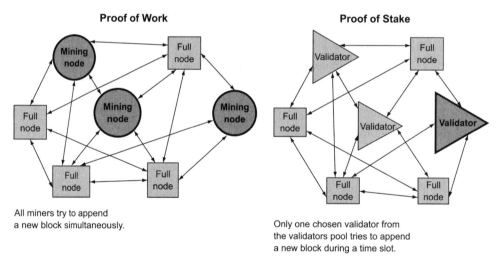

Proof of Work

All miners try to append
a new block simultaneously.

Proof of Stake

Only one chosen validator from
the validators pool tries to append
a new block during a time slot.

Figure 15.1   PoS versus PoW. Whereas under PoW, many miners perform work (and consume electricity) simultaneously to append a block, under PoS only one node, called a validator, proposes a new block during a time slot.

---

[2]   See "Proof of Stake FAQs" on the Ethereum wiki on GitHub at http://mng.bz/jO48.

Validators submit a deposit in Ether, which represents their stake in the infrastructure. The chosen validator, selected through a randomizer or round-robin function weighted on the stake, proposes a new block. Then, depending on the specific implementation of the PoS algorithm, the validator submits the proposed block to several secondary validators for approval. They vote on the block (the vote might be weighted on their stake) and, if the outcome is positive, the block is appended to the blockchain and the validator is rewarded in Ether. On the other hand, if the block is found to be incorrect, the initial (main) validator might get blacklisted and lose their deposit. Also, secondary validators are encouraged to be honest: if their vote diverges too much from that of their peers, they might get penalized and lose some of their deposit, as you can see in figure 15.2.

The PoS algorithm, with its incentives and disincentives, might provide various benefits, such as reductions in dependency of the network on advanced hardware, risk of centralized processing by a few miners, and likelihood of a 51% attack (which would become much costlier). The project name for the PoS algorithm is called Casper, and the project released a test network in January 2018.

PROOF OF AUTHORITY

Many practitioners and researchers have criticized the nature of PoS's incentives for being potentially unbalanced because they don't take into account the total holdings of each validator. A state-sponsored validator, for example, might have committed an amount of Ether considered large by the designers of the algorithm. But if that amount is relatively small with respect to the value of their total assets (including cryptocurrency and conventional assets), they might not be discouraged from acting dishonestly.

Proof of Authority[3] is an alternative form of consensus algorithm that is still based on a pool of validators, but in this case each validator puts at stake their reputation rather than their Ether. Nodes that want to take part in the validators pool apply through a formal identification process: they disclose their real identity, which is verified through the same checks a conventional notary would perform. Once a node has been approved as a validator, it becomes an *Authority* (hence the name of the algorithm). The idea is that linking the block verification process to the node's reputation rather than to the perceived value of their deposit is more robust, as shown in figure 15.3.

Currently, two public test networks support different implementations of PoA: Rinkeby and Kovan. In August 2018, Microsoft released Ethereum PoA on Azure, targeting private and consortium permissioned networks. (See section 15.2 for more details on permissioned networks.)

---

[3] See the Wikipedia "Proof-of-Authority" page at https://en.wikipedia.org/wiki/Proof-of-authority.

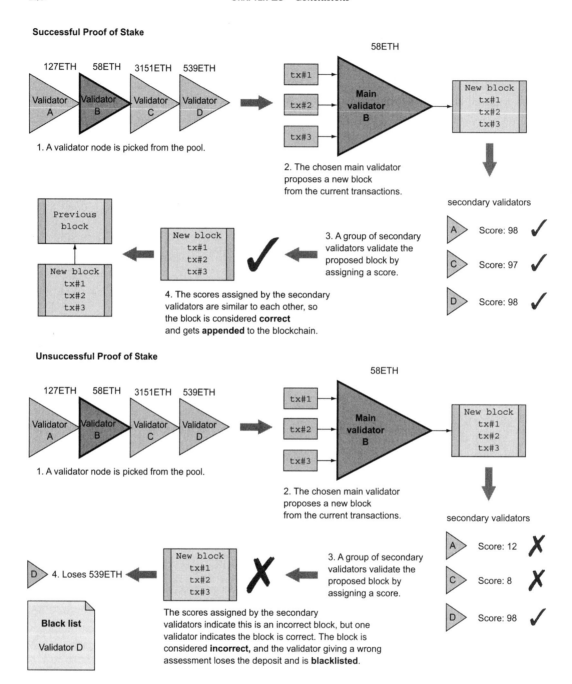

Figure 15.2   PoS algorithm. First, validators submit a deposit. Then the selected validator proposes a new block and submits it to secondary validators for approval. If they score the block as correct, it's appended to the blockchain. The main validator or secondary validators might get penalized in Ether if they're found to be dishonest.

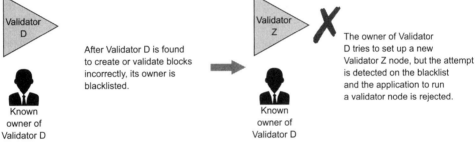

Figure 15.3   PoA versus PoS. When a malicious node loses their Ether deposit under PoS, their sponsor can set up a new node and continue with malicious behavior. Under PoA, once an authority has been detected as malicious, their sponsor (and all associated identities) is prevented from reentering the network.

15.1.5   *Evolution of the ecosystem*

Many of the components of the Ethereum ecosystem I presented in chapter 9 are evolving. For example, on the ENS website (https://ens.domains/), you can find a roadmap that indicates the production ENS registrar, currently based on a commit–reveal auction, will be replaced in the next few months with a simplified version. Also, the Swarm team has published a roadmap[4] for the future development of the decentralized file system. A more dramatic evolution is that of Zeppelin. What started as an open source Ethereum smart contract library is becoming ZeppelinOS (https://zeppelinos.org/), a full-blown operating system for smart contracts.

---

4   See the Swarm "Roadmap" on GitHub at https://github.com/ethersphere/swarm/wiki/roadmap.

15.2   *Alternative Ethereum implementations*

Although you might have been fascinated by the technology, if you work in an enterprise, you might think Ethereum would be difficult to adopt. One good reason is that it doesn't offer out of the box three features most enterprise applications require: scalability, permissioning, and data privacy. The Enterprise Ethereum Alliance is an organization trying to extend the public Ethereum implementation with such features.

15.2.1   *Enterprise Ethereum Alliance*

The Enterprise Ethereum Alliance (EEA) (https://entethalliance.org/) is a nonprofit consortium of around 500 companies that formed in March 2017 from a core of 30 founding members, including technology corporations (Microsoft, INTEL), research institutes (Toyota Research Institute), consultancies (Deloitte, Accenture, Samsung SDS), and financial institutions (Banco Santander, ING). The mission of the consortium is to propose and drive a roadmap for enterprise features and requirements; to shape a governance model for licensing around the open source technology; and to provide businesses with resources to help them learn Ethereum and address industry use cases that can take advantage of the technology.

The EEA has published the Enterprise Ethereum Architecture Stack (EEAS), which presents a standardized view of the Enterprise Ethereum ecosystem, from the network layer to the application layer. This is illustrated in table 15.1, which compares the public Ethereum building blocks with the corresponding Enterprise Ethereum ones. (A more comprehensive view is available in the official documentation.)

Table 15.1   Public Ethereum versus Enterprise Ethereum building blocks

Level	Public Ethereum	Enterprise Ethereum
Permissioning and credentials	Key management	Permissioning and authentication
Integration and deployment tools	Integration libraries	Enterprise management systems
Privacy	On-chain	Private transactions and off-chain transactions
Storage	On-chain public state and storage; off-chain storage	On-chain private state
Execution	EVM	Trusted execution
Consensus	Public consensus	Private consensus
Network	DevP2P	Enterprise P2P

The first version of the Enterprise Ethereum Client Specification (EECS), detailing extensions to the public Ethereum blockchain to support permissioning, privacy, and scalability required for enterprise deployments, was published in May 2018, and you can download it from the EEA website. The objective of this specification, whose broad requirements are summarized in table 15.2, is to serve as a flexible standard that can allow different vendor implementations. For example, the specification defines various levels of privacy, identified with A, B, and C, that depend on the requirements for connectivity between nodes, permissioning, and transaction privacy. The vendor can decide which level to target and gets certified accordingly.

Table 15.2 Broad requirements of EECS

Requirement	Description
Permissioning	A blockchain system is defined as permissioned when its network isn't public, but its nodes are owned by a restricted group of known participants.
Privacy	The content of a transaction should be visible only to the parties involved in the transaction.
Scalability	The performance of the blockchain infrastructure shouldn't degrade with an increasing number of transactions, and it should ideally be equivalent to that of major enterprise systems, such as those handling credit card transactions.

15.2.2 Quorum

One of the first Enterprise Ethereum implementations is Quorum (www.jpmorgan .com/global/Quorum). This is a fork of Ethereum that two members of the EEA—AMIS (a joint venture of Taiwanese financial institutions) and the bank JP Morgan—created in 2016. Quorum extends a shared private Ethereum network with a *constellation network* that handles permissioning and data privacy, as you can see in figure 15.4. When a transaction takes place between two or more participants, the constellation network deploys the relevant smart contract only across the members of the transaction. The content of the transaction is encrypted and stored off-chain by a transaction manager, and a hash is stored on the shared Ethereum blockchain.

Quorum has been one of the first Ethereum-based platforms to

- take advantage of geth's pluggable consensus interface to allow a *configurable consensus algorithm.*
- use *zk-SNARKs'* cryptographic privacy technology to provide zero-knowledge verification of smart contract transactions, which means verification of the correctness of the execution of a transaction without learning what has been computed. The project's participants have used this technology to build the *zero-knowledge security layer* (ZSL), which provides Quorum the ability to transfer digital assets on the blockchain without revealing any information about the sender and recipient assets themselves, therefore guaranteeing complete privacy.

NOTE   zk-SNARKs is the technology that makes ZCash a truly anonymous cryptocurrency, contrary to Bitcoin, whose transactions can be traced to their owner.

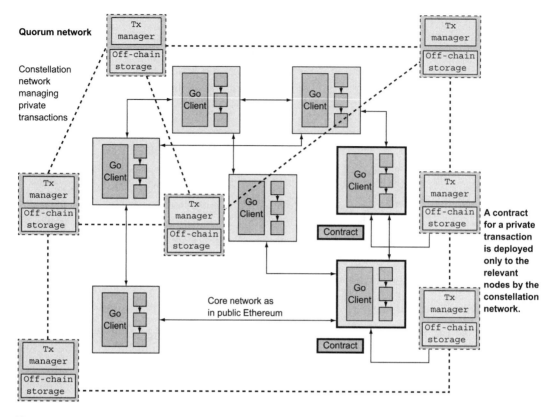

Figure 15.4   A constellation network allows Quorum to handle permissioning and privacy. A smart contract is deployed only across the parties involved in a transaction; the transaction is encrypted and stored off-chain, and its hash is stored on the shared Ethereum blockchain.

15.3   *Beyond the Ethereum blockchain*

As you know, blockchain technology is well suited to solving problems related to proving ownership and traceability of assets. But as you learned earlier, public blockchains like Ethereum might not be suitable for enterprise applications designed to solve these problems because of their lack of focus on enterprise needs, such as those listed in table 15.2: permissioning, privacy, and scalability. Although the EEA is trying to fit the Ethereum blockchain to such requirements with various extensions (Quorum is one such example), other organizations have decided to take a completely different approach. Vendors agree that a decentralized database would be the core component of any solution, but they disagree on many implementation aspects of an architecture:

- *Decentralized database technology*—This isn't necessarily based on a blockchain structure, so the industry has come up with the more general term of *distributed ledger technology* (DLT).

- *Permissioning*—Vendors agree that a distributed ledger can be accessed securely and with acceptable scalability only through a restricted network of known participants.

- *Consensus*—Consensus in the blockchain space has evolved from PoW, based on a large group of anonymous miners processing the same transactions simultaneously, to PoS, based on a smaller group of participants that have submitted a deposit and process different sets of transactions in a coordinated fashion, to PoA, based on a limited set of known participants. The commonality among these approaches is they involve fundamentally two network roles: transaction submitters (any node) and validators (or miners). Consensus in a distributed ledger, on the other hand, might involve a more complex interaction among many roles to provide better scalability without compromising the integrity of the stored data.

- *Cryptocurrency*—The consensus algorithm of distributed ledgers not based on a blockchain structure isn't based on PoW or PoS, so cryptocurrency isn't needed, but some platforms still allow the generation of cryptocurrency or tokens to facilitate the exchange of monetary value, when needed.

Two distributed ledger initiatives that have gathered considerable traction are Hyperledger and Corda. I'll briefly sketch what they offer so you can get a better idea of what's happening with alternative blockchain-based distributed ledgers.

15.3.1 *Hyperledger*

Around December 2015, the Linux foundation started a project called Hyperledger, whose strategic objective is to stimulate cross-industry collaboration through the development of distributed ledgers. Various distributed ledger frameworks have been tested under this successful project, sponsored by around 250 member organizations that provide funding and technical expertise. Two examples are Hyperledger Burrow, which includes its own implementation of the Ethereum Virtual Machine, and Hyperledger Iroha, whose focus is on mobile applications.

Hyperledger Fabric (www.hyperledger.org/projects/fabric), probably the most popular among the Hyperledger projects, was started with the objective of building a framework for enterprise blockchain applications. Its codebase was seeded with code developed by IBM, Digital Asset, and Blockstream during a hackathon that had taken place a few months earlier. Hyperledger Fabric is based on blockchain technology, but it's designed on an open plug-and-play framework that allows you to change and customize many components of the architecture and adapt the platform to many industry use cases. For example, the consensus algorithm is pluggable by design, and you can write smart contracts in a variety of mainstream languages, such as Java, JavaScript, and Go. If you have time, the official documentation (https://hyperledger-fabric .readthedocs.io) provides comprehensive information, from the high-level architecture to low-level implementation details of the platform.

Here are the main characteristics of Hyperledger Fabric that differ from traditional blockchain systems, such as Ethereum:

- Up to four roles could take part in a transaction and contribute to the consensus:[5]
  - *A submitting client* is a node that submits a transaction.
  - *An endorser* (or endorsing peer) is a node that verifies the electronic signature and endorses a transaction through an endorsing policy before it gets committed on the ledger; endorsers are generally all the parties that have to approve the transaction.
  - *An orderer* is a node that runs the messaging service that provides ordering and delivery guarantees, when the transaction requires it.
  - *A committer* (or peer) is a node that commits a transaction and holds a copy of the ledger.
- The details of a transaction are private to only the interested participants. This is achieved through *channels*, subnetworks that provide isolated and confidential communication only among a number of authorized participants—a little bit like a WhatsApp group.

Another interesting blockchain framework that the Hyperledger project has developed under its umbrella is Hyperledger Sawtooth,[6] which introduces the following innovative features:

- *Parallel transaction execution*—Most blockchain systems can only process transactions sequentially.
- *On-chain governance*—Participants can actively configure their network through smart-contract–based voting.
- *Ethereum support*—As Hyperledger Burrow does, Sawtooth offers a compliant EVM capable of running Solidity contracts.
- *Dynamic consensus*—This goes beyond Fabric's plug-in consensus design, as you can change consensus algorithms on the fly.
- *Wider smart-contract language choice*—On top of the languages that Fabric supports, Sawtooth also supports Python.

The Hyperledger initiative has also coordinated the development of blockchain tools such as Hyperledger Composer, focused on helping users create smart contracts, and Hyperledger Explorer, which allows users to view and analyze block and transaction information.

15.3.2 Corda

R3 is a consortium of companies formed in 2015 that has grown to around 200 members, initially mainly from the financial sector but increasingly from other industries. They started Corda in 2016 as an open source project.

---

[5] See "Transaction Flow" in the Hyperledger Fabric documentation at http://mng.bz/Wadl.
[6] See "Hyperledger Releases Hyperledger Sawtooth 1.0," January 30, 2018, http://mng.bz/Ee2X.

The approach they took for creating Corda was different from that taken in the EEA and Hyperledger initiatives. In the first place, the technical stack is made of standard off-the-shelf parts, such as the Java Virtual Machine, relational databases, and message queues. Second, Corda achieves privacy by sharing data not among a group of participants, such as those interacting in a Hyperledger channel, but only at the level of individual transactions. Specifically, two or more nodes can share one or more facts, and each node maintains its own local copy of such facts. There's no central database containing all facts, as illustrated in figure 15.5 and described more extensively in the official documentation.[7] This fine level of data sharing is provided through a *notary*, a network role that provides transaction ordering and timestamping.

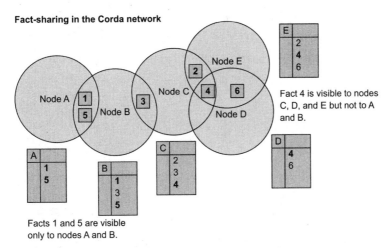

Fact-sharing in the Corda network

Fact 4 is visible to nodes C, D, and E but not to A and B.

Facts 1 and 5 are visible only to nodes A and B.

Figure 15.5 How facts are shared in the Corda network. Each node maintains its own copy of its own facts, but it can share some facts with other nodes. For example, facts 1 and 5 are shared between nodes A and B; fact 4 is only visible to nodes C, D, and E, but not A and B.

As you can see, this is a domain that's constantly evolving, and there are many different ways to solve problems. Hold tight and expect further innovation!

Summary

- The EVM is being upgraded to a more general version supporting eWASM that ultimately will be able to execute code compiled from Rust and C.
- Continuous improvements in Solidity syntax are resulting in changes such as the deprecation of `send()` and `call()` in favor of `transfer()`.

---

[7] See "The ledger" in the Corda documentation at https://docs.corda.net/key-concepts-ledger.html.

- Web3.js version 1.0, which is in beta at the time of writing, is about to become the official version to be used across the Ethereum ecosystem. I strongly advise you to reference it as soon as it's released.
- Some alternative Ethereum networks are based on consensus algorithms different from Proof of Work: Kovan and Rinkeby support Proof of Authority, whereas the Casper project is introducing Proof of Stake.
- An Enterprise Ethereum platform, such as Quorum, supports enterprise Dapp requirements such as scalability, permissioning, and privacy.
- Other distributed ledger platforms, such as Hyperledger or Corda, offer alternatives to Enterprise Ethereum.

Listing A.1 Refactored `SimpleCoin` contract, inherited from `Ownable`

```
pragma solidity ^0.4.16;
pragma solidity ^0.4.24;

import "./Listing6_4_Ownable.sol";

contract SimpleCoin is Ownable {                ⟵
    mapping (address => uint256) public coinBalance;
    mapping (address => mapping (address => uint256)) public allowance;
    mapping (address => bool) public frozenAccount;

    event Transfer(address indexed from, address indexed to, uint256 value);
    event FrozenAccount(address target, bool frozen);

    constructor(uint256 _initialSupply) public {
        owner = msg.sender;

        mint(owner, _initialSupply);
    }

    function transfer(address _to, uint256 _amount) public {
        require(_to != 0x0);
        require(coinBalance[msg.sender] > _amount);
        require(coinBalance[_to] + _amount >= coinBalance[_to] );
        coinBalance[msg.sender] -= _amount;
        coinBalance[_to] += _amount;
        emit Transfer(msg.sender, _to, _amount);
    }
```

The owner state variable and the onlyOwner modifier are inherited from the Ownable contract.

```
function authorize(address _authorizedAccount, uint256 _allowance)
  public returns (bool success) {
  allowance[msg.sender][_authorizedAccount] = _allowance;
  return true;
}

function transferFrom(address _from, address _to, uint256 _amount)
  public returns (bool success) {
  require(_to != 0x0);
  require(coinBalance[_from] > _amount);
  require(coinBalance[_to] + _amount >= coinBalance[_to] );
  require(_amount <= allowance[_from][msg.sender]);
  coinBalance[_from] -= _amount;
  coinBalance[_to] += _amount;
  allowance[_from][msg.sender] -= _amount;
  emit Transfer(_from, _to, _amount);
  return true;
}

function mint(address _recipient, uint256  _mintedAmount)
  onlyOwner public {

  coinBalance[_recipient] += _mintedAmount;
  emit Transfer(owner, _recipient, _mintedAmount);
}

function freezeAccount(address target, bool freeze)
  onlyOwner public {

  frozenAccount[target] = freeze;
  emit FrozenAccount(target, freeze);
}
}
```

Listing B.1 Full SimpleCrowdsale application, including crowdsale and coin contracts

```solidity
pragma solidity ^0.4.24;

import "./Listing5_8_SimpleCoin.sol";
import "./Listing6_4_Ownable.sol";

interface ReleasableToken {
    function mint(address _beneficiary, uint256 _numberOfTokens) external;
    function release() external;
    function transfer(address _to, uint256 _amount) external;
}

contract ReleasableSimpleCoin is ReleasableToken, SimpleCoin {
    bool public released = false;

    modifier canTransfer() {
        if(!released) {
            revert();
        }

        _;
    }

    constructor(uint256 _initialSupply)
        SimpleCoin(_initialSupply) public {}

    function release() onlyOwner public {
        released = true;
    }
```

```
    function transfer(address _to, uint256 _amount)
        canTransfer public {
        super.transfer(_to, _amount);
    }

    function transferFrom(address _from, address _to,
        uint256 _amount)
        canTransfer public returns (bool) {
        super.transferFrom(_from, _to, _amount);
    }
}

contract FundingLimitStrategy{
    function isFullInvestmentWithinLimit(uint256 _investment,
        uint256 _fullInvestmentReceived)
        public view returns (bool);
}

contract CappedFundingStrategy is FundingLimitStrategy {
    uint256 fundingCap;

    constructor(uint256 _fundingCap) public {
        require(_fundingCap > 0);
        fundingCap = _fundingCap;
    }

    function isFullInvestmentWithinLimit(uint256 _investment,
        uint256 _fullInvestmentReceived)
        public view returns (bool) {

        bool check = _fullInvestmentReceived + _investment < fundingCap;
        return check;
    }
}

contract UnlimitedFundingStrategy is FundingLimitStrategy {
    function isFullInvestmentWithinLimit(uint256 _investment,
        uint256 _fullInvestmentReceived)
        public view returns (bool) {
        return true;
    }
}

contract SimpleCrowdsale is Ownable {
    uint256 public startTime;
    uint256 public endTime;
    uint256 public weiTokenPrice;
    uint256 public weiInvestmentObjective;

    mapping (address => uint256) public investmentAmountOf;
    uint256 public investmentReceived;
    uint256 public investmentRefunded;

    bool public isFinalized;
    bool public isRefundingAllowed;

    ReleasableToken public crowdsaleToken;

    FundingLimitStrategy internal fundingLimitStrategy;
```

```
constructor(uint256 _startTime, uint256 _endTime,
 uint256 _weiTokenPrice, uint256 _etherInvestmentObjective)
 payable public
{
    require(_startTime >= now);
    require(_endTime >= _startTime);
    require(_weiTokenPrice != 0);
    require(_etherInvestmentObjective != 0);

    startTime = _startTime;
    endTime = _endTime;
    weiTokenPrice = _weiTokenPrice;
    weiInvestmentObjective = _etherInvestmentObjective
        * 1000000000000000000;

    crowdsaleToken = createToken();
    isFinalized = false;
    fundingLimitStrategy = createFundingLimitStrategy();
}

event LogInvestment(address indexed investor, uint256 value);
event LogTokenAssignment(address indexed investor, uint256 numTokens);
event Refund(address investor, uint256 value);

function invest() public payable {
    require(isValidInvestment(msg.value));

    address investor = msg.sender;
    uint256 investment = msg.value;

    investmentAmountOf[investor] += investment;
    investmentReceived += investment;

    assignTokens(investor, investment);
    emit LogInvestment(investor, investment);
}

function createToken()
    internal returns (ReleasableToken) {
        return new ReleasableSimpleCoin(0);
    }

function createFundingLimitStrategy()
    internal returns (FundingLimitStrategy);

function isValidInvestment(uint256 _investment)
    internal view returns (bool) {
    bool nonZeroInvestment = _investment != 0;
    bool withinCrowsalePeriod = now >= startTime && now <= endTime;

    return nonZeroInvestment && withinCrowsalePeriod
        && fundingLimitStrategy.isFullInvestmentWithinLimit(
        _investment, investmentReceived);
}

function assignTokens(address _beneficiary,
    uint256 _investment) internal {

    uint256 _numberOfTokens = calculateNumberOfTokens(_investment);
```

```
            crowdsaleToken.mint(_beneficiary, _numberOfTokens);
    }

    function calculateNumberOfTokens(uint256 _investment)
        internal returns (uint256) {
        return _investment / weiTokenPrice;
    }

    function finalize() onlyOwner public {
        if (isFinalized) revert();

        bool isCrowdsaleComplete = now > endTime;
        bool investmentObjectiveMet = investmentReceived
            >= weiInvestmentObjective;

        if (isCrowdsaleComplete)
        {
            if (investmentObjectiveMet)
                crowdsaleToken.release();
            else
                isRefundingAllowed = true;

            isFinalized = true;
        }
    }

    function refund() public {
        if (!isRefundingAllowed) revert();

        address investor = msg.sender;
        uint256 investment = investmentAmountOf[investor];
        if (investment == 0) revert();
        investmentAmountOf[investor] = 0;
        investmentRefunded += investment;
        emit Refund(msg.sender, investment);

        if (!investor.send(investment)) revert();
    }
}

contract TranchePricingCrowdsale is SimpleCrowdsale  {

    struct Tranche {
        uint256 weiHighLimit;
        uint256 weiTokenPrice;
    }

    mapping(uint256 => Tranche) public trancheStructure;
    uint256 public currentTrancheLevel;

    constructor(uint256 _startTime, uint256 _endTime,
     uint256 _etherInvestmentObjective)
     SimpleCrowdsale(_startTime, _endTime,
        1, _etherInvestmentObjective)
     payable public
    {
        trancheStructure[0] = Tranche(3000 ether, 0.002 ether);
        trancheStructure[1] = Tranche(10000 ether, 0.003 ether);
        trancheStructure[2] = Tranche(15000 ether, 0.004 ether);
        trancheStructure[3] = Tranche(1000000000 ether, 0.005 ether);
```

```
            currentTrancheLevel = 0;
        }

    function calculateNumberOfTokens(uint256 investment)
        internal returns (uint256) {
        updateCurrentTrancheAndPrice();
        return investment / weiTokenPrice;
    }

    function updateCurrentTrancheAndPrice()
        internal {
        uint256 i = currentTrancheLevel;

        while(trancheStructure[i].weiHighLimit < investmentReceived)
            ++i;

        currentTrancheLevel = i;

        weiTokenPrice =
            trancheStructure[currentTrancheLevel].weiTokenPrice;
    }
}

contract FixedPricingCrowdsale is SimpleCrowdsale {

    constructor(uint256 _startTime, uint256 _endTime,
     uint256 _weiTokenPrice, uint256 _etherInvestmentObjective)
     SimpleCrowdsale(_startTime, _endTime,
     _weiTokenPrice, _etherInvestmentObjective)
     payable public {
    }

    function calculateNumberOfTokens(uint256 investment)
        internal returns (uint256) {
        return investment / weiTokenPrice;
    }
}

contract UnlimitedFixedPricingCrowdsale is FixedPricingCrowdsale {

    constructor(uint256 _startTime, uint256 _endTime,
     uint256 _weiTokenPrice, uint256 _etherInvestmentObjective)
     FixedPricingCrowdsale(_startTime, _endTime,
     _weiTokenPrice, _etherInvestmentObjective)
     payable public {
    }

    function createFundingLimitStrategy()
        internal returns (FundingLimitStrategy) {

        return new UnlimitedFundingStrategy();
    }
}

contract CappedFixedPricingCrowdsale is FixedPricingCrowdsale {

    constructor(uint256 _startTime, uint256 _endTime,
     uint256 _weiTokenPrice, uint256 _etherInvestmentObjective)
     FixedPricingCrowdsale(_startTime, _endTime,
     _weiTokenPrice, _etherInvestmentObjective)
```

```
        payable public  {
        }

    function createFundingLimitStrategy()
        internal returns (FundingLimitStrategy) {

        return new CappedFundingStrategy(10000);
    }
}

contract UnlimitedTranchePricingCrowdsale is TranchePricingCrowdsale {

    constructor(uint256 _startTime, uint256 _endTime,
     uint256 _etherInvestmentObjective)
     TranchePricingCrowdsale(_startTime, _endTime,
     _etherInvestmentObjective)
     payable public  {
     }

    function createFundingLimitStrategy()
        internal returns (FundingLimitStrategy) {

        return new UnlimitedFundingStrategy();
    }
}

contract CappedTranchePricingCrowdsale is TranchePricingCrowdsale {

    constructor(uint256 _startTime, uint256 _endTime,
     uint256 _etherInvestmentObjective)
     TranchePricingCrowdsale(_startTime, _endTime,
     _etherInvestmentObjective)
     payable public  {
     }

    function createFundingLimitStrategy()
        internal returns (FundingLimitStrategy) {

        return new CappedFundingStrategy(10000);
    }
}
```

Listing C.1 SimpleCoinTests.js

```javascript
const fs = require('fs');
const solc = require('solc');
const Web3 = require('web3');
const web3 = new Web3(
    new Web3.providers.HttpProvider("http://localhost:8545"));
var assert = require('assert');

const source =
    fs.readFileSync('c:/Ethereum/mocha/SimpleCoin/SimpleCoin.sol',
    'utf8');
const compiledContract = solc.compile(source, 1);
const abi = compiledContract.contracts[':SimpleCoin'].interface;
const bytecode = '0x' + compiledContract.contracts[':SimpleCoin'].bytecode;
const gasEstimate = web3.eth.estimateGas({ data: bytecode }) + 100000;

const SimpleCoinContractFactory = web3.eth.contract(JSON.parse(abi));

describe('SimpleCoin', function() {
  this.timeout(5000);
  describe('SimpleCoin constructor', function() {
    it('Contract owner is sender', function(done) {
        //arrange
        let sender = web3.eth.accounts[1];
        let initialSupply = 10000;

        //act
        let simpleCoinInstance =
            SimpleCoinContractFactory.new(initialSupply, {
```

```
                  from: sender, data: bytecode, gas: gasEstimate},
                  function (e, contract){
                  if (typeof contract.address !== 'undefined') {
                      //assert
                      assert.equal(contract.owner(), sender);
                      done();
                  }
            });
    });

    it('Contract owner balance is equal to initialSupply', function(done) {
        //arrange
            let sender = web3.eth.accounts[1];
            let initialSupply = 10000;

            //act
            let simpleCoinInstance =
                SimpleCoinContractFactory.new(initialSupply, {
                    from: sender, data: bytecode, gas: gasEstimate},
                    function (e, contract){
                    if (typeof contract.address !== 'undefined') {
                        //assert

    assert.equal(contract.coinBalance(contract.owner()), initialSupply);
                        done();
                }
            });
    });
});

describe('transfer', function() {
   it('Cannot transfer a number of tokens higher than number of tokens
➡ owned', function(done) {
        //arrange
            let sender = web3.eth.accounts[1];
            let initialSupply = 10000;
            let recipient = web3.eth.accounts[2];
            let tokensToTransfer = 12000;

            let simpleCoinInstance =
                SimpleCoinContractFactory.new(initialSupply, {
                    from: sender, data: bytecode, gas: gasEstimate},
                    function (e, contract){
                    if (typeof contract.address !== 'undefined') {
                        //act and assert
                        assert.throws(
                            () => {
                                    contract.transfer(
                                        recipient, tokensToTransfer, {
                                        from:sender,gas:200000});
                            },
                            /VM Exception while processing transaction/
                        );
                        done();
                }
```

```
                });
            });
        it('Successful transfer: final sender and recipient balances are
    correct', function(done) {
            //arrange
                let sender = web3.eth.accounts[1];
                let initialSupply = 10000;
                let recipient = web3.eth.accounts[2];
                let tokensToTransfer = 200;

                let simpleCoinInstance =
                    SimpleCoinContractFactory.new(initialSupply, {
                        from: sender, data: bytecode, gas: gasEstimate},
                        function (e, contract){
                        if (typeof contract.address !== 'undefined') {

                            //act
                            contract.transfer(recipient, tokensToTransfer, {
                                    from:sender,gas:200000});

                            //assert
                            const expectedSenderBalance = 9800;
                            const expectedRecipientBalance = 200;

                            let actualSenderBalance =
                                contract.coinBalance(sender);
                            let actualRecipientBalance =
                                contract.coinBalance(recipient);

                            assert.equal(actualSenderBalance,
                                expectedSenderBalance);
                            assert.equal(actualRecipientBalance,
                                expectedRecipientBalance);

                            done();
                    }
                });
        });
    });

    describe('authorize', function() {
        it('Successful authorization: the allowance of the authorized account
    is set correctly', function(done) {
            //arrange
                let sender = web3.eth.accounts[1];
                let initialSupply = 10000;
                let authorizer = web3.eth.accounts[2];
                let authorized = web3.eth.accounts[3];
                let allowance = 300;

                let simpleCoinInstance =
                    SimpleCoinContractFactory.new(initialSupply,
                        {from: sender, data: bytecode, gas: gasEstimate},
                        function (e, contract){
                        if (typeof contract.address !== 'undefined') {
```

```
                              //act
                              let result = contract.authorize(authorized,
                                      allowance,
                                      {from:authorizer,gas:200000});

                              //assert
                              assert.equal(contract.allowance(
                                  authorizer, authorized), 300);

                              done();
                          }
                      });
              });
          });

      describe('transferFrom', function() {
          it('Cannot transfer number of tokens higher than that owned by
     authorizer', function(done) {
                  //arrange
                  let sender = web3.eth.accounts[1];
                  let initialSupply = 10000;
                  let authorizer = web3.eth.accounts[2];
                  let authorized = web3.eth.accounts[3];
                  let toAccount = web3.eth.accounts[5];
                  let allowance = 300;
                  let initialBalanceOfAuthorizer = 400;
                  let tokensToTransferFromAuthorizerToAuthorized = 450;

                  let simpleCoinInstance =
                      SimpleCoinContractFactory.new(initialSupply,
                          {from: sender, data: bytecode, gas: gasEstimate},
                          function (e, contract){
                              if (typeof contract.address !== 'undefined') {

                                  //arrange
                                  contract.authorize(authorized, allowance, {
                                      from:authorizer,gas:200000});

                                  contract.transfer(authorizer,
                                      initialBalanceOfAuthorizer,
                                  {from:sender,gas:200000});

                                  //act and assert
                                  assert.throws(
                                      ()=> {
                                          contract.transferFrom(authorizer,
                                              toAccount,
                                              tokensToTransferFromAuthorizerToAuthorized,
                                              {from:authorized,gas:200000});
                                      },
                                      /VM Exception while processing transaction/
                                  );

                                  done();
                              }
```

```
              });
          });

      it('Cannot transfer tokens from an account that has not authorized any
⇒ account', function(done) {
          //arrange
              let sender = web3.eth.accounts[1];
              let initialSupply = 10000;
              let authorizer = web3.eth.accounts[2];
              let authorized = web3.eth.accounts[3];
              let toAccount = web3.eth.accounts[5];
              let allowance = 300;
              let initialBalanceOfAuthorizer = 400;

              let fromAccount = web3.eth.accounts[4];
              let initialBalanceOfFromAccount = 400;

              let tokensToTransfer = 250;

              let simpleCoinInstance =
                  SimpleCoinContractFactory.new(initialSupply, {
                      from: sender, data: bytecode, gas: gasEstimate},
                      function (e, contract){
                          if (typeof contract.address !== 'undefined') {

                              //arrange
                              contract.authorize(authorized, allowance,
                                  {from:authorizer,gas:200000});

                              contract.transfer(fromAccount,
                                  initialBalanceOfFromAccount,
                                  {from:sender,gas:200000});

                              //act and assert
                              assert.throws(
                                  ()=> {
                                    contract.transferFrom(fromAccount,
                                        toAccount,
                                        tokensToTransfer,
                                        {from:authorized,gas:200000});
                                  },
                                  /VM Exception while processing transaction/
                              );

                              done();
                          }
                      });
          });

      it('Cannot transfer tokens by an account that has not been
⇒ authorized', function(done) {
          //arrange
              let sender = web3.eth.accounts[1];
              let initialSupply = 10000;
              let authorizer = web3.eth.accounts[2];
```

```
        let authorized = web3.eth.accounts[3];
        let toAccount = web3.eth.accounts[5];
        let allowance = 300;
        let initialBalanceOfAuthorizer = 400;

        let transferExecuter = web3.eth.accounts[4];

        let tokensToTransfer = 250;

        let simpleCoinInstance =
               SimpleCoinContractFactory.new(initialSupply,
                  {from: sender, data: bytecode, gas: gasEstimate},
                  function (e, contract){
                    if (typeof contract.address !== 'undefined') {

                       //arrange
                       contract.authorize(authorized, allowance, {
                          from:authorizer,gas:200000});

                       contract.transfer(authorizer,
                          initialBalanceOfAuthorizer,
                          {from:sender,gas:200000});

                       //act and assert
                       assert.throws(
                          ()=> {
                             contract.transferFrom(authorizer,
                                toAccount, tokensToTransfer,
                                {from:transferExecuter,gas:200000});
                          },
                          /VM Exception while processing transaction/
                       );

                       done();
                    }
                 });
       });

   it('Successful transfer from authorizer to authorized: final source
   and destination balances are correct and allowance is reduced as
   expected', function(done) {
        //arrange
        let sender = web3.eth.accounts[1];
        let initialSupply = 10000;
        let authorizer = web3.eth.accounts[2];
        let authorized = web3.eth.accounts[3];
        let toAccount = web3.eth.accounts[5];
        let allowance = 300;
        let initialBalanceOfAuthorizer = 400;

        let tokensToTransfer = 250;

        let simpleCoinInstance =
               SimpleCoinContractFactory.new(initialSupply,
                  {from: sender, data: bytecode, gas: gasEstimate},
```

```javascript
                    function (e, contract){
                      if (typeof contract.address !== 'undefined') {

                        //arrange
                        contract.authorize(authorized, allowance,
                              {from:authorizer,gas:200000});

                        contract.transfer(authorizer,
                            initialBalanceOfAuthorizer,
                        {from:sender,gas:200000});

                        //act
                        contract.transferFrom(authorizer, toAccount,
                            tokensToTransfer,
                              {from:authorized,gas:200000});

                        //assert
                        assert.equal(150,
                            contract.coinBalance(authorizer));
                        assert.equal(250,
                          contract.coinBalance(toAccount));
                        assert.equal(50,
                            contract.allowance(authorizer, authorized));

                        done();
                      }
                    });
    });
});

describe('mint', function() {
    it('Cannot mint from nonowner account', function(done) {
        //arrange
        let sender = web3.eth.accounts[1];
        let initialSupply = 10000;

        let minter = web3.eth.accounts[2];
        let recipient = web3.eth.accounts[3];
        let mintedCoins = 3000;

        let simpleCoinInstance =
                SimpleCoinContractFactory.new(initialSupply,
                  {from: sender, data: bytecode, gas: gasEstimate},
                  function (e, contract){
                    if (typeof contract.address !== 'undefined') {
                      //act and assert
                      assert.throws(
                        () => {
                            contract.mint(recipient, mintedCoins,
                              {from:minter,gas:200000});
                        },
                        /VM Exception while processing transaction/
                      );

                      done();
```

```
                }
            });
    });


    it('Successful minting: the recipient has the correct balance',
        function(done) {
            //arrange
            let sender = web3.eth.accounts[1];
            let initialSupply = 10000;

            let recipient = web3.eth.accounts[3];
            let mintedCoins = 3000;

            let simpleCoinInstance =
                SimpleCoinContractFactory.new(initialSupply,
                    {from: sender, data: bytecode, gas: gasEstimate},
                    function (e, contract){
                        if (typeof contract.address !== 'undefined') {
                            //act
                            contract.mint(recipient, mintedCoins,
                                {from:sender,gas:200000});

                            //assert
                            assert.equal(contract.coinBalance(recipient),
                                mintedCoins);
                            done();
                        }
                    });
        });
});

describe('freezeAccount', function() {
    it('Cannot freeze from nonowner account', function(done) {
        //arrange
        let sender = web3.eth.accounts[1];
        let initialSupply = 10000;

        let freezer = web3.eth.accounts[2];
        let frozen = web3.eth.accounts[3];

        let simpleCoinInstance =
            SimpleCoinContractFactory.new(initialSupply,
                {from: sender, data: bytecode, gas: gasEstimate},
                function (e, contract){
                    if (typeof contract.address !== 'undefined') {
                        //act and assert
                        assert.throws(
                            ()=> {
                                contract.freezeAccount(frozen, true,
                                    {from:freezer,gas:200000});
                            },
                            /VM Exception while processing transaction/
                        );

                        done();
```

```
                          }
                    });
        });

        it('Successful freezing: verify the account has been frozen',
          function(done) {
                //arrange
                let sender = web3.eth.accounts[1];
                let initialSupply = 10000;

                let frozen = web3.eth.accounts[3];

                let simpleCoinInstance =
                    SimpleCoinContractFactory.new(initialSupply,
                        {from: sender, data: bytecode, gas: gasEstimate},
                        function (e, contract){
                            if (typeof contract.address !== 'undefined') {
                            //act
                            contract.freezeAccount(frozen, true,
                                {from:sender,gas:200000});

                            //assert
                            assert.equal(contract.frozenAccount(frozen),
                                true);
                            done();
                        }
                    });
        });
    });

});
```

Listing D.1   SimpleVoting.sol: full voting contract

```solidity
pragma solidity ^0.4.22;

contract SimpleVoting {

    struct Voter {
        bool isRegistered;
        bool hasVoted;
        uint votedProposalId;
    }

    struct Proposal {
        string description;
        uint voteCount;
    }

    enum WorkflowStatus {
        RegisteringVoters,
        ProposalsRegistrationStarted,
        ProposalsRegistrationEnded,
        VotingSessionStarted,
        VotingSessionEnded,
        VotesTallied
    }

    WorkflowStatus public workflowStatus;
    address public administrator;
    mapping(address => Voter) public voters;
    Proposal[] public proposals;
    uint private winningProposalId;

    modifier onlyAdministrator() {
        require(msg.sender == administrator,
```

```
            "the caller of this function must be the administrator");
        _;
    }

    modifier onlyRegisteredVoter() {
        require(voters[msg.sender].isRegistered,
            "the caller of this function must be a registered voter");
        _;
    }

    modifier onlyDuringVotersRegistration() {
        require(workflowStatus == WorkflowStatus.RegisteringVoters,
            "this function can be called only before proposals registration
    has started");
        _;
    }

    modifier onlyDuringProposalsRegistration() {
        require(workflowStatus ==
            WorkflowStatus.ProposalsRegistrationStarted,
            "this function can be called only during proposals
    registration");
        _;
    }

    modifier onlyAfterProposalsRegistration() {
        require(workflowStatus == WorkflowStatus.ProposalsRegistrationEnded,
            "this function can be called only after proposals registration
    has ended");
        _;
    }

    modifier onlyDuringVotingSession() {
        require(workflowStatus == WorkflowStatus.VotingSessionStarted,
            "this function can be called only during the voting session");
        _;
    }

    modifier onlyAfterVotingSession() {
        require(workflowStatus == WorkflowStatus.VotingSessionEnded,
            "this function can be called only after the voting session
    has ended");
        _;
    }

    modifier onlyAfterVotesTallied() {
        require(workflowStatus == WorkflowStatus.VotesTallied,
            "this function can be called only after votes have been
    tallied");
        _;
    }

    event VoterRegisteredEvent (
            address voterAddress
    );
```

```
event ProposalsRegistrationStartedEvent ();

event ProposalsRegistrationEndedEvent ();

event ProposalRegisteredEvent (
    uint proposalId
);

event VotingSessionStartedEvent ();

event VotingSessionEndedEvent ();

event VotedEvent (
    address voter,
    uint proposalId
);

event VotesTalliedEvent ();

event WorkflowStatusChangeEvent (
    WorkflowStatus previousStatus,
    WorkflowStatus newStatus
);

constructor() public {
    administrator = msg.sender;
    workflowStatus = WorkflowStatus.RegisteringVoters;
}

function registerVoter(address _voterAddress)
    public onlyAdministrator onlyDuringVotersRegistration {

    require(!voters[_voterAddress].isRegistered,
        "the voter is already registered");

    voters[_voterAddress].isRegistered = true;
    voters[_voterAddress].hasVoted = false;
    voters[_voterAddress].votedProposalId = 0;

    emit VoterRegisteredEvent(_voterAddress);
}

function startProposalsRegistration()
    public onlyAdministrator onlyDuringVotersRegistration {
    workflowStatus = WorkflowStatus.ProposalsRegistrationStarted;

    emit ProposalsRegistrationStartedEvent();
    emit WorkflowStatusChangeEvent(
        WorkflowStatus.RegisteringVoters, workflowStatus);
}

function endProposalsRegistration()
    public onlyAdministrator onlyDuringProposalsRegistration {
    workflowStatus = WorkflowStatus.ProposalsRegistrationEnded;
```

```
        emit ProposalsRegistrationEndedEvent();
        emit WorkflowStatusChangeEvent(
            WorkflowStatus.ProposalsRegistrationStarted, workflowStatus);
}

function registerProposal(string proposalDescription)
    public onlyRegisteredVoter onlyDuringProposalsRegistration {
    proposals.push(Proposal({
        description: proposalDescription,
        voteCount: 0
    }));

    emit ProposalRegisteredEvent(proposals.length - 1);
}

function getProposalsNumber() public view
    returns (uint) {
    return proposals.length;
}

function getProposalDescription(uint index) public view
    returns (string) {
    return proposals[index].description;
}

function startVotingSession()
    public onlyAdministrator onlyAfterProposalsRegistration {
    workflowStatus = WorkflowStatus.VotingSessionStarted;

    emit VotingSessionStartedEvent();
    emit WorkflowStatusChangeEvent(
        WorkflowStatus.ProposalsRegistrationEnded, workflowStatus);
}

function endVotingSession()
    public onlyAdministrator onlyDuringVotingSession {
    workflowStatus = WorkflowStatus.VotingSessionEnded;

    emit VotingSessionEndedEvent();
    emit WorkflowStatusChangeEvent(
        WorkflowStatus.VotingSessionStarted, workflowStatus);
}

function vote(uint proposalId)
    onlyRegisteredVoter
    onlyDuringVotingSession public {
    require(!voters[msg.sender].hasVoted,
        "the caller has already voted");

    voters[msg.sender].hasVoted = true;
    voters[msg.sender].votedProposalId = proposalId;

    proposals[proposalId].voteCount += 1;

    emit VotedEvent(msg.sender, proposalId);
}
```

```solidity
function tallyVotes() onlyAdministrator onlyAfterVotingSession public {
    uint winningVoteCount = 0;
    uint winningProposalIndex = 0;

    for (uint i = 0; i < proposals.length; i++) {
        if (proposals[i].voteCount > winningVoteCount) {
            winningVoteCount = proposals[i].voteCount;
            winningProposalIndex = i;
        }
    }

    winningProposalId = winningProposalIndex;
    workflowStatus = WorkflowStatus.VotesTallied;

    emit VotesTalliedEvent();
    emit WorkflowStatusChangeEvent(
        WorkflowStatus.VotingSessionEnded, workflowStatus);
}

function getWinningProposalId() onlyAfterVotesTallied public view
    returns (uint) {
    return winningProposalId;
}

function getWinningProposalDescription()
    onlyAfterVotesTallied public view
    returns (string) {
    return proposals[winningProposalId].description;
}

function getWinningProposaVoteCounts() onlyAfterVotesTallied public view
    returns (uint) {
    return proposals[winningProposalId].voteCount;
}

function isRegisteredVoter(address _voterAddress) public view
    returns (bool) {
    return voters[_voterAddress].isRegistered;
}

function isAdministrator(address _address) public view
    returns (bool) {
    return _address == administrator;
}

function getWorkflowStatus() public view
    returns (WorkflowStatus) {
    return workflowStatus;
}
}
```

index

MORE TITLES FROM MANNING

Grokking Bitcoin
by Kalle Rosenbaum

ISBN: 9781617294648
450 pages
$39.99
April 2019

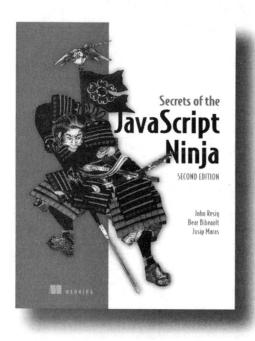

*Secrets of the JavaScript Ninja,
Second Edition*
by John Resig, Bear Bibeault,
and Josip Maras

ISBN: 9781617292859
464 pages
$44.99
August 2016

*Get Programming with
JavaScript Next*
*New features of ECMAScript 2015, 2016,
and beyond*
by JD Isaacks

ISBN: 9781617294204
376 pages
$39.99
April 2018

Get Programming with JavaScript
by John R. Larsen

ISBN: 9781617293108
432 pages
$39.99
August 2016

For ordering information go to www.manning.com

MORE TITLES FROM MANNING

Grokking Deep Learning
by Andrew W. Trask

ISBN: 9781617293702
336 pages
$49.99
January 2019

Deep Learning with Python
by François Chollet

ISBN: 9781617294433
384 pages
$49.99
November 2017

For ordering information go to www.manning.com

MORE TITLES FROM MANNING

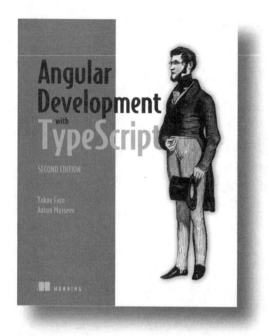

Angular Development with Typescript, Second Edition
by Yakov Fain and Anton Moiseev

ISBN: 9781617295348
560 pages
$49.99
December 2018

Angular in Action
by Jeremy Wilken

ISBN: 9781617293313
320 pages
$44.99
March 2018

Learn Linux in a Month of Lunches
by Steven Ovadia

ISBN: 9781617293283
304 pages
$39.99
November 2016

Linux in Action
by David Clinton

ISBN: 9781617294938
384 pages
$39.99
August 2018

For ordering information go to www.manning.com

MORE TITLES FROM MANNING

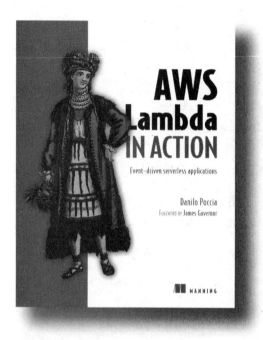

AWS Lambda in Action
Event-driven serverless applications
by Danilo Poccia

ISBN: 9781617293719
384 pages
$49.99
November 2016

Google Cloud Platform in Action
by JJ Geewax

ISBN: 9781617293528
632 pages
$59.99
August 2018

For ordering information go to www.manning.com

*Classic Computer Science Problems
in Python*
by David Kopec

ISBN: 9781617295980
224 pages
$39.99
March 2019

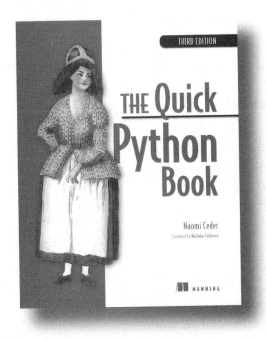

*The Quick Python Book,
Third Edition*
by Naomi Ceder

ISBN: 9781617294037
472 pages
$39.99
May 2018

MORE TITLES FROM MANNING

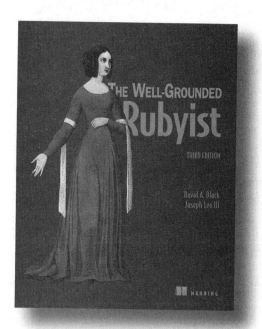